Frontispiece (1)   **Left lateral view of the brain**

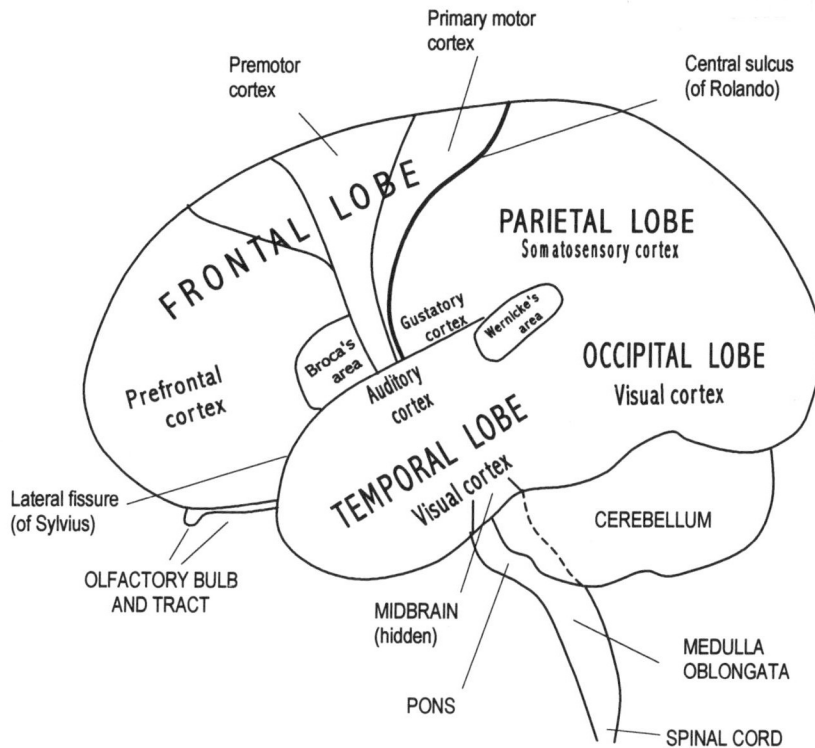

Broca's (motor speech) area occupies the opercular and triangular portions of the inferior frontal gyrus (approximate areas 44 and 45 of Brodman.)

Wernicke's ('language comprehension') area occupies the posterior part of the superior temporal gyrus and the adjoining angular gyrus of the parietal lobe. Note that this area is not specialized cortex for interpreting language (an evolutionary improbability) but overlies a major crossroads of inter-sensory fibre connections essential for forming memory associations which give meaning to sensory experiences, including linguistic and other symbols.

Frontispiece (2) **Midsaggital (longitudinal, vertical midline) section showing medial side of right half of the brain**

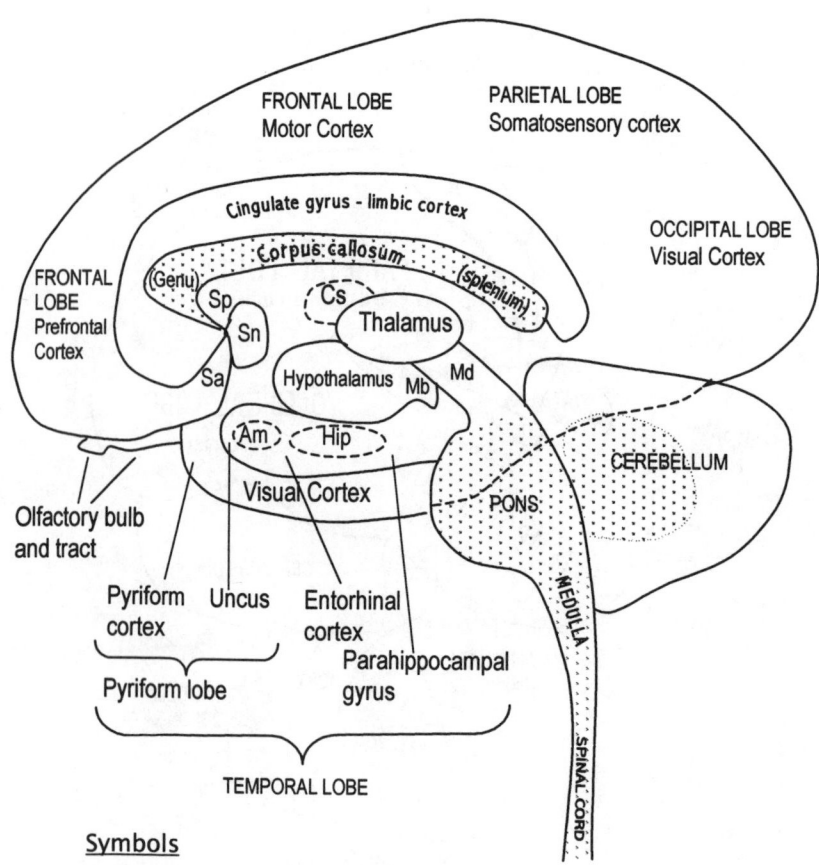

Symbols

Am = amygdala
Cs = corpus striatum
Hip = hippocampal formation
Mb = mammillary body
Md = midbrain
Sa = septal area
Sn = septal nuclei
Sp = septum pellucidum

Dashed outlines indicate position of structures deep to the surface
Stippling represents structures continuous across midline cut by sectioning the brain

Frontispiece (3)   **Inferior view of the brain**

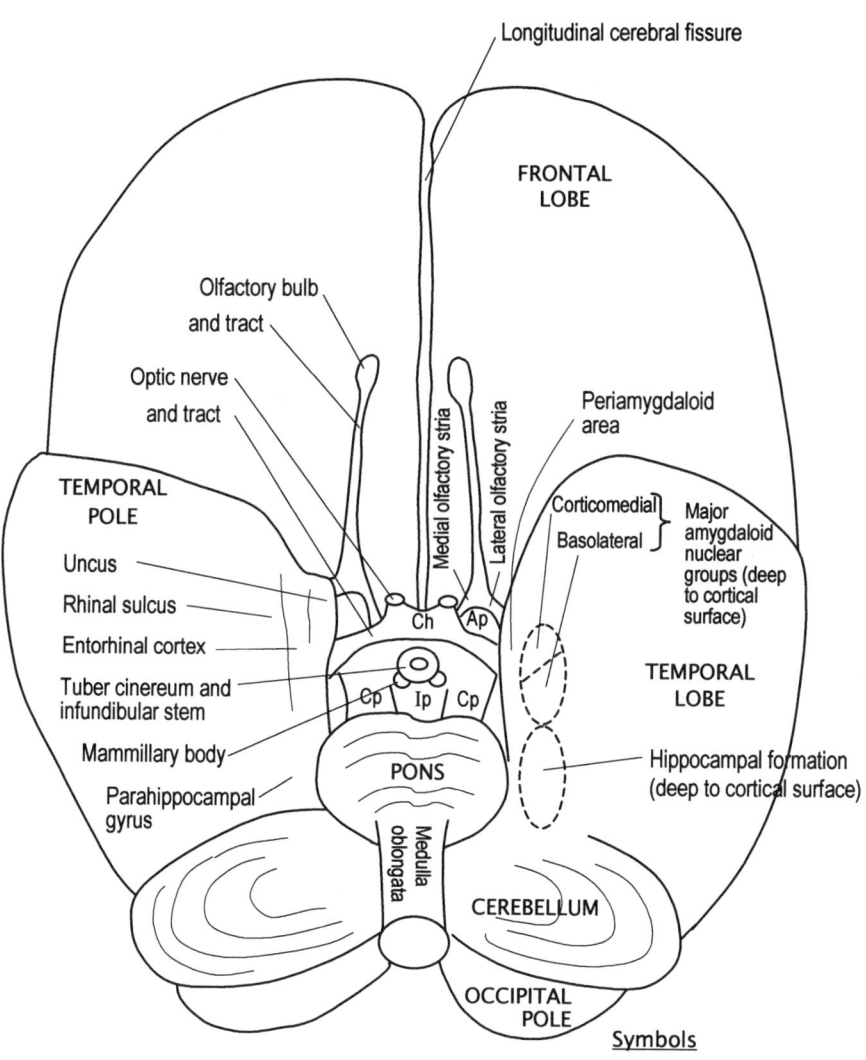

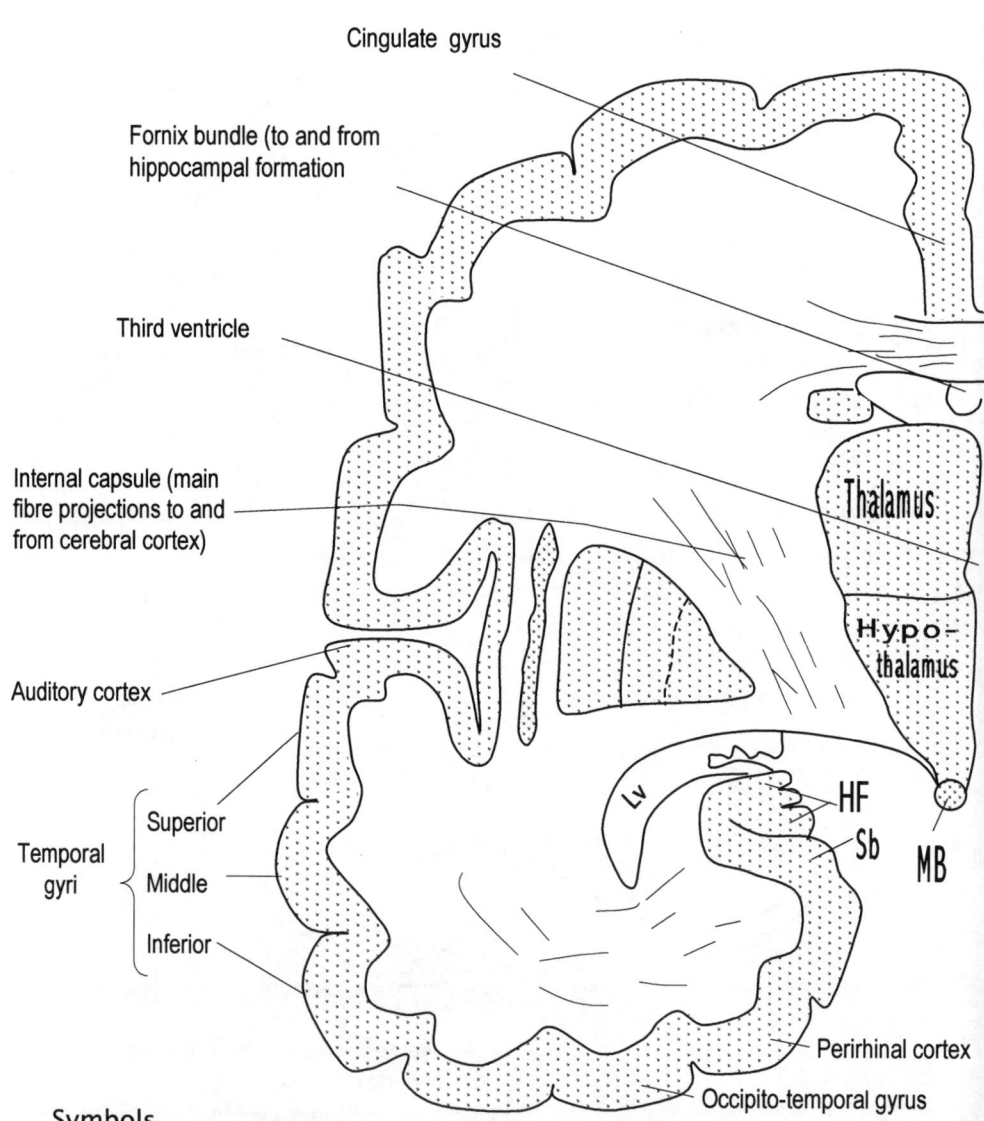

Frontispiece (4-A) **Frontal (transverse, vertical) section through hippocampus (relative positions are approximate)**

Symbols
HF = Hippocampal formation
Lv = Lateral ventricle (temporal horn)
Mb = Mammillary body
Sb = Subiculum

<u>Hippocampus</u> has a part to play (not yet understood) in the consolidation of new memories

Frontispiece (4-B) **Frontal section through amygdala (slightly rostral to 4-A)**

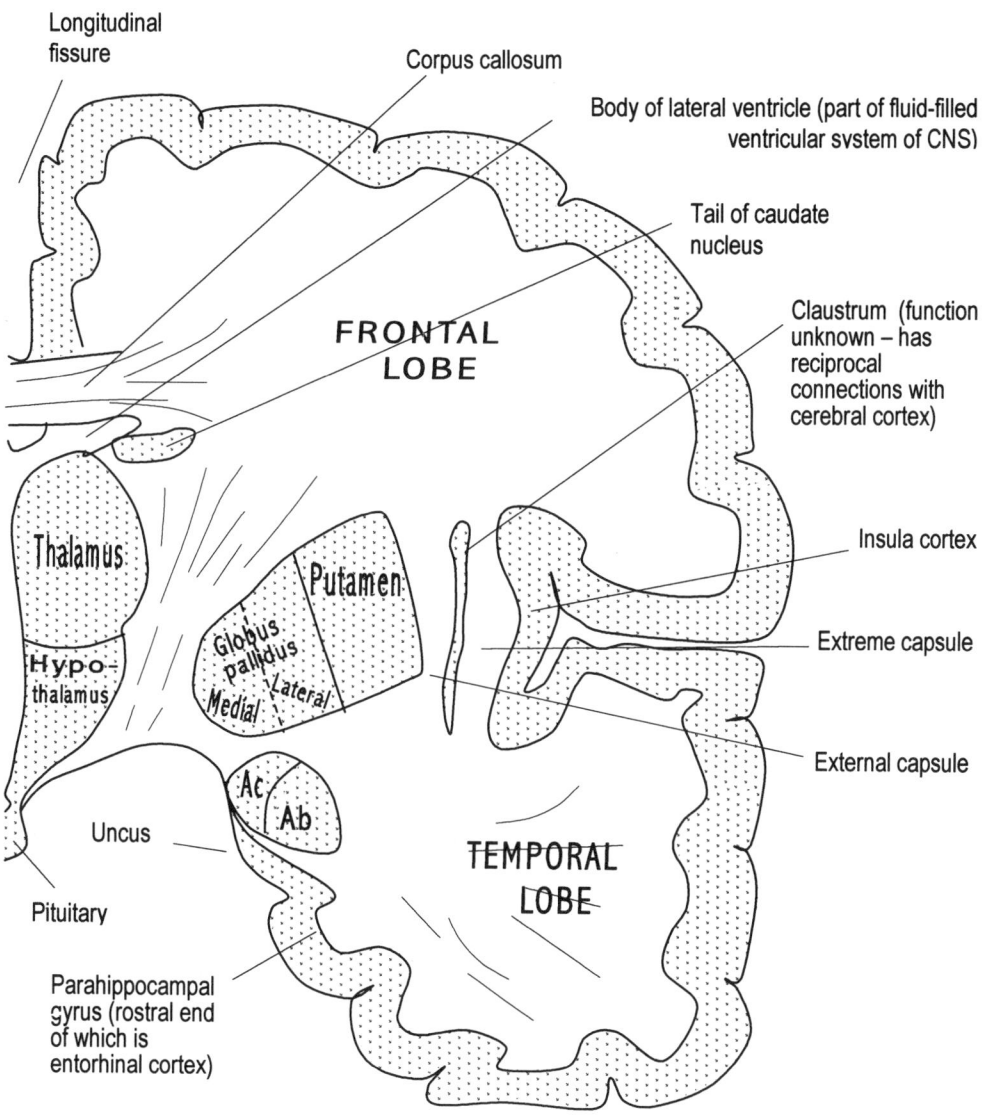

Amygdala is the principal gateway to the emotional system – it receives input from all sensory modalities

Symbols

Ac = Amygdala (corticomedial group of nuclei

Ab = Amygdala (basolateral group of nuclei)

MECHANISMS OF THE MIND

You can't hope to understand the $\begin{Bmatrix} \text{mind} \\ \text{brain} \end{Bmatrix}$

until you've understood the $\begin{Bmatrix} \text{brain} \\ \text{mind} \end{Bmatrix}$

(With apologies to Prof. Robert Mills)

This book:

Written for my own satisfaction and pleasure, but also in the hope it may influence the thinking of some young people embarking on careers in the life sciences,
and
dedicated to my extended family.

MECHANISMS

OF THE

MIND

AN EVOLUTIONARY PERSPECTIVE

Malcolm I. Hale

1999
HALE – van RUTH
Pittsburgh, PA

© Copyright- Malcolm I. Hale, 1999. All rights reserved

LIBRARY OF CONGRESS CATALOG CARD NUMBER 98-92639

ISBN 0-9623691-1-X

Published by Hale-vanRuth, 2424 Huntington Drive, Pittsburgh, PA 15241

Printing and binding by Hignell Book Printing Ltd.

Printed in Canada

FOREWORD

Having emerged from the 'dark ages' of behaviorism during which mind was considered to have no place in biology – when, in fact, to be seen taking an interest in consciousness was to risk one's academic reputation – the last decade or two has seen a scramble by several authors to make up for lost time (somewhat akin to religious revival in the former Soviet empire!)

Even so, there is residual caution in venturing into what was once forbidden territory, particularly noticeable among neurobiologists: the psychological scars of behaviorism remain. In consequence there is failure to recognize, or reluctance to accept, that consciousness is at the core of biology of the mind and must therefore be a physical phenomenon, and that the bulk of the mammalian forebrain evolved to generate and utilize consciousness; or, put another way, utilizing the properties of consciousness documented in this book (and which, it will be argued, we seem forced to accept from consideration of the empirical data) was the principal adaptive 'strategy' of the evolutionary process in the line that led to man.

The author is a physician. By the nature of their work physicians are realists – they can neither afford to engage in abstract theorizing nor ignore troubling facts. Also, being outside academia they perhaps feel less restraint in pursuing the implications of empirical data. They are, however, due to the often urgent necessity to act before all the facts are in, disposed to opine without full thought. The author hopes he has taken sufficient care to avoid this pitfall.

Although a somewhat detailed knowledge of the anatomy of the nervous system may be required for critical evaluation of parts of this book, it is not so for understanding most of its main ideas and proposals.

M.I.H.
P.O.Box SS-5222
Nassau, Bahamas
E-mail: Phale@100jamz.com

Acknowledgements
I wish to particularly thank my son Michael for much arduous work in the preparation of this book, my sister Margaret Warren for handling much correspondence, my son Pieter for electronically connecting me with the outside world, and as always my wife Ank for being there and keeping my spleen under control.

Credits
I thank the following authors and publishers for their courtesy in allowing me to use their material. For positions in text see Index.

Section 1.1 (1) Jean-Pierre Changeau: "Neuronal Man", Pantheon Books, 1985. (2) R.W. Sperry: "Mental Phenomena as Causal Determinants in Brain Function"; E.M. Dewan: "Consciousness as an Emergent Causal Agent in the Context of Control System Theory"; Karl H. Priabram: "Problems Concerning the Structure of Consciousness", in G.G. Globus et al, eds. Plenum Press, 1976. (3) J.Z. Young: (a) "An Introduction to the Study of Man", 1971; (b) "Philosophy and the Brain", 1986, Oxford University Press. (4) Semir Zeki: "The visual image in mind and brain", Scientific American, Special Edition, Sept. 1992. (5) John R. Searle: "Minds, Brains and Science", Harvard University Press, 1984. (6) Donald R. Griffin: "Animal Thinking", Harvard University Press, 1984. (7) Arthur C. Guyton: "Basic Neuroscience", W.B. Saunders, 1987. (8) Vernon B. Mountcastle: "Medical Physiology" 14th Ed., C.V. Mosby Co., 1980. (9) Keith Oatley: "Representations of the physical and social world"; David A. Oakley: "Animal awareness, consciousness, and self-image"; Freda Newcombe: "Neuropsychology of consciousness: a review of human clinical evidence"; David A. Oakley and Lesley C. Eames: "The plurality of consciousness", in "Brain and Mind", David A. Oakley, ed. Methuen and Co. (Routledge Ltd.) London, U.K., 1985.

Section 1.4 L.L. Glen and M. Steriade: "Discharge rate and excitability of cortically projecting intralaminar thalamic neurons during waking and sleep states", Jour. Neurophysiology, 48(2), 352-371, 1882.

Appendix A Morris Kline: "Mathematics and the Search for Knowledge", Oxford University Press, New York, 1985.

Appendix C (1) D.G. Amarel et al: Figs C(2) and C(3) and several short quotations form "Anatomical Organization of the Primate Amygdaloid Complex", in: "The Amygdala", J.P. Aggleton, ed. Wiley-Liss, N.Y., 1992. (2) M.L. Barr and J.A. Kiernan: "The Human Nervous System", fifth edition, J.P. Lippincott, Philadephia, 1988.

Various sections (1) Malcolm B. Carpenter: "Core Text of Neuroanatomy", Williams and Wilkins, Baltimore, 1991 (2) Harvey B. Sarnat and Martin G. Netsky: "Evolution of the Nervous System", Oxford University Press, 1981.

Additional credits   Renée Rosenberg; Hee Jung Yoon, Nuntanee Satiansukpong, Renny Shih, Aaron Rosenberg.

Concerning those few authors and publishers whom all my efforts to reach had failed I had these choices: to paraphrase their quotes with of without attribution, to remove them from the manuscript, or to quote on the assumption that they had died. I chose the last because their views had been put before the public, and as these in my opinion merited critical assessment it was desirable to quote verbatim for accuracy. I beg the indulgence of the copyright holders.

CONTENTS

Frontispieces, i – v
Foreword, xi
Acknowledgements, xii
Introduction, 1

PART I   FEATURES OF THE MIND

1.1   Theories of Consciousness – A Critical Review   9
1.2   Sensation, Perception, and Consciousness   27
1.3   Toward an Heuristic Characterization of Consciousness   30
1.4   Consciousness and Natural Selection   33
1.5   Localization of Consciousness Generation   34
1.6   The Status of Consciousness   37
1.7   The Evolutionary Biology of Perception   41
1.8   Visual Mechanisms and Sight Consciousness   49
1.9   The Memory System and the Elaboration of Consciousness   58
1.10 Consciousness of an Objective World and Other Forms of Complex consciousness   73
1.11 Evolution of the Neural Substrate for Elaborated Forms of Consciousness   80
1.12 Focusing (or Selective Generation) of Consciousness   85
1.13 Role of Reticular Activating System in Focusing   101
1.14 The Generalized Thalamocortical System   103
1.15 The Evolution of a Focusing Function   106
1.16 Focusing Mechanisms   107
1.17 Recognition and Response Mechanisms for Priority Information   116
1.18 Competition for Focusing – Priority Processing   123
1.19 The Prefrontal Cortex and Focusing in Thinking   128
1.20 Switch-Focusing in Thinking   130
1.21 Relationship Between Prefrontal Cortex and Limbic System   134
1.22 Relationship Between Prefrontal Cortex and Thalamus   135
1.23 Sleep, Consciousness, and the Reticular Formation   138

1.24 Volition   141
1.25 Thinking and Understanding   143
1.26 Symbolism in Thinking   155
1.27 The Language Function and Thinking   157
1.28 The Imaginative Function   168
1.29 The Emotional System   179
1.30 The Neuroanatomy of the Emotional System   199
1.31 Recognition Circuitries for the Newer Emotions   210
1.32 Cortical Cytoarchitecture and Mental-Cognitive Functions   212
1.33 AI, Consciousness, and Thinking   222

PART 2   STAGES IN EVOLUTION OF THE MIND

Introduction   226
2.1 The Origin of Consciousness and Memory   230
2.2 Origin of the Linkage Systems of Memory   238
2.3 Origin of Recognition Memory and Memory Retrieval   241
2.4 The Origin of Mental Processing Mechanisms   248
2.5 The Beginning of Higher Mental Functioning   250
2.6 Origin of Anticipatory Ability   255
2.7 The Expansion of Memory Capacity   257
2.8 The Linkage Systems of Memory   259
2.9 The Further Evolution of Higher Mental Functioning   269
2.10 The Origin of Curiosity and 'Purposeful' Behaviors   271
2.11 The Evolution of Mental Control of Fine Peripheral Movements   273
2.12 The Initiation of Mentally Determined Movements   275
2.13 The Conversion of Thoughts to Action   278
2.14 The Faculty of Intention   282
2.15 The Origin and Nature of Volition   284
2.16 Evolution of Capacity for Motor Program Formation and Storage   289
2.17 The Development of Monitoring by the Mind   300
2.18 The Evolution of Response to Unfamiliar Items In Familiar Contexts   302
2.19 Thinking and Understanding   308
2.20 Mental Processing and Behavior   308

2.21 The Evolution of The Human Mind   310

APPENDICES

    (A) An Heuristic Model of Consciousness   314
    (B) The Olfactory System   330
    (C) The Limbic System   334
    (D) Corpus Striatum and Associated Structures –
        the Motor Arm of the Emotional System   353
    (E) Evolution of the Brain:
       (1) Flow-chart Illustration   362
       (2) In Sketches   365

    Bibliography   375
    Index   387

FIGURES

1.7 46	2.1(1-8) 233-237	B(1) 333
1.8(1) 53	2.2(a,b) 239	C(1) 337
" (2) 55	2.5(1) 252	C(2,3) 339
1.9 59	2.13(1,2) 280-1	C(4,5) 341-2
1.12(1-8) 94-100	2.16(1-3) 295-6	C(6,7) 347-8
1.16 111	2.18(1-3) 305-7	C(8) 350
1.17(1-3) 117-119		C(9) 352
1.29(1-3) 185-7		D(1-8) 357-361
" (4) 193		E(1-21) 362-373
1.32(1) 214		
" (2,3) 216		

INTRODUCTION

Preliminary Statement

There is a degree of ambivalence among neuroscientists towards the concept of mind, or even the propriety of using the word in brain science. This is in part a residuum of decades of behaviorism, which, in reaction to the pseudo-scientific methods of psychoanalysis and psychic phenomenalism, banned consciousness and mind from the field of science.

This stricture has had a powerful influence on brain research right down to the present; a young Ph.D. seeking advancement would jeopardize his chances by showing undue interest in consciousness! Yet, ironically, much of the brain is concerned with the generation and uses of consciousness; it is not mere hyperbole to state that the brain exists to support the mind.

Viewed in this light one may say that the enormous amount of neurophysiological and anatomical data being collected will have their true scientific use when the biology of consciousness emerges from its present prescientific status. Towards that end this book seeks to identify and explore those brain systems concerned with the major features of the mind, features that can only, or mainly, be known through introspective analysis. It is not enough to know, for example, that lesioning the amygdala in an experimental animal produces certain behavioral effects, or that its connections are such and such, or that a mere thought may set the heart racing, or that the sight of the female form may produce a welter of emotions. All of these things must be tied together to grasp the wholeness of the emotional system; and to more fully understand this system we must also know, or conjecture, how and why it evolved.

Various authors (e.g. Ornstein, Ryle, Dennett) use the word 'consciousness' in reference not to the phenomenon itself but to wisdom, knowledge, level of education, enlightenment, etc.. Others even maintain that consciousness arose with language and art. It is evident that many people are averse to thinking biologically; biologists seek to explain the mechanisms of the mind solely on the basis of evolutionary and physiological principles.

In this study it is maintained that the mind can be properly understood only if it is treated as a biological function owing its characteristics entirely to the processes of biological evolution, as much as, say, the digestive system.

The evolution of the mind to the level of man was not a uniform process but one of critical steps each of which allowed a breakthrough to a higher level of versatility in coping with the challenges of life. If in looking back from man's position there seems to have been an inevitability in the steps that led to his level it is because we are apt to ignore the multitude of life forms that remained trapped at various primitive levels, or to overlook the chanciness of breakthroughs occuring and of taking root. Tens of millions of years elapsed between some of the most significant breakthroughs, each probably followed at first by rapid evolutionary change as natural selection took advantage of the new possibilities, then a more or less prolonged period of consolidation which brought the lineage to a condition of preadaptation for another breakthrough. Obviously the potential to reach the human level of intelligence, and no doubt beyond, was in the first seed of life, but conditions had to be right in innumerable ways for hundreds of millions of years for the result to be 'inevitable'.

Consciousness – The Key To Brain Development

It will be suggested in this study that the size and complexity of advanced brains are the evolutionary consequences of the properties of consciousness; that it may have been impossible for such complexity to evolve without the agency of consciousness; and, further, some basic neuronal properties may have evolved because they facilitated the utilization of consciousness. This position is in direct opposition to the idea that consciousness emerged only when neural network complexity reached some critical level; arguments will be advanced to show why such a view is untenable, being incompatible with biological principles.

The attempt here is to relate consciousness to the particulars of neuroanatomy and to the various functions of advanced central nervous systems in which consciousness is apparently an essential ingredient. The approach is guided by the simple assumption, *hitherto almost universally discounted, when considered at all*, that consciousness is a form of energy with unique properties that the evolutionary process utilized in building complex brains: the details of neurostructure and function will be reviewed in terms of how they relate to the subjective conscious experience, because the particular form of these structural details may be dependent on their contribution to that experience. It will be argued that treating consciousness as a form of energy interchangeable with other forms of energy is both a natural position, given the empirical evidence, and perhaps the only way of escaping the traditional mind-body dilemma.

In evaluating the biological status of consciousness we may work from the position of our own subjectivity. In our attempt to characterize those basic properties of consciousness which may be causally involved in processes of the brain we take into account what we construe to be the essentials of subjective conscious experience and ignore all constructs that in mental life arise from these. These properties appear introspectively to be physically causal and therefore under genetic determination and subject to the operation of natural selection.

At every level of central nervous system functioning the pattern is input followed by appropriate output, carried out by mechanisms evolved through the process of natural selection. Unless shown to be an ineradicable epiphenomenon every feature found in all normal members of a species may on principle be presumed to be genetically determined and therefore to have been contributory to ancestral adaptation and survival. If consciousness is present in all normal members of a species it must on the above principle be provisionally accepted as being genetically based and therefore causally involved in at least some of the responses of the organism to input (environmental, corporeal, social) in the major domains of life.

In empirical neuroscientific research it is generally found unnecessary to think of consciousness per se. Consciousness is implicit in much of such research, but it has proven profitless to pursue it as an object of study. Thus, a typical investigation might measure fluctuating scalp potentials or cerebral blood flow in response to sensory stimuli (or to internally generated imagery or cognitive tasks) and relate these to particular cortical areas.

Empirical data, not conjecture, is what counts in the real world; only the former have the potential for practical applications, and in the realm of human affairs utility is of first importance. In science (as in politics, industry, and commerce) honour usually goes to conjecture only when such conjecture leads to knowledge of potential utility. This is no doubt as it should be; yet, fortunately, people will speculate, on rare occasions producing some pearl of wisdom that might forever have eluded narrow experimentation and the compilation of factual material.

Not that mainstream neuroscientific research is pursued blindly. This is far from being the case. Every effort is directed to answering specific questions, and while these tend to become increasingly narrow, thus moving away from the broad picture, it is the hope and expectation that this painstaking route will inexorably lead to a grand edifice that is complete down to the last detail, with little left to conjecture.

The Goal And Method Of The Analysis

The task in this analysis is to relate the major features of the mind to the structures of the brain and to put forward a credible, hypothesized account of the crucial evolutionary steps that led to the 'finished' product, the mind of man. The approach, though necessarily inferential, is based on, and endeavors to be compatible with, the principles of biological evolution, neurological knowledge, and the first-hand acquaintance we all have with the workings of the mind. It assumes that *everything* about the mind is explicable in terms of natural phenomena, and since consciousness is the basis of mind yet is so seemingly unlike natural phenomena a special effort is made to define it in natural terms; it must be so characterized that it can be treated as a material agent in the functioning of the nervous system. Such a characterization is a working hypothesis – a mental picture or model which serves as an aid in the development of a theory of consciousness. This, in turn, provides a base from which to seek an understanding of the structure of the brain's cognitive processes.

It will not be claimed that the characterization of consciousness adopted in this study is structurally definitive, but only that it is logically valid and by conferring biological status on the elusive properties of subjectivity, an act which is anathematic to both academic neurobiologists and metaphysicians, we take the only route which can possibly lead to a sound and satisfactory understanding of the mind and its evolutionary history.

In trying to understand the cognitive functions of the brain the approach may either be by introspective analysis or by neuropsychological research – from the inside out or the outside in. In the former method the mind is able to look at its own functions and surmise what physical mechanisms underlie them. For example, it knows that items of consciousness are retrievable, therefore, by analogy with phenomena of the external world, they must be stored in some manner and must have some means of returning from storage to consciousness. A theory of how neurons may do this is constructed and search is then made among the data of neuroscience for structures that might perform these functions. Further analysis brings the realization that the actual consciousness that existed is not, strictly speaking, what is stored. Such consciousness ceases to exist after the briefest moment, so 'storage' is a misnomer for the actual process. What must obviously happen is that consciousness produces a lasting change in the biochemical structure of some part of the brain, so that when that part is subsequently activated the new biochemical arrangement is a necessary instrument in the process that generates consciousness anew, this being identical or nearly so to the original consciousness in its subjective characteristics.

Numerous theoretical and epistemological considerations arise from the above line of thought; for example, if consciousness exists at one moment, then disappears, and there invariably follows a structural change in the brain, must it not have been physically causal, and thus have done work, and therefore to have possessed energy obeying the laws of physics? Also, we may immediately see that a certain minimal set of neuronal structures and connections must exist to carry out this function.

The alternative approach depends on empirical investigation of the physical structures and attempts to assign to them cognitive functions by searching among the data of verbal report and behavior, which of course can only have meaning for the investigator by virtue of his own subjective experiences. The search for empirical data tends to become preoccupying and an end in itself, due to the enormous complexity of detail in the material, so that relevance to the subjective world is of diminishing concern. In like manner introspective analysis tends to remain locked in introspection, with little regard for the results of brain research.

Approaches to the mind

It is out of place here to review even a few of the numerous attempts to understand the mind, or even give a summary of the wide range of its definitions. Many of these efforts are clearly non-scientific in that they make no attempt at, and have no relevance to, biological explanation. In this group must be included various philosophies and theologies.

At the opposite pole are the standard neuroscience texts, most of which either avoid the subjects of consciousness and mind or make only oblique reference to them. Theories of mind are not often proposed by researchers in basic neuroscience; as Cowan (1981:xix) put it... "it is almost as if neurobiologists as a group not only have eschewed theory, but even despise it." Yet, paradoxically, a full and accurate understanding of the mind must be in conformity with the established data of neuroscience. For example, the faculty of imagination, an obviously important feature of the mind, is totally dependent on normally functioning neural mechanisms – neurons are active during the process and without them the act could not occur; yet neuroscience has so far been unable to identify the particular neurons or the neural processes involved, further than very general localization in sensory cortices, while introspective analysis, which may be as elaborate as one wishes, cannot gain acceptance unless bolstered by factual data or until its predictions are fulfilled.

As in other areas of science, theory and experimentation are helping one another towards a common understanding. For example, many scattered neurological data may be adduced in support of the theory of the focusing of consciousness ('attending') put forward in this study, such as recordings of shifting vascular activity with thinking. On the other hand the theory may encourage and guide research for more specific data; for example, the reticular activating system (RAS) may, through its widespread neocortical projections, discriminate narrowly among areas of cerebral cortex for preferential activation at any moment in response to focusing needs; it seems very improbable that in man the RAS has, as neurology texts suggest (mainly based on data from the cat), only a general, non-specific influence on the whole cerebral cortex.

The localization of function is the domain of clinical and experimental neuroscience. Large areas of the brain which were formerly designated 'silent' are now tentatively, even confidently, labeled with functions, most recently so the large prefrontal cortical mass modern man has in excess of that of pre-man or of modern apes and other less cerebrally evolved species. Undoubtedly we must seek in this enlarged region some of the neural bases of his advanced mental faculties of thinking, imagining, remembering, communicating, understanding, etc. We must take particular note of the several brain structures that show progressive enlargement and complexity of structure as we move from non-mammalian vertebrates through taxonomically lower mammals to monkeys, pongids, and finally man.

The terminology in this book is straightforward. The one or two coined terms are clearly defined in the text, but 'artefactual (artificial) niche' needs some justification. Strictly speaking it is a niche only in the sense that it is a way of life which may be entered and exploited. Its essence is that natural materials and forces are utilizable in various ways to improve success in life. Many organisms have done so in limited ways, but only man has fully entered and exploited this niche because to do so requires an understanding faculty which no other species has evolved.

Man's ancestral line had fortuitously become pre-adapted for this final step, then a happy conjunction of factors carried him over the threshold and this proved (no doubt at first it was touch-and-go) so successful that explosive evolutionary development followed. The advantages of a thinking, understanding brain proved so great that nature 'undertook' a crash program to develop it as fast and fully as possible, using every means available, inventing others, sacrificing much, and bearing many costs (such as a lumbar region forever breaking down, a tendency to choke on food, a pelvic outlet often too small for the fetal head, and a tendency to many physiological, emotional, and developmental defects).

Man's mind (and therefore his brain) is in its post-pithecoid features the result of evolutionary adaptation to the artefactual niche.

'Teleonomy' refers to a way of speaking of the evolutionary process as though it were goal-directed. It is not, of course, but because it so often seems to be it is sometimes convenient to employ this manner of speaking.

PART 1

FEATURES

OF THE MIND

1.1 THEORIES OF CONSCIOUSNESS – A CRITICAL REVIEW

".... our current understanding of the phenomenon of consciousness is probably even less adequate than our understanding of the foundations of quantum mechanics" (A.J. Leggett, 1987).

"No one understands quantum mechanics" (R.P. Feynman, 1985).

".... knowledge cannot be acquired without consciousness, which seems to be a crucial feature of a properly functioning visual apparatus. Consequently, no one will be able to understand the visual brain in any profound sense without tackling the problem of consciousness as well" (Semir Zeki, 1992).

In view of the absence of consensus among workers in the neuro-mental sciences as to the nature of the process(es) generating consciousness I consider it appropriate and of general interest to present the published views of several participants in the mind-brain debate. I have taken pains to extract from their material only what seems pertinent, and despite the risk of distortion I believe I have succeeded in preserving their meanings. After each presentation I offer a brief critical assessment.

GUYTON, A.C. (1987).   In his textbook of neuroscience Guyton reports that the elicitation of severe pain appears to occur with electrical stimulation of certain areas of the hypothalamus and mesencephalon in animals, but not with the human cerebral cortex. "On the other hand loss of the visual cortex causes complete inability to perceive visual form or colour." The 'holistic theory of thoughts' is that "a thought probably results from the momentary 'pattern' of stimulation of many parts of the nervous system at the same time, probably involving most importantly the cerebral cortex, the thalamus, the limbic system, and the upper reticular formation of the brain stem". "The stimulated areas of the limbic system, thalamus, and reticular formation perhaps determine the general nature of the thought, giving it such qualities as pleasure, displeasure, pain, comfort, crude modalities of sensation, localization to gross areas of the body...On the other hand, the stimulated areas of the cerebral cortex probably determine the discrete characteristics of the thought such as specific localization of sensations of the body and of objects in the field of vision, discrete patterns of sensation...". "And consciousness can perhaps be described as our continuing stream of awareness of either our surroundings or our sequential thoughts"(pp.232-3).

The word 'thought' is apparently used here to mean conscious experience and not the process of thinking. No effort is made in this textbook to specify or speculate on the neuro-physiology of consciousness generation. The last sentence is virtually empty of meaning in that 'consciousness' and 'awareness' are, in most common usages, interchangeable words.

MOUNTCASTLE, V.B. (1980). "In dealing with the problem of consciousness, neurobiologists assume that they deal with a certain aspect of the functional organization of brains that will eventually be defined in terms of neural mechanisms". "Consciousness is a neural phenomenon". "Consciousness exists in other animals as well as man". "Consciousness presupposes perception, a continual updating of the central neural reflection of the state of events in the external world...Whether total reduction of input leads to total loss of consciousness is unsettled, perhaps because complex nervous systems may replicate afferent input by imagery, thus maintaining the conscious state". "The neural mechanisms involved in ... actions that give evidence of consciousness are little understood", e.g. the act of attention and capacity to shift attention selectively, the manipulation of abstract ideas, the capacity for expectancy, self-awareness and the recognition of other selves, esthetic and ethical values, memory (pp.299-300).

This view can be simply stated: Consciousness results from the activity of brains. I suspect the verbal expansion reflects the tentative nature of intellectual exploration. In the end it is frustrated by caution and we are told what everybody already knows. The statement "consciousness presupposes perception" is, however, open to question; after all, percepts (i.e., perceptions) *are* forms of consciousness – a

1.1 Theories of Consciousness 11

percept (perception) is a more-or-less complex consciousness. (Failure to appreciate that the act of perceiving is one and the same with *what* is perceived has been, and continues to be, the cardinal error blinding workers to a valid understanding of the mind).

> YOUNG, J.Z. (1988). "Consciousness is an aspect of the functioning of the brain" (p.12) "We can probably all agree that consciousness is not the name of a thing but of a state or condition" (1971:127).

A state or condition of what? The neurons of the brain, presumably. But states and conditions are open to observation and measurement; consciousness is not, except to itself. We can probably all agree (to borrow Young's phraseology) that consciousness is generated by brains, but once so generated cannot be a state or condition but must have a separate existence or being – must, in fact, be, in some sense, a 'thing'. The product of a manufacturing process cannot be that process itself. Young, like so many others, is in the grip of a false dilemma: having to choose between 'immaterial' spirit and 'material' brain in providing an account of consciousness.

> CHANGEUX, J.P. (1985). "While we are awake and attentive, we appreciate and pursue the formation of percepts and concepts. We can store and recall mental objects ... We are conscious of all this ..." "... what we might call *consciousness* can be defined as a kind of a global regulatory system dealing with mental objects and computations using these objects" (p.145). "Consciousness, then, corresponds to a regulation of the overall activity of cortical neurons and, more generally, the entire brain" (p.151). "During dreaming, images and concepts form and link together without significant interaction with the outside world, but this imagery ... only rarely reaches consciousness" (p.252). "The hypothesis adopted here is that percept, memory image, and concept constitute different forms or states of the basic material infrastructure of mental representation, which we gather together under the general term 'mental objects'" (p.133). "Operations on mental objects, and above all their results, will be 'perceived' by a *surveillance system*, composed of very divergent neurons ... and their reentries. The existence of regulatory loops with reentries at several organizational levels of the brain could lead to high-amplitude oscillations. These linkages and relationships, these 'spider webs', this regulatory system would function as a whole. Can one say that consciousness emerges from this? Yes, if one takes the word 'emerge' literally, as an iceberg emerges from the

water. But it is sufficient to say that consciousness is the functioning of this regulatory system. Man no longer has a need for 'spirit'; it is enough for him to be Neuronal Man" (p.169).

Changeaux says we are conscious *of* mental objects. But presumably these mental objects are already forms of consciousness, so we must be conscious of consciousness. Similarly, he distinguishes between the imagery of dreaming and consciousness. To him consciousness and the contents of consciousness are distinct phenomena. He says consciousness is a global regulatory system, but it is also the *functioning* of this system and it *corresponds* to the regulation of overall activity. Also, consciousness 'emerges', 'literally', which must mean that it has a distinct existence in some sense, which seems to contradict the previous (already ambiguous) positions.

I think it is fair to say that the views of the above neuroscientists and biologists do not advance our understanding of consciousness in any fundamental way. Their views besides being internally inconsistent here and there are somewhat wooly and represent common ideas dressed up in technical language. Writing as professional biologists they are naturally cautious, but one would like to have their speculations on how neurophysiological processes, biochemical and electrochemical, generate the subjective conscious experience, which obviously they do. (But A.F. Huxley, 1983:18 writes: "I do not see a way through neurophysiology: however much we may know about what nerve cells are doing, I do not see how it can tell us how their activities relate to conscious phenomenon, although clearly, of course, they do relate").

GRIFFIN, D.R. (1984). "We know next to nothing about how the brain functions that do lead to human consciousness are distinguished from those that do not". "It seems very unlikely that there are 'consciousness neurons' or special biochemical substances, perhaps neurotransmitters, that are uniquely correlated with the conscious state, so that a person is conscious when and only when these cells are active or those substances present. It seems far more likely that consciousness results from patterns of activity involving thousands or millions of neurons" (p.44)

In this proposal it is not the activity of neurons that produces consciousness, but the 'patterns' of such activity. But how can a pattern of anything be generative? It obviously cannot. On the other hand if it were allowed that neural activity, that is the physico-chemical processes of individual neurons, generates consciousness then it follows that different patterns of such activity would result in different patterns of consciousness.

His first sentence, quoted above, blunt though it may be, is an understatement – we know *nothing* of the distinction, in spite of all the looking that may have been done. People react to this fact in different ways, the commonest, among neuroscientists, being simply to ignore consciousness, while among philosophers and many psychologists it is to ignore that aesthetically offensive lump of offal, the brain. An alternative to these positions, adopted in this study, is to assume that the failure to find a distinction will eventually be overcome and in the meanwhile to propose properties of consciousness that would, if valid, help resolve the mind-brain dilemma.

> KENT, E.W. (1981). "The subject of consciousness may be divided into two questions. The first concerns the mechanism of consciousness per se, and the second concerns the mechanisms that determine the content of consciousness at any one time". Concerning the existence of the state of awareness or consciousness itself: "Consciousness has as a requirement the functioning of the brain, and probably the forebrain ... a blow to the head or reduction of oxygen or blood supplies, eliminates conscious awareness. Damage to the brainstem reticular formation also eliminates consciousness in the absence of any damage to the forebrain". It thus appears "that the operation of the forebrain is a necessary substrate for consciousness and that its occurrence is regulated by lower brainstem centers" (pp.264-5). "Given what is known about the relationship between reported states of conscious awareness and arousal and the physical measures of forebrain activity such as the EEG, it seems reasonable to identify the existence of a state of consciousness as a primitive, mental experience with the operation of this reticulo-cortical circuitry, and a state of maintained conscious activity with the physical activity around the feedback loop" (pp.264-5).

As with most authors with a background of academic neuroscience Kent discusses consciousness from the point of view of the structures and circuits involved, in particular the importance of the reticular activating system. The importance of this system is now generally known to students of the mind, including philosophers, but there still remain puzzles about its precise functioning. Is any consciousness generated in this system? Or is its function solely to influence the generation of consciousness elsewhere? Even amphioxus, a very primitive chordate, possesses a reticular formation, though poorly differentiated, which it uses for transmission of signals via many synapses from its primordial brain (Sarnat and Netsky,1981:204). Does this formation have an influence on whatever consciousness this primitive organism may generate? If not when and how did it acquire such an influence in more cerebrally developed organisms? Did it originally generate consciousness, this function being taken over by the developing cerebrum?

These are interesting and important questions which are likely to become more relevant when more is known about the precise physiological processes involved in the generation of consciousness and its control by mechanisms of sleep.

> SPERRY, R.W. (1976). "[By] consciousness I mean the kind of experience that is lost when one faints or sinks into a coma. It is the subjective experience that is lacking during dreamless sleep (p.163) .... [The] conscious experience [is] like seeing red, or hearing a musical tone, or feeling pain" (p.164). ".... our ... view can be classified broadly as an 'emergent' theory of mind ... the phenomena of subjective experience are not thought to be derived from electrical field forces or volume-conduction effects, or any metaneural by-product of cerebral activity. Our view relies on orthodox neural-circuit and related physiological properties ... I have conceived the mental properties to be *functional* derivates that get their meaning from the way in which the brain circuits and related processes operate and interact....[The] conscious subjective properties ... are interpreted to have a causal potency in regulating the course of brain events; that is, the mental forces or properties exert a regulative control influence in brain physiology. The subjective conscious experience on these terms becomes an integral part of the brain process, rather than a correlated phenomenon .... mental events are *causes* rather than correlations ... [our] view can be said to involve a form of mental interactionism ... The mental forces are direct causal emergents of the brain process"(p.165). "...the holistic conscious properties that I think of as the mental properties of the brain processes ... [are] different from and more than the neural events of which they are composed ... colors, sights, sounds ... pain ... are .... phenomena in their own right. Rather than being identical to the neural events .... they are emergents of these events"(p.166). "Wholes and their properties are real phenomena ... [with] causal potency ..." "[The] relationships of the parts to

each other in time and space are of critical importance in causation ..." "[The] pattern properties are just as real and important as are the properties of the parts ..."(p.167). "Consciousness ... is strictly a property of brain circuits specifically designed to produce the particular conscious effects .." "[A] mutual interdependence is recognized to exist between the neural events and the emergent phenomena. In other words, the brain physiology determines the mental effects and the mental phenomena in turn have causal influence on the neurophysiology"(p.168). "[For example] pain sensation is ... a real emergent phenomenon ...Although built of neural events the pain sensation as a larger whole is not itself the same as the neural and glial events"(p.169). "The conscious subjective qualities ... derive from the selective operational interactions of brain events in a matrix of brain activity"(p.174).

Sperry denies that consciousness is a "metaneural by-product of brain activity", which, if it were the case, would (by my interpretation of the language) make it an emergent epiphenomenon. He further disclaims epiphenomenalism when he goes on to say that "mental forces are direct causal emergents of the brain process" and in turn have "causal potency", thus apparently maintaining that consciousness has a causal role. However, his views seem to have some internal contradictions. He says that "color...pain... are phenomena in their own right", which must mean an independent existence, yet "consciousness is strictly a property of brain circuits"; logically, anything that is a property of something cannot be a phenomenon in its own right, as this implies independent existence. When he says that "the brain physiology determines the mental effects and the mental phenomena in turn have causal influence on the neurophysiology" this, it seems to me, can only be the case if they are physically separate and distinct entities, which, logically, must mean that if one were to disappear the other, however briefly, would continue to exist; but earlier he says that "the subjective conscious experience .... [is] an integral part of the brain process", which, however generously interpreted, means that it is a brain process, and not a phenomenon "in its own right". Brain processes are in principle observable and measurable by instruments; consciousness is known directly only to itself and only indirectly to observers by it effects; it obviously takes part in brain processes but to identify it with such processes is illogical and meaningless.

Sperry attempts to be more specific in his speculations than several other authors I have reviewed. But he does not, possibly from ingrained psychological inhibitions, or fear of peer ridicule, or sober scientific caution, take the final step which would both preempt lethal criticism and largely (in principle) settle the mind-brain debate: he fails to postulate that emergent consciousness is a unique and independent form of energy which is transformable into other forms of energy and which takes part in the conservation of energy. Sperry's position is obviously incomplete in that he has no *mechanism* to show how emergent subjective experience becomes something separate from the neural events causing it and none to show how it in turn can influence those events. In the end his thesis carries no explanation but is merely a reiteration in technical language of what the man-in-the-street already knows, and is in essence no different from the ideas of some of the other authors quoted here.

DEWAN, E.M. (1976). Dewan employs as analogy the phenomenon of "mutual entrainment oscillations" in which feedback harmonizes the elements of control systems. He emphasizes how prevalent mutual entrainment is in nature and technology. He uses the example of a power grid, in which "the stability and accuracy of a system is far greater than any single unit. This mutual entrainment is a splendid example of *self-organization* ... such a system can be regarded as a *single unit* so far as its function is concerned .. [Out] of mutual entrainment has emerged a '*virtual governor*' which controls the entire system in a manner which uses feedback"(pp.183-5). "[The] grid acts *as if* there were a virtual governor but 'in reality' the virtual governor *doesn't exist*". From the above and other considerations he summarizes the ontological status of consciousness as a "holistic emergent property of the interactions of neurons which has power to be self-reflective and ascertain its own awareness" and as such "its reality must be taken as axiomatic to epistemology"(pp.187-8). Out of the tremendous ongoing interaction and mutual control between the system and between subsystems "it is possible to imagine the emergence of an 'inner awareness' which can 'supervene' ... This consciousness would be the ultimate embodiment of ... a virtual governor. Its unique property would be self-reflexive *awareness* and its 'self-identity'. I am proposing that our 'inner world' which we 'perceive' within 'ourselves' is the emergent self-controlling virtual governor resulting from generalized entrainment of large numbers of superadaptive optimum control systems arranged into hierarchical mutually cooperative structures .." "Since the virtual governor does not have a physical existence in the usual sense, but is a property of the system as a whole... consciousness must somehow emerge from physical neuronal activity but not have a physical existence in the usual sense"(p.193). He admits that this view is completely without technical detail, and in a footnote asks "Does a neuron have consciousness? How could you find out? What are the necessary and sufficient conditions for awareness?"

If, as Dewan says, "consciousness must somehow emerge from physical neuronal activity but not have a physical existence in the usual sense", and if "its reality must be taken as axiomatic", and if it has the "power to be self-reflective and ascertain its own existence", then from these properties (which we can hardly disavow) we must conclude that we are dealing with a paradox: a real yet phantom entity with functional capability, of an 'other-worldly' nature. Dewan finds it possible to imagine the emergence, out of the interaction and mutual control between system and subsystems, analogous to the emergence of the 'virtual governor' in his example, of an 'inner awareness' which can 'supervene'. But acts of imagination of this sort, unsupported by other acts of imagination as to how, are no better than the stuff of dreams.

It seems to me that the fatal flaw in all such spin-off ideas is that, whether the authors intend it or not, they make of consciousness an epiphenomenon, or in some sense a paraphenomenon therefore beyond the reach of biological explanation, whereas the evidence is overwhelming that consciousness is causal in biological processes; its existence as an epiphenomenon simply makes no sense.

> PRIBRAM, K.H. (1976). "My proposal is that the basic function of brain is to generate the codes by which information becomes communicated. Some of these codes are like those used in optical information processing – they are holographic. Thus image construction and projection occurs, and, when the system becomes sufficiently complex, it no longer functions only as a self-contained unit, but begins to act more like an open parallel processing mechanism. Characteristic of such open systems is that when they are endowed with memory they generate feed-forward processes that select, become voluntary, rather than just respond to input. It is therefore readily conceivable that an open parallel processing system would generate images ...The question remains whether such images are simply epiphenomena...." "Conscious awareness is a realization as real as brain. In understanding the origins of the organization of consciousness we employ reductive

procedures leading to the structure of brain, but in understanding the organization of the brain we employ procedures that are equally reductive and which lead to the structure of awareness. And who is to say that one of these reductions is more fundamental than the others?"(pp.301-3). "Ordinary consciousness is ... achieved by a mechanism (somewhat like a hologram) that disposes the organism to locate fresh experiences and performances at some distance from the receptive and expressive interfaces that join organism and environment"(p.306).

I find Pribram's ideas difficult to follow. I take him to mean that consciousness emerges from complexity in some way that is due to the nature of complexity itself. This idea is completely false, because although a machine that becomes more complex can perhaps do many things better than when it was simple, these things are of the same class, not things of a qualitatively different nature – a machine that does not generate electricity when simple will not start doing so simply as a result of becoming more complex; for it to do so new *kinds* of things would have to be put into it, like a magnetic source. It is the nature of the ingredients, not complexity, that determines the *kind* of output. As Lloyd (1989:191) put it: "Suppose we decide the toad is not perceptually aware [in that] we have found nothing for consciousness to do in the toad – neurons take care of the toad's needs ... The problem with this [is that] surely bats are open to the same argument, and if bats, then cats, monkeys, and, ultimately, man. The burden of proof is on those who would deny consciousness to the toad. It is up to them to explain what the toad lacks. And it is not open to say simply that the toad isn't complex enough".

SEARLE, J.R. (1984). "In my view, the mind and body interact, but they are not two different things, since mental phenomena just are features of the brain. One way to characterize this position is to see it as an assertion of both physicalism and mentalism. Suppose we define 'naive physicalism' to be the view that all that exists in the world are physical particles with their properties and relations. The power of the physical model of reality is so great that it is hard to see how we can seriously challenge naive physicalism. And let us define 'naive mentalism' to be the view that mental phenomena really exist. There are really mental states ....and many of them function causally in determining events in the world. The thesis ... can be stated quite simply. Naive mentalism and naive physicalism are both consistent with each other ... (and) they are both true." "Consciousness is a real property of the brain that can cause things to happen" (pp.26-7). "Mental phenomena, all mental phenomena ... are caused by processes going on in the brain" (p.18). "Pains and other mental phenomena just are features of the brain" (p.19).

Searle does not allow that the consciousness produced by the brain is a separate, independent entity. But, if it is not different from the brain but just a feature or just an activity of the brain and yet is causal on the brain this simply means that the brain is active on itself, and subjectivity becomes biologically irrelevant.

OAKLEY, D.A. (1985). In discussing awareness, consciousness, and self-awareness Oakley does not speculate on the neurophysiological generation of consciousness. For him 'simple awareness' is simply neurophysiological responsiveness, e.g. reflexes, homeostatic systems, etc., and as for 'consciousness': "...the ability to create central representations of external events ... corresponds to the emergence of mind, and ... the activity of processing information ... constitutes consciousness" (p.132-3). "Consciousness is qualitatively different from simple awareness in that it depends on different information processing strategies ... [it] emerged after the evolution of the hippocampus and neocortex or their homologues"(p.137).

Oakley's definitions are somewhat idiosyncratic, as he himself admits. Since consciousness is generated by the impact, indirectly, of external events on specialized nervous tissue such consciousness *ipso facto* 'represents' these events; the first spark or unit of consciousness, even if it occured in a unicellular organism, would be a representation of the external event that (indirectly) caused it. (I take this opportunity to anticipate a main thesis of this book: that representation of the external world by consciousness is one of the principal factors that allowed the evolution of advanced brains).

It is unclear how the activity of 'processing information' can 'constitute' consciousness, unless by 'consciousness' is meant not the basic phenomenon but elaborate patterns of the latter; e.g. a simple smell would not be a legitimate instance of consciousness, but a rich blend from the kitchen with associated visions would somehow be. If this is what is meant it is either false or a trivial, arbitrary distinction. To suggest or imply that 'consciousness' only appears when the nervous system is advanced enough to generate elaborate patterns of consciousness representing relatively complex external events is to violate the basic principles of evolution and invoke magical intervention.

> OATLEY, K. (1985). "Human consciousness involves the creation of a reality partly composed by the rules of our particular culture" (p.52). "Consciousness is largely a social consciousness, though used for technical purposes too" (p.54).

It is obvious that in this and so many other approaches to consciousness it is not the basic phenomenon that is being discussed but the patterns built up from the elemental kinds of the basic phenomenon, and this ambiguity plagues much of the discussion on consciousness. A person emerging from anaesthesia, coma, or deep sleep may first experience a tiny point of light, or the faintest sense of nausea, or a simple isolated odour. This is consciousness as near to the unit level as is likely to occur in humans; it doesn't have context and has the minimum of pattern. And when we say the 'person' experiences such isolated, minimal consciousness we speak loosely; logically there is nothing 'experiencing' it; there is nothing apart from itself which is conscious 'of' it; it exists of itself following its generation by the recovering brain and (we may conclude from various evidence) immediately ceases to exist by reconversion to neural energy which 'imprints' a downline memory neuron; and so long as the generating function is active a continuous stream of the same elementary units of consciousness is in existence. All we can legitimately say about someone 'experiencing' consciousness is that it is a convenient use of language indicating that the consciousness is generated in a particular individual organism, in whom it has reconversion effects on downline neural mechanisms.

> NEWCOMBE, F. (1985). "The putative neural substrate of conscious activity is dependent on our operational definition. The function of wakefulness is dependent on structures that include mammillary bodies or the neighbouring posterior hypothalamus and anterior mesencephalon, and the intralamilar and midline nuclei of the thalamus. But our major interest is in a wider definition of consciousness, embracing the concept of selective attention and volitional control" (p.183). "Consciousness may be but the culmination of a complex continuum of operations in which orientation, detection, recognition and choice interact ..."(p.184). "[The] ghost in the machine may turn out to be a higher level of neuronal patterning" (p.185).

Once again here is an author skirting the central issue of the neurophysiological generation of consciousness per se and dealing with the secondary manifestations, that is, with operations of the mind. When it comes to the core biology of consciousness there is, among academics, a universal shrugging of the shoulders.

> OAKLEY, D.A. AND EAMES, L.C. (1985). "One of the most persuasive [sic] aspects of what we intuitively label as 'consciousness' or 'conscious awareness' is its unity." These authors then propose "... to review evidence which suggests that the unity of consciousness is illusory"(p.217).

Since consciousness is entirely subjective then if there is an 'illusion' of unity there is unity. The unity is directly experienced and no amount of gainsaying can nullify this. The unity of consciousness is a fact. When the neural substrates of consciousness are physically divided multiple consciousnesses result, each of which is a unity separate from and unknowable by the others.

The real problem is in determining the mechanism coalescing units of consciousness generated in different areas of the intact brain. On the face of it one may conclude that the generated consciousness moves or extends itself along the axonal branches to meet with the consciousness generated in other neurons, to coalesce with these to form a compound unitary consciousness. This apparently commonsensical, 'naive' interpretation of the facts is rejected out of hand or simply not considered by the authors I have consulted, the reason presumably being that consciousness has not shown up in any laboratory investigation of brain tissue! Those who have proposed a biological mechanism for the unification of consciousness (e.g. Edelman,1989;Zeki,1993) have generally invoked the agency of reciprocal (reentrant) neural signals in performing a binding or mapping function. But neural signals per se cannot unify consciousness unless they serve to put consciousness generated and 'residing' in one area into contact with that in another, and there has been no suggestion as to how this might be accomplished.

I have already denied that consciousness can be created by *patterns* of neural *activity*; being inert, patterns cannot create anything. So the neural activity does the creating. But what activity? Biochemical? Electrochemical? Some other? Does this unknown activity fail to produce consciousness when occurring in a single or a few neurons but somehow produces it when large numbers of neurons (how many?) are simultaneously active? Attempts at answering these questions will be made later.

Searle's (1984) idea is that consciousness is the surface characteristic of microevents in the brain, and that these are simply different aspects of the same thing. His analogy is with liquidity and the molecules in the fluid: a single molecule cannot be said to be liquid but at the macro-level numerous such molecules by their behavior produce liquidity. This analogy seems to me logically invalid in that all the stages from non-liquid single molecules to the stage of liquidity are revealed, directly or indirectly, by observation, whereas consciousness is only observable by itself and must have an independent existence, however transiently, from the neural activity generating it. The surface *feature* of anything is not an energetic entity – it cannot *do* anything; it would require some energetic process to detect it and use this information for causal processes; it would require, in the case of the brain, consciousness, which would 'detect' it by representation, having been generated into independent existence by cellular metabolism associated with the neural substrate that itself constituted the 'feature'. This argument opposes all ideas that do not accept consciousness as an independent energetic agent.

The various views quoted above appear to have two things in common: they avoid dualism, the idea that the conscious mind is separate from the brain and has a continued existence independent of it, and with which it interacts in some way; and they hold that in some manner consciousness may be equated with the brain – that consciousness is the brain or the brain's activity as observed in the laboratory, or some feature or reflection of the brain.

I consider both dualism and identity ideas to be untenable for the following reasons: Dualism is biologically untenable because it removes consciousness and mind from genetic determination, whereas it is abundantly inferable, if not empirically demonstrable, that they are genetically determined. On the other hand identity and spin-off ideas are untenable because they either do not succeed in accounting for consciousness or give it epiphenominal status.

A valid explanation of consciousness and the mind-brain dichotomy must accomodate the following: 1/ Consciousness is generated by the metabolic activity of brains. 2/ The subjective conscious experience is causal (is an essential precipitating factor) in some metabolic, physiological, and behavioral processes. 3/ Mind is the product of evolution by natural selection and consciousness is the basis of mind. 4/

The ability of certain biologically active tissues to generate consciousness allowed the evolution of an organ capable of more effectively utilizing data extracted from the environment (external and corporeal) in adjusting behaviors for optimal survival chances for the individual and therefore its genetic continuance. 5/ The unique properties of consciousness as known to introspection, such as privacy, unity, self-experiencing, importance-in-itself, other dimensionness, etc. must be accepted as natural phenomena subject to natural laws (some of which remain to be discovered).

There is a general dismissive attitude towards the idea that specialized neurons generate consciousness. This may stem from the fact that all the histo-biochemical studies of neurons in the sensory cortices reveal nothing distinctive. The more details discovered of nerve-cell functioning the more improbable it seems that there is anything in it that can be singled out as a generator of consciousness. But the *absence* of evidence *for* something is not as weighty as the *presence* of evidence *against* it; there is only indirect evidence that neurons generate consciousness (inferred from the facts that brains generate consciousness and that brains are composed of neurons), but there is no fact of any kind disqualifying neurons as generators of consciousness.

The following points and inferences must be considered: 1/ The brain generates consciousness; the brain is composed of neurons (and glial cells); therefore neurons (and/or glial cells) generate consciousness. 2/ Neurons are specialized for many different functions; therefore some neurons may be specialized for the generation of consciousness, there being no a priori reason why this cannot be so. 3/ Consciousness is inviolately private; its presence is not detectable by probing instruments. 4/ Consciousness exists only so long as metabolic brain activity is occurring, therefore such activity is a necessary requirement for consciousness. 5/ This activity is dependent on chemical energy, therefore energy is required to generate consciousness. 6/ Consciousness is now in existence, but undetectable by the investigator: it is invisible yet from the evidence of introspection it is instrumental in the transference of the energy of sensory input to the energy of cortical motor output, and further evidence for such a role is provided by the investigator's finding that verbal report of conscious experience is accompanied by observable behaviors. 7/ Energy in any form is undetectable except by its effects; consciousness is undetectable except by its effects; when conventional energy acts on matter it produces electron motion or heat; the evidence leaves open the possibility that consciousness produces electron movement in neurons, and there is evidence that consciousness may produce heat (see below).

From these considerations we would seem to have some justification for provisionally accepting consciousness as a form of energy. Conventional forms of energy occur in units or 'quanta', so conscious energy may be assumed to be quantal. A *pattern* of neuronal activity is not consciousness, but generated units of consciousness form complex 'higher order' patterns of consciousness limitless in variety and behavioral effects. Mere neuronal activity cannot be consciousness — the neuronal activity must 'manufacture' consciousness which then becomes, like all manufactured products, something separate from, and independent of, the manufacturing process. By analogy, the active electric organs of some teleosts and the electric current they produce are not identical, nor are they different faces of the same thing; nor are organs of bioluminescence identical with the light they produce. Consciousness, if produced by specialized neurons, would similarly be distinct from the neuron; it would simply have the strange properties listed earlier and further discussed in this analysis.

We have to accept the 'strangeness' of consciousness as a fact of nature and not let that strangeness be a bar to our dealing with it as such; it is not for us to display metaphysical prejudice, which is what we do in an inverted sort of way when we refuse to make the provisional conclusion, from the evidence, that consciousness is a form of energy generated by specialized neurons. We may legitimately, from the evidence, take this as a working hypothesis and use it as a model for heuristic purposes. We may not invent or imagine evidence, but in searching for a mechanism we may be guided by analogy with known mechanisms, such as bioluminescence. The search for a mechanism may prove futile, as many have predicted, and for working neuroscientists a distraction they cannot afford, but for those with the time and the inclination it is easy to become absorbed by this greatest of scientific teasers.

With the rise of neuroscientific knowledge mind became increasingly associated with brain, but eventually became lost in the neuronal jungle, and disappeared altogether during the decades of behaviorism. Until recent times neuroscientists dared not whisper the word 'consciousness' for fear of academic ostracism and peer ridicule. Now consciousness is out in the open, but there remains a psychological barrier to considering it, even in fanciful hypothetical terms, as an independent form of energy of such a nature that it can only be investigated by introspective analysis and verbal report in order to properly understand its role in the functioning of the central nervous system.

Examples of the kinds of supporting evidence for the characterization of consciousness put forward in this study are the following:

1/ During vivid visual dreaming the temperature in the core of the brain rises quite precipitously, and single unit activity in the cerebral cortex may increase but doesn't acquire the irregular patterning that is characteristic of wakefulness (Evarts,1962, cited in Legg 1989:182). A possible interpretation of these findings is that consciousness is being very actively generated in the haphazard manner of dreaming but cannot reconvert to useful neuronal functioning because the sleep process has shut down the downline mechanisms, so the consciousness dissipates as heat.

However, a more prosaic explanation is that the neural process that leads to the imagery of dreaming is overactive, having been released from inhibition by the sleep process, and if at the same time the mechanism of conversion of neural energy to that of consciousness, i.e., to the actual imagery, is not able to fully cope, the excess pent-up neural energy will be converted to heat. The dream state is, of course, a conscious state; the mechanism that transduces sensory impulses to consciousness is probably also the same mechanism that transduces internally generated neural signals to the imagery of dreams. There is support for this from experiments showing that the same cortical areas involved in sensory experiencing are involved in the internal generation of imagery during imagination (Farah et al,1989;Kosslyn et al,1993).

2/ Work by Zeki (1983 a,b) on the reaction of cells in monkey visual cortex to wavelength (colour) lends support to the idea that consciousness is generated by single neurons. "The significant point to emerge from his work is that a perceptual phenomenon once believed to be the result of high level cognitive processing now turns out to have a single cell correlate at an early stage in the visual pathways" (Legg,1989:76).

3/ "It has long been known that during arrest of behavioral responsiveness to external stimuli during states of sleep or light barbituate anaesthesia, primary evoked potentials from cortical sensory receiving areas are preserved ... In the classical microelectrode studies of Hubel and Wiesel (1965) the feature selectivity of even the more complex cells in visual cortex were present even in animals immobilized by barbiturate anaesthesia, presumably without perceptual awareness" (Jasper, 1981:379).

Anaesthetics work by their suppressive physico-chemical effects on cellular metabolism of the brain. The clear inference is that this metabolism generates consciousness and is separate from, and perhaps superimposed on, the more primitive and robust metabolism that allows the passage of signals detected by microelectrodes.

It has been established (Glen and Steriade, 1982) that intralaminar thalamic neurons projecting to neocortex terminate chiefly in superficial cortical layers with some axonal collaterals to layer 6, and (Jones,1981) that specific thalamic projections go to middle layers with collaterals to layers 5 and 6. Now, the deeper layers contain mostly pyramidals which are corticofugal; that is, they do not take part in further activities in their own cortical columns (except for the recurrent axonal branching of some). It is suggested that some of these may mediate relatively primitive reflexive functions not involving consciousness, via the direct input of the collaterals noted above. It is further suggested that light anaesthesia and synchronized sleep shut down the activity of the middle and superficial layers which are presumed responsible for the generation of consciousness and for the modulatory control of such generative activity respectively, and therefore behaviors driven by consciousness cannot occur. The more primitive reflex circuits of the deeper layers are presumed to be more robust and less affected by light anaesthesia and sleep.

4/ Specific neurophysiological mechanisms for focusing (i.e. the selective regional generation) of consciousness would not exist if consciousness were an epiphenomenon or even (it may be argued) if it were due (in some way) to patterns of neural activity, but only if specific consciousness-generating neurons exist. It will be shown in this work that elaborate and highly evolved mechanisms for the selective generation (focusing) of consciousness exist in the central nervous system. Clearly, the existence of these would make no sense if consciousness were epiphenominal.

Zeki(1993) has reviewed the physiological and anatomical data showing increasing levels of cellular responsiveness and connectivity from striate (V1) to prestriate (V4,etc.) cortical areas. He refers to 'experiential' cells, the responses of which 'correlate' with the perception of colour (pp.300-3). Epistemologically, this statement is in the same category as the statement that the activities of the brain as a whole correlate with consciousness, yet the anatomical and physiological details he cites carry us close to the threshold the crossing of which (prudently avoided by Zeki) would be made by the statement 'the experiential cells *generate* consciousness', which is the basic premise of the present work and which, I maintain, cuts the Gordian knot of the mind-brain dilemma.

Taken together the several points and inferences noted thus far form the basis for the ideas on consciousness developed in this work, guided by the principle that the utilization of consciousness in biological systems is subject to the process of evolution through natural selection.

The characterization of consciousness as a form of energy generated in quantal units by specialized neuronal activity, reconvertible to downline neural energy and governed by the law of conservation of energy, will be used as if factually established, it being understood that this is an hypothetical construct not at present, if it ever will be, empirically verifiable. Its use is as an heuristic aid; by 'resolving' the mind-brain dilemma it becomes easier and more comfortable to deal with mind-brain phenomena.

1.2 SENSATION, PERCEPTION, AND CONSCIOUSNESS

Kolb and Whishaw's 1990 "Fundamentals of Human Neuropsychology", a tome of some 900 pages, does not list 'consciousness' in its subject index. 'Sensation' and 'perception' are listed and discussed in the text. This is orthodox terminological practice among neuropsychologists for distinguishing between hierarchical levels in the organization of consciousness, a matter possibly of some importance in clinical work. These authors (p. 223) distinguish between sensation and perception as follows: "Sensation is the *result* of activity of receptors and their associated afferent pathways to the corresponding neocortical sensory areas; perception is the *result* of activity of cells in the cortex beyond the first synapse in the sensory cortex". The italics are added to spotlight the caution exercised in these definitions in avoiding the tabooed word 'consciousness'; an effect, one suspects, of the psychological scars carried by psychologists since the era of behaviorism. They also (p. 223) define 'perception' as "our subjective experience of the physical energy" (physical energy having been transduced into nervous activity), and state that "it is perception, rather than sensory transduction, that is of most interest to the psychologist".

Subjective experience, sensation, perception, no matter how defined, imply consciousness. The subject matter of psychology is the mind, and consciousness is the basis of the mind, so any reticence in the treatment of consciousness is a self-imposed handicap in the analysis of mind. It is almost a contradiction in terms to speak of a behavioral approach in psychology, since the psychological data used are verbal reports of subjective experiences or physical responses to subjective experiences (which we vicariously share with the subject); the essential ingredient is consciousness, and the essential findings are the forms of consciousness (i.e. kinds of subjective experience) under normal and abnormal conditions. When a strict behaviorist reports on findings following damage to the occipital lobes he will not speak of blindness but of failure of the subject to respond appropriately to visual stimuli. For him the victim's cry of "I cannot see" has no scientific significance. His approach is mechanistic, not psychological.

One of the obvious, somewhat naive but nonetheless legitimate, questions about the nature of sensory perception is how the convoluted cortex is able to generate a stable image of geometric proportions corresponding accurately to the external world, instead of an image as seen in a distorting mirror. A simple answer is that the perception does not have to be geometrically congruent with the features of the external world to be functionally effective, but need only be topographically reliable, and different brains almost certainly produce different perceptions of the same feature. It is sufficient that perceptions are functionally reliable, which means that the external feature will be subjectively experienced in the same way today as yesterday, because responses are determined by perceptions. (We leave aside the question of how perceptual constancy is maintained in the face of a shifting external world).

And, of course, we don't perceive the external world; we only 'perceive' our perceptions, the 'we' here being that part of the composite, global unitary consciousness in relation to those other parts which come under the category of perceptions. This idea is difficult to grasp but is fundamental: Consciousness is self-experiencing; consciousness can only be experienced by itself, therefore for the 'self' to experience consciousness other than itself, i.e. to have perceptions and sensations, requires that the units of consciousness generated by different parts of the brain and constituting self-consciousness on the one hand and perception on the other must coalesce into a unitary consciousness which experiences itself *in toto*. This is incontrovertible, for if the experiencing self were something totally separate from the brain's percepts it would have to get inside those percepts to experience them – the self's consciousness (the conscious self) would have to include the percepts; but percepts are already forms of consciousness –*seeing* (objects), *hearing* (organized sounds), etc. – which would mean the absorption of consciousness by consciousness, which is what coalescence is, or first the conversion of the conscious percept into some non-conscious neural state which is then reconverted to a percept within the self's embrace by some arcane process, a biologically unparsimonious double step. Furthermore, "anatomical studies have yet to reveal a single cortical area to which all the visual areas connect exclusively" (Zeki,1993:123), and Kinsbourne (1995), in citing evidence against a 'centered brain', writes: "A centered cortical neuroanatomy .... is not to be found". Furthermore, by considering the evolution of the vertebrate nervous system as successive additions of parallel reflex arcs with interconnections for cooperative functioning we virtually eliminate the possibility of a structural ego evolving.

Perceptions may be altered by abnormal conditions (e.g. toxic states, diseases, special glasses) with resulting inappropriate responses. But the brain is capable of some degree of compensation through relearning and probably by means of innate mechanisms evolved to compensate for normal perturbations. It is obviously important that such compensating mechanisms should exist, otherwise behavioral responses would be dangerously erratic.

The brain may also create its own perceptions (i.e., consciousness generated in response to internal signals) as part of the compensatory mechanisms, and in doing so may override the sensory perception. If, e.g., a brain 'knows' that in a certain situation it should be experiencing a certain perception, yet because of interference of some sort is not properly doing so, it may have a mechanism to instruct the imaginative function to generate an appropriate image.

It is of course unknown how the myriad units of consciousness widely generated at any moment by different parts of the brain coalesce and self-experience as visual and other sensory patterns of infinite detail all in proper place and not a featureless smear. As already mentioned it is vital that such order should exist and correspond with the external order, because a huge number of innate and acquired responses are driven by percepts which must reliably represent the external order for survival. Astronomical numbers of connections and physiological transactions must function with precision for perceptual stability to be maintained, not to mention the functioning of non-conscious parts of the CNS, and we know that many chemical and physical agents can distort perception and result in inappropriate responses.

If we could follow the evolution of sensory and perceptual systems step by step from the emergence of the first spark of consciousness we would no doubt grasp how nature works its wonders in this matter.

1.3 TOWARD AN HEURISTIC CHARACTERIZATION OF CONSCIOUSNESS

We have this impasse: numerous efforts to approach the mind, but reluctance to accept physical status and a causal role for its central constituent, consciousness. There is abundant circumstantial evidence that consciousness is generated by metabolic activity of the brain – this is now beyond reasonable doubt. As securely established is that all metabolic processes are genetically based. We seem forced to the conclusion that the function of generating consciousness is a phenotypic result of genetic determination.

The idea of saltationism in evolution is generally regarded as a false doctrine; the orthodox view is that complex structures and functions have the simplest of beginnings and evolve by small changes, sometimes faster, sometimes slower. The mind, with its core constituent, consciousness, could not have appeared *de novo* as an elaborate going concern. It must of necessity have arisen at the most elementary level as a result of changes in the genetics underlying cellular metabolism, and its appearance must have conferred some definite benefit, however slight, to permit its retention and elaboration in subsequent generations.

1.3 Toward an Heuristic Characterization of Consciousness

One must reject as mystical, or at least un-biological, the idea that consciousness first appeared as an emergent phenomenon of neural *complexity*. This notion probably suggested itself to its originators from analogy with the many instances in which growth and increased complexity in physical systems result in something new. But what is new in such cases is appearance or range of function, or both, not a fundamental entity. For a change in a system to produce such an entity the system itself must undergo a structural change at a fundamental level, not that of mere complexity, and this is presumably what happened in the primitive metabolism as a result of genetic changes, resulting in the generation of consciousness.

If progress is to be made in the study of consciousness and its role in the brain it must be modeled in a form that can be treated scientifically, and one way of doing this is to assume that it is composed of basic units with a property spectrum encompassing the whole range of possible elements of subjectivity or 'qualia', with each species being able to generate a particular range of the spectrum as a result of its evolutionary history. We may speculate that the primitive cellular biochemistry which was the precursor of nervous function had variations able to generate these units of consciousness which then took part in the nervous activity. In order to accomodate the naively accepted self-evident properties of consciousness we must endow the units with privacy, subjectivity, essential selfhood, and the ability to coalesce with one another to form a compound unitary whole able to self-experience all of its parts simultaneously without loss of the properties and specific neural activities of the individual units.

Such a model is apt to be seen as going beyond reasonable speculation. What, for example, can be the justification for postulating units or quanta of consciousness? There are at least three possible answers to this: First, the probability that some neurons are specialized to generate consciousness, and neurons function in bursts; second, using this assumption makes it easier to explain a great deal of higher mental functioning, as well as its evolutionary development; and third, if consciousness is a form of physical energy then by analogy with the other forms of energy it should be quantal.

A further objection: Surely the coalescence of such units into a compound unitary whole is an idea entirely too far-fetched and without foundation? Far-fetched, yes, yet an unavoidable consequence of transferring subjectivity and selfhood from a nebulous entity pervading the brain to individual, quantized units. The unity of consciousness is a universally recognized phenomenon of mind, introspectively self-evident and undoubtedly evolved because of its effectiveness in serving the survival interests of a unit, the individual organism. It therefore must have a physical basis by which this is achieved, and, by extension of this argument, must exhibit genetically determined variations permitting natural selection to be operative. A corollary to this is that there may be forms of consciousness operating in other parts of the central nervous system separate from, and therefore unknowable to, the mind.

Having said all this it is still undeniable that there is no compelling evidence for accepting consciousness as an energetic entity. Until, if ever, such evidence is forthcoming the position is purely speculative, put forward as an exercise in heuristics to see where it leads. But after a while one may get comfortable with this idea to the point of acceptance, particularly as with it so much seems to fall nicely into place; having a well-defined mental picture, however emblematic, of the essentials of any complex situation is always helpful in banishing confusion of thought.

It will undoubtedly be asked: "How can consciousness, characterized as a physical property, be demonstrated? Where in neuronal histology and biochemistry is the transducer of neural activity to consciousness to be found?" These questions cannot now be answered. If a probing instrument interacts with a quantum of consciousness the latter might dissipate as heat. Because of the inviolable privacy of consciousness no external probe can reveal the conscious self-experience. Only by the coalescence of elementary units of consciousness to form a compound unitary whole which self-experiences all of its parts can one consciousness 'know' another, and it would be carrying conjecture too far to imagine how the bringing of two minds together might be achieved! Clinical and experimental evidence for divided consciousness is obviously a relevant topic here, but such evidence must be very carefully evaluated to avoid drawing wrong conclusions. What may *seem* to be divided consciousness, i.e., two separate and independent minds occurring in the same brain following structural disconnections, may be the effect of separation of a part of the memory system from the rest.

1.4 CONSCIOUSNESS AND NATURAL SELECTION

Where consciousness is concerned the apparently metaphysical may be materially empirical. Take, for instance, the statement: "Feeling (i.e. feeling consciousness) is intrinsically important," or, as Dennett (1991:31) put it, "*mattering* (enjoying, etc.) ... depend[s] on consciousness". This is the kind of statement one is inclined to dismiss as trivial rambling. Yet natural selection has operated intensively on genetically based variations in feeling consciousness to evolve behaviors assuring maximum success in the struggle for life by utilizing the unfathomable fact that feelings are intrinsically desirable or undesirable. There is, admittedly, difficulty in understanding how a particular category of feeling can become functionally tied to an appropriate response, but an attempt will be made later in this study to account for this.

The target for natural selection has historically been, and continues to be, a matter much debated, much of the time at cross purposes. Although feelings (i.e. varieties of feeling-consciousness) are private they are accessible to natural selection. In identical circumstances different individuals may experience relevant feelings (that is, feelings which will in part determine their behavior) in different degrees, due (in part) to genetic differences, with corresponding differences in behavioral effects. There will be, in the circumstances, an optimal type of behavior and this will be precipitated, or catalysed, by a particular level or mix of feeling which will in effect be targeted by natural selection. Of course, it is not only subjectivity that is a target for selection in such cases, but also non-conscious neural and somatic mechanisms taking part in the response. But all these belong to the individual and it is the genetic make-up of successfully reproducing individuals which determines the next generation's gene pool.

The point is that as private and inaccessible to the external observer as feelings are they are yet potent, perhaps the most potent, actors in the evolution of many behavioral responses. To reiterate, subjective experience, or consciousness, dismissed for decades by behavioral scientists, is urged as the great invention of Nature which permitted the construction of advanced central nervous systems.

1.5 THE LOCALIZATION OF CONSCIOUSNESS GENERATION

The anatomical location of consciousness generation in the brain, which would be the first step in its physical investigation, is still uncertain. Neurosurgeon W. Penfield, a pioneer in the localization of brain functions, placed it in the highest level of the brainstem, claiming that circumscribed lesions in this area are invariably accompanied by loss of consciousness. This is in keeping with experimental findings in various mammals, but it is now considered that the effect is due to damage to the reticular activating system which indirectly controls conscious activity in the cerebral cortex. It must always be borne in mind when trying to locate brain functions that interfering with some part of the brain does not prove that it is the seat of the function that may be disrupted. For example, loss of consciousness will result if all input to the consciousness-generating areas is blocked, despite the putative consciousness neurons remaining entirely untouched, and except for any spontaneous activity they may incidentally exhibit.

Obviously no progress can be made in investigating the physiology of consciousness generation until its anatomical localization is achieved. Assuming such knowledge the physiology of the neurons under different conditions of activity would have to be measured in detail not presently possible, in particular the energy levels when quiescent and during strong sensory input, in order to detect discontinuities through micro-level energy bookkeeping. Unique features in the cellular metabolism would have to be sought and, if found, homologous metabolism in other species could then be investigated with the chance of more rapid progress.

The idea of energy discontinuity or discrepancy is this: In the generation of consciousness there is increased metabolic activity in restricted parts of the brain. Whatever amount of consciousness is in existence at any moment as a result of this is hypothesized to be energy in a form that disappears from conventional instrumental detection and measurement, taking the form of subjective experiencing (i.e., according to this idea, the new form of energy is the experiencing self), so that a conventional energy count will show a deficit. This deficit will be rectified when the energy of consciousness reconverts to downline neural energy for transmission to the memory neurons or to effector neurons.

1.5 Localization of Consciousness Generation

Of course, the technical difficulties of such measurement would make it virtually impossible of accomplishment: as consciousness is being generated it is also reconverting to conventional energy to drive neuronal functioning (recollect that this process is selectively abolished by light barbituate anaesthesia); the measurement would have to be made in the extraordinarily brief interval between the generation of a quantum of consciousness (in a neuron quiescent up to that moment) and its reconversion to neural energy.

Although the localization of the supposed consciousness-generating metabolism in the brain has not been achieved, so strengthening dismissive attitudes to this idea, the true position is that it has never been rigorously sought, principally because one would need cooperating human 'preparations' for such an investigation. Additionally, the technical difficulties would be extremely formidable. For example, to trace sensory signals to the part of the brain where they become sensory consciousness one may start by temporarily blocking input from the sense organ, e.g., by local anaesthesia or cooling. This would result in loss of that sensory consciousness, but restoring the sense organ would return consciousness to normal as reported by the subject. One would proceed in this way more and more centrally, first removing then restoring signals. At each level the sensory consciousness would at first be lost then restored as we pass through those central nervous system (CNS) structures which conduct and process sensory signals but do not generate consciousness. We finally block some neurons and find that consciousness is not lost; blocking these structures alone does not eliminate consciousness. We have in this way identified the preceding ones as the consciousness-generating neurons. (A difficulty with this is that downline from the consciousness-generating neurons are the effector systems, including communication and memory, inactivation of which may prevent the examiner from discovering that consciousness is being or has been generated).

Assessing consciousness clinically is notoriously problematic. Part of the difficulty is the unreliability and crudeness of much of the data, and also there is the possibility that clinicians and psychologists have no precise agreement on what is meant by consciousness; but, more importantly, widely scattered lesions, or a variety of pathologies, may affect consciousness in some manner, and it is not known except in a speculative way how these have their effects. This is particularly so with complex perceptual and cognitive forms of consciousness, the parts of which may be generated in widely separated cerebral areas.

We would like to use the clinical data to help us locate in the CNS the site or sites where consciousness is generated. The presence of consciousness and its level are established by verbal report from the patient and by inference from the patient's behavior. Loss or diminution of consciousness may be global or regional. Full global loss precludes verbal witness, but we may often not be sure from the evidence of absent verbal or other behavior that the loss is complete, while in regional or partial global loss we may, for various reasons, not be sure of the reliability of the verbal report.

Identifying the boundaries of histological damage or physiological impairment can seldom be better than roughly approximate in the human subject, thereby limiting the accuracy of attempts at correlation with subjective and behavioral effects, and in animal studies although lesions can be made more precise subjective information is unavailable for correlation.

Prefrontal lobectomy and removal of some large areas of cerebral cortex have been reported not to result in loss of consciousness, although mental and behavioral functions are disturbed. Such disturbances may in fact be due to loss of the ability to generate advanced and subtle forms of consciousness, which crude neuropsychological testing fails to reveal. If an area is destroyed or removed and consciousness is not lost or reduced then that area is not one that generates consciousness. Bilateral damage to the primary auditory cortices in man (but apparently not in the least encephalized mammals) results in deafness (Guyton 1987:229). In the case of the lower mammals sound consciousness may be generated in the medial geniculate nuclei of the thalamus, possibly with the 'primary' cortical areas subserving secondary auditory functions. Removal or pathology of the primary visual cortices in humans results in blindness as reported by the subject. These findings are generally accepted as sufficient evidence that these cortical areas generate auditory and sight consciousness respectively.

If all consciousness generation is lost the organism is totally unconscious. If some consciousness is retained in the absence of cerebral cortex it obviously is generated in lower structures, presumably the thalamus; phylogenetically older reflexive systems may utilize consciousness without memory and without access to language centres, and on evolutionary grounds this seems probable, although impossible to prove until the metabolism of consciousness generation has been elucidated.

Loss or diminution of consciousness means failure or partial failure in the generation of consciousness. Abnormalities of consciousness result either from abnormal conditions affecting the basic transducing metabolism which generates consciousness or from disturbances in the complex neural machinery which coordinates the signals vying for access to the transducer, producing subjective effects such as confusion, strangeness, depersonalization, and other mental disturbances.

1.6 THE STATUS OF CONSCIOUSNESS

The various anatomical and functional findings (assuming their reliability) must be interpretable in terms of our own subjective experiences and the conclusions drawn from these. When there is seeing it means that sight consciousness is being generated by brain activity. 'I am seeing' is language certifying that sight consciousness is being generated in this individual. The accumulated evidence shows that this sight consciousness is generated by primary (striate) visual cortex and specialized, distinct secondary (prestriate) areas (Zeki, 1993).

When an object slips from our hand and a few milliseconds later we catch it in midair the occurrence is over 'before we know what is happening' – we apparently see and feel what has happened 'after the fact'. The evidence suggests that this feat is a non-conscious reflexive action, but also that in the intact brain visual and somesthetic signals that trip the reflex go on to generate sight and somatic consciousness; the reflexive act may be completed before consciousness of the event is generated. Similarly, we may react to a sound before we hear it. Several levels of reflexivity are present in advanced nervous systems; each newly evolved level in effect lies piggy-back on the earlier levels and mediates more complex responses. The highest levels operate via consciousness of the mind; any consciousness operative at a submental level is not part of the unified consciousness of the mind and therefore not open to introspection.

We may see, hear, feel, etc. passively or actively. Passive seeing, for example, is the mere generation of sight consciousness. Sensory signals are constantly arriving in varying strengths at the consciousness-generating neurons of all the sensory modalities. The 'focusing' mechanisms of consciousness will largely determine to what degree such incoming signals are allowed to generate consciousness, and this is the first stage of active seeing. *'Noticing' or 'attending' or 'focusing' at the mental level is nothing more than an increase in the generation of the relevant consciousness.* We 'notice' or 'attend' *to* one set of neural signals from an external source by means of the several focusing mechanisms of the brain boosting or facilitating the generation of consciousness by those signals derived from that set, at the same time suppressing the generation of consciousness by other signals. Other elements of active sensing include various automatic perceptual 'interpretations' (e.g. spatial judgements, detection of the direction of sounds, shifting illusions), as well as recognitions, memory retrievals, etc.

I hold that the generated visual consciousness (to take one sensory modality) *is* the *seeing*; it is both the seeing *and* what is seen. A visual signal that does not generate consciousness produces no seeing. All facets of consciousness generated at any moment (seeing, hearing, feeling, etc.) *are self-experiencing* – there is nothing outside such consciousnesses that can experience them, except that the process of unification allows the multifaceted whole to experience itself and its parts. The conviction of self in relation to a non-self world is a dichotomy (perhaps partly evolved, partly acquired) within the global, unitary consciousness; it is an internal representation of external reality (of the corporeal self vs. the environment) enabling effective responses at second-hand. Self in this sense may be a subjective composite – of memories, of the operation of innate and acquired mental and physical reflexes, etc., all exaggerated by the use of language and thinking.

There is no mechanism within the conscious experience itself that 'selects' for 'attention'. The different parts of the compound unitary consciousness engage downline neural mechanisms according to their strength and/or the existence of specific receptive programs. No inhibitory or augmentory mechanisms operate on already generated consciousness, but only on the pathways and processes that contribute to the further generation of such consciousness and on downline neural mechanisms engageable by consciousness. This is necessarily so if consciousness is a form of energy momentarily independent of the neural substrate; the hypothesis here holds that interaction between consciousness and matter results in disappearance of the former with transference of its energy either to useful neural activity or to heat.

When some part of the panorama of conscious experience at any moment 'catches our attention' what happens is that for such a part there is some neural circuitry or 'program' (innate or acquired) present in the CNS which is triggerable by it, and this program having a position in the hierarchy of priority for focusing will gain access to the focusing master-control apparatus (to be described later) if at that moment it has top priority, in which case it instructs the control apparatus to more strongly generate that part of the panorama of consciousness that triggered it (the program circuitry) and to suppress the generation of others. This is in a sense a form of selection, but it is self-selection and not selection by an independent agency.

This idea may be expressed slightly differently for emphasis and clarity as follows: The term 'sensation' in psychological practice refers to passive sensory consciousness; the processing that leads to this is of course active, but the *consciousness* is passive – it does nothing. Active seeing, hearing, etc. occurs when generated consciousness has effects on downline neural mechanisms. This begins when consciousness reconverts to neural energy and activates memory neurons and various response mechanisms and programs, acquired or innate. These in turn will, in addition to any executive effects, have access to a 'priority processing' function to compete for stronger focus, i.e. for increased generation of the relevant consciousness.

A concrete example may further clarify these ideas. Suppose the global unitary consciousness, that is, the panorama of the total conscious experience at any moment, includes a particular sound, say a slight rustling sound. Although this may constitute only a small fraction of the total at that moment, yet if it has through either genetic inheritance or learning special significance for the individual, for example indicating danger, this significance is embodied in the form of neural pathways constituting a recognition-response program of a certain degree of strength, giving it a particular priority position among the innumerable recognition-response programs in that individual's nervous system. If it has the highest priority among the programs being engaged at that moment by other aspects of the current global conscious experience it will be accommodated to the exclusion of the others.

In this example the rustling sound may by this means capture focus, so that the part of the auditory sensory cortex generating this sound consciousness will be maximally activated and competing cortical areas inhibited, with the result that signals coming from the sound source are able to fully reach other relevant recognition-response programs, including marginal ones, and in addition become subject to whatever higher level processing capability (thinking, etc.) the brain possesses.

As much as it may seem, introspectively, that when I select for concentrated attention some item in my current panorama of conscious experience 'I' am some literally independant conscious ego surveying then choosing, this cannot be so. It would mean that the ego as a separate entity is conscious of the details of consciousness – that 'I' am seeing what is being seen, which is redundant; and the only way that separate consciousnesses can experience or 'know' one another is by coalescence to form a global unitary consciousness via intact neuronal connections, the mechanism of which remains unsolved. The subjective ego that represents the individual organism as a whole is an evolved illusion necessary so that the sensory part of conscious experience, which is a *representation* of the external world, can be treated by the brain's cognitive mechanisms as if it were the external world; the very same level or type of neural substrate that generates the illusion that the sensory part of conscious experience *is* the external world also generates the illusion of the ego as a separate entity observing this external world. In certain pathological conditions this highly sophisticated mechanism is disturbed, with depersonalization and unreality effects.

It is necessary to further belabour this point as it is the core thesis of this book: In the theoretical model each of the postulated quantal units which constitute consciousness is in and of itself both the sensation (e.g. blue) *and the experiencing of the sensation* (i.e., seeing blue) – the unit of consciousness experiences itself; it is its own ego. The corporeal person (whether neuron, brain, or whole body) has no part to play in conscious experiencing but only in the non-conscious activity that generates consciousness and in non-conscious activity triggered by the reconversion of energy of consciousness to downline neural energy.

Furthermore, it is necessary to postulate that units of consciousness coalesce into composite, or higher order, *units*. A composite unit would be, for example, seeing blue and feeling pain, *and* this would represent the simplest level of global unitary consciousness. Multiply these and add varieties in sufficient numbers and one arrives at the human mind in which one part of the global unitary consciousness is the feeling of conviction of a separate ego corresponding to the corporeal entity in causal relationship with other parts corresponding to an external environment. Furthermore, the behavioral effects arising from this relationship are experienced through feed-back and reinforce the subjective dichotomy

1.7 THE EVOLUTIONARY BIOLOGY OF PERCEPTION

The term 'perception' as used in experimental psychology refers to active seeing, hearing, etc. in a narrower sense than above. This sense is demonstrated by the use of visual sketches and patterns which may be interpreted in different ways (e.g., either a vase or two faces in silhouette) or from which some significant feature may be extracted. In Kolb and Whishaw (1989) "perception is the result of activity of cells beyond the first synapse in the sensory cortex", and "in the neocortex sensory information is transformed into a percept by such factors as experience and context". It is evident that processing of sensory data takes place so that higher level illusion-consciousness is generated, illusional in that the contents of sensory consciousness although only representations of reality are treated (by the self part of consciousness and its associated neural mechanisms) as if they are reality. How this process functions, that of having within the same totality of consciousness at any moment a part which represents the organism inspecting another part which represents the external world is something of a mystery, but it can hardly be doubted that this illusion evolved, or develops with maturation and experience, because of its effectiveness for the organism in coping with its world.

Understanding this is crucial to understanding the mind. It is vital that the percept (i.e., the higher-level illusion constructed from the sensory data) be the same today as yesterday given the same external circumstances, because the organism depends on this reliability in its committal to action. The evolutionary process utilized variations in genetically based neuronal configurations which permitted the presence of certain features in the sensory data to have behavioral effects resulting in differential survival. New neuronal configurations giving rise to certain elaborations of the primitive sensations proved most reliable in representing significant external features and were selected. When these features are present in the sensory data the organism's response will determine its fate. Genetically based responses to a particular combination of basic features (lines, angles, shadows, etc.) will vary from individual to individual and natural selection will operate on these.

The response itself is determined by the kind of illusion consciousness generated, but how this secondary or higher level of consciousness (the 'percept') is fabricated – the 'binding' problem – remains unclear. It is doubtful that consciousness-generating cells are functionally linked so that activation of one part of such an ensemble results in activation of the whole thus giving the percept – seeing the tail of an animal does not result in *seeing* more than the tail, although of course it would commonly result in an image of the whole from memory. It is in the memory system with its specialized synaptic properties (as will be discussed later) that sensory configurations are stored, with the consciousness-generating neurons remaining unbound and free to be selectively activated to generate the percept.

The numerous illusional tricks with line drawings, e.g. that an object is near or far or the silhouette is a face or a vase, show that the percept is to some degree constructed by neural mechanisms responding to the raw sensory data. It is possible that some of these neural mechanisms are 'hard-wired' in that neuronal maturation allows particular patterns of sensory data to generate a stable percept which influences behavior in some vital way, but in many other situations the neural mechanism is moulded by experience, particularly experiences involving different sensory modalities, and by feedback from physical responses.

The percept is obviously a representation of the external world, and responses to the percept are responses to the external world at second hand. As already emphasized , it is vital that the percept be reliable in its representation, and this imperative acts as a selecting agency both in the evolution of mechanisms able to distinguish among the minutiae of sensory data those which are clues to the structure of the external world, and in the evolution of mechanisms for constructing the conscious experience or percept of sufficient distinctness to unhesitatingly drive appropriate behaviors.

For the survival of the organism it may hardly matter what form the percept takes, so long as the chain of reliability is maintained, unlike the specific relevance of particular feelings, physical and emotional. The intrinsic subjective experience, for example, of 'farness' for a perceptual object as opposed to that of 'nearness', is perhaps irrelevant and not analytically reducible, but the aura of nearness or farness must be stable under stable external conditions.

There must, of course, be certain essential correspondences, for example geometric: for three objects in the external world the one in the middle must remain so in the representing perception. The complete list of such essential correspondences would amount to all we can directly experience or really know about the external world, but while such a list may be somewhat small it yet enables us to invent mathematics and construct deep theories about the nature of reality.

But where is the consciousness (the percept) generated? If in the secondary sensory areas these must be equipped with more advanced consciousness-generating neurons and neuronal architecture derived presumably by evolutionary elaboration of the neuroblasts giving rise to the primary areas. There would in the secondary areas be new consciousness-generating neurons. The alternative would be newly evolved circuitries in the secondary areas which function to manipulate the individual consciousness-generating neurons in the primary areas to produce patterns of consciousness we term 'percepts'. I am not aware of any available empirical data useful in deciding between these alternatives, nor any theoretical grounds for doing so, but a percept is a coherent, advanced form of consciousness, generated by orchestrated consciousness-generating neurons, of a form evolved to trigger appropriate behavioral responses. A.R. Damasio (1989) has expressed views similar to the second alternative, his designated 'convergence zone' being a neural apparatus which feeds back to sensory cortex instructions for object delineation from elementary sensory fragments.

The secondary (prestriate) visual cortex is said (in one neuroscience text) to 'organize' conscious data from the primary cortex, a typically unhelpful generalization. We do not know if it (prestriate) also receives and processes unmodified sensory data via striate cortex. There are uncertainties around this question. According to Zeki (1993:111) "V1 must act as a segregator, parceling out different signals to the different specialized visual areas". The general evolutionary principle is easily enunciated: The evolving brain adds new structures to the old to provide more sophisticated representations of, and responses to, the external world – striate cortex extends the visual competence of the lateral geniculate nucleus (LGN), and prestriate cortex does the same for striate cortex.

Retinal ganglion cell axons do not extend all the way to the striate cortex; all synapse in the LGN. What does LGN do with the optic signals? Does it process and parcel? Are its signals to striate cortex affected by input from other thalamic structures? Was consciousness ever generated by LGN, and if so does it still do so or has this function been wholly taken over by neocortex?

A recent overview of the subject (Zeki, 1993) has magnocellular (M) layers 1 and 2 of the LGN going to layers 2 and 3 of striate (V1) cortex, thence to areas V2 and V4 by separate routes, with V2 also going to V4, and with some, but lesser, input to V3 and V5. On the other hand the parvocellular (P) layers 3 to 6 of LGN go to striate layer 4B, thence to areas V3 and V5 and some input to V4. There is parcellation but also significant overlap. What it all means has yet to be worked out, including the functional properties of the ultra-structures within cortical columns which receive input from several sources and transmit the results of their internal operations to several destinations to take part in various functions. We know from introspective analysis what the brain has to do; the accumulating details from neuroscientific research indicate how the brain actually works. Unraveling the machinery that provides the functioning mind is what such research is all about.

There is obviously an enormous amount of specialization of cellular structure required to produce the human level of conscious experience, but we may simplify the visual cortex (and similarly other sensory cortices) by proposing that it is structured so as to carry out up to four levels of reflexivity in parallel: 1/ The simplest level, possibly via input to layer 6, thence after one pyramidal cell synapse to contribute to head, neck, eye movements, etc. Primordial sight consciousness generated at the thalamic (LGN and pulvinar) level may exist and have a similar role.

2/ The simplest of the unequivocally conscious levels of reflexivity is engaged by input to layer 4 of V1, and possibly layers 2 and 3, and produces primitive visual sensations which may trigger or augment more complex, but still promptly acting, responses than 1/.

3/ More elaborate responses, commonly termed 'instinctive', to the most complete forms of visual sensory consciousness, often referred to as

1.7 The Evolutionary Biology of Perception   45

'percepts', generated by the combined functioning of striate and specialized prestriate cortical regions.

4/ Responses to the products of the thinking function involving widespread cerebral structures and operating voluntarily through the motor corticospinal tract. (The reflexivity of voluntariness is of course a moot point).

All of the neocortical sensory modalities are structured in this manner, a product of their evolutionary histories. The different levels and the different modalities influence one another in several ways for cooperative functioning, necessarily so because the brain, and indeed the nervous system as a whole, essentially functions as a single, massive reflex arc. The principal influence between the levels is probably inhibitory on their effector pathways to allow expression of the most relevant level of the moment, but the structural composition of each level on the sensory side of the reflex necessarily includes all levels beneath it.

It is by the combined functioning of the primary and secondary sensory visual areas that lines, corners, angles, wavelengths, movements, gradations of shading, stereoscopic data, and the relative positions of numerous such cues determine what class of object the individual 'sees' and his experience of space. If insufficient data are being received the interpretation may oscillate from one class to another, e.g., whether it is the inside or the outside of a box. This is a common happening both in real life and psychology classrooms – we often have to 'look twice'. Natural selection has made frequent use of the limitations of the neuroperceptive mechanisms by devising various forms of mimicry.

The interesting question is what happens when we shift from one class of perception to another during interpretation of a particular set of sensory cues. The simplest explanation seems to be the following: We have memory stores of, say, birds and leaves (which may be of similar size, shape, colour, and spatial context). When the sensory data are sufficiently unequivocal for bird or for leaf there is strong retrieval of the correct memory image which 'meshes' (Section 2.3) with the incoming sensory data to produce conscious recognition, which is a 'feeling' of familiarity, and there is immediate retrieval of linked details from memory which merge with the corresponding details in the sensory data giving secondary recognition, thus increasing the conscious experience of 'bird' or 'leaf' as the case may be, plus the beginning engagement of

Fig 1.7 **Primary and secondary recognitions** (From Hale, 1989)

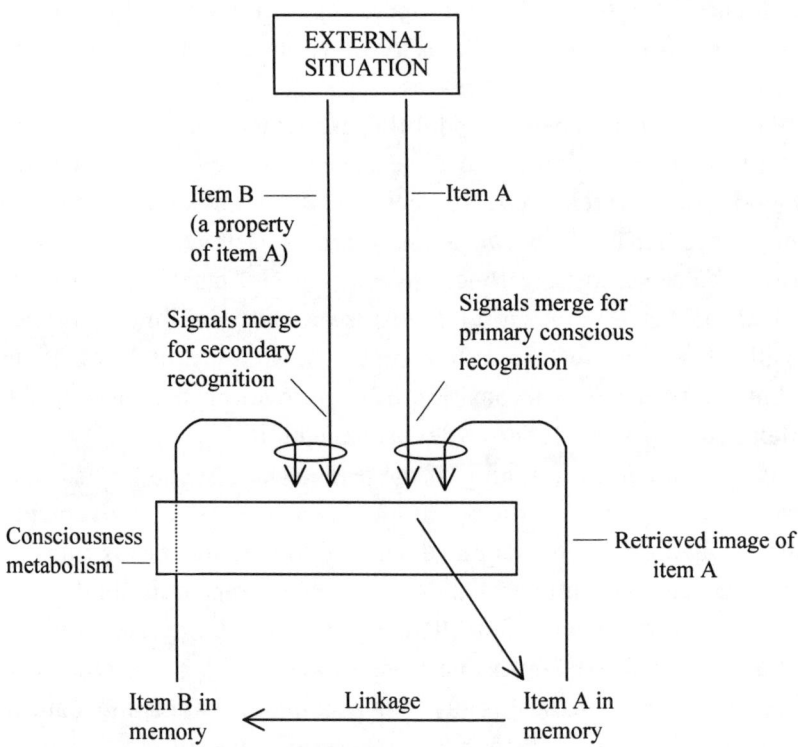

In primary conscious recognition the item itself is first recognized, but not its properties or associations, which are still in unretrieved memory. More or less shortly, and more or less completely, such retrievals take place, and those that have their origin in currently arriving sensory data combine with the latter to produce secondary recognition. Of course if these secondary items had captured focus first they would have resulted in the primary recognition. Also two or more recognitions may be primary in succession before secondary recognitions occur to link them (reveal their relatedness) in consciousness.

acquired and innate responses (however faintly), adding further to the conscious package of 'birdness' or 'leafness'.

But when the data are equivocal or insufficient the recognition oscillates from one category to the other, or both may be trying to operate simultaneously, with a resulting feeling of confusion. The adverse consequences of wrong interpretation must have acted powerfully to select against imperfect neuronal feature-extracting mechanisms, and the selective advantage of more discriminating mechanisms in neuronal technology, when reliable, would lead to great improvement in the mechanism of conscious recognition.

In the case of bird and leaf, each category has, through repeated exposure, more-or-less strongly bound a large number of individual memory neurons through grooved (potentiated) synaptic connections, with some overlap between the two categories, i.e. they share certain neuronal assemblages. When these shared assemblages are the ones mostly being activated at a given moment they will send streams of excitatory impulses in both directions, viz. to activate assemblages giving rise to bird and leaf recognitions, with mutual nullification of response mechanisms, until the matter is resolved by additional sensory data tipping the scale in one direction. When this happens the assemblages of synaptically-bound neurons representing the other feature will be reflexly inhibited so cease to have functional effects.

Obviously such overlap and sorting-out, excitations and inhibitions, functional compartmentalization yet rapid reshaping of compartments, all require a very high degree of specialization in neuronal properties – physiological, morphological, connectional, etc.. We know by introspection what sorts of mental faculties and experiences we have. The next step is to provisionally attribute to the anatomical elements we find in the brain these various functions, but ".... the manner in which large interacting networks of these nerve cells produce a mental activity remains almost a complete mystery" (Cooper,1981:479).

The neuroarchitectonics of perception is a branch of science still in its infancy; at present it consists of little more than tentative interpretive generalizations from clinical and experimental data, including single cell recordings. For example, in the bizarre clinical condition of sensory neglect following injury to the region of the right inferior parietal lobe the patient although receiving sensory information from the left side of the world behaves as if this side does not exist, e.g. in copying pictures will leave out features on the left side, or may ignore tactile sensations from the left side of the body, or may even deny that anything is wrong (Kolb and Whishaw,1990:424 ff). There are various theories to account for this neglect, e.g. that it is caused by defective sensation or perception, or it is caused by defective attention or orientation. On the face of it, each is possible, but no support for any is offered of the sort that would be determinitive, as such support would have to be in the form of detailed functional micro-anatomy of the cortex, such as which cells in which layer of the cortex are essential for the generation of consciousness; which act as memory stores; which are involved in intercortical connections for the kinds of intermemory linkages that form the basis of object delineation and object characterization; which intracortical connections allow memory retrieval into image form; how the mechanism of 'coalescence' of elements of consciousness into a compound unitary consciousness functions; what particular cortical cells are involved in the transmission of signals from a percept to downline responses (mental, motor, emotional); which connections relate somatosensory information to visual information to create spatial consciousness and how such consciousness is generated and how it is tied into various instinctive and acquired behaviours, etc..

It is hard to see how indepth knowledge of this sort is to be obtained. In the meantime speculation should not be discouraged despite its historical tendency to ruin reputations, for out of the controversy that such speculation is likely to cause there surely would arise ingenious new approaches to empirical research. For example, an interesting point may be brought up in the case of sensory neglect mentioned above. Such patients on making drawings from memory also neglect the left side of the picture. This can be explained on the assumption that the neurons generating the conscious percept have closely associated with them downline neurons responsible for storing the ingredients of the percept and for feeding them back to the consciousness-generating neurons for imagery, this imagery guiding the drawing the subject makes on paper. Damage to the area giving rise to the sensory percept will almost inevitably damage its associated memory neurons. This, then, can be adduced as evidence that individual consciousness-generating neurons have their own memory neurons which by recurrent axonal branching can re-stimulate the consciousness neuron independently of sensory input, to generate units of consciousness of the type it is specialized for. By

1.7 The Evolutionary Biology of Perception 49

extension of this argument, all memory neurons are tied functionally and anatomically to specific consciousness-generating neurons; if the latter are destroyed the memories can no longer be retrieved. Bilateral loss of cortical area V4, for example, results not only in loss of colour vision, but also of the ability to remember or even imagine colours (Zeki,1993). (Some classes of pyramidal neurons in the deeper layers of sensory cortices have such recurrent axonal collaterals to neurons in the more superficial layers. Since these neurons must obviously be doing something, almost certainly concerned with mental activities such as perceiving, remembering, and imagining, it seems eminently sensible to provisionally assign specific functions to them. To do so at least gives us targets to shoot at critically).

1.8 VISUAL MECHANISMS AND SIGHT CONSCIOUSNESS

Loss of the primary visual (striate) areas of the cerebral cortex results in blindness, i.e., loss of sight consciousness. The conclusion is that sight consciousness is generated by neurons in these areas of the cortex. Loss only of the secondary visual areas of cortex (prestriate cortex) does not result in loss of all sight but disorganizes or even abolishes specialized sight consciousness such as motion, colour, spatial relationships, etc.(Zeki,1992,1993; Kolb and Whishaw,1990); presumably the supplementation of primary subjective visual experience by increasingly complex percepts is carried out in these areas. Loss of prestriate cortex bilaterally in the monkey is reported to result in inability to learn, which suggests that visual memory function is located here or that this is a route to visual storage (Poggio,1980:555), although more likely the learning disability following such crude experimental damage results from loss of higher visual consciousness-generating function.

On the other hand, after loss of only the primary visual areas the monkey, though presumably without sight consciousness (but see Barbur et al, 1993), is able to accurately respond to moving objects in its environment, but does not 'recognize' still objects. Similarly the high decerebrate cat, in which the superior colliculi and the input to these from the optic nerves are intact, responds to moving objects accurately but will walk into static objects, which it apparently does not 'see'. It may be concluded from these findings that the removed higher structures evolved in part because the ability to 'notice' details of the static environment was profitable. But primitive organisms with no homologue of these structures do not walk into obstructions, so the conclusion loses credibility unless it can be shown that there is a 'law' governing the evolution of complexity in nervous systems to the effect that preadapted structures on evolving more elaborate function are deprived, in their retained primitive parts, of behavioral responsibility. In the present example when the relevant neural mechanism in the preadapted organism evolves a more advanced 'noticing' capability the new supporting neural structure may during the course of its elaboration become physically distanced from the original structure and so be cut off in the high decerebrate preparation.

The primary visual (striate) decorticate human and the high decerebrate animal cannot 'see' but are able to follow moving objects with their eyes and to more or less accurately react to them. The question then arises as to whether any kind of consciousness is involved in this lower level capability. The answer would seem to be that we cannot know (but see Beckers and Zeki, 1995, for experimental findings relevant to this topic). The ability to learn would require a memory function and therefore, almost certainly, consciousness, but I know of no report on visual learning in such 'blind' subjects. Consciousness can only make itself known to an observer by the existence of such learning ability or by language communication from the subject or by behavioral effects which we believe to be impossible without it.

Similar in some ways to this visually functioning but 'blind' capability (so-called 'blind sight') is the finding in commissurotomy (split-brain) subjects, who are 'blind' to objects in the left visual field (served by the right cerebral hemisphere) as reported by left cerebral-dominant patients, of being able to respond appropriately to some visual cues presented in the 'blind' field. A straightforward (if unlikely) interpretation of the findings in this case is that in the intact brain only the dominant hemisphere generates sight consciousness, receiving visual signals directly from the contralateral field and indirectly from the ipsilateral field via collaterals across the corpus callosum from axons synapsing in the corresponding visual cortex. If this is the case the dominant hemisphere presumably inhibits the generation of consciousness by the other side via inhibitory transcallosal fibres. Such inhibitory activity may in time result in loss of functional competence of the inhibited neurons, so that the later in life loss of the dominant hemisphere takes place the

1.8 Visual Mechanisms and sight Consciousness 51

poorer, one would expect, would be the ability of the suppressed visual cortex to resume the function of generating sight consciousness. The fact that right occipital lobe damage results in left visual field blindness is not proof that sight consciousness is generated there, for such damage will almost certainly interrupt the collateral signals to the left side.

On the other hand if left occipital lobe damage occurs at any stage of life left visual field sight (served by the right occipital lobe) remains intact and can be verbally attested by the subject, thus arguing against the above ideas. Furthermore, anatomical studies have shown that the primary visual cortices of the two sides are not, or only very sparsely, interconnected via the commissures (Carpenter,1991:393); however, Berlucchi and Sprague(1981:431) have shown transfer of visual information between areas 17 and 18 of the two sides.

An experiment on the human which would shed much light on this problem would be temporary inactivation of corpus callosal function by local anaesthesia, producing a reversible split brain condition. If any visual experience from the left visual field to the right cerebral hemisphere occurring during the effects of the local anaesthetic can later be recollected in visual imagery it would prove that divided consciousness had truly occurred, and it would strongly support the idea that preoccupation with the corporeal 'self' is a function of the language dominant hemisphere. Although corporeal self-awareness is a highly evolved or, more likely, acquired form of complex perceptual consciousness which undoubtedly develops pari passu with the faculties of volition and language, it is a separate process from language, but the intimate working relationship between these faculties would seem to favour their concentration in the same hemisphere. Nonetheless, and complicating the picture, in split-brain patients "although the hemispheres function independently they both do so at a high level" and specific tests show that each has "its own sensations, percepts, thoughts, and memories that are not accessible to the other hemisphere" (Kolb and Whishaw, 1990:509). Specific tests also indicate that the non-speaking hemisphere has knowledge of self and has language comprehension.

Bilateral loss of both the primary and secondary (striate and prestriate) visual cortices results in loss of all visual competence (except pupillary and blink responses to bright flashes). Loss of the secondary areas alone results in impairment of spatial judgement, confusion of moving objects, and inability to learn pattern discrimination tasks. From the evidence of animal (and more recently human – e.g. Barbur et al, 1993, and Beckers and Zeki, 1995) studies the secondary area has visual functions which are independent of input from the primary ('seeing') area, and this is supported by the connections it has with subcortical structures (superior colliculus, pulvinar, etc.) which in turn receive sensory visual input independently of the main geniculo-striate visual pathway. In man, however, these subcortical connections of the parallel visual system are believed to have relatively little importance, being in fact vestigial.

It has been established (see review by Zeki,1993) that prestriate visual cortex has several subdivisions, designated V2 through V6, specialized for different functions – colour, movement, etc.. Specific classes of cells in V1 and V2 send projections independently to the specialized areas, evidently to build up more comprehensive perceptual representations of the external world since damage to these areas impoverishes visual perception.

Each small area of V1 (striate cortex) receives all the input that a correspondingly small area of the retina (with which it is anatomically and functionally associated) is able to transmit (leaving aside the role of the lateral geniculate nucleus (LGN)). These retinal areas first receive all the light stimuli from a correspondingly small, fixed region of the field of view, the information within such light stimuli probably being far richer than can be utilized by any visual system so far evolved.

Each such small area of V1 has evolved to be able to handle just so much of the information reaching it – it can generate just so much seeing consciousness (of wavelength, movement, shape, etc.) Each of these small areas of V1 with its associated small area of retina is in effect a complete, though primitive, visual system able to sample the entire visible world, tiny sections at a time, by moving the eye around, but evolution has provided large numbers of these unit systems placed and operating in parallel so that a wide visual field can be seen at a glance. Evolution has also provided connections between these numerous parallel units so that their perceptual (seeing) functions are in some unknown manner joined (coalesced) to provide a united, single percept – the so-called unity of consciousness. Unit areas (retinal or cortical) are not all identical; some handle certain types of optical information better than others.

The point of all this is that for a lineage to enjoy a richer seeing capability evolution must add to and elaborate what is already there, all

Fig. 1.8(1) Each small area of retina has some or all of the following projections

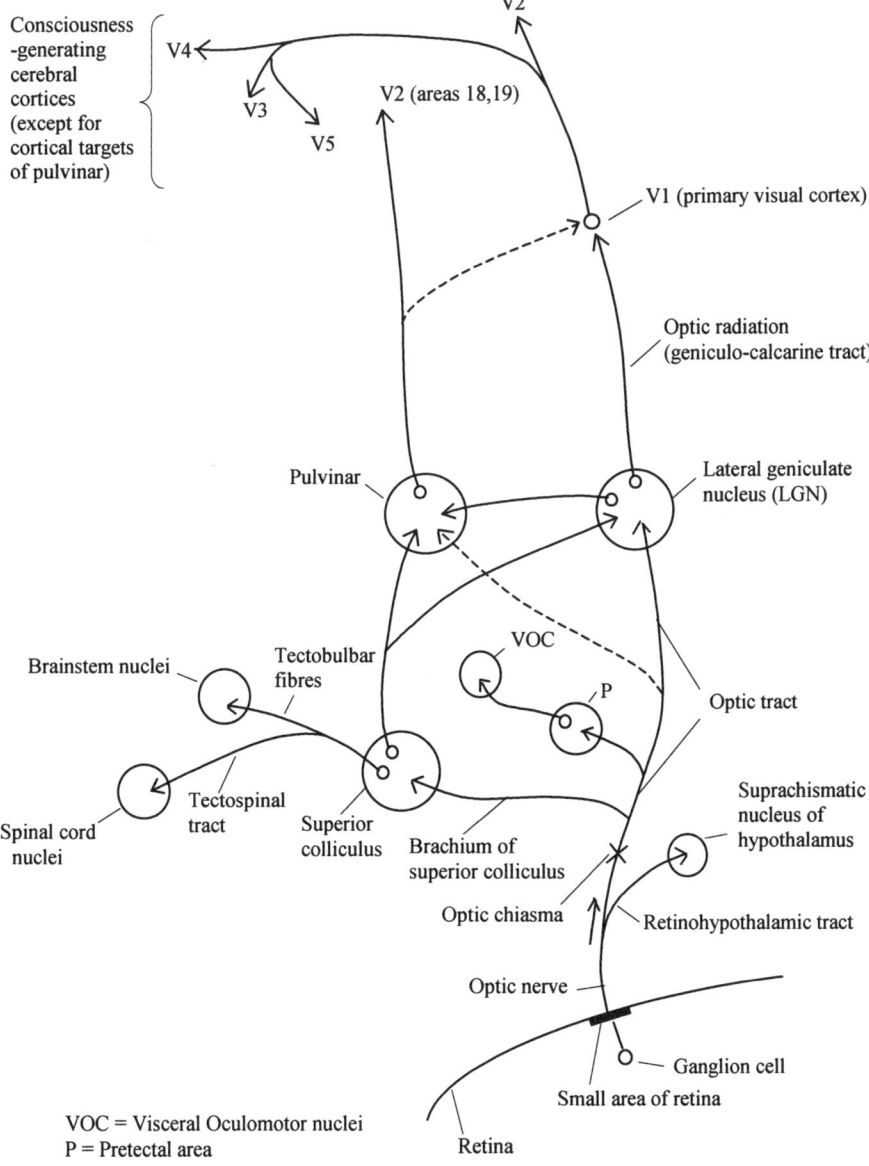

the way from the optics of the eye to the mechanism that transduces neural signals into consciousness. The way this has been achieved, so far as the cortex is concerned, has apparently been for each unit area of V1 to parcel out tasks to newly evolved cortical areas beyond the boundaries of V1. For example, the cells responsible for wavelength discrimination within each V1 unit area pass on signals to cells in V4 which have evolved the ability to use such signals to generate colour consciousness, thus enriching the internal representation of the external world; similarly, other cells in the same V1 unit area responsible for elementary motion consciousness pass signals to V5 for more complete motion consciousness. And so on.

Many details of genetic blueprinting have yet to be worked out, but there is evidence that genetic variation can involve the whole sensory system from receptor to cortex in 'one go'. E.g., mice bred with supernumerary vibrissae are found to have enlarged cortical representations for vibrissae (Welker and Van der Loos,1986). This makes the evolutionary elaboration of complex systems easier to understand, in that it does not so fully depend on the fortuitous appearance simultaneously of several critical phenotypic variations separately controlled genetically.

We know from introspection that a visual image (sensory or from memory-imagination) may have several effects: triggering of innate or acquired reflexive responses, elicitation of emotions, retrieval of other memories, engaging the imaginative and thinking functions, etc. This means that the visual image on reconversion to neural energy must have open to it pathways to several different parts of the brain; and since the image precipitating these effects may vary from being simple and poorly organized (thus probably generated in the striate cortex) to the most complex (thus generated by much of the visual consciousness-generating cortex) every part of the visual cortex must have such access, directly or indirectly. The elucidation of these pathways is still at an elementary stage, although considerable progress has been made in recent years. Unfortunately, progress is limited by the necessity of investigating the substrate of these functions in poorly encephalized mammals, for example the connections between sensory neocortex and amygdala in the rat, an animal with a primitive emotional system.

Fig.1.8(2) Flow-chart of the visual systems

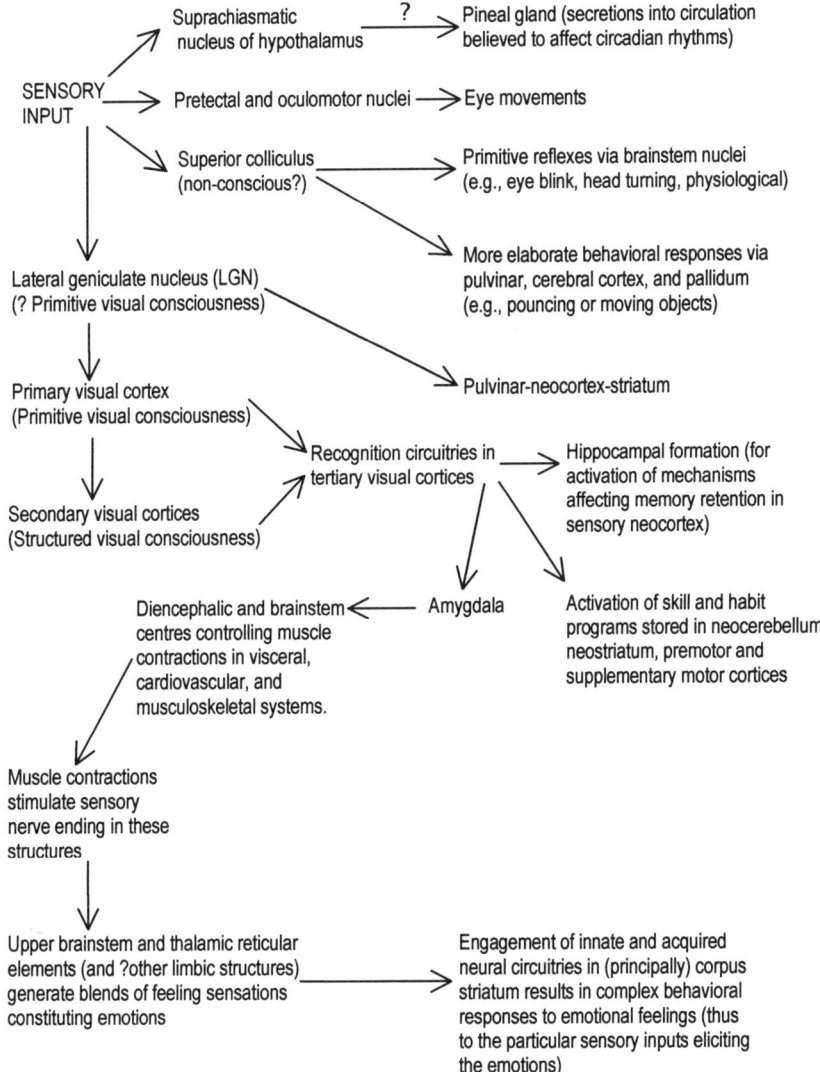

Agnosias, the "partial or complete inability to recognize sensory stimuli, unexplained by a defect in elementary sensation or by reduced level of alertness" (Kolb and Whishaw,1990) dramatize the degree to which evolution has elevated the sensory systems for the provision of conscious representation of the external world.

In no instance is this better demonstrated than in prosopagnosia, the inability to recognize familiar faces. There are, as is usual in the interpretation of clinical findings, some differences of opinion about what prosopagnosia tells us about the workings of the brain. There is evidence that inferomedial temporal cortex and adjacent occipital cortex are crucially involved in such recognition (Tranel and Damasio,1993; Guyton,1987; Barr and Kiernan,1988), while other workers have found the right parietal cortex to be important (Kolb and Whishaw,1990).

Essentially we are dealing here with a highly evolved learning and recognition capability which allows individual visual patterns differing in minor details to be easily discriminated and recognized. This is probably no more than advanced development of the basic mechanisms of conscious recognition, or recognition memory, which is discussed in Section 1.9. The pattern differences that make up individual faces are recordable in human memory. Reexposure to the patterns elicits narrow responses which prominently include a sense or feeling of familiarity. This direct conscious recognition is rapidly supplemented by retrieval of a host of associated memories as well as engagement of various acquired response programs (behavioral, linguistic, mental, and emotional) which are more-or-less consciously experienced, adding to the recognition.

The essentials of this process may be present in primitive form at early stages of sensory processing, possibly as early as the level of primary visual cortex, becoming progressively more sophisticated through secondary and tertiary visual areas. If we speculate on the evolution of such stages we may get a better idea of the nature and location of the present mechanisms. If, at each stage of evolution, genetically based variations occur in the capacity for storage and recognition of sensory patterns, and if for a particular lineage there is adaptive value in continued improvement in such capacity, then, according to established principles, greater complexity of structure and function will evolve.

The actual form such elaboration takes will be constrained by the resistance of older structures and functions to internal change, therefore internal reorganization is less likely than peripheral elaboration and expansion, giving rise to new structures. More complex patterns of stimuli emanating from environmental entities having particular significance for the genealogical line over evolutionary time will come to be specifically memorizable and recognizable; the presence in the environment of such relevant entities mandates the direction of evolutionary adaptation.

Applying these ideas to the human capacity for recognizing faces (or, for that matter, to any faculty in any species for high-level performance) we see that new structures allowing more sophisticated functioning are added to the old; first the early sensory neocortex to preexisting sensory elements of the thalamus, then extension of this early neocortex to secondary and tertiary visual areas, each stage allowing more elaborate visual memory and recognition functions, with increasingly wide connections to other cortical and subcortical structures.

It follows that the location and severity of damage will determine the nature of the observed behavioral effects. In the case of prosopagnosia the disability may range from slight hesitancy in recognizing familiar faces to inability to recognize that a nose, a mouth, and eyes, which are individually recognizable, constitute a specific entity, a face.

How ancient is the specific ability in humans to recognize individual faces? Is the temporal visual cortex more recent in origin than the occipital? What is the significance of its close anatomical relation to the limbic and diencephalic systems? Presumably the earliest visual cortex operated in part through these latter systems and would have been in close anatomical relation to them. But as new visual cortex appeared this would necessarily be positioned between the older visual cortex and these systems, with more elaborate connections, yet with the early cortex still retaining at least some of its original connections, allowing response to different levels of sensory and perceptual complexity, as illustrated in Appendix E, Fig(5).

It should be noted that anatomical studies have shown some of the more primitive pathways to be vestigial in humans.

Does temporal visual cortex generate consciousness? Or does it act to integrate smaller perceptual segments generated in earlier stages of the visual cortex? What is the significance of the finding that electrical stimulation of temporal visual cortex may result in the elicitation of vivid visual memories?

The ability to recognize, of necessity requiring the ability to store in memory, increasingly complex sensory patterns requires that synaptic properties evolve to be able to functionally link smaller ensembles of memory neurons into larger units. Thus the component parts of faces are linked in memory in such detail that not only are they recognized on exposure as constituting a whole face but a unique whole face. Again the question arises of why new cortex is required for such additional specialized function, and the provisional answer as before is that internal reorganization of existing structures is severely constrained by limits of space and genetic variability. If, therefore, damage to 'association' cortex results in failure to recognize previously learned unique sensory patterns it need not be that memories of these patterns are stored here but that such cortex contains neuronal elements that link memories stored in the consciousness-generating areas of cortex.

It is improbable that inferotemporal cortex generates sight consciousness or stores visual memories. An attempt will be made later to show that the generation of consciousness and the memory of such consciousness are functions of closely juxtaposed neurons situated in the same cortical columns in sensory cortices. Electrical stimulation of temporal visual cortex will activate memory ensembles situated elsewhere, and it is not surprising that the effects of such blunderbuss stimulation tend to be bizarre.

(Does the sense or feeling of familiarity that comes with recognition have a biological function? It will be proposed (Section 2.18) that it has a crucial role in the evolution of advanced minds. It should be noted that basic recognition is a purely functional, one might say mechanical, process – simply that a stimulus is able to activate some neural circuitry. The subjective experience, as we know it, that is 'correlated' with this process may originally have been an ineradicable epiphenomenon).

1.9 THE MEMORY SYSTEMS AND THE ELABORATION OF CONSCIOUSNESS

General considerations

The evidence from introspection and common experience tells us that the conscious state is recorded in some non-conscious form which can be re-converted back to image consciousness. Experimental and clinical

Fig. 1.9 **Inter-sensory connections subserving memory functions (and probably the unification of consciousness)** – left lateral view of brain

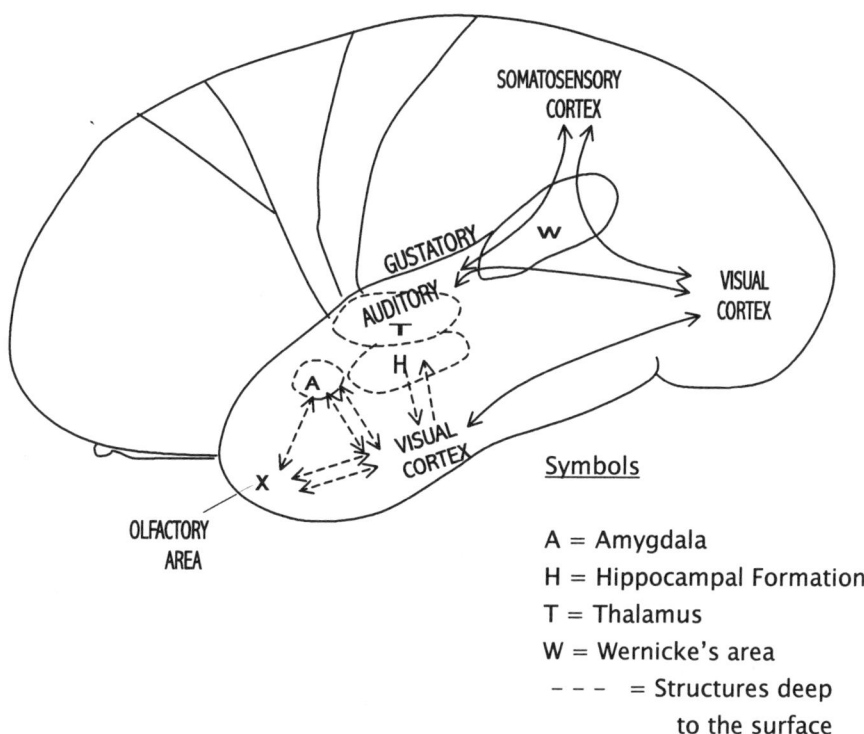

Symbols

A = Amygdala
H = Hippocampal Formation
T = Thalamus
W = Wernicke's area
- - - = Structures deep to the surface

All sensory modalities (visual, auditory, somatosensory, olfactory, gustatory, vestibular) as well as all feeling modalities (emotional and physical) are in contact with one another via intact axonal-dendritic connections to allow inter-modality associations to form. The same pathways may also play a part in integrating consciousness to form the unitary mind.

Note that Wernicke's area overlies the main crossroads. Numerous lesser crossroads exist but damage to this area (or, more specifically, to its underlying white matter) virtually stops mental functioning.

Each sensory area sends deep fibres to amygdala (A) and hippocampal formation (H) for access to emotional, behavioral, and physiological functions of limbic-diencephalic-brainstem systems. Also, each area receives its sensory input from relay cells in thalamus (T), except for the olfactory area.

investigations have shed disappointingly little light on how and where these processes occur. The cerebral cortex of Homo sapiens has been estimated to be composed of some 10 billion neurons, and possibly 5 to 10 thousand times that many synapses. This is an astronomical number, yet presumably they perform functions contributory to the individual's survival. Given man's huge memory capacity, probably very much greater than his retrieving ability, and its versatility, we may look to the neocortex for the bulk of these functions.

The vast range and complexity of sensory consciousness generated by our brains must require an unimaginably large number of neurons involved in consciousness-generation. Each such neuron must in principle have access to another neuron for storage of its product (i.e. recording of its activity) by means of some cellular (somatic and/or synaptic) mechanism. Vast numbers of the latter are therefore required for human memory function. These conclusions seem incontrovertible. It is extremely unlikely, given the close evolutionary and functional correlation of consciousness and memory, that the consciousness-generating neuron and its memory neuron are physically much separated, and it is even possible, though unlikely, that a single neuron carries both functions. We must therefore expect to find the basic memory function in the sensory areas of the cortex, in the same cortical columns as the consciousness neurons, and probably in deeper cortical layers since the general flow of information in the cerebral cortex is from upper to lower layers.

We may also expect to find primitive consciousness-memory functions in the more ancient parts of the cerebral cortex and perhaps in the even more ancient structures from which cortex evolved, but these functions may be too feeble to be introspectively distinguishable. (However, on wakening from sleep or recovering from head injury, anaesthesia, etc. the first resumption of consciousness-memory function may be in the primitive areas, these being more robust and the last to succumb to, and the first to recover from, adverse conditions, or so we believe. What we do not know is to what extent more recently evolved structures usurp functions belonging to the structures from which they are supposed to have evolved).

1.9 The Memory System and the Elaboration of Consciousness

The basic structure

The simplest, most commonsensical picture of the basic consciousness-memory function is that of a specialized neuron which on being activated generates units of consciousness which reconvert to neural energy to 'imprint' its downline memory neuron. This memory neuron is now altered in such a way that when it is subsequently activated (whether by impulses from other neurons or again by its consciousness neuron) it sends impulses via its axonal branches to (1) other memory neurons, (2) back to its consciousness neuron to generate more of the same consciousness, and (3) possibly (unless inhibited) to effector mechanisms. The other memory neurons it activates in this way will each on discharging do these same three things. It seems very probable that a major part of all corticocortical pathways in the sensory areas consists of linkages between memory neurons, for only by such connections can memory associations form and retrieval of dormant memories occur. See Figs. 2.1(1)-(8)

Localization of function

The primary sensory areas of cerebral cortex in man comprise a relatively small proportion of the whole cortex. Precise mental functions must be assigned to the remainder, but this becomes more difficult as the functions become more complex and subtle. We must try to localize functions such as the memory linkages between different sensory modalities, and explain how complex memories and understandings are stored. We must also determine where emotion consciousness and subtle forms of consciousness are generated, and the neural mechanisms controlling (activating or inhibiting) the various regions of consciousness generation. Every innate mental process must have a genetically determined neural substrate, perhaps with the more recently evolved functions, such as thinking and voluntary imagination, being supported by widespread subfunctions. It obviously requires great complexity of structure and much cellular material to store complex memories such as visual scenes, musical pieces, and understandings of all kinds.

Matching the introspectively derived model to the currently accepted anatomy

In making an effort to fit an introspectively based model of the mind in all its activities to the known, or currently accepted, empirical data of neuroscience perhaps the greatest difficulty is in determining where to locate the generation of subtle forms of consciousness associated with cognitive activities such as wonder, curiosity, interest, will, amusement, etc. It seems unlikely that these forms of consciousness are generated in the primary sensory areas, but if they are generated elsewhere, in the secondary and tertiary (or 'association') sensory areas, we must suppose, as discussed earlier, that either these areas somehow manipulate the elementary consciousness-generating cells in the primary areas to build up complex patterns or new blends of consciousness, or such forms are generated in the secondary and association areas by more recently evolved consciousness neurons. And, complicating the picture, many of these subtle forms of consciousness associated with higher cognitive functions such as wonder, curiosity, etc. may be emotionally tinged, therefore almost certainly involving the limbic system, and this may contribute importantly to behavioral effects.

New blends of consciousness

A 'unit' of consciousness if generated in the primary area presumably cannot travel to another region of the brain to take part in a mixing process or synthesis; if it is an energetic entity, as hypothesized here, it reconverts to neural energy at the site of its origin. The genetic blueprint for the primary generating neurons may, however, in the course of evolution have spawned off-shoot neurons generating different flavours of consciousness and these and others slightly dissimilar may be anatomically and physiologically associated so as to function in unison to generate a new blend of consciousness having a useful behavioral effect. New areas of cortex and possibly limbic (e.g. amygdaloid) circuitries thus appear in the evolution of the lineage, downstream from the more primitive 'parental' (ancestral) areas, and will be retained if any elaboration of behavior they may give rise to is of selective value.

Pertinent to the above ideas is the discovery of a mosaic of visual field representations in areas bounding the primary visual cortex in all the mammals so far studied. Detailed studies of these representations have shown that they differ from one another in several important ways

(Maunsell and Newsome,1987). One of the features of these areas is that the receptive field properties of their cells appear to repeat properties already present in primary visual cortex. These findings taken at face value support the idea that secondary visual areas evolved as extensions of the primary and that they are elaborated for more comprehensive perceptual functions. In general one may say that the evolutionary process has painstakingly moved toward representing by means of consciousness more and more of the features and properties of the world in which the organism lives which are relevant to its vital interests, such representation evidently being the only means by which appropriate behavioral responses to complex external features can be engineered. The responses are engaged by the conscious representation, therefore only indirectly (at 'second-hand') by the external situation.

Various other studies (e.g. Cowey,1981) have revealed in secondary cortical sensory regions a multiplicity of semi-independent 'association' islands which have profuse internal interconnections, with strong but fewer connections between the islands. It is again tempting to propose that such structuring (if they are not the same as the above mosaics) evolved to represent more properties of the external world through increasingly elaborate forms of consciousness ('percepts') which act on equally evolved downline mechanisms for more effective behaviors. Each island is presumably specialized to generate a particular attribute of perception, or some perceptual category in cooperation with other islands. In the visual system several distinct functional areas responding to different stimuli (wavelength, motion, form) have been identified in prestriate cortex (Zeki,1993). Whatever the nature of the physics underlying the coalescence or integration of elements of consciousness into a unitary whole, it is evidently necessary that intact connections between the generating neurons must exist, and there is a profusion of these within and to a lesser extent between the cortical association islands.

Cooperative functioning of dispersed processing areas

A situation or subject matter which contains visual, somesthetic, auditory, and olfactory elements will, despite being a circumscribed whole, be represented by consciousness being generated in widely separated areas of the brain, viz. the occipital, parietal, temporal, and olfactory cortices, either by sensory input or activation of their associated memory structures. Damasio's (1989) idea of convergence zones where multimodal concepts are created is attractive but probably untenable: it would require, for example, the different modes of consciousness to travel from their sites of origin to some other part of the cortex for a mixing process, which seems highly improbable, or that these zones are multimodal sensory cortices able themselves to generate every type of consciousness, which is even more improbable.

It is extremely doubtful that any individual neuron is able to generate more than one modality of consciousness, and it is difficult to see what advantage would be gained by having islands of cortex containing a mix of neurons belonging to different sensory modalities, not to mention the unlikeliness of such a system evolving. The responses of some neurons (e.g., in inferior area 6 of frontal lobe and 7b of parietal lobe) in single electrode studies to more than one modality of sensory input is not evidence that they generate more than one type of consciousness, or any consciousness at all, but only that they partake in multimodal cooperative functioning; e.g., in one study 24% of tested cells in putamen responded to both visual and somatosensory input (Graziano and Gross, 1995), and putamen almost certainly does not generate consciousness.

The most rational explanation for the existence of cortical zones of multimodal activity is either that these contain cells that (as suggested above) exercise switching functions for intermodal cooperative functioning or are otherwise local crossroads of corticocortical medullary fibres connecting adjacent sensory modalities for more specialized memory linkage functions, including sequential ones essential for the storage of understandings (i.e., they are satellites of the main Wernicke junction which is located in the region of the angular gyrus).

Islands of 'association' cortex

The above multimodal zones must be distinguished from the islands of tertiary ('association') cortex described above which, it was speculated, serve advanced cognitive functions, possibly also as recognition networks for complex environmental and social situations. Whether such recognition networks are hard-wired, requiring only maturation to become functional, or are partly hard-wired, requiring priming, or are plastic and able to be shaped by experience, are matters completely uninvestigated, while the more basic question of the function of 'association' cortices remains unresolved. The flow of neural current from these areas funnels through paralimbic cortex to hippocampus, or more directly to amygdala, and these in turn engage limbic, diencephalic, striatal, and brainstem autonomic and reticular systems to evoke emotions, behaviors, and physiological changes. Learning and conditioning no doubt play important roles in shaping such responses, but the innate elements may be very much more significant than we think, requiring a large number of complex evolved circuitries for the numerous recognition-responses. Much of the stereotyped responses or mannerisms of humans, such as smiling and a feeling of benevolence at the sight of young at play, may be largely innate, and the 'association' areas are logical places to look for the recognition circuitries for these.

For an individual the meaning (or significance) of an object (or word) is the totality of more-or-less strong linkages its memory storage neurons have with other memory storage neurons, and these may be widely scattered in the brain. When such an object (or word) is consciously experienced these linkages will tend to be engaged, in leisurely or rapid sequence, and short-term (holding, working) memory will tend to keep them 'in mind' as a unified whole.

The 'binding' problem

How can one account for the finding that wavelength, form, and motion are processed by different areas of visual cortex yet are accurately combined in the subjective sensory experience? We know that objects in the external world have these phenomena conjoined, and that such conjunction is maintained in the retina and the primary visual cortex (V1).

Although V1 is said not to generate colour consciousness, it nonetheless receives and transmits (presumably processing in some manner) the impulses that are used in cortical area V4 to generate colour consciousness. A possible explanation is that V1 receives information emanating from the external object to the limit that the retina can transduce the light stimuli it receives, but itself can only generate fairly simple consciousness out of this data, and this does not include colour consciousness. But more recently evolved cortex, in V4, is able to generate colour consciousness from the transmissions it receives from V1.

Somehow this colour consciousness is matched appropriately to the simpler conscious representation of the external object generated in V1. That is, light stimuli from an external object activates, via the retina, an ensemble of cells in V1 which cannot generate colour consciousness but which transmit neural signals to the newer cortex, V4, which can do so, and this in turn is somehow fitted appropriately to the consciousness generated by the V1 ensemble.

But how? Does V4 send signals back to the ensemble in V1 saying, "Use these return signals to generate colour consciousness in the appropriate parts of yourself, eg. blue in this part, red in that part, etc."? But this is unlikely because V1 would have to have evolved a capacity for generation of colour consciousness, which kind of evolution within the structure of older regions hardly ever occurs, but also because it would be redundant in that there is strong evidence that V4 does generate colour consciousness (Zeki, 1993).

So how else? My suggestion is that the colour consciousness generated in V4 remains in V4 but necessarily fits with whatever consciousness is generated in the V1 ensemble, colour-to-part appropriately. Light reflected from an external object contains all the information about that object available for use by visual mechanisms, irrespective of the possibility that neural signals in parallel pathways responding to adjacent light sources may influence one another before the stage of actual perception, as apparently happens with colour vision, and quite apart from cognitive embellishments. Since the perceptual object must correspond to the external object (if the organism is to survive and prosper) then each evolutionary improvement in the transduction of neural signals to consciousness for circumscribed object perception must operate on the same stream of light stimuli reflected from the external object as used by the older (earlier) parts of the processor. This must mean that neural pathways from retina to 'experiential' cells remain coherent, no matter how many new stages of such cells evolve for more complete conscious (visual) representation of the object, and no matter how much branching for specialization this 'tree of cohesion' may take, and irrespective of the distribution of return pathways.

1.9 The Memory System and the Elaboration of Consciousness 67

The modular unit of the visual system

It would seem to follow that there must be component areas of retina of critical minimum size each having the complement of cellular elements able to transduce to neural signals all the information that corresponding areas of V1 and their branches of specialization need for complete visual perception. Each such retinal area subtends a small field of view, rather like looking through a keyhole, but can register every visual quality that passes across that field of view. Such a segment of retina and V1 would be a functional unit, and, as mentioned earlier, there are large numbers of these in parallel, though not all functionally identical. So each, with its specialized extensions, is a more or less complete visual system able to sample only a tiny section of the world at any moment, but by the as yet little understood mechanism of integration these parallel perceptual pathways are combined to give panoramic perception representing more efficiently the external world.

So when light comes from the external world each narrow tree of specialization is activated as a unit, all parts virtually simultaneously, giving of necessity precise coherence of perceived attributes within the boundaries of its field of view. Form, colour, size, movement, etc. must all cohere within that tree. Linearly, from retina to specialized visual cortex, cohesion is built in because every type of consciousness generated along the way 'covers' the same field of view.

Since each attribute of consciousness in the experiential tree is self-experiencing it is perceptually distinct from every other attribute, but is necessarily co-joined with them; they are bound together so long as the pathways have developed normally and remain intact.

Functional integration of modular units

Distinct from this is the problem mentioned above of integrating laterally the component, linear trees of perception into unified perceptual objects and panoramas corresponding to those in the external world, but how this is done and the allied problem of how different sensory modalities can become unified into the global conscious experience remain unsolved. Intact neuronal connections are certainly required, and these connections carry nerve impulses, but it is *consciousness* that is unified and nerve impulses and consciousness are different entities. Also, simultaneity of generation determines only what is unified and is irrelevant as an explanation of the process. If back-and-forth nerve impulses have a part to play in the unification of consciousness it is hard to see what this might be – the passage of nerve impulses occurs throughout the nervous system and its essential function is either excitation or inhibition of target neurons, so when impulses from consciousness-generating areas 'A' and 'B' are exchanged the most that could happen would be an increase in the type of consciousness each generates, and we are no closer to a solution of integration.

Evolutionary elaboration of sensory consciousness and downline mechanisms

It is evident that the totality of passive sensory consciousness generated by any species is first due to the efficiency of its sense organs in transducing physical stimuli to neural signals and last to the efficiency of its 'experiential' (i.e., consciousness-generating) cells in transducing neural signals to consciousness. It is this consciousness that the brain's downline mechanisms respond to, and therefore, as previously mentioned, this is response to the external world at second-hand, and ranges from being a fairly simple reflex to one that has a processing stage consisting of thinking and understanding, the results of which in order to engage the executive mechanisms and thereby fulfil its function as a reflex arc requires the triggering agency which we call 'volition'. (Understanding the external world by thinking takes the brain's activities so far away from direct responding that natural selection necessarily evolved the functions of intention and volition; that is, for thinking to be selectively advantageous its results, understandings, can only be effectively applied through newly evolved executive functions).

Each new variety or form of consciousness the newly elaborated brain is capable of generating must have an associated memory capability. Thus if the newer cortex is capable of generating object consciousness (i.e. the 'percept' of discrete objects), then we must suppose that its associated memory neurons are able to store such information by means of specialized synaptic linkages between them. (I think of such specialized linkages as 'internal' linkages. Levitan and Kaczmarek (1991) have summarized the extraordinary amount of synaptic and other neuronal specializations revealed by recent research, the end of which is not nearly in sight. See also Shepherd (1990)). The new complex consciousness must also become part of the total unitary consciousness of the individual, and, in addition, as a result of being co-experienced

1.9 The Memory System and the Elaboration of Consciousness   69

with other aspects of consciousness, become linked to these via their respective memory neurons (by 'external' linkages). Only by the latter is retrieval of relevant dormant memories possible.

Further, the new arrangement, permitting the generation of more elaborate percepts representing external reality in more detail, must have useful behavioral effects if it is to be retained. As this requires an almost concomitant elaboration of response mechanisms it poses a theoretical difficulty of a sort frequently encountered in biological evolution: how to account for the apparently simultaneous elaboration of cooperative organic features which are under separate genetic control, none of which is of use in the new function without the others. The most likely explanation seems to be that in rapidly evolving species there is such a high level of genetic variability, even if of small range, among the individuals of each generation, in at least their rapidly evolving areas , that a potentially useful variation in some subfeature might, before being genetically lost, become associated in some descendant individual with a variation in another subfeature which results in functional benefit. Figuratively, there is a kind of entrepreneurial alertness among the various organs to seize on any new and viable business opportunity.

Inter-modality connections and mental functioning

There is an area of cerebral cortex of crucial importance in mental functioning which is not precisely defined and agreed upon in different texts (e.g., Kolb and Whishaw,1990 vs. Guyton,1987), possibly because of anatomical variations encountered and different investigatory techniques employed by the basic researchers. In Guyton this is Wernicke's area located in the posterior part of the superior temporal gyrus. In Kolb and Whishaw it is the angular gyrus and the posterior part of the parietal cortex, roughly Brodman's areas 39 and 40. This area is surrounded and 'fed' by the 'association' (or tertiary) areas of the visual, auditory, and somesthetic sensory modalities. It is believed that processed sensory information is 'integrated' here in most intellectual functions of the brain, and that it is the most important part of the brain for the higher function we call 'cerebration'. Loss of this area in the adult is said to result in a life of almost demented existence (Guyton,1987:230).

The strategic position of this area strongly suggests that it is concerned with memory linkages between the different sensory modalities, and that such linkages are between complex memories. For example, the sight of a bird (a complex visual object) may retrieve the memory of a bird song (a complex auditory experience) or vice versa. *Inasmuch as intellectual activities consist largely of sequential retrieval into consciousness of linked memories between (and within) the different sensory modalities, the disruption of the main crossroads will inevitably stop most mental functioning.* Hearing, seeing, feeling, etc. will each have no *meaning* outside its own modality: the sight of a bird will elicit visual associations, but no auditory ones; similarly words, read or heard, will be recognized (in the restricted sense of seeming familiar) but their meanings will not be elicited. In the reading disability known as dyslexia, of which there are several subvarieties, there is failure to recognize the meaning of written words. The obvious explanation for this is dysfunction or paucity of intermodal connections, and recent imaging techniques, notably magnetic resonance imaging (MRI), have shown reduced activity in the angular gyrus and Wernicke's and satellite intermodal areas (e.g., Shaywitz and Shaywitz, 1998.)

Also worth considering is that interrupting the physical connections between the different sensory modalities may destroy the unity of consciousness, thereby contributing to the 'demented' state. Such a suggestion is highly reasonable in view of the demonstrated loss of conscious unity following commissurotomy. There will be a hearing self, a seeing self, etc. all unknown to one another, each as truly distinct as the selves of different individuals. The pure form of such dissociations is unlikely to be seen clinically as this would require precise pathological interruption of all intermodal connections bilaterally.

When a memory substrate is activated by signals from sensory cortex of a different modality the image consciousness generated is presumably in the cortical region of the activated modality, not in Wernicke's area unless the cortex there is actually part of this modality. It is more likely that the crucial crossroads consists of sub-cortical corticocortical fibres and that the cortex itself does not serve any 'integrative' function between modalities as some textbooks suggest; there may be some intermingling of cells from adjacent modalities due to accidents of ontogenetic development, i.e., randomness in the final stages of neuronal maturation, but multimodal cortex as an adaptive evolutionary product is probably mythical. We must of course distinguish here between consciousness-generating cells, which are extremely unlikely to be able

1.9 The Memory System and the Elaboration of Consciousness

to generate more than one type of consciousness, and bimodal cells which respond to two modalities of input. These latter do not generate consciousness but, as suggested elsewhere, serve to coordinate the response systems serving different sensory modalities.

Cross-modal matching

The repeated congruence of visual, tactile, and other sensory data leads to strengthened object identity and conviction of objective reality. In man the neural basis of such integration is highly evolved in conjunction with other neural processes and permits the acquisition and use of greater details of environmental features and their properties, which is the principal advantage of highly evolved minds. Man, other primates, and perhaps some less encephalized mammals have the ability to identify by touch objects previously experienced only visually and vice versa. This 'cross-modal matching' is lost or impaired by damage to the angular gyrus and/or to Wernicke's area (Davenport et al.,1973; Jarvis,1977). The conclusion that these areas generate multimodal object consciousness is, as has been argued above, almost certainly wrong. The probably correct conclusion is that intermodal memory linkages form so firmly that, for example, a particular touch sensation very strongly elicits its corresponding visual image, and an image of an object can be built up in this way by tactile exploration. This intermodal linkage can become so strong and sensitive to triggering that introspectively we tend to give a unitary objective identity to the multimodal experience, and this may be strengthened by the use of language: tactile exploration may elicit the name of an object, and this in turn may elicit its visual image.

Blind-sight

As discussed earlier (p.50) the phenomenon of 'blind-sight' occurs when both occipital poles containing the primary visual cortices are damaged and there is total subjective blindness. In such cases various visual performances are possible without the knowledge of the victims, which seems to suggest that consciousness cannot be generated in the secondary visual areas when visual signals reach them only by the colliculo-pulvinar pathway, which bypasses the main geniculostriate route. It was suggested earlier that richer consciousness may be generated in these areas by activation of specialized neurons and neuronal circuitries receiving input from the primary sensory areas. In the intact brain such consciousness may participate in conjunction with signals coming via the parallel visual (collicular) pathways in various innate responses to visual stimuli. In other words the secondary visual areas may have evolved an advanced recognition-response capability for certain complex environmental cues, the recognition in part operating consciously but also in part with a non-conscious component of primitive origin able to function, if somewhat clumsily, in the absence of the conscious component.

There is support for this idea from comparative studies. The cat, which in comparison with man has a limited mind, has considerable, presumably non-seeing, visual competence via the retino-colliculo-pulvinar pathway to the secondary visual areas outside areas 17 and 18 (Graybiel and Berson,1981). These pathways become progressively smaller and less influential concomitantly with the development of the geniculostriate system and, presumably, an increased seeing (conscious) capability as phylogeny 'ascends' through primates to man, in whom they are very sparse. In evolving minds, therefore, visual competence appears to be increasingly that of conscious representations controlling behaviors, and this may be true of all sensory modalities.

A recent study (Beckers and Zeki, 1995) has shown that temporarily inactivating V1 with transcranial magnetic stimulation does not fully eliminate conscious motion perception associated with activity in V5, whereas inactivating V5 does so, indicating that some projection from LGN bypasses V1 to reach V5. If this is confirmed it would mean that in the evolution of prestriate cortex the new cells took with them some direct projections from LGN. The finding in this study is in apparent conflict with total absence of all verbally reported sight consciousness in the contralateral field of view in patients with unilateral loss of striate cortex (Kolb and Whishaw, 1990:230).

Destruction of all primary and secondary visual cortices results in complete visual incompetence, except for blink and pupillary reflexes; these primitive reflexes are not mediated by cerebral cortex. Somewhat more elaborate responses such as eye movements in following objects may also, in primitive organisms, be mediated by striate cortex and not require consciousness, and this non-conscious capability may partly be retained in advanced brains with superadded elaboration utilizing consciousness.

According to these ideas there is a limit to an evolved capability in non-conscious neural systems for recognizing and responding to environmental features of more than a certain complexity.

1.10 CONSCIOUSNESS OF AN OBJECTIVE WORLD AND OTHER FORMS OF COMPLEX CONSCIOUSNESS

Self and world: a fundamental perceptual dichotomy

The cognitive act of being conscious 'of' something is an evolved illusion contributing to greater effectiveness of the individual organism in its interaction with the environment; those aspects of consciousness which represent and characterize self are distinguished from those which represent and characterize environment. Although this is an evolved dichotomy it probably requires maturation and experience to develop in the individual, and it is known that abnormalities of brain function, and even environmental deprivation in early life, may lead to disturbances of apprehension of reality and self.

Both self-related and environment-related forms of consciousness consist of multiple units of generated consciousness coalesced into a global unitary consciousness. The environment-related units are generated in the brain no differently from the self units, but to each set become associated subtle forms of consciousness with the qualities 'out there' and 'in here'. The phenomenon of dreaming demonstrates this clearly. All aspects of dreams are internally generated by populations of neurons over wide areas of sensory cortices. These cells generate ego consciousness in relation to situational consciousness; this is incontrovertibly so, but neurophysiology has not yet been able to elucidate the details of this accomplishment.

These forms of consciousness are generated by evolved neural structures, malfunctioning or maldevelopment of which leads to various depersonalization and unreality effects. The analysis of superadded specialized forms or 'auras' of consciousness can be tricky, as they may have components acting subtly or indirectly.

A multiplicity of factors contribute to the 'percept' of a spatial, extra-corporeal, independent objective world, even though all forms and 'contents' of conscious experience are composed of units generated in the brain.

Thus a particular visual shape or size or texture may be experienced frequently without varying much and may be associated with somatosensory, olfactory, or auditory sensations to result in object identity; i.e. there is expectation of occurrence of these sensations on exposure to the visual 'object'. Also the repeated and often surprising and unexpected appearance of the 'object' independently of volition and imagination reinforces its non-self character, as does the discovery of causal properties of the 'object' and the changes that can be produced on it by voluntary activity, and finally confirmatory information from other individuals.

The problem of localization of function

Where in the brain does all of this take place? Numerous structures are obviously involved: the primary sensory areas, the secondary sensory areas where or by which more complex patterns of consciousness are built up, the medullary fibre tracts (cerebral 'white matter') which allow different sensory modalities to take part in object identification through memory linkages so that, for example, on seeing an object there is, however faintly, a 'sensing' of its weight, texture, odour, composition, uses, causal properties, etc., and tertiary (most recently evolved) areas which support advanced cognitive functions. Seeing (or hearing, feeling, etc.) the object sends impulses through vast axonal-dendritic networks via synapses differentially conditioned by previous co-experiences involving the different sensory modalities, thus allowing fuller object recognition through memory retrieval of associated features.

Although lesion studies in man and laboratory animals have contributed greatly to the location of areas involved in some manner in the generation of different forms of consciousness, for example, spatial consciousness in the parietal lobe and object recognition in the temporal lobe, the findings must be evaluated very carefully since different theories may be able to 'explain' the facts. And, potentially even more misleading, the 'facts' may not be what they seem to be; for example, is it really spatial perception that is impaired by the parietal lesion, or is it perhaps a more general disruption of mental functioning caused by this lesion? Disruptions within the multifaceted global consciousness caused by various lesions may have bizarre effects on the subjective experience in its different parts.

1.10 Consciousness of an Objective World and Other Forms of Complex Consciousness

Obviously the parts of the cerebral cortex where the different sensory modalities meet are the likely regions for the presence of subcortical inter-modal connections. Whether the cortex of these areas is specialized for multisensory integration of some kind in object identification and object characterization is probably unknown, but unlikely on developmental grounds and on grounds of parsimony and redundancy. Also, does such junction cortex generate consciousness? If so does it generate consciousness of a tertiary level of complexity which when superimposed on the primary and secondary levels of complexity constitutes highest level 'perception' with advanced behavioral effects? And if so does it have specialized efferents to the executive parts of the CNS to initiate behaviors, acquired and innate, voluntary and reflexive?

Terminological pitfalls

In the neuroscientific literature there is much terminological confusion, in part the result of the subject's historical development but also due to uncertainty over the anatomical details. The term 'association' should logically be reserved for inter-modality transactions, and therefore should be applied only to cortico-cortical fibre pathways serving the memory function; there is thus no association cortex, or at the most only very short intracortical connections across modality boundaries. As Killacky (1995) put it: "The name *association area* is more the reflection of a theoretical bias and a paucity of experimental evidence than an accurate reflection of the functional role of the cortical area so named." Within a particular sensory modality the terms 'primary', 'secondary', and 'tertiary', seem most acceptable for designating increasing complexity of network specialization for advanced functions. 'Integration' implies an operation on two or more inputs to produce a coordinated output with a useful function; all cellular groupings in the CNS may perform some integrative function, so the term carries no special significance when applied to specific cortical areas. Its use for the unification of consciousness is unfortunate but probably here to stay. On the other hand 'interpretive' implies some kind of transformation or translation of information to bring out meaning and generate understanding; these are general functions of the brain involving all non-motor cortical elements in mental activity – no specific cortical area can lay claim to having a specialized interpretive function; even the auditory language 'interpretive' centres merely act to retrieve from other modalities linked memory material. 'Processing' is another very general term used in reference to whatever goes on within any structure between input and output of neural signals.

Wernicke's area in the posterior part of the superior temporal gyrus and the adjoining angular gyrus of the parietal lobe are considered to be the main association areas of the cerebral cortex. Intermodal subcortical connections are probably densest in these areas, so it is not surprising that their destruction results in severe cognitive disabilities. Several other 'association' areas have been proposed (e.g., by Pandya and Seltzer, 1982) but the functional significance of these remains obscure. Also doubtful is the existence of cortex generating multimodal consciousness, despite the finding of sensory overlap in some areas (op. cit.). It is difficult to see how such a function could have evolved and how it would work; and the unity of consciousness in the normally functioning intact brain already provides multi-modal experience. Tooby and Cosmides (1995) have emphasized the pitfalls in pursuing research in cognitive neuroscience without due attention to the principles of biological evolution.

The problem of assigning specific functions to specific cortical cells

Consciousness is evidently generated in the sensory cortices, and sensory afferents to the primary areas from the thalamus and from the primary to the secondary areas synapse mainly on stellate cells in layer 4. Do these stellate cells generate consciousness? If a single sensory fibre to one cortical column is stimulated does the organism have a unit of sensory experience, e.g. a point of light, a pure auditory note, a single itch, etc.? Probably yes – and this argues against the various 'spin-off' and 'patterns of neural activity' ideas for the generation of consciousness. And do cells in cortical layer 5 or 6 perform the memory function? If so they must send axonal branches back to the consciousness-generating cells (Lund, 1981), there being no other way to account for the incontrovertible facts of consciousness and memory: these are functions of the brain, and in the brain the cerebral cortex is the most likely candidate structure for performing them, and the cerebral cortex is composed of neurons of several kinds, suggesting high specialization.

On the other hand some brainstem reticular elements, some 'non-specific' thalamic nuclei, and limbic archi- and paleocortices are

1.10 Consciousness of an Objective World and Other Forms of Complex Consciousness

candidate structures for the generation of emotional and physical feelings. Also, primitive consciousness of the various sensory kinds and their associated memory functions, especially 'working' memory (Friedman et al.,1990), may still occur subcortically.

Very popular in neurophysiological research is the recording by micro-electrodes of the activity of single neurons to sensory input, and a great body of empirical data has accumulated. The problem has been in interpreting these findings in terms of subjective experience and adaptive functions, and most particularly how the individual cells cooperate to achieve these ends.

Projections of the generalized thalamocortical part of the reticular activating (RA) system (principally from the central lateral and paracentral intralaminar thalamic nuclei) synapse mainly in the outermost cortical layers (1-3) on dendrites whose cell bodies lie in deeper layers. This is the prime candidate system for modulation or selective control of the generation of consciousness, as discussed in later sections. It seems likely that signals from this system are modulatory; they determine to what degree sensory or memory input will be allowed to generate consciousness. (La Berge, 1995, proposes pulvinar as the central structure controlling selective attention. A contrasting view of the role of pulvinar is put forward in the next sections).

In the visual cortex connections from the primary area to the secondary and tertiary areas synapse in layer 4, possibly with the function of generating more complex patterns of consciousness in these areas, while return pathways to the primary area synapse in layers 2 and 3 (Kolb and Whishaw, 1990:196) possibly for feed-back modulation, although Zeki (1993) has shown that the return distribution is much wider, a finding also of the amygdala's return fibres to the cerebral cortex, the significance of which has not yet been clearly established. Kass (1987), Mishkin et al.(1984), and several other workers have identified numerous cortical areas and cells responding specifically to various sensory inputs, as well as specific directions of information flow. For example, in the rhesus monkey 12 visual areas, 4 auditory areas, and 8 somatic areas have been defined (Kass, 1987), many of these areas re-duplicating the representation of the sensory environments, with a tendency for individual cells to respond to more complex inputs and to have larger receptive fields the further away from the primary sensory areas they are located.

Generally, the further along a cell is in the visual system the more elaborate the visual stimulus must be to excite it: cells in the primary cortex may respond to lines, changing light intensities, and simple motions, while those in the inferotemporal cortex to complex stimuli such as faces. These facts come from single electrode recordings (e.g. Held et al., 1978) and therefore may be misleading. It is impossible for a single cell to 'recognize' a complex stimulus – the stimulus must activate large numbers of cells which are bound together by facilitated synaptic linkages to form a recognition program, acquired or genetic; all or most of the participant cells in the group tend to become activated even though the complex stimulus may only partially or weakly engage the sense organ. ('Recognition' in this sense must be distinguished from perception – an object may be recognized even if only part of it engages the sense organ, but in such a case only that part is sensually perceived, although the imaginative function may supply imagery of the remainder).

It is obvious that the more detail we have of cortical make-up the better for neuroscience, but a time must come when we must attempt to see the relevance of such detail to mental functioning: e.g., which cells generate consciousness; which perform memory functions; how the conscious experience is converted into a memory store; by which connections memory data are returned to consciousness; which afferent fibres and cortical cells are involved in modulating the receptivity of the consciousness cells to signals from sensory and memory sources; how the consciousness cells function cooperatively to generate discrete object representation and more intricate or subtle forms of consciousness; how multiple cortical representations translate into a unitary conscious experience; etc.

It is the functioning neural structures, from their molecular to their gross anatomical levels, which carry out all the processes of the central nervous system, from simple reflex responses to the highest cognitive functions, and it has been possible, in a general way, to view these processes entirely in terms of the empirical findings of anatomy and physiology. But our explanations have barely scratched the surface, and the formidable details of structure and function so far revealed are conceded to be a minute part of what is yet to be found. If the role of consciousness is in part that of a servo-mechanism upon the neural substrate this fact may never be revealed by the irreducible crudity of laboratory investigations: the investigations will show continuous connections and continuous passage of neural signals from A to Z, without being able to demonstrate that the whole system cannot function without the energy of consciousness. As an analogy, the basic braking system of a modern car is mechanically complete and demonstrably functional from A to Z, but virtually useless without the energy of the servo-system. Laboratory investigations may forever be too crude to detect at the molecular level that a non-conscious brain is at best only functional for the lowest reflexive tasks.

An evolutionary perspective

A target for natural selection is the conscious experience (together with its effects) in response to happenings in the outside world; the neural substrate exists because it produces the right kinds of conscious experience, including global conscious unity. We must therefore look at each aspect of neural structure from the point of view of how it may contribute to, or influence, the subjective conscious experience. This is not to overlook the obvious rejoinder from behaviorists that natural selection acts on variations of morphology and behavior, and that it is entirely spurious to invoke subjectivity. But we can have no more certain knowledge than that what we feel, see, etc. (i.e., the particular variety of consciousness generated by our brain) under particular conditions influences our responses to these conditions.

New qualities or 'flavours' of consciousness for the driving of advanced cognitive functions may not be generated by neurons specialized for this purpose, but by neural programs (evolved circuitries) which direct the generation of certain patterns or mixes of elemental consciousness. Experiential components of the mental states of intention, belief, enlightenment, whimsy, irony, etc. are probably complex consciousnesses composed of patterns of elemental consciousness under the control of neural mechanisms which if not quirks of mental-emotional ontogenetic development have evolved because the executive effects of the complex consciousness proved beneficial by contributing to the success of a behavior. Thus the conscious component of intentional behavior, i.e. the subjective experience of intention, is now in man an essential trigger for the behavior, which is essential in turn for utilizing understandings acquired by experience or generated by thinking: the understanding 'faculty' is the result of an enormous evolutionary undertaking and would be valueless without the 'faculty' of intention.

It must be realized, therefore, that brain damage disrupting an advanced form of consciousness may occur at any one of several sites which are contributing to the assembly of the complex consciousness; conversely, localized damage may not be entirely disruptive. While the broad outlines of the evolution and functioning of the various faculties of advanced brains may easily be discerned, the search for structural detail is soon thwarted by technological limitations. Although, for example, it can hardly be doubted that the phenomenon of intention is the functioning of a neural substrate with an evolutionary history its precise demonstration may never prove feasible.

Only by introspection do we know of the existence of the faculty of intention and other higher mental faculties. In neuropsychology we are largely dependent on the reports of patients about their introspective knowledge and their conscious experience. No amount of behavioral studies can reveal these; our own introspection having self-revealed these faculties we are then able to infer their existence in other human and non-human individuals. If having gotten into the habit of using this inferred knowledge in our experimental work we then deny the role of introspection as a legitimate investigatory tool, and ignore or dismiss the causative power of consciousness, it is because our concern is with utility not basic knowledge.

1.11 EVOLUTION OF THE NEURAL SUBSTRATE FOR ELABORATED FORMS OF CONSCIOUSNESS

Thoughts, broadly defined as parades of imagery, occur in the consciousness-generating areas of the brain, the primary and secondary sensory neocortical areas, each of which probably has its own system of memory neurons. The level of complexity in the structure of sensory consciousness (i.e. percepts) of which a brain is capable will presumably determine the highest raw-material available for basic thinking. Since it is, in part, the conscious representation of the external world that drives behaviors which act upon and within that world, for better or worse, there is, in animals relying on their minds for coping with the world, constant pressure to evolve the capability for generating more elaborate conscious representations which enable more specific and appropriate behaviors.

1.11 Evolution of the Neural Substrate for Elaborated Forms of Consciousness

The evidence from comparative studies, neurophysiology, and other approaches indicates that the secondary cortical areas evolved after the primary areas, each new area being able, in combined functioning with the older areas, to generate more complex forms of consciousness to represent more of the various realities of the external world, or to represent them in greater detail, each advance being selectively beneficial by enabling the individual to respond to the challenges and opportunities of its world in ways that better serve its interests.

It is worth considering the idea that, among other functions (such as recognizing emotionally significant social situations), tertiary or 'association' areas of cerebral cortex, evidently the most recently evolved areas, undertake higher-level mental functioning by orchestrating via retrograde connections to sensory cortices the recording of sequential events in a manner that constitutes understanding; i.e., the ability to store, and from this to use, experiences of causal relationships.

We can only guess how this might be done. If we had to invent such a function and were given a brain able to respond to complex visual situations through innate and learned behavior programs, we might start by elaborating the memory system so that situations affecting the organism (i.e., causal relationships) were more readily remembered and recognized. We might from this develop anticipatory mechanisms, including a sense or feeling of expectation, and from this appropriate anticipatory responses. Notice that this would be more than the Pavlovian conditioned reflex in that it depends on the retrievable memory system and one exposure may be sufficient for its establishment.

This is *basic understanding* and out of it, but not out of the classic Pavlovian conditioned reflex, can evolve a thinking and understanding function, which may have been an exclusively mammalian achievement.

We next must take a major step: that of inventing a propensity to notice, record, and use environmental causal happenings not involving the organism directly, which would amount to an impersonal understanding of the world, a faculty present only in humans and possibly the higher apes.

The evolutionary process is uncompromisingly pragmatic; it will adapt the organism to respond only to those aspects of its world which affect its vital interests, and in different lineages it does so in different ways. If it employs the mind it will ultimately, unless constrained, evolve a capability for conscious representation and storage of cause-effect happenings in the world, and it will evolve faculties able to use such knowledge to act on the world with benefit.

The first stages of sensory cortical functioning in the visual mode may give forms of consciousness such as shape, size, possibly some colour, and movement. A higher stage may give object consciousness of increasing cohesiveness and detail: the brain is able to generate forms of consciousness representing discrete objects in the environment. A yet higher stage enables significance or meaning to be attached to objects and events by elaborate processes of memory linkages and reflex responses. These are acquired through experience and require extremely intricate connections within and between the sensory modalities and highly refined physiological capabilities for signal passage through the neuronal jungle, almost certainly utilizing different neuronal properties to provide various forms of memory linkages and signal characteristics. (For review see Levitan and Kaczmarek,1991; Shepherd (ed), 1990).

The understanding function, depending as it does on the recordings of sequential events, must be heavily dependent on specialized neuronal/synaptic properties and circuit arrangements permitting widely separated areas to be linked so as to provide sequential conscious imagery representing environmental causal happenings.

At these higher levels normal functioning involves much wider areas of cortex, so that precise localization of function becomes increasingly difficult with the consequence that gross damage may disrupt mental functioning in unpredictable ways, or various subtle mental disabilities may not be discovered by the examiner.

What is the underlying neural principle allowing the generation of forms of consciousness representing discrete entities in the external world? Despite various claims to the effect that the brain creates its own reality it is a fact that so far as sensory perception is concerned the reality that the brain creates, that is, the actual sensory image or percept, is proportional in detail and clarity to the efficiency of transduction by the sense organ and the efficiency of transmission of the neural signals.

The signals reaching the consciousness-generating areas carry information about the structure of external reality. If such signals manage to generate consciousness the information will therefore materialize in imagery. It follows that for further evolutionary elaboration of passive sensory consciousness there must be concomitant

1.11 Evolution of the Neural Substrate for Elaborated Forms of Consciousness

evolutionary elaboration of all the structures involved in sensory transduction and transmission.

There remain some puzzles. If each putative consciousness-generating cell produces units of consciousness specific to that cell, e.g., a particular shade of red, how can we account for the continuous gradations of sensations that can be produced and for after-images? We can easily see how mixing colours externally can result in different patterns of neural signals in the optic pathways, but how can we account for the precise cortical transduction of these into corresponding subjective experience if there is only one specific type of consciousness that each transducing cell can produce? We seem forced to postulate either some interaction between units of consciousness (i.e. interactions within consciousness) which alters their nature, or that the individual consciousness-generating cells are able to generate units of consciousness varying in their spectral range, at least to a limited degree.

Furthermore, since the entire visual field of view may be occupied by a uniform colour which may change gradually through the entire visual spectrum we must conclude that there is a uniform distribution of consciousness cells throughout the visual cortical areas collectively able to transduce to imagery almost infinitely small gradations of wavelength over the visible spectrum.

We need more physiological data. Do cortical columns in colour cortex V4 all respond to all wavelengths? If so does each consciousness-generating cell in each column have such an ability, or does each cell only respond to a very small range, there being enough variety of cells in each column to cover the entire range? One possibility is that if the whole visual field is occupied by one shade of colour (i.e., emanates a narrow wavelength of light) then only those experiential cells in colour cortex activable by the resulting neural signals will generate consciousness, all others remaining quiescent. The resulting global subjective experience will therefore be of that colour.

Finally, how can we account for after-images? When we stare at a red patch for a while then look at a white surface we see green, and *vice versa*. The *seeing* is the conscious experience; it may be illusory but it is still conscious reality. Somehow when the colour looked at is removed there is a rebound generation of activity in other cells exposed to the same visual field; the generation of red consciousness may be accompanied by inhibition of the generation of green consciousness, so when the input of red wavelength is removed and replaced by white light the red component of this is now too feeble to generate consciousness, but the green component is released from inhibition and generates green consciousness.

Whatever the mechanism(s) for the generation of gradations of colour consciousness, and all other categories of consciousness, each species by virtue of its cellular endowment is able to transduce to neural signals only a selection of the physical information reaching it from the outside world, and to consciousness perhaps also only a selection from these signals. (That is, there may be more information in the signals reaching the consciousness-generating cells than these are able to use, although this would be non-adaptive). What each species can do depends on its evolutionary history and therefore on its particular transducing and transmitting neurons. Significant improvement restricted to one or a few elements of the entire linear system – from sensory receptor through intermediate subsystems to output physiological and behavioral systems – is unlikely to be adaptive if the other elements are already working at full efficiency. Either sufficient variations in the capacity and efficiency of all the elements occur with each generation, with the chance that in some descendant individuals all will improve more-or-less simultaneously with consequent selective advantage, or some other genetic explanation must apply.

It is easy to accept that the first primordial reflex arc was in its entirety under single or unified genetic control. There obviously has evolved an enormous amount of genetic material to code for the mammalian eye, let alone all the elaborate visual processing structures through to physiological and behavioral functions. But at each stage of their evolutionary histories the different parts of the genome concerned with vision may have evolved to some degree as a functional unit – elements of this genomic packet may have tended to evolve under some unitary control, so that the morphology of the components of the entire reflex arc would be capable of undergoing in-step incremental elaboration, from sense organ through the intermediate processing structures to effector structures.

1.12 THE FOCUSING (OR SELECTIVE GENERATION) OF CONSCIOUSNESS

Definition

'Focusing' of consciousness (or, more accurately, selective or differential control over the generation of consciousness) is of the greatest importance in functioning of the mind; it is the means by which the organism's processing and responding capabilities are brought to bear on the most important challenge of the moment. The mechanisms controlling it are probably extremely intricate. *Its basis is the selective activation of neurons concerned with consciousness generation.*

As this point is crucial for a proper understanding of the mind, its implications must be clearly spelled out. When the brain is generating consciousness this consciousness is the organism's subjective world. When some aspect of this subjective conscious experience succeeds in 'catching attention' it is simply that the brain increases its generation of this particular aspect of the panorama of consciousness and reduces or discontinues the generation of the remainder.

A simple analogy may clarify this further: a comparison between a picture on a TV screen and a picture on canvas. The former is like the brain – when the mechanism focuses on some aspect of the picture it simply increases the energy devoted to the generation of that aspect, so that it becomes brighter and larger, while discontinuing or reducing the generation of the remainder. By contrast, 'focusing' on or 'attending' to, some aspect of the canvas is a function of some agent external to and separate from it, which is what the organism does when it indulges in optical focusing or behavioral attending. These fundamentally distinct mechanisms have, of course, evolved to function cooperatively.

Behavioral attending vs. central focusing

Optical focusing does not generate consciousness – it is simply one of the several mechanisms that contribute to the flow of neural signals that result in the activation of some part of the brain's consciousness-generating grey matter, where the actual visual experience is created. And, as will be emphasized often, there is nothing in the brain 'looking at' this sensory consciousness except the consciousness itself – it is the peculiar nature of consciousness to be self-experiencing, and no agent outside itself can inspect it. But the brain has evolved to generate a form of consciousness which is that of 'self' in interactive relationship with other aspects of the global unitary consciousness. And it was 'necessary' that evolution should have done this, since within global unitary consciousness there must be a representation of the corporeal organism in relation to the representation of the external world. Interaction between the organism and its environment takes place directly via non-conscious vegetative reflexive functions and indirectly (at secondhand) by means of the conscious system.

This is not an original thought. Philosopher David Hume (1711-1776) who knew little of biological evolution and probably less of neuroscience claimed that there are simple and complex impressions and ideas, but the latter are merely combinations of simple ones, and that the mind is identical with its collection of impressions and ideas; the conviction of an external world separate from the mind is an illusion attending the relationships between different subfeatures of the mind.

Self-consciousness

We must distinguish three kinds of 'self-consciousness': (1) The proposed individual unit of consciousness (which we may call a 'menton') is self-experiencing in that, for example, a unit of red is, in and of itself, both the colour red *and the seeing* of the colour red – there is no entity outside it which *sees* it, except that a double unit formed by coalescence, for example that of red and that of pain, is a unitary system which is both the seeing of red and the feeling of pain, and there is nothing outside this double unit which can experience or know its 'contents'; (2) the innate conviction of self in relation to an outside world, which must have an evolved neural basis; and (3) accumulated knowledge of the corporeal self. Both (2) and (3) are elaborated forms of (1).

The adaptive 'need' for specialized focusing mechanisms

Since each putative consciousness-generating neuron (or its functional equivalent) may be activated to produce a unit of consciousness either by an impulse from its sensory source or from its associated memory neuron, the selective activation of vast numbers in focusing must be under the control of special neural mechanisms which permit or block access to these consciousness-generating neurons. Sensory information under normal conditions reaches the brain in amounts proportional to the engagement of the various sensory receptors by the current environmental situation. Just which parts of such information are allowed to generate consciousness is determined, at least to some degree, by what may be figuratively called a priority processing system which 'instructs' some complex neural equivalent of a master control mechanism to use its subsystems to modulate the transmission of such information and the receptivity of the consciousness-generating areas chosen. The functioning of these subsystems probably includes 1) a capability for varying blood flow to the different areas of sensory cortex, 2) inhibition of neuronal pathways carrying unwanted sensory information, 3) facilitation or amplification of the chosen pathways and signals, 4) inhibition of unselected consciousness-generating neurons, and 5) facilitation or sensitization of the selected.

Behavioral response to sensory input via consciousness

The consciousness-generating neurons activated at any moment produce a kaleidoscopic pattern of consciousness representing features in the world or in memory, ranging from the simplest of objects to some part of a sequence constituting the most complex of subject matters. At the human level it presumably takes many millions of simultaneously generated units of consciousness to maintain even simple mental activities.

Any part of the total pattern of consciousness existing at any moment will have an influence on behavior if there is in the CNS an acquired or genetic effector program or neural circuitry engageable by that part. This means that the energy from conversion of a particular unit of consciousness to downline neural activity must work in concert with the several other units comprising that part of the pattern to activate some neuronal ensemble which directly or indirectly engages the behavior. The point is that just as the first primeval consciousness-driven or consciousness-assisted reflex arc would have had a specific function, so would the first combined pair of such arcs, and so on. Each elaboration of the consciousness system was a phenotypic variation which only became established in the evolution of the lineage if genetically based and if tied to some useful function; and the more consciousness-assisted reflex circuits harnessed in this way the greater the behavioral options available for natural selection. In advanced brains huge numbers work cooperatively in a unitary fashion to engage specific behaviors in response to stimuli from external situations which may be very complex in detail but which have a unitary relevance for the animal. Similarly, mental functions in advanced brains employ circumscribed patterns of imagery composed of innumerable units of consciousness in thinking, remembering, and imagining.

Constraints on the direction of evolution of a focusing system

From an early stage in evolution of the mind a focusing function must have existed, becoming more intricate as the mind evolved increasingly specialized functions. Differences in importance among incoming data must be distinguished in some way due to the mind having evolved to process and utilize information linearly. (This *linear* activity is carried out by possibly large numbers of neural channels operating in *parallel*; a trivial point, but the lack of contradiction in this needs emphasizing because of the fuss made over the 'discovery' of parallel processing in the brain).

Strength of stimulus is probably the most primitive 'attention-getter'. Strength alone is probably sufficient to force the generation of consciousness so may not need the aid of a priority-determining mechanism, but subsequently evolved behavioral and mental mechanisms which utilize consciousness are able through the priority system to engage mechanisms which inhibit to some extent the generation of consciousness due to strength of sensory stimuli.

The great biological importance of being able to select from the environment particular features for attention is of course attested by the several evolved mechanisms and behaviors for the positioning of sensory exteroceptors: visual accommodation and eye movements, swivelling of pinnae, tasting, following scents, tactile exploration, etc.. These mechanisms are of ancient evolutionary heritage and bring innate behavioral responses into play. More recent evolution provided mechanisms for focusing by the selective generation of consciousness, making possible more versatile behavioral responses.

Reciprocal connections for cooperative functioning between these two systems no doubt evolved as the systems evolved. In man these connections are obviously extremely elaborate and sensitive – we may consider, for example, the neural mechanisms that allow a particular thought, the product of specialized central focusing, to reorient in an instant the various sensory receptors for the purpose of extracting some desired data from the environment.

(We may look to the pulvinar for a major contribution to this cooperative functioning. Pulvinar's disproportionally large size in the human has always been a puzzle: it takes up roughly one-third of the bulk of the thalamus, much less so in other primates, and is barely detectable in the cat (LaBerge, 1995). The puzzle is that the collicular-pulvinar-cortical (extrageniculate) visual system is generally considered to be almost vestigial in the human, yet the large relative size of the pulvinar proclaims some vital function for this organ contributory to higher cognitive capacities. Now the extrageniculate system is largely concerned with non-conscious visio-motor competence as in 'blindsight'. LaBerge (1995) has argued that the experimental data and the cortical connections of some parts of the pulvinar nuclear complex, which he cites, can be interpreted as giving pulvinar a central role in selective activation of target neurons in the cortex by inhibition of surround neurons, above and beyond simple orienting to stimuli. This interpretation overlooks the requirement by an advanced brain for a highly specialized mechanism enabling the targeting of narrow elements of the environment by the orienting sense organs in response to advanced cognitive needs. The cat's mind is primitive and has no need for (i.e., cannot profit from) scrutiny of the minutae of the environment, so its pulvinar consists of relatively few cells; on the other hand the human pulvinar may have the circuitries enabling it to integrate the requirement for sensory detail with brainstem circuitries controlling the specialized orienting of sense organs.)

Consciousness is its own ego and puts in its own claim for focusing

It must be reiterated that the roughly equivalent terms – focusing, attending, selective attention, paying attention, concentrating, etc. – all tend to mislead us in that we envisage some form of independent ego looking at the panorama of experience and selecting this or that for special attention. Indeed, there is a selective process, but the selecting agent is none other than the selected item itself – it selects itself by being able to command for itself the mechanisms that control the regional generation of consciousness, so that the consciousness-generating neurons giving rise to this item of conscious experience are maximally activated, and all others inhibited.

When neurons that generate consciousness are activated, e.g. by external stimuli, they *produce* consciousness which in a sense *represents* the activating agent, and this is spoken of as focusing or attending; removal of focus simply means preventing stimuli from gaining access to their consciousness-generating neurons or suppressing the metabolism of these neurons by various inhibitory mechanisms. In the case of focusing on the imagery of thinking or imagining, once the memory neurons have been activated and in turn activate their parent consciousness-generating neurons the imagery will continue to reelicit itself via the focusing mechanisms if it represents a subject with priority at that moment; that is, if it is part of a theme with strong motivational status.

The dilemma for the evolutionary process in developing linear processing

In the individual organism numerous physiological systems function simultaneously, and in theory organisms could evolve separate minds that function in parallel; possibly some have done this, defining as 'mind' any functional consciousness, however primitive. Natural selection, if it were ever faced with such a choice in the vertebrate line, favoured the single mind (i.e. unitary consciousness) with its serial processing. The fundamental usefulness of the mind is in enabling the animal to better cope with the challenges and dangers it encounters in its life. Such situations come singly or together, seldom or often, urgently or of low priority. Processing and behavioral mechanisms will evolve which most successfully cope with these often competing environmental challenges, within the constraints of genetic variability. Natural selection must deal with the problem of satisfying two mutually exclusive needs: the need to stay with a situation for maximum processing and the need to move from situation to situation in the interests of safety and opportunity.

Nature's solution to this problem is one of the most interesting features of the apparatus of mind. Two mechanisms must be perfected: the narrowing of the focus of consciousness and the ability to rapidly switch focus, and these must be made responsive to a priority-determining mechanism. (One can immediately see that we are faced here with having to develop a system that must utilize several neuronal properties. It is even possible that some of these properties evolved – or were 'invented' by the evolutionary process – because of the specific requirements of a focusing system which was inexorably evolving because of its enormous selective value. Inhibition, facilitation, augmentation (or amplification) and other basic neuronal properties are no doubt very ancient, but the origin of consciousness may have preceded them and the need to vary the activity of different areas of consciousness generation may have resulted in selection of useful varieties of proto-neurons).

The evolutionary 'need' for a priority-determining system

Where two or more environmental situations evoke conflicting responses in the reflexive systems mediated by consciousness not only must the less urgent reflexive activities be inhibited at the post-conscious level (i.e. the vegetative motor control systems), but it helps if the neural pathways leading to such activities are also inhibited at the conscious and even pre-conscious levels. At the same time the highest priority response must be accommodated as fully as possible. These requirements are essential to prevent indecisiveness or paralysis of action (or confused mental functioning).

It is obviously also desirable that the appearance of a more urgent situation should promptly evoke its reflexive response. There therefore must evolve a priority recognition (or determination) system. In the evolutionary history of each species there would have been particular environmental and social situations of vital importance in the major domains of life. In most species life-threatening situations were the most important, and we find that these have the highest priority. Strength of stimulus is probably the most primitive and potent attention-getter, but a large variety of alarm and vital cue recognition-responses are to be found in nature. Many of these may trigger response at the pre-conscious level, with consciousness being generated too late to be the primary mediator of the response. These ancient vital cue recognition-responses are retained by most if not all species, including man, and they in addition probably continue to command the highest priority for the capture of conscious focus in subsequent evolution of the mind, and through such focusing obtain the services of higher mental processing.

Only through conscious representation can complex situations be recognized and responded to

More complex environmental patterns and situations which have been of significance to a lineage over evolutionary time may be responded to by genetically determined reflexes *engaged via consciousness*. These may include such instances as courtship display, sight of prey or predator, etc. They are generally of high priority and will tend to engage focus strongly. In some of these instances seasonal and other physiological changes in the animal may influence responsiveness and level of focusing.

The existence and biological importance of this more advanced reflexive system utilizing consciousness needs emphasizing. It involves consciousness but no thinking. The utilization of consciousness in neural circuitry made possible the evolution of stereotyped responses of increasing complexity to more complex situations than was within the genetic potential of the non-conscious system. It is therefore a 'higher' but less 'vital' level of reflexivity superimposed on the latter, with which it exchanges regulatory, mostly inhibitory, influences.

It may always remain a matter of debate how far down the phylogenetic scale (and individual nervous systems) we may find a consciousness-mediated reflexive system. In the visual system of nonmammalian vertebrates most fibres of the optic tract terminate in the tectum (superior colliculus) while in mammals by contrast most fibres end in the lateral geniculate nucleus of the thalamus (with relays to the occipital cortex for sight consciousness) (Sarnat and Netsky, 1981:251). Does the retino-tectal visual system utilize consciousness? It obviously supports a high, if limited, degree of visual competence: in the frog the visual system is organized for the recognition of a few stereotyped patterns, such as those that denote flying insects, and there is evidence that it possesses a weak memory capability for these (op.cit.:282). There are the following possibilities: In mammals the retino-tectal system may originally have been a conscious system, the subsequently developed thalamocortical system usurping this property; it may never have been conscious, visual consciousness arising for the first time in the thalamocortical system; or it may utilize consciousness, with this consciousness functioning separately and not being part of the unitary consciousness of the mind, or being too feeble to be introspectively distinguishable.

The basic function of an emotional system

Emotions strongly engage focus on the situations that cause them; it is evident that natural selection has operated on genetic variations of that unique property inherent in feeling (i.e. feeling consciousness) of being desirable or undesirable to force the individual into behaviors favourable

1.12 Focusing of Consciousness

to its well-being and therefore to its genetic continuance, and this is achieved in part by the ability of emotions to command focus. Each individual in a species with an emotional system is born with a potential for emotional arousal and response, this potential being genetically provided, the vicissitudes of life determining whether they will be evoked or not.

Greater learning capacity leads to greater noticing of environmental details

Finally, the ability to learn results in a wider range of environmental events acquiring significance and thus being able to capture focus. This property is at the leading edge of evolution of the mind and may be considered the watershed for the advanced development of mental functioning. It is therefore important to try to understand how it works. First, the fact that a previously experienced event or feature is now in memory is no guarantee that it will engage focus on re-encounter and conscious recognition. The recognition must either become tied to one or more of those environmental situations which reflexly engage focus through their own genetically based recognition programs, or some new mechanism must evolve to allow acquired recognitions to compete for focus. That is, either the feature the animal has learned to recognize must become linked in memory to some feature biologically important to it through their being consciously co-experienced, or, possibly, genetic variations in exploratory behavior may have been such that a tendency to linger over certain kinds of environmental features was of adaptive value in that the serendipitous consequences were sufficiently often of benefit to the individual.

In the former case the linkage may work by evoking an image of the biologically important feature, this image engaging focus because of a built-in reflex enjoying a particular status in the focusing priority system. Improvement in the neuro-physiology underlying this linkage process may allow even one co-exposure to be subsequently effective. The individual in time may by this means come to attach importance to many environmental features, which thereby will tend to capture focus. It is even possible that these acquired, indirectly operating, multistage recognition-responses may now gain direct access to the priority determining system, by-passing the primary genetic recognition, or operate through the latter with great speed, evoking little or no imagery.

Fig. 1.12(1) **Sensory input and focusing mechanisms**

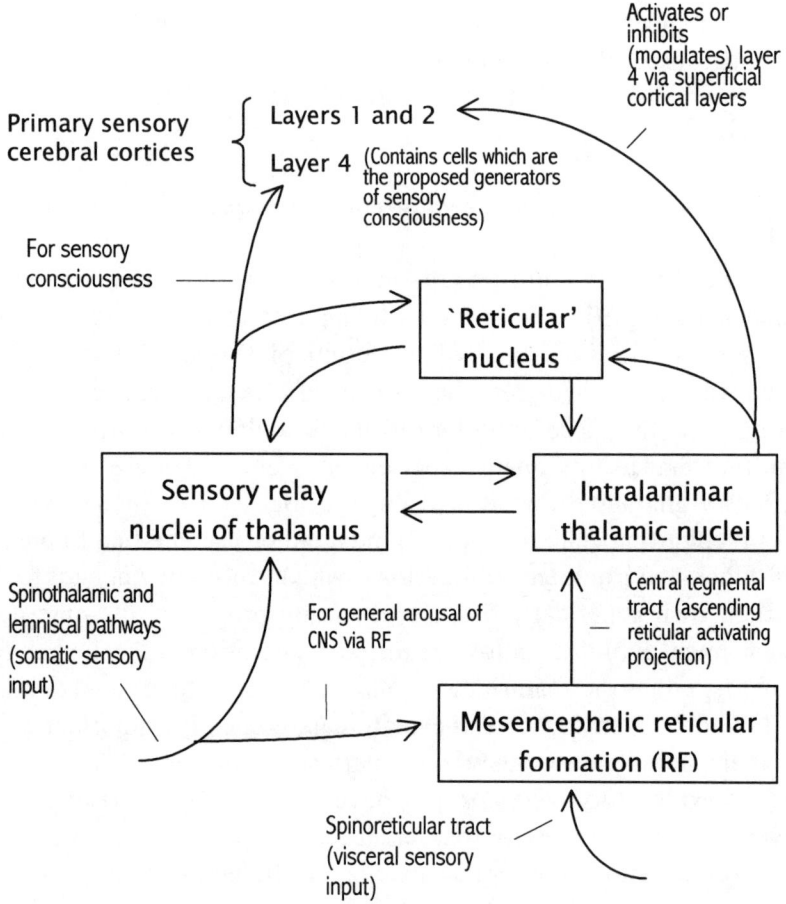

The 'reticular' nucleus is not part of the reticular formation or the ascending reticular activating system (Carpenter,1991:277). Its inputs are from thalamic nuclei (relay and intralaminar) and all areas of cerebral cortex. Collaterals from thalamic sensory relay projections to cortex go to the same portions of the reticular nucleus that in turn receive collaterals from the cortical projections (Figs. 2 and 3) to the thalamic relay nuclei it (the cortical cells) received from. Reciprocal projections from reticular nucleus to thalamic nuclei are to and from the same areas (op.cit.:278). Reticular nucleus has no projections to cerebral cortex but "is situated so as to sample neural activity passing between the cerebral cortex and nuclei of the dorsal thalamus"(op.cit.:278).

The reticular nucleus may be partly responsible for determining the address of the cortical neurons that have priority for selective activation (focusing), and in turn informs the focusing mechanisms. It may be concerned with the specialized switch-focusing of the thinking process in association with other structures. Its cells are GABAergic so its effects may be by indirectly suppressing activation of the unwanted consciousness-generating cells of the moment.

Fig. 1.12(2) Projections from cortex to focusing mechanisms

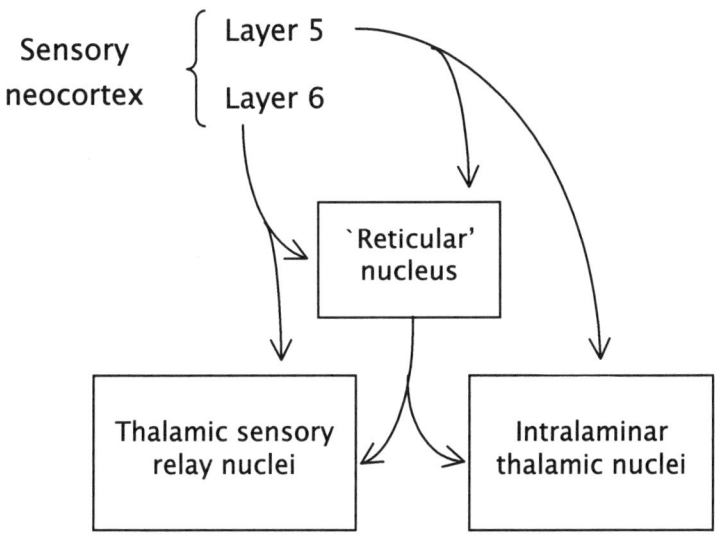

Fig. 1.12(3)

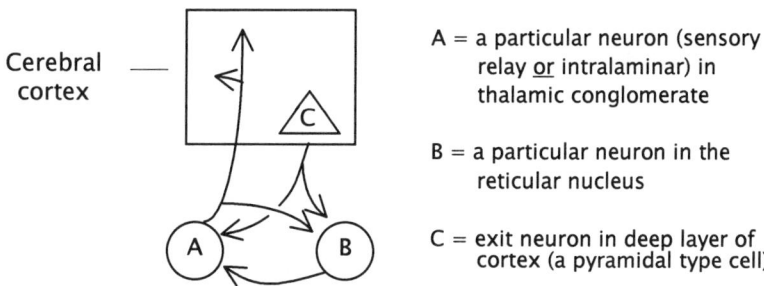

A = a particular neuron (sensory relay or intralaminar) in thalamic conglomerate

B = a particular neuron in the reticular nucleus

C = exit neuron in deep layer of cortex (a pyramidal type cell)

Neuron B 'samples' information from cortex to neuron A, and in turn sends information to this same neuron which in its turn sends information to cortex with a sample back to B. The possible function of such interconnectedness may be to control cortical activity according to need. When A is active on cortex it lets B know of this activity. B can then modulate A's activity according to the type of information it receives from C. There may be several varieties of B for specific functions; e.g., for giving the cortical address to the various varieties of A for accurate application of modulatory influences.

Fig.1.12(4) Structures able to modulate the activity of sensory neocortex

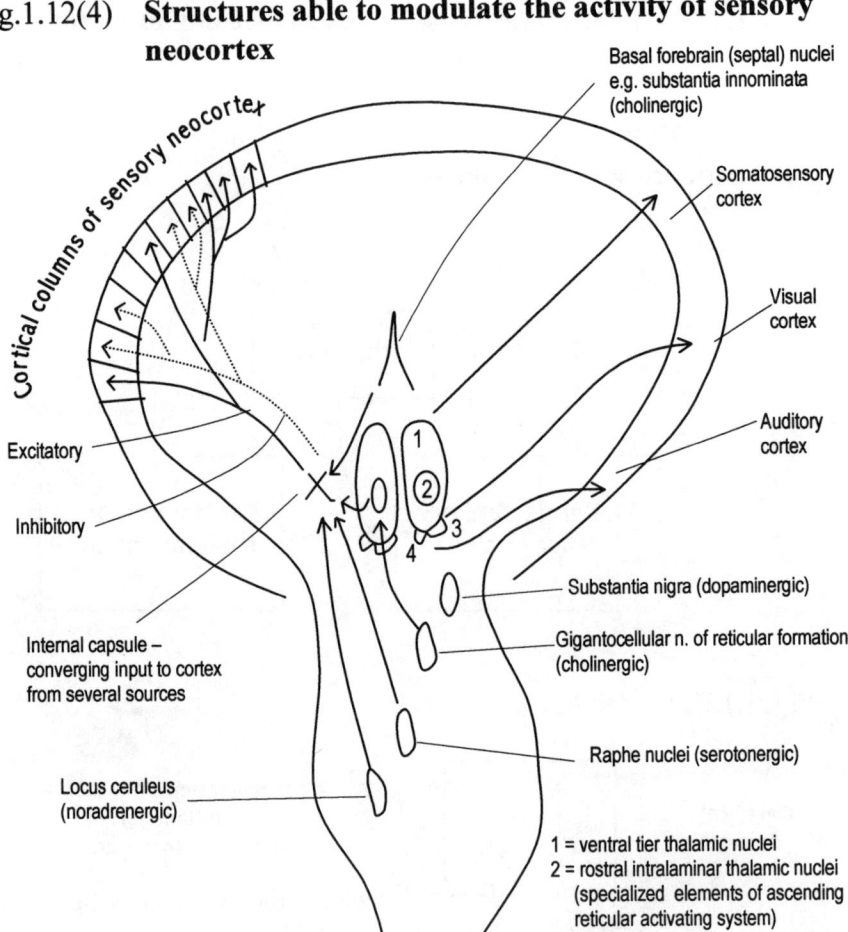

All modulatory projections on sensory cortices may partake in focusing functions, e.g., from locus ceruleus (noradrenergic), raphe nuclei (serotonergic), basal forebrain (septal) nuclei (cholinergic), as well as rostral intralaminar thalamic nuclei (which are specialized elements of the ascending reticular activating system.) Some central mechanism must coordinate all of these functions for precise operation in augmenting or inhibiting the same sets of consciousness-generating cells.

The evolutionary process must have been under intense pressure to advance the faculty of selective regional generation (focusing) of consciousness, and any genetically based phenotypic variation contributing to this would have tended to be selected, but it must be noted that no specific structure for carrying out this coordination has been identified — in all probability multiple interconnections do so, involving different phylogenetic levels.

97

Fig. 1.12(5) Putative cortical receptive, distributive, and modulatory circuits

Cortical Layers | Primary Sensory Cortices | Secondary Sensory Cortices

1
2 — C_1 — C_2
3 — B_1 — B_2
4 — A_1 — A_2 ·Etc.
5-6

From thalamic sensory relay cells

Modulatory inputs from ascending RA systems, locus ceruleus, raphe nuclei, septal nuclei

Transmission of sensory information (?'raw' and 'processed') through primary sensory cortices to secondary cortices from more elaborate and specialized processing

Symbols

A_1 = Putative consciousness-generating neurons in layer 4 of primary sensory cortices

A_2 = Putative consciousness-generating neurons in layer 4 of secondary sensory cortices (which are evolutionary extensions of A_1, allowing more specialized representations of sensory information.)

B_1, B_2, etc = Pyramidal cells in layer 3 transmitting sensory information to consciousness-generating neurons in secondary sensory areas. All (or most) sensory information transduced to consciousness in secondary areas arrive via primary areas.

C_1, C_2, etc. = These cells receive input from different sources which project widely on all sensory cortices to modulate the activity of all metabolic processes, including the generation of consciousness.

Note: The various modulatory influences have probably been active on the CNS generally from early evolutionary times, and their widespread projections on cortex are a consequence of this.

Fig. 1.12(6) **Recognition circuitries for priority processing**

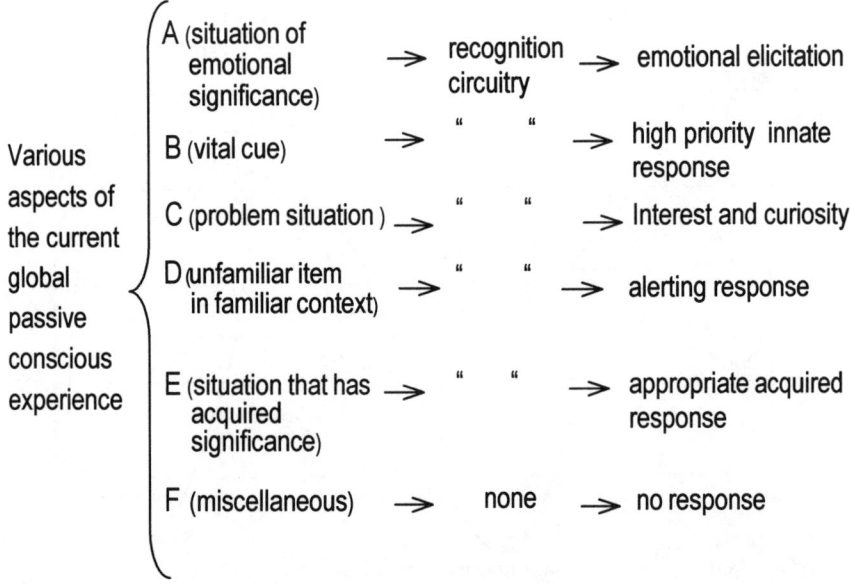

For some aspect of the total passive sensory conscious experience of the moment to gain access to downline effector mechanisms it must first be 'recognized'; that is, it must be of a form that when converted to neural signals is able to activate some downline neural circuitry. Such circuitry may be innate (hard wired) or acquired (i.e., new patterns of synaptic facilitations), ranging from primitive vital cue recognitions (such as for alarm cries) to intellectual concepts elicited from dormant memory through linkage to recognition memory.

Since mental processing (i.e., the processing of items of consciousness) is linear, whatever 'gains attention' at any moment is what has highest priority and such priority status is determined by the evolutionary history of the individual's lineage and by the individual's personal experience.

The details of priority processing have not been worked out. It is clear that the item of highest priority of the moment is able, directly or indirectly, to inhibit the effector pathways of all other items, although at what point(s) such inhibition is applied it is unknown, as also is whether such inhibition is directly from the item's recognition circuitry or comes from a central priority-recognition mechanism (such as may be constituted by the rostral intralaminar-thalamic reticular nuclear complex.)

Fig. 1.12(7) The utilization of emotion in competition for focusing

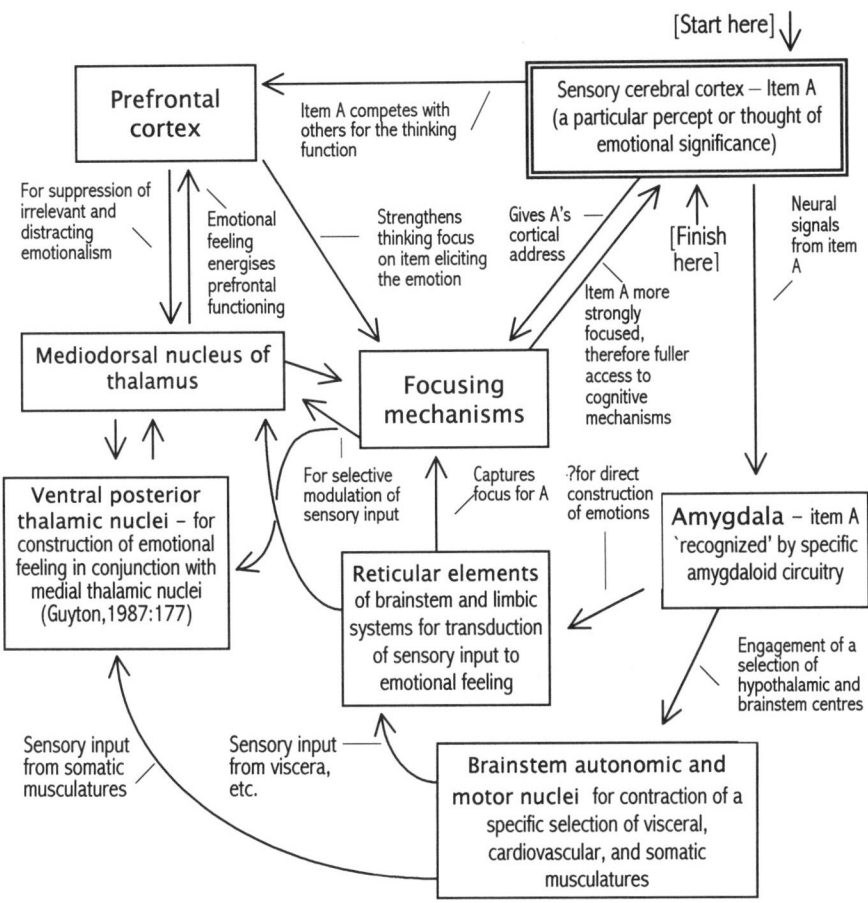

Some sensory or thought item, e.g., item A, will capture focus ('attention') if it has significance for the individual (Fig.1.12(6)) and has highest priority of the moment. An item of emotional significance will be 'recognized' by a specific amygdaloid circuit which in turn will activate specific internal amygdaloid circuitries to selectively engage appropriate downline structures (see text) for the construction of a specific emotional feeling.

Since an emotion very strongly brings focus on the item eliciting it, certain systems must be intimately interconnected. According to Carpenter (1991:259) "The mediodorsal (MD) nucleus [of the thalamus] is thought to be concerned with integration of somatic and visceral activities... and with aspects of affective behavior." This is somewhat vague, but MD seems well connected for such integration; it is strongly connected with prefrontal cortex on the one hand, and on the other with structures which are candidate generators of feeling consciousness and others housing central focusing mechanisms. Both MD and prefrontal cortex are more massively developed in humans than other primates, and in primates than other mammalian orders.

Fig.1.12(8) **Interconnections that may underlie the relationship between the emotional system and the thinking function**

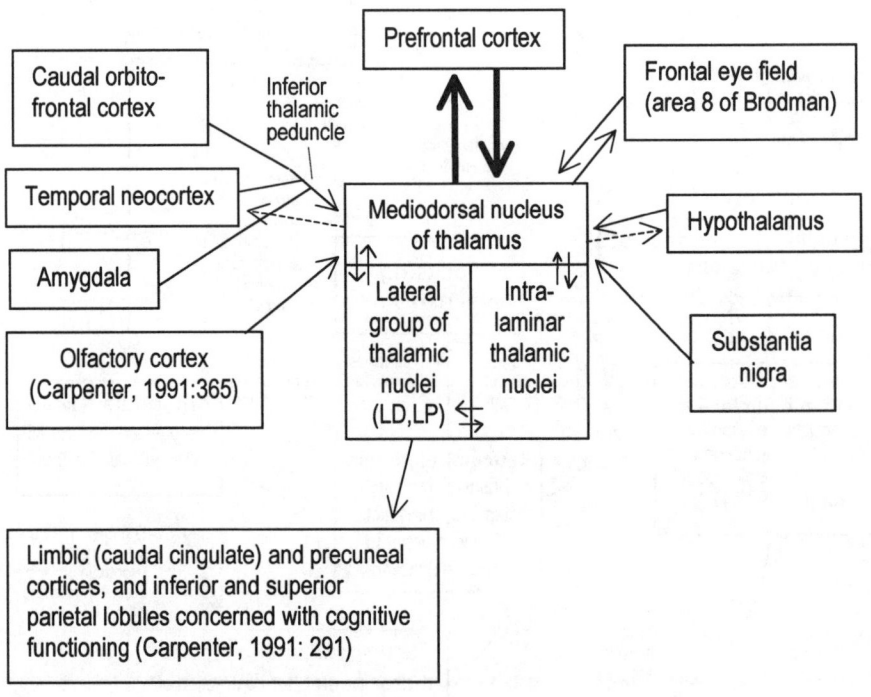

Note: The thalamic mediodorsal (MD) nucleus is highly developed in primates and especially in humans (Carpenter, 1991: 291)

It is put forward in this study that the massive development in prefrontal cortex in humans is best explained by assigning the role of the specialized thinking function to this area, in association, especially, with the rostral intralaminar thalamic nuclei, the thalamic reticular nucleus, and (possibly) the zona incerta, all of which are also disproportionately enlarged in humans.

Since emotion very strongly brings focus on the particular aspect of the current global consciousness which elicits the emotion these systems must be intimately interconnected, and anatomical studies show this to be the case. MD is massively connected with prefrontal cortex and its direct connections are entirely within the forebrain (telencephalon plus diencephalon.)

Furthermore, other environmental features similar in some way to those with acquired capability for capturing focus will, in proportion to the similarity, tend to attract focus.

Figs. 1.12(1)-(8) illustrate those mechanisms described in this and following sections which are involved in the selective regional generation (focusing) of consciousness.

1.13 ROLE OF RETICULAR ACTIVATING SYSTEM IN FOCUSING

Prima facie evolutionary evidence

General facilitation (priming, awakening, alerting, readying) of the consciousness system may have been the first step in the evolution of focusing. Some groupings of the diffusely spread cells in the brainstem which constitute the reticular formation (RF) have a general stimulating effect on the entire CNS and are themselves subject to inhibition and activation by various inputs. When the organism is receiving sensory stimuli this system is activated by collaterals from the ascending sensory tracts and in turn acts to facilitate receptivity of the signals and perhaps amplify strength of response. In the evolution of this system it is very probable that natural selection operated on variations of neuronal properties, particularly of synapses and transmitter substances, and such selected properties became increasingly important actors in the evolution of focusing mechanisms.

In tracing the evolution of the faculty of selective generation of consciousness the reticular formation is therefore the most obvious system to study for evidence of increasing specialization that might serve this faculty, and various pieces of evidence support this idea. Diffuse electrical stimulation in experimental animals of parts of the mesencephalic and pontine reticular formation causes immediate activation of the cerebral cortex. Extending upward from the mesencephalic reticular formation are multiple pathways terminating in almost all areas of the diencephalon and cerebrum. This whole system is called the 'reticular activating system (RAS)'. It is now known that certain regions of the reticular formation as well as portions of the upward radiating distribution system have discrete anatomical organizations, discrete distribution pathways, and different effects on different parts of the brain (some causing increased, others decreased activity) and utilize different transmitter substances (Guyton,1987:241).

Pathways of the upward reticular activating system

There are two main pathways to the cerebrum from the mesencephalic portion of the reticular activating system. One pathway synapses in the intralaminar, midline, and reticular nuclei of the thalamus, thence to essentially all parts of the cerebral cortex and basal ganglia (note that the 'reticular nucleus' is a separate structure external to the thalamus and is not part of the reticular nuclei of the latter; it receives its input from cortex and thalamic structures and projects back to the latter but not to cortex (Carpenter, 1991:277-8; Desmedt, 1981:464).) The second pathway (believed to be less important) passes through the subthalamus, hypothalamus, and adjacent areas. Animal experiments indicate that elements of the reticular formation of the mesencephalon and upper pons provide intrinsic activation of the brain, while the system below this level can inhibit the upper system (Guyton,1987:242).

Electric stimulation of different areas of the thalamic portion of the activating system activates specific regions of the cerebral cortex more than others, whereas stimulating the mesencephalic portion excites large areas of the brain at the same time. It seems reasonable to suppose from this that selective stimulation of portions of the thalamus by the internal signals of the brain might be the cause of specific activation of certain areas of cerebral cortex (op.cit.:242).

The reticular activating system receives input from most parts of the CNS, including most parts of the cerebrum (particularly the somatic sensory cortex, the motor cortex, the frontal cortex, the basal ganglia, hippocampus and other limbic structures) and the hypothalamus.

Certain distinct cellular groupings of the brainstem RF have special importance in controlling specific activities of the diencephalon and cerebrum. They include the gigantocellular nucleus of the mesencephalic reticular formation which releases acetyl choline which normally functions as an excitatory transmitter; the substantia nigra, secreting dopamine which functions as an inhibitory transmitter, although some dopamine receptors are excitatory; the locus ceruleus whose projections secrete noradrenaline and are spread widely if sparsely through the diencephalon and cerebrum (as well as the cerebellum and brainstem), having either excitatory or inhibitory effects; the raphi nuclei, secreting serotonin which in the diencephalon and cerebrum may play an essential role in causing normal sleep, while its cord influence may reduce pain (op.cit.:243). Refer to fig.1.12(4)

1.14 THE GENERALIZED THALAMOCORTICAL (RETICULAR ACTIVATING) SYSTEM

"We believe that depolarization evoked by axons of CL-PC [central lateral-paracentral thalamic intralaminar nuclei] origin in distal parts of apical dendrites of cortical neurons is a major factor of activation, defined as a tonic state of readiness in neuronal networks, thus creating the necessary background for potentiation of neuronal responses during attentive behavior" (Glen and Steriade,1982).

All sensory signals to the cerebral cortex, except olfactory, are relayed in the thalamus by so-called specific thalamic nuclei, giving the 'specific' thalamocortical system. There is in addition the 'generalized' thalamocortical system discussed above – the projections of the mesencephalic reticular activating system to the cortex via mainly the thalamic intralaminar nuclei. The latter (the CL-PC) are composed of multiple small diffusely distributed neurons lying between the specific thalamic nuclei or on the surface of the thalamus. These project fibres to all parts of the cerebral cortex, except the primary visual areas, *and also have multiple connections with the specific thalamic nuclei* (Bentivoglio et al,1988; Jones,1975; Macchi and Bentivoglio,1986; Steriade and Glenn,1982). These data are mostly from cat and monkey; the human details are unknown but presumed to be broadly similar.

Comparison of the ways in which the generalized thalamocortical system and the specific sensory systems activate the sensory cortex (in the cat) shows that the sensory systems act and cease action promptly, whereas the generalized system develops its effects more gradually and these also cease more gradually. Also the sensory signals mainly go to layer 4 of the cortex, whereas the fibres from the generalized system go to layers 1 and 2 where they synapse profusely with dendrites belonging to deeper cortical neurons thus probably having a modulating effect on the latter which renders them more (or less) sensitive to signals from other sources (Glen and Steriade,1982).

However, these authors also report that a lamina analysis of cells involved in the detection of relevant and irrelevant stimuli showed that *attention* rarely modified unit discharge in the middle layers, but affected cells at the junction of layers 1 and 2, and layer 6. On the other hand they report that high frequency stimulation of midbrain RF or medial-intralaminar thalamic areas was shown, by intracellular recordings, to produce first a generalized excitatory response in layers 1 and 2, which then move to deeper cortical layers. More refined studies are clearly needed, if possible on human subjects undergoing neurosurgery. Finally, stimulation of points in the thalamus of the generalized system affects a wider area of the cortex than stimulation of points in the sensory systems, although the generalized system is capable of some degree of regional or selective facilitation of cortical activity (Mountcastle, 1980:301).

These data were mostly obtained from work on the domestic cat, a species with a relatively primitive brain; in higher primates, and especially in man, this system is probably very highly specialized to subserve advanced cognitive functions, in particular with much narrower and rapid cortical responses to pinpoint intralaminar stimulations. Intralaminar thalamic nuclei "show a striking development in primates and man, in relation to thalamic relay nuclei, suggesting they constitute a complex intrathalamic regulatory mechanism concerned with diverse functions" (Carpenter 1991:263).

In addition, the generalized thalamocortical system modifies the activity of the specific nuclei of the thalamus, the basal ganglia, the hypothalamus and other structures of the cerebrum and diencephalon. Also the reticular nucleus (RN) of the ventral thalamus receives collaterals from the axons of both the specific and generalized thalamocortical cells and from corticothalamic axons, and distribute their own axons very widely back to the thalamus, constituting a re-entrant system possibly modified by cortical activity.

This 'reticular' nucleus (or 'complex' of Jones, 1975) is thought to be a derivative of the ventral thalamus and not related to the reticular formation of the brainstem. It lies between the external medullary lamina of the thalamus and the internal capsule; its cells are heterogeneous in type, many of which are similar to those of the brainstem reticular formation. Its main axons project medially into the principal thalamic nuclei. Inputs to the RN are derived from the principal thalamic nuclei and from the cerebral cortex. Fibres from the dorsal thalamus to specific cortical areas give collateral branches to specific parts of the RN. Corticothalamic fibres to a particular nucleus of the dorsal thalamus give collaterals to the same portion of the RN as does the thalamic nucleus. Cells in particular parts of the RN exchange fibres with cells in particular parts of the thalamic nuclei. Both the intralaminar and relay nuclei of the dorsal thalamus exchange fibres with the RN. Cortical projections to the RN arise from the entire cerebral cortex. The RN has no projections of its own to the cerebral cortex but its connections allow it to 'sample' neural activity passing between the cerebral cortex and nuclei of the dorsal thalamus (Carpenter,1991:277-8). It clearly has a role in the functional relationships between cortex and thalamic structures, possibilities including indirect modulation of consciousness by its projections on sensory and intralaminar thalamic nuclei which project to cortex and as a device for the switching of activity in sensory cortices via its effects on these thalamic nuclei in response to cortical needs. It is therefore a strong candidate structure for a critical role in the selective regional generation (focusing) of consciousness. See Figs. 1.12(2,3)

Ventrally the RN becomes continuous with the zona incerta, a strip of grey matter composed of diffuse cell groups, which receives fibres from precentral cortex (Carpenter, 1991:350). Its claim to interest is that as one 'descends' the phylogenetic scale from man it becomes more poorly differentiated then absent (Sarnat and Netsky,1981:6), and this suggests the possibility that it plays some role in higher mental functioning; it may, we might speculate, represent the most recently evolved refinement for the focusing of consciousness, notably in the function of thinking-to-understand. The generalized thalamocortical system, the reticular nucleus, and possibly the zona incerta, may be highly specialized in man to perform some of the major functions in the focusing of consciousness.

The generalized thalamocortical system receives input from the cerebral cortex and all major afferent (centrally projecting) systems (either directly via the paleospinothalamic system or indirectly via the brainstem reticular system). It has been suggested that this global input to a relatively ancient system may allow gross regulation of the level of excitability of cortical neurons (Mountcastle,1980:303). This is probably true as no other candidate neural mechanism for this function at this level is known, but we may go further and point out that in the evolution of the faculty of focusing of consciousness (i.e. control over regional generation of consciousness) there obviously was a progression in the elaboration of structural and functional complexity from that of a general, non-specific capability for modulating the responsivity of consciousness-generating neurons up to the human level of enormous focusing versatility.

1.15 THE EVOLUTION OF A FOCUSING FUNCTION

Amphioxus (lancelet) is a primitive chordate with no forebrain and very little differentiation of its neural tube – the rostral end of its central canal is slightly enlarged. Whatever consciousness it generates – possibly only olfactory and somatosensory – presumably requires little focusing although it is believed to have a primitive homologue of the vertebrate reticular formation. Further evolution of the neural tube in other lineages produced medulla, midbrain, and diencephalon rostrally as sense organs appeared in this region. It has been suggested that evolution of the forebrain (here meaning telencephalon plus diencephalon) occured when filter-feeding protochordates became active seekers of food, and that the earliest true vertebrates therefore already had a forebrain. In mammalian embryos the hemispheres develop from lateral outgrowths of the rostral end of the neural tube, as continuations of the ventral thalamus (Sarnat and Netsky, 1981).

In primitive mammals, e.g. the tree shrew, the thalamus (a diencephalic structure) is considered to be the highest centre for 'analysing' specific sensory information, the cortex of the primitive cerebrum supposedly serving to inhibit inappropriate response selectively (Sarnat and Netsky,1981:322). Such speculations do not touch upon the question of where consciousness is generated at this animal level, thalamus or cortex.

This raises an important principle governing development of the central nervous system: New structures are superadded to the old to produce more advanced functions. The balanced view is that old and new are fully integrated wholes, with more or less of the older structures and functions still remaining identifiable; this implies that primitive consciousness and its focusing mechanisms are probably still operative in the old structures in advanced mammals. These are elemental functions, e.g. involving primitive physical and emotional feelings, therefore indispensable. The life of any organism is carried on at different levels at different times but it is very likely that at whatever level it is functioning at any moment the structures below this level are either involved or actively inhibited; it seems unlikely that where ancient structures have been retained they ever entirely lose their original function to the newer structures. For example, there is strong evidence that pain sensation is generated not only in thalamic but more primitively in brainstem reticular structures (Barr and Kiernan,1988:189,295; Carpenter,1991:289).

The reticular activating system, including its subdivision, the generalized thalamocortical system, may be largely responsible for general alertness and some focusing of consciousness well down the phylogenetic scale. A strong sensory input by activating these systems via axonal branches will heighten general CNS responsivity to all stimuli in addition to forcing the generation of consciousness in its own target area by virtue of its strength of stimulus. But it is probable that even at an early stage in the differentiation of nervous systems the focusing mechanisms evolved preferential responsivity to certain classes of stimuli of vital importance to the organism, so that even when these are relatively weak they are able to gain access not only to promptly acting pre-conscious reflexes by also to consciousness-mediated reflexive responses.

Such vital cues, e.g. a slight scratching sound, may be responded to pre-consciously by promptly acting reflexes of ancient origin. Consciousness is secondarily generated, both by neural signals from the cue and by feed-back signals from the reflex action. Only then can cognitive functions be engaged. There is a resulting general alertness of the nervous system as well as narrow focusing on the cue signals which will by this means be recycled through the consciousness-memory loop thus allowing the brain's more recently evolved reflexive and cognitive systems to function on the cue situation.

1.16 FOCUSING MECHANISMS

General considerations

The faculty of focusing (i.e., the selective regional generation) of consciousness in man and higher mammals retains these primitive mechanisms and almost certainly is an evolved elaboration of them. Versatility, strength, and narrowness of focusing, speed of switch-focusing, and the enormous complexity of the required neural and haemodynamic control mechanisms are the 'new' features. The focusing control mechanisms are probably of three main types: 1/ Those operating at various levels of sensory signal transmission, to inhibit or facilitate the signal passage; 2/ those operating on the putative consciousness-generating neurons, to inhibit or facilitate signal access or even to suppress or sensitize their metabolism; and 3/ those operating through intrinsic cerebral vascular control.

That as many as three distinct, major mechanisms are employed in support of the same function argues strongly for the great adaptive value of that function, and indicates that not one of these mechanisms by itself was able to support that adaptation; for example, the centralis lateralis and paracentralis (CL-Pc) intralminar thalamic nuclei were possibly not able to evolve a sufficient number of constituent neurons projecting on the cortex in the crash evolutionary 'endeavor' to expand the thinking function.

There may indeed be other structures contributing to control over the selective generation of consciousness, e.g., the locus ceruleus with its noradrenergic projections on the cortex which may have both inhibitory and excitatory effects (Glen and Steriade, 1982), and nuclei of the basal forebrain, e.g., the substantia innominata of the septal area, with their cholinergic projections on cortex (Carpenter, 1991:383), which may contribute to the focusing of consciousness in response to emotional feelings elicited by the latter. Robbins and Everitt (1995) review in detail the contributions of these structures and their chemical neurotransmitter substances to cortical functions, characterizing them as a complex, multifaceted system operating parallel to the thalamic intralaminar system.

As all *sensory* signals except olfactory pass to the cerebral cortex via thalamic synapses, and as the reticular activating 'generalized' thalamocortical system has numerous and intimate connections with many of these sensory relay neurons, it is reasonable to seek a primary focusing function here. Similarly, as the generalized system innervates almost all parts of the cerebral cortex it is a prime candidate for modulatory influence on consciousness-generating neurons. There is also anatomical and physiological evidence that collaterals from the generalized system synapse intrathalamically with cells (e.g., of the mediodorsal nucleus) having connections with 'association' cortex (Carpenter,1991:291).

Stimulation of various parts of the generalized nuclei in the cat tends to produce, after a relatively long latent period, rather widespread activation of the cortex. This is really not surprising as the cat lacks those advanced mental-cognitive capacities requiring intense localized focusing (i.e., selective regional generation of consciousness) and rapid switch-focusing. One may confidently expect that when detailed data on the human generalized thalamocortical system become available they will show the kind of precise and delicate modulation of cortical activity essential to human mental functioning.

If, as postulated in this study, there are cortical neurons specialized for the generation of consciousness it follows that they will be under modulatory control by various mechanisms. Layer 4 spiny stellates receive the bulk of *sensory* input to the cortex. Whether or not they are generators of consciousness ('experiential' cells:Zeki,1993) they and the spiny pyramidals of the same layer are at least as good candidates as any others; in mammalian cortex the population of interneurons (mainly stellate cells in layer 4) increases as phylogeny is 'ascended' (Barr and Kiernan, 1988:229). From such anatomical evidence as we have it appears that the rostral intralaminar thalamic nuclei (CL-Pc) may project to layers 1 and 2 on the dendrites of layer 4 spiny stellates and pyramidals which arborize in these more superficial layers (Lund,1981).

In addition, the intralaminar thalamic projections are thought to be operative on the cortical VIP (vasoactive intestinal peptide) neurons whose radial processes influence vascular supply and metabolism of whole cortical columns (Emson and Hunt,1981:339). Similarly, GABA-containing (inhibitory) non-spiny stellates are activated by thalamic stimulation, "and the horizontal spread of their axons may provide a mechanism for limiting the outward spread of activity induced by thalamic activity" (Op.Cit.:339).

There is obviously closely integrated functioning of all the subsystems involved in the selective control of consciousness generation. Following a separate look at the transmission and vascular subsystems several sections will be devoted to analysing the system as a whole, including its vital role in higher mental functioning.

Control Over Sensory Transmissions

There is anatomical evidence in support of the idea that the modulation of sensory transmissions operates at different levels of the nervous system, not only for filtering of sensory stimuli for non-conscious neural reflexes but as part of the mechanisms involved in focusing of consciousness. There is even evidence that a prefrontal-thalamic mechanism exists that exerts a modality-specific suppression of sensory input to primary cortical regions (Yingling and Skinner, 1977).

The submechanism of the complex faculty of focusing we are concerned with here is that which operates on the transmission of sensory information transduced by the sense organs from external stimuli. Feedback modulation from upline stations may operate on any neuron transmitting information from the sensory periphery to the consciousness-generating centre. We may cite the auditory system as an example of this principle.

The auditory transducer is the organ of Corti in the cochlea of the inner ear. Neural signals originating here encounter two or more of the six synaptic way-stations before reaching the auditory cortex in the temporal lobe. These are the two cochlear nuclei, the superior olivary nucleus, nucleus of the lateral lemniscus, the inferior colliculus, and the medial geniculate body. Paralleling this upward flow of information is a downward flow through the same nuclear pools from the auditory cortex to the organ of Corti, and this downward flow may modify through inhibition or release of inhibition the strength of any part of the upward flow. For example, control is exerted over the initiation of nerve impulses in the transducer (the organ of Corti) via the olivocochlear bundle originating in the superior olivary nucleus of the pons; the endings of these inhibitory fibres are applied to the transducing hair cells and the first part of the nerve fibres carrying the signals inward from these (Barr and Kiernan,1988:323).

The consensus view is that in centripetal transmission the various cell stations process acoustic data for refinement of pitch, timbre, and volume of sound *perception*, with feedback inhibition sharpening the *perception* of pitch, especially by inhibition of transmissions from those parts of the organ of Corti's basilar membrane not maximally vibrating to some particular frequency of sound waves. It is also thought that central inhibition probably suppresses background noise when *attention* is being concentrated on a particular acoustic stimulus (op.cit.:323). These ideas seem reasonable answers to the question of why the return pathways exist; they must serve *some* function through modulatory effects, ranging

Fig. 1.16 Control over sensory transmissions – auditory pathways

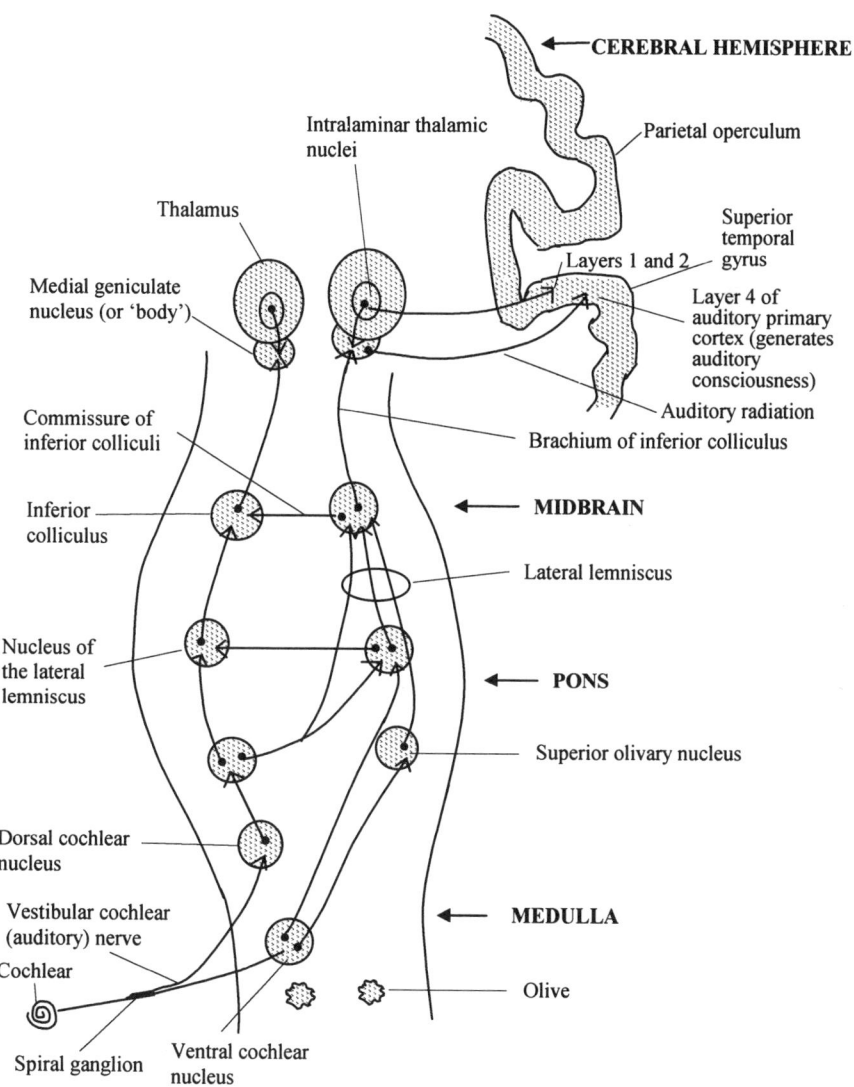

This diagram shows the flow of sensory (auditory) information from receptor to and through neuronal pools mediating increasingly complex reflexive functions. Not shown are the reciprocal pathways (present in all sensory systems) which exercise downward modulatory control of transmissions and reflexive functions. When exercised from the highest level (the central focusing mechanism) this controls the degree and specificity of auditory consciousness.

from inhibition to augmentation, possibly by varying a median baseline inhibitory activity.

As the first level of origin of feedback activity is at the cochlear nucleus which, so far as we know, does not employ consciousness, we may presume that in evolutionary history if the primitive homologue of this cellular grouping carried out the highest level of auditory processing, the refinement of the auditory signals served the purpose of narrowing the engagement of non-conscious reflex programs by eliminating or reducing the impact of all but the most prominent or biologically relevant environmental sound stimuli.

If, on the other hand, consciousness had a very ancient beginning, then the leading edge of nervous system evolution at any stage would presumably employ consciousness. If this were the case then conscious hearing would best serve reflexive functions by being selectively maximized in those parts of its spectrum most relevant at the moment to priority information carried by sound vibration. This generation of relevant consciousness could in part be achieved by control over the transducer by the modulatory mechanism noted above.

Subsequent evolution would increase the complexity and connectivities of the leading edge of the brain and its use of consciousness. The primordial homologue of the cochlear nucleus would increase in complexity and extend more rostrally, but the newer function and the older would become more distinct, particularly as the newer developed wider cooperative connections with other neural systems, and as a result the nucleus would tend to become physically divided into two parts, the rostral now becoming the ancestral homologue of the superior olivary nucleus. We may speculate that the newer structure would usurp the conscious function, or possess a separate but more complex organization of consciousness and the reflexive mechanisms it participates in, requiring , *inter alia*, more selective control of the signals reaching it to improve strength and definition of its representation of the external events for more precise engagement of more advanced reflexive functions. This selective control would be achieved in part by return fibres with inhibitory function on the cochlear nucleus. And, again, if such fibres in the neutral state maintain a chronic inhibitory tone, simply increasing or decreasing this will have inhibitory *or* augmentary effects peripherally. We may suppose that the transducer will evolve *pari passu* with the central structures, as will the repertoire of behavioral responses.

The utilization of consciousness may be essential for the evolution of new structural complexity permitting more comprehensive representation of, and appropriate responses to, environmental events, this being selectively advantageous in organisms relying on the mind for dealing with the challenges of life. But if consciousness is essential for the functioning of the leading level of the evolving nervous system does it continue to operate there when that level is superceded? The idea of the existence of separate 'minds' at different levels of the central nervous system cannot be dismissed peremptorily in view of the findings in commissurotomy (split-brain) patients.

In all of the sensory modalities influence on sensory transmission is exercised by each stage on the earlier, more peripheral stages (with some exceptions; e.g., the medial geniculate body does not give rise to fibres influencing lower auditory relay nuclei – Carpenter,1991:427), ultimately by the cerebral cortex on the transducer. I suggest that this has evolved to become a major mechanism in the focusing of consciousness, functioning cooperatively with the intrathalamic modulatory mechanisms discussed in the previous sections.

We may follow the evolution of the brain as it elaborated more and more functions utilizing consciousness, each stage establishing increased cooperative functioning among the different sensory systems, as exemplified by the increasing number of connections and complexity of function in the auditory system as we ascend from the inferior colliculus to the medial geniculate body thence to the auditory cortex with its vast network of connections subserving perceptual, behavioral, and intellectual functions. Each nuclear level, to repeat, may be the remnant of the leading edge of the auditory system at some stage in its evolutionary history, being left behind as new extensions evolved to serve more elaborate reflexive functions and for cooperative functioning with more recently evolved higher levels.

Hillyard et al (1995) employing event related potentials (ERPs) in their studies of attentional responses to auditory and visual stimuli conclude that "attention acts to modify processing in cortical areas that encode elementary stimulus features rather than fully analysed pattern or object representation." But this can hardly be the case, at least for mental attending. Responses to stimuli occur at different levels of processing, from the simple non-conscious reflex to the fullest level of conscious (perceptual) representation, and 'true' mental attending operates only at the latter level. Once an item of consciousness has gained access to the focusing master-control system several submechanisms are employed to focus that item and suppress the rest of the current conscious experience.

Furthermore, the rostral intralaminar thalamic nuclei, postulated in this study to control cortical receptivity to sensory signals, do not project to primary visual cortex (where elementary stimulus features are encoded), so very little attention (selective generation of consciousness) occurs at this level. These and other authors do not always clearly specify that it is *somatic orienting* (of eyes, pinnae, etc.) and not mental focusing that they are investigating; the former 'attending' does indeed funnel stimuli to the primary sensory areas.

It must be argued again that it flies in the face of evolutionary principles to suppose that human-level consciousness arose *de novo*, anymore than did complex morphological structures.

Vascular Control Of Focusing

On theoretical grounds one would expect to find a vascular control mechanism as part of the processes involved in the selective generation of consciousness. The evidence that such a mechanism exists includes the following: 1/ The distribution of radioactive material in the cerebral circulation has been monitored during mental passivity and various sensory and motor activities and characteristic shifts demonstrated (Reivich, 1982). 2/ Radioactively labeled glucose concentrates in active brain tissue and can be monitored. 3/ Radioactive labels in positron emission tomography (PET) scanning allow observation of patterns of neural activity; e.g., Pardo *et al*, (1991) in 23 healthy volunteers found blood flow to the right prefrontal and superior parietal cortices increased during mental concentration on certain tasks. 4/ Thermoelectric probes in the cat showed that illumination of one retina caused an increase in blood flow restricted to the opposite visual cortex. 5/ In mammals the sensorimotor, visual and auditory areas of the cortex normally have relatively greater blood flow than other regions, and thiopental anaesthesia depresses this flow and abolishes the regional differences. 6/ Regions of 'functional' hyperemia have been detected in conscious humans subjected to various physical and emotional stimuli (Sokoloff and Kety, 1960). 7/ Vasodilating nerves to cerebral vessels exist (Schmidt, 1950; Chorobski and Penfield, 1932). 8/ Circulation through the brain is somewhat independent of extra-cerebral circulatory events

(Forbes and Wolff, 1928). 9/ The dilator effect of the products of metabolism greatly exceeds any other factor in the control of cerebral vessels (Shapiro *et al.*, 1966) – this suggests a blood supply *response* to neuronal metabolism. 10/ Tissue CO_2 levels are more influential than arterial CO_2 in cerebral blood flow.

Roland and Friberg (1985) with blood-flow and PET studies showed variations in localization of cortical blood flow and cortical metabolic activity during specific types of thinking. Their main findings were: 1/ Regional blood flow outside the primary sensory and motor areas was increased by thinking; 2/ different types of thinking activated different cortical fields, with areas of the prefrontal cortex activated in all tasks in all subjects; and 3/ the results showed that thinking required more metabolic brain activity than making voluntary movements or processing sensory data (thus supporting what we all know: hard mental effort is much more tiring than passive sensing). Also, Roland et al (1995): "In normal brains the rCBF [regional cerebral blood flow] is monotonically related to the regional metabolism. This relation is spatially very accurate and can be seen at the columnar level". See also Roland (1982).

It has not been established that there is a specific central neural mechanism with control over regional vasodilation and vasoconstriction in the focusing of consciousness (but see next paragraph), and autonomic innervation appears to play only a small part in control of cerebral vessels (Milnor, 1980). That such a mechanism exists is suggested by the shifts in vascular flow to areas of specific cortical activity occurring too rapidly to be fully accounted for by the effects of the products of metabolism. There exists the possibility of local neurogenic control of circulation – that each area of cortex has dilating and constricting neural control over its own blood supply. This would imply that increasing the blood supply to a tissue may initiate activity in that tissue, an antecedant event that has its equivalent in large scale redistribution of the body's blood supply in instantaneous response to emotions elicited by the merest thought in physiological preparation for action. Even if the trigger for dilation of local vessels is rise in tissue CO_2 or fall in O_2 or changes in levels of other metabolites these may act as promptly as they do by the quicker route of triggering local neurogenic effects on the vascular musculature.

Finally, the possibility exists that the generalized thalamocortical system has direct influence not only on neuronal activity of the cortex but on its blood supply, and if in man it has evolved a highly specific targeting capability for cortical activation such specificity may include circulatory control. In the cortex there is a class of excitatory interneurons with long vertical axons containing the powerful vasoactive intestinal polypeptide (VIP) which may spread a focus of excitation in a columnar fashion through the layers of the cortex (Colonnier,1981:145). And, "the ability of VIP to enhance local blood flow in the cortical area influenced by the radial processes of the VIP neurons could produce the marked regional differences in metabolic activity in the cortex revealed by the deoxyglucose technique" (Emson and Hunt,1981:339). But at present there are no data establishing specific RA projections on these interneurons.

1.17 RECOGNITION AND RESPONSE MECHANISMS FOR PRIORITY INFORMATION

Recognition circuitries

The selective generation of consciousness with its various enabling mechanisms is a biological function with parallels in other systems of the organism, from internal cellular processes to whole body activities: the body's innumerable systems and subsystems are geared to act in specific ways in response to their respective inputs. The individual organism's focusing (attentional) mechanisms are geared to be responsive to signals enjoying the highest current priority. When neural signals (sensory or from memory) activate the consciousness-generating neurons some part of the resulting pattern of consciousness may, on reconversion to downline neural energy, activate, or be 'recognized' by, an innate or acquired neural program with a fixed place in the hierarchy of relevance for the individual, and the signals carrying information with top priority of the moment will in this indirect manner gain access to the executive mechanisms of focusing directing them to maximise the consciousness generated by these priority signals. See Figs. 1.12(6) and 1.17(1),(2),(3)

Where are such recognition programs stored and how do they engage focus? That is, where in the CNS are the neural circuitries or programs which 'recognize' that some particular kinds of information the organism becomes conscious 'of' are relevant to its interests. One way to tackle this question of storage is to look at the evolutionary development of the

Fig.1.17(1) **Competition for capture of focus** (From Hale, 1989)

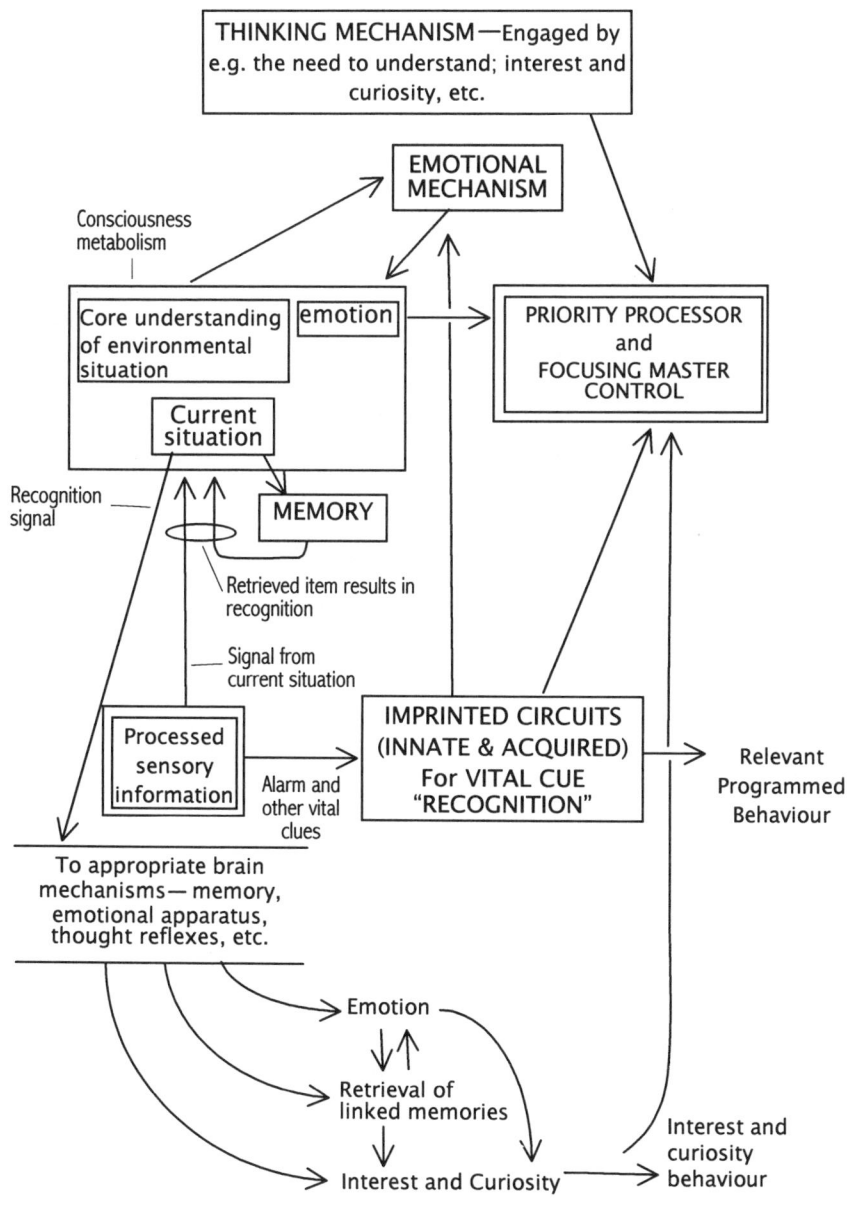

Fig.1.17(2) **Capture of focus: priority processor**
(Highly schematic and conjectural)(From Hale, 1989)

Each input axon sends branches to activate inhibitory interneurons

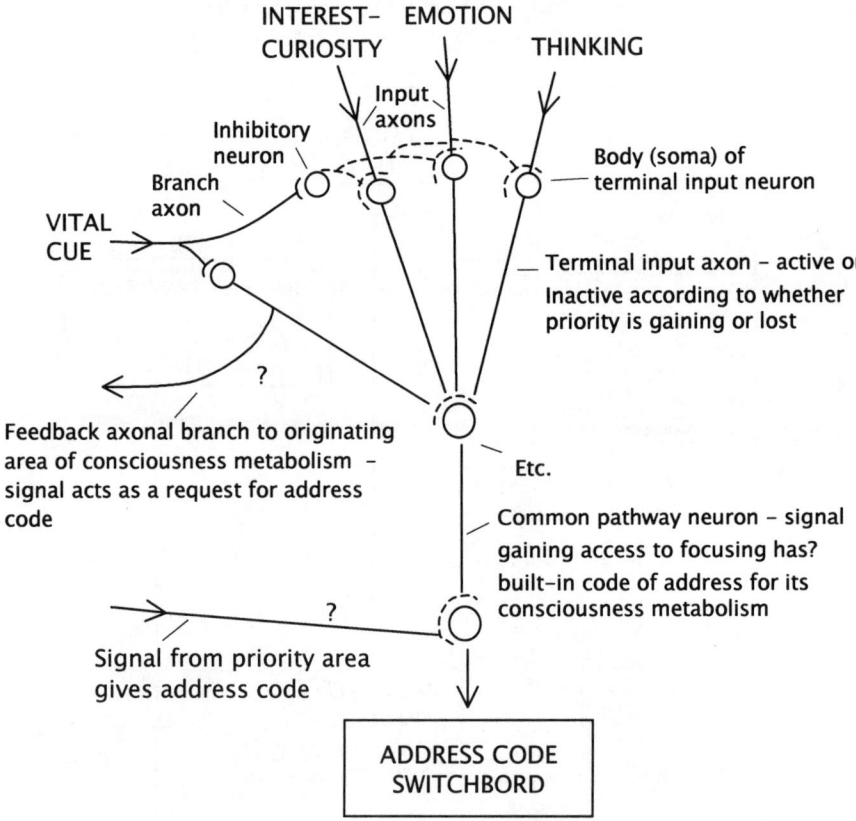

According to the species and the learning history some inputs will have greater power for gaining focus (e.g. a slight rustling sound; a teasing intellectual problem, etc.). Such inputs either have (genetically) or acquire greater or more efficient access pathways and/or greater inhibiting capability on other inputs.

Fig.1.17(3) Consciousness focusing—master control system
(From Hale, 1989)

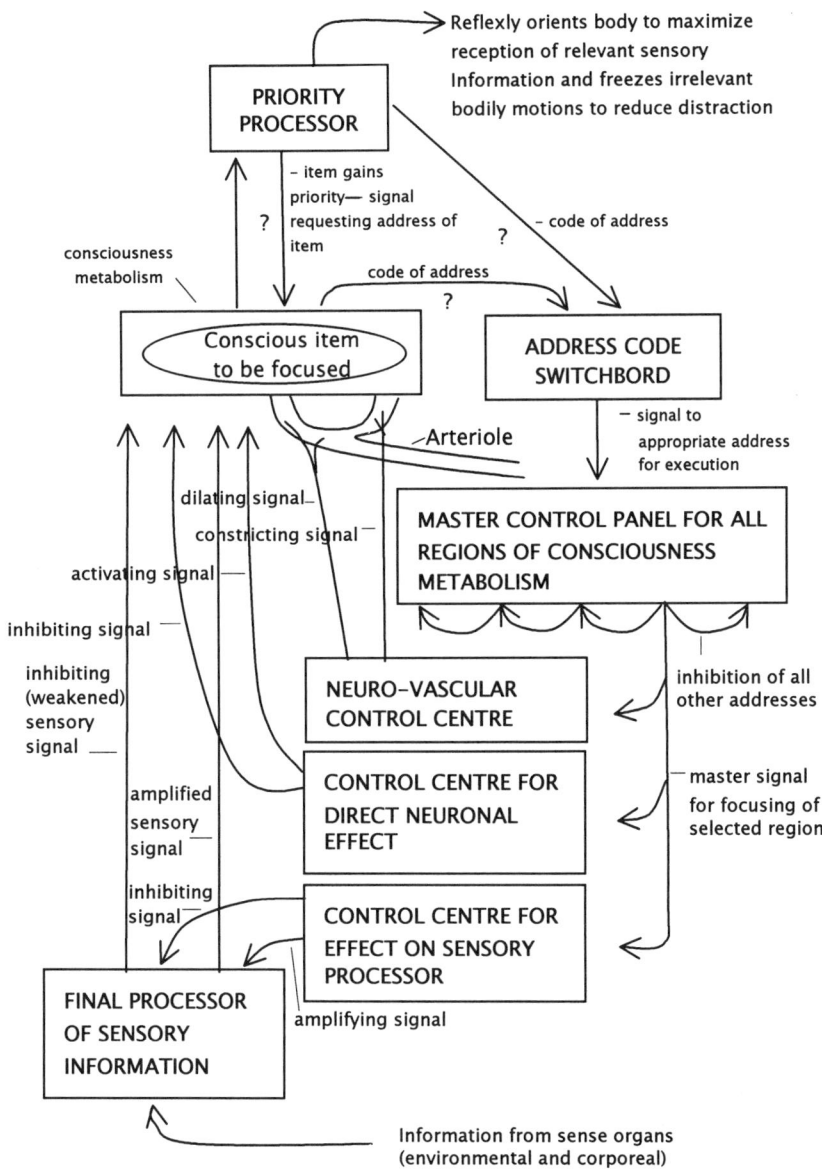

nervous system. At each stage there will be found evolved (fixed) responses to particular exteroceptive stimuli which have been of importance to the lineage over evolutionary time. The neural substrates for such responses will continue to be found in the same parts of the nervous system when they constituted the leading edge of development, and they will continue to function in much the same way (Sarnat and Netsky,1981:39). Further evolutionary change will tend toward more complex mechanisms better adapted or more competitively successful, and these in their turn will generally be retained as the elaboration continues.

Therefore, in accordance with the principle of conservatism in evolution, the most primitive responses will be found in the most ancient parts of the nervous system, and these will be supported by the simplest neural architecture; the structural arrangements and connections ('hard-wiring') of neurons will determine the effects of a stimulus, and will constitute both a recognition and a response program.

Levels of reflexivity in the CNS

In keeping with these ideas we may distinguish the following levels of reflexivity in operation in advanced nervous systems: 1/ Simple reflex arcs triggerable by unorganized sensory stimuli. 2/ More complex reflexes sensitive to specific simple environmental cues of organized stimuli such as sounds, cries, movements, patterns of light intensity, etc. which are recognized by evolved (hard-wired) neural circuitries and which trigger evolved response programs stored, at least in part, in the archicerebellum or the paleocerebellum. Each recognition circuitry will be in a primitive part of the pathways of the sensory modality concerned; for example, in the inferior colliculus or the medial geniculate nucleus for auditory cues. 3/ Yet more complex reflexes triggerable by more elaborate environmental situations. The ability to pounce on moving prey, which may have its recognition circuitry in the superior colliculus of the mesencephalon and the pulvinar nuclei of the thalamus and its motor program shared by several structures (e.g. basal ganglia, substantia nigra, red nucleus, paleocerebellum), is an example of this level. 4/ Innate recognition-responses to conscious representations; for example, to secondary sexual characteristics. The recognition circuitries for these may reside in the cerebral cortex, perhaps with some aspects of the recognition handled by subcortical centres. The recognition network is therefore probably multifocal. Likewise the response package is probably a functional assemblage of several neural networks in many parts of the brain, including the supplementary motorcortex, neocerebellum, neostriatum, and limbic structures. 5/ Finally, acquired recognitions and responses also operating through consciousness but utilizing conventional (retrievable) memory and motor (skill acquisition) 'memory', the former being a function of the cerebral cortex and the latter principally of the neocerebellum and/or neostriatum.

It should be noted that all exteroceptive stimuli, including those triggering non-conscious reflexes, have access to consciousness. This is necessarily so because complex environmental situations the brain evolved to handle by means of consciousness are compounded of simple stimuli.

The conscious experience representing complex environmental patterns of stimuli is the result of the coordinated and simultaneous generation of large numbers of units of consciousness. For a particular pattern or item of consciousness (and therefore the external feature it represents) to be 'recognized' there must exist in the cerebral cortex an engageable downline circuitry composed of large numbers of neurons functionally bound by synaptic linkages. Such a circuitry is either acquired (i.e., is a memory) or has evolved (i.e., is an innate 'hard-wired' recognition-response behavior program).

In all probability only a fraction of the conscious experience is needed to engage the recognition program because the neuronal package comprising the latter is likely to be sparse in securely linked components relative to the vast number of units comprising the conscious experience. In other words, although the vast number of consciousness-generating neurons activated by the sensory data in principle involve an equal number of recognition program neurons, a one-to-one correspondence is unlikely to exist owing to the limited genetic potential allowing such elaborate neuronal circuitry to evolve. Despite this, however, storage capacity in the conventional memory system is probably very much greater than retrievability would lead us to believe.

Competition for focusing of consciousness

Each of the currently activated recognition circuitries must in turn generate neural signals that 1) compete with the others for access to the focusing mechanisms of consciousness, the outcome of which will depend on priority status, and 2) engage behavior programs, innate or acquired, unless these programs are reachable directly from consciousness via neural pathways bypassing the recognition and memory systems. On this topic much remains obscure: skill acquisition can occur in cases where the ability to acquire retrievable memory is apparently lost (after bilateral hippocampectomy), a finding open to various interpretations (Glickstein and Yeo, 1990).

Presumably, when some incoming data are recognized there are signals relayed to the focusing mechanisms requesting that these data be 'given attention', which in effect means that the incoming data be given every facility for maximizing their generation of consciousness, i.e. the representation of themselves in consciousness, and, through this, full access to processing mechanisms (e.g., thinking) and to acquired and innate behavior programs (mental, emotional, or physical) relevant to themselves. This means shutting down uninvolved cortical areas and maximally facilitating the involved ones so that relevant reflexive behaviors and relevant memory stores are fully accessible. See Figs. 1.12(6) and 1.17(1),(2),(3)

In man, and primitively in higher primates, the recognition may also trigger interest and curiosity which in turn act on the focusing mechanisms to allow the relevant material to more strongly generate conscious activity. Note the principle involved here: Interest and curiosity may be called the 'intellectual emotions'. Natural selection has evolved these 'feelings' to force or encourage (in the 'teleonomic' sense – McNaughton, 1989) the individual to use its higher mental faculties on any situation able to engender the feelings. This is an extension of the more primitive general emotional system which operates to force the individual into behaviors important for its survival and genetic continuance. The principle is the use of feelings to engage and/or catalyse vital functions.

It should be noted that some neural mechanism must exist which informs the focusing mechanisms precisely which areas of consciousness-generating cortex are to be selectively activated. This may in part be the function of the priority-determining mechanism itself, possibly acting through the reciprocal pathways from the sensory cortices back to the specific thalamic relay neurons innervating those areas of cortex and their connections with intralaminar thalamic nuclei.

1.17 Recognition and Response Mechanisms for Priority Information

In all of this there is obviously much dependence on reciprocal control and monitoring mechanisms and on feed-back and feed-forward information requiring enormous complexity and delicacy of operation of neural networks. The elaborate perceptual and intellectual functions of man and his enormous capacity for storage and linkage of memories and for acquired behavior programs go some way to accounting for the astronomical number of neurons present in his brain.

1.18 COMPETITION FOR FOCUSING – PRIORITY PROCESSING

How does competition for the selective generation of consciousness work? The various competing items are forms or patterns of consciousness, generated either by sensory input or from memory stores in thinking, imagining, or dreaming. Each area of sensory cortex may be able to give its address to the focusing mechanisms by virtue of its reciprocal connections, via the primary sensory areas, with the specific thalamic nuclei which in turn have reciprocal connections with the intralaminar thalamic nuclei of the generalized thalamocortical system and the associated reticular nucleus (or complex) which we hypothesize constitute in part the *master control system* for focusing. This system will receive claims, via the recognition circuitries discussed above, from different aspects of consciousness at any moment, and it has to decide which of these will be chosen for full focusing – that is, which ensemble of consciousness-generating neurons will be maximally activated by incoming signals.

It is unlikely that the conscious experience can directly capture focus. In the neutral state input is passively received and the intensity of consciousness in the different parts of the global conscious experience of the moment will simply be a function of the strengths of the different sensory or memory inputs. For some aspect of the conscious experience, i.e. a particular ensemble of consciousness-generating neurons, to gain sole access to the focusing system it must be of a form able to engage (i.e., to be recognized by) one or more mechanisms that can commandeer the resources of the master control system for focusing, such as recognition circuitries for alarm and vital cues, acquired recognition-response programs, disposition to respond to unrecognized items in otherwise familiar settings, interest and curiosity reactions, and any kind of emotion. If a particular aspect of conscious experience is able to elicit any of these mechanisms it will by doing so put in a claim for preferential augmentation; that is, for selective activation of the relevant consciousness-generating neurons.

The focusing master control mechanism is very probably a system of enormous complexity. Not only must it be responsive to the clamour of myriad competing claims but it is probably composed, as discussed earlier, of many disparate elements co-opted by the evolutionary process to cooperatively serve a single function, and the neuronal connectivities underlying this integration may be very difficult to identify. For example, how do the various agents, such as vital cue recognition circuitries, which are putting in claims on behalf of their client items of consciousness, engage all the sub-elements of the focusing master control system? Do they do so via a single doorway, or to each separately, or do they first act to nullify one another with the victor getting sole possession of the field and sending signals to all the sub-elements giving addresses of the areas of cortex whose activities are to be promoted, all other areas being automatically inhibited?

So there may exist a neuronal system acting as a final pathway to the focusing master control to which all forms of consciousness competing via their recognition circuitries for selective augmentation have access, this pathway becoming closed to the unsuccessful claimants; or, there may be different pathways to the master control system, and when one competitor is able to engage this system all others are automatically excluded. But the enabling (middleman) mechanism (emotion, vital cue program, etc.) is the actual agent which gains control on behalf of the particular aspect of the conscious experience.

We may speculate that the reason for this lies in the brain's evolutionary history, in that at a primitive stage, before the appearance of higher level reflexivity involving elaborate patterns of consciousness, the various lower level recognition-response mechanisms (emotional, vital cue, etc.), because they operated linearly, needed some central mechanism able to augment or suppress neural activity according to priority. This basic focusing or switching mechanism presumably evolved in that part of the reticular formation in closest association with the pathway crossroads of the emerging special senses at the most rostral end of the neural tube, the resulting conglomerate constituting the developing thalamus.

With the evolution of a new structure – the cerebral cortex – able to generate new elaborations of consciousness representing the external

1.18 Competition for Focusing – Priority Processing 125

world in greater detail and variety, the 'need' for versatility in the selective generation of consciousness gradually became more imperative (that is, there was strong adaptive advantage in such a development), but it was equally important that the representation of most relevance to the welfare of the individual at any moment should be the one focused, and this relevance is determined by evolutionary history or acquired through experience and is embodied in the form of the agencies mentioned above.

The focusing master control system will be instructed as to which aspect of the conscious experience of the moment to focus (that is, which ensemble of consciousness-generating neurons to selectively potentiate) either by the agency that gains access to the focusing mechanisms on behalf of the highest priority aspect of the conscious experience, or on gaining that access the agency may send a message to these neurons directing them to send their address to the focusing master control, which would presumably be done via the reciprocal connections they have with the thalamic nuclei, as suggested earlier.

To be more specific and to illustrate how the various agencies may gain access to the focusing control mechanisms we may select one of the vital cue categories. There are numerous such categories in the different sensory modalities of most species: auditory (alarm cries, rustling sounds); visual (changes in light intensity, certain movements and shapes); somatosensory (touch, changes in ambient pressure and temperature); olfactory (odors from food or excreta); gustatory (bitterness).

In the case of sound cues a preconscious response may operate through any of the lower reflexive levels; that is, through any of the subcortical nuclear stations discussed earlier, from cochlear nuclei to inferior colliculi. The reflex response will be progressively more elaborate, e.g., from simple swivelling of pinnae to full flight or fight, the latter controlled by motor program circuitries in the older parts of basal ganglia and cerebellum. The central 'processor' is hard-wired circuitry in one or another of the nuclear stations and is activated by input from the relevant cue – it 'recognizes' the cue – and in turn engages the motor response. 'Focusing' in these subcortical systems is a general non-specific alerting of the nervous system by widespread projections of the brainstem reticular activating (RA) system which itself is activated by sensory input generally, but more particularly by input from cue recognition circuitries.

In the latter case there may be elements of the brainstem RA system specifically engageable by the activated recognition circuitry and in its turn specifically augments both the responsivity of the motor program to signals from the recognition centre and the responsivity of the recognition centre itself to the vital cue signals. When cerebral cortex later evolved to handle more complex input these primitive selective activation functions of the RA system evolved to function at this new level, becoming the rostral intralaminar thalamic group of specialized nuclei.

In species with auditory cortex all sound signals may go on to generate sound consciousness, but when auditory cortex is still primitive vital cue signals alone are able to attract specific attention, and there are two routes by which they do so. One is by evolved connections, via the putative (theoretically required) cortical recognition circuitry, to the mechanisms that control the regional generation of consciousness, principally the rostral intralaminar thalamic nuclei in conjunction with the reticular nucleus and lesser participants, as discussed earlier. The cue's hierarchy status is determined by evolutionary history, and whether or not it gains control will depend on the strength of competition from other claimants. It should again be noted that this high-level focusing is an evolutionary extension of the primitive general alerting function, carried out by increasing specialization of elements of the rostral reticular formation.

The second route is by eliciting an emotional response, such as startle-fear, which acts as a catalyst both on the motor response and the receptivity of the focusing mechanisms to the cue signal. Access to the emotional apparatus is via amygdala by connections from the cue's recognition circuitry. (The emotional system is extremely complex and will be discussed fully in later sections, but it may be noted here that primitive emotion consciousness may antedate the evolution of cerebral cortex and special sensory consciousness).

As the brain continues to evolve, newer circuitries able to recognize more complex environmental phenomena appear in the anatomy, and in neocortex such circuitries are engaged by increasingly elaborate sensory consciousness; the properties of consciousness allow it to represent complex external phenomena and this is the means by which the brain can evolve recognition circuitries to phenomena of more than a certain complexity.

In summary, some aspect of the global conscious experience of the moment has greatest importance due to its ability to activate a downline mechanism which in turn gains control of the master mechanism for focusing which then selectively amplifies that part of the conscious experience, this amplification allowing maximum access to the processing and executive mechanisms of the brain.

See Figs. 1.12(6) and 1.17(1),(2),(3)

A sense organ may transmit more patterns of neural signals than the organism's brain is hard-wired to recognize and respond to. The less encephalized the organism the less potential it has for transducing non-vital stimuli and making use of them; there is presumably a balance between these functions; they must evolve *pari passu* or nearly so, possibly with a slight improvement in one allowing any improvement in the other to become established, in accordance with the upward spiral principle. Thus a mutational improvement in the transducing sense organ would allow more information to flow centrally, and this extra information would be of potential value if there were a concomitant improvement in, for example, the memory system. There is also evidence (e.g., in the case of an extra vibrissa in the mouse) that the transducer and the central processor are a functional unit, to some degree under common genetic control.

The faculty of focusing (or selective regional generation) of consciousness evolved from simple beginnings to eventually serve complex mental processing functions enabling increasingly versatile and appropriate behaviors. When such processing involves focusing on retrievals from memory a new level of mental functioning has been reached: in addition to the improvement in efficiency and range of innate and acquired recognition-responses there now is the additional benefit conferred by enabling relevant memory stores of past experiences to further modify behavior; focusing on a retrieved memory not only enables it to influence behavior but secondarily retrieves related memories which may add to the appropriateness and success of the behavior. This is the basic thinking process. Its nature and advanced development will be explored in the following sections. See Figs. 1.12(1)-(8)

1.19 THE PREFRONTAL CORTEX AND FOCUSING IN THINKING

The higher control of the focusing mechanisms which forms the basis of thinking within the confines of a subject matter is a candidate function for the prefrontal cortex. Damage to this area is characterized by extreme distractability – the inability to concentrate attention on particular tasks for any length of time. The numerous intellectual (or 'cognitive') deficits noted after such damage can probably all be explained in part by loss of this function. All intellectual functions depend on the abilities of acquiring, storing, and using *understandings*, that is, acquaintance with causal relationships in the real world or their operational equivalents in symbolic worlds (of language, mathematics, imagination, abstraction), and these basic abilities are dependent on a highly evolved capability for strong, narrowly localized activation of consciousness-generating neurons, as well as the ability to maintain this focus, and, at the highest level, to shift focus rapidly within a range governed by a theme, subject matter, problem, etc. If any part of this intricate control is lost or damaged productive thought and several forms of normal behavior are impaired.

The ability to handle new data against the background of accumulated understandings and factual material is also crucial for higher mental functioning, including judgement of the relevance of the data in various fields of experience, the possible consequences of contemplated behaviors, and the choice of behavior in present circumstances. Allied to this is the ability to suppress the expression of some vegetative functions and lower-level acquired and innate behavior programs.

To repeat, all of these higher mental, behavioral, and intellectual capabilities are dependent on specialized focusing: the ability to sustain focus on relevant sensory data and memory retrievals. It is therefore important to consider how prefrontal cortex might orchestrate such focusing and inhibit lower level behaviors, and also what processes control prefrontal cortex.

First it may be stated that there is no evidence that prefrontal cortex is conscious; i.e., that consciousness is generated in this part of the brain. When we say it may exercise control over higher mental processes we are not suggesting that some volitional ego resides here. We are simply proposing that when certain types of situation confront the individual his subjective experience of these may trigger an evolved neural mechanism in his prefrontal cortex which directs the control systems to undertake

1.19 The Prefrontal Cortex and Focusing in Thinking

the specialized focusing of consciousness we call thinking. This mechanism almost certainly operates via the basic mechanisms controlling selective generation of consciousness discussed in previous sections and not by having any direct selective control or duplicate focusing mechanism of its own on the sensory cortices. An essential part of the functioning of this proposed prefrontal mechanism is concomitant inhibition of spontaneous behaviors. Shimamura (1995) goes further and argues that the many cognitive deficits following damage to frontal lobe prefrontal cortex are due not only to this cortex suppressing primitive responses but to dissociation of various functions of the sensory cortices with runaway activity of these areas.

The engagement of the prefrontal mechanism for initiating thinking would be brought about by signals originating in other parts of the brain, and it may be suggested that this occurs when the situation the individual is experiencing has some aspect which is unfamiliar or unrecognized, or which presents an obstacle to achieving a goal. There must therefore be neural pathways from those areas and mechanisms of sensory cortex most highly evolved for mental functioning to the prefrontal cortex thence to the generalized thalamocortical system, or, if frustration is aroused, to the limbic system thence to prefrontal cortex.

At the same time the 'emotions' of interest and curiosity may be aroused by such situations, and these may facilitate or 'catalyse' the thinking process, or even initiate it. These 'emotions' may have a long mammalian history, having evolved through their propelling effect on purposive exploratory behavior. They may be generated by the limbic-diencephalic emotional apparatus and since thinking-to-understand is an exploratory process they naturally take the role as the 'intellectual emotions'.

The long association axonal bundles or fasciculi (the uncinate, arcuate, superior longitudinal, cingulum) which connect the major lobes carry fibres from sensory cortices to the prefrontal cortex. Since prefrontal cortex is in the executive lobe of the brain yet does not have a motor function we may speculate that its executive function is that of mediating the thinking function. Memory dysfunction following injury to this cortex may not be due to loss of any memory storage facility but, as suggested earlier, to extreme distractability due to some impairment of the focusing function.

We have no detailed knowledge of the role played by prefrontal cortex in thinking. That it has such a role is inferred from its disproportionately large size in man, and this is supported by studies such as those of Roland and Friberg (1985) which show that some part of prefrontal cortex is always active in different kinds of thinking involving different intermediate and remote 'association' cortices.

We have assigned the function of controlling the differential generation of consciousness in the sensory cortices to a complex of structures including elements of the intralaminar thalamic nuclei, the reticular thalamic complex (Jones,1975), and the ascending components of the brainstem reticular formation. Projections of the adrenergic locus ceruleus and the cholinergic basal forebrain nuclei may also be participants. We have suggested that these structures, which in the cat have a general alerting influence on the cortex with only moderate capacity for regional activation, became specialized in the primate, particularly the hominid line, for modulationary control allowing narrower and stronger regional generation of consciousness as part of the evolutionary elaboration of mental processing capability.

This trend is most advanced in man and includes the capability for rapid switch-focusing, momentarily allowing one or another set of incoming information, whether sensory or from memory, to preferentially represent itself in generated consciousness.

Since mental processing is linear the top priority item must compete successfully with other contemporaneous aspects of the situation. By this process some aspect of consciousness representing a particular environmental situation (or subject matter from memory) is selectively generated. That is, the ensemble of consciousness-generating neurons (or whatever process generates consciousness) comprising the subject matter is selectively activated. This allows the latter maximum access to *relevant* understandings and factual material in memory storage, as well as to mental and physical responses and to the brain's thinking function for the internal generation of new understandings, all of which may be used to guide behavior with benefit.

1.20 SWITCH-FOCUSING IN THINKING

We now come to the specialized switch-focusing which is the basis of the most highly evolved mental function of the brain: thinking-to-understand. The functional essence of this is the facile switching of focus

1.20 Switch-Focusing in Thinking 131

within the boundaries of a subject matter from the present image to the first image it retrieves from memory, and from *this* to the first *it* retrieves, and so on. This is a crucial specialization of basic thinking, the latter being random, open-ended memory retrievals and imagined scenarios, a process that is autonomous in the human, albeit influencable by mood, incidental sensory input, etc..

It must be noted that this is more than a switching of focus as forced by changing priorities among incoming sensory or memory information; thinking-to-understand is a specialized *parade* of memory retrievals and imagined scenarios *within the framework of a theme*, and mechanisms exist to prevent the straying of focus outside the boundaries of the theme, even to the extent of suppressing to some degree the influence of high priority stimuli.

We may wonder at the enormous selective value of this specialization and the huge demands it made on the preadapted structures and functions for its evolutionary achievement, an achievement evidently just within the competence of natural selection. The resulting faculty made possible the exploitation of the artefactual niche and once that threshold had been crossed it proved so competitively advantageous that natural selection 'undertook' a crash program to advance it as fully as possible in the face of many developmental constraints.

Posner et al. (1987) concluded from their studies of human stroke victims that the parietal cortex has a function in disengaging attention, while the brainstem is involved in the shift phase and a third mechanism in fixing a new thought. They also demonstrated that performing a mental task such as counting backwards slowed the reaction time for shifting visual focus, a not surprising finding which supports what we all know: that mental processing operates 'linearly', one task at a time. (That submechanisms which may be involved in this processing operate simultaneously, i.e. in parallel, is a trivial point).

But what mechanism has the specific function of orchestrating the shifting of focus from a *memory* image to the one it retrieves through linkage connections, and how is such a function not the same as shifting focus from one *sensory* item to another? It seems to me that these involve identical *central* focusing mechanisms – whether the item of consciousness is sensory or from memory the process of focusing is the same and both the sensory item and a *random* memory item are focused if they enjoy the highest priority status of the moment. This is probably the highest level of central 'attending' achieved by non-primate species. It must of course be distinguished from *somatic* orienting in sensory attending which is a separate mechanism carried out at a pre-conscious reflexive level (subject to voluntary override in humans; and of course the sensory signals go on to generate consciousness) and this is what Posner et al investigated (and what passes as 'attention' in the majority of studies in rats, cats, and monkeys by neurophysiologists). Shift-focusing within the boundaries of a theme on the other hand is a new, superimposed mechanism operating on the central focusing mechanisms. The phylogenetic level at which it first appears is difficult to determine (its pre-adaptations may be present in primitive mammalian species) but it is behaviorally discernible in the higher primates and is greatly developed in man, or sufficiently so to enable him to open-endedly exploit the artefactual niche.

The situation which becomes subject to the operation of thinking-to-understand is, it has been suggested, one which frustrates goal-directed activities, or elicits the 'emotions' of interest and curiosity, or constitutes a puzzle or dilemma. By leading to a solution of these problems through understanding the individual's fitness is sufficiently, and sufficiently often, enhanced for the mechanism to be strongly adaptive.

In the function of thinking-to-understand not only is focus shifted from image to image as these retrieve one another, but the focus is both narrow and strong, an evolved refinement which both excludes distractions (i.e. 'noise') and allows weak but possibly significant memory associations to be flushed out and themselves be subject to the process.

There is in basic thinking a facile movement of focus from one image to another, which undoubtedly is an evolved facility in lineages increasingly relying on the mind and its processes for adaptive behaviors. But are Posner et al. correct in inferring that the parietal area is specialized for such disengagement? A cognitive function lost after destruction of some large area of brain does not necessarily mean that that area was specialized for such a function. It may simply be that the focusing master control system is so sensitive to changing priorities that the emergence of a new image triggered by the one currently being generated may capture focus if it elicits the slightest participation of a priority-gaining agent, such as a 'feeling' of interest or an emotion. Grossly traumatizing the brain (e.g. by a stroke, which inevitably involves various subcortical structures) may indirectly disrupt such delicate functioning.

To repeat, in the most specialized form of thinking, thinking-to-understand, a new type of control is imposed on the focusing mechanisms. This control restricts focus on retrieved images to those which are within the boundaries of some subject matter – a problem, a social situation, some event, etc.. Sequential retrievals therefore go back and forth within a circumscribed field.

It was proposed above that the neural mechanism which maintains this specialized shift-focusing is situated in prefrontal cortex; that it is an executive function of the highest order, and prefrontal cortex is the most recently evolved part of the executive lobe of the brain. Prefrontal cortex must send signals to the focusing system to maintain switch-focusing. Only material pertinent to the subject matter is focused. This requires feed-back information so that the performance can be monitored for compliance. The way this may work is through the theme of the subject matter being 'in mind' at all times during the thinking operation, as a background consciousness, and thoughts not relevant to the present subject matter will tend to introduce conflicting subject matters, and this conflict alerts the system to more strongly focus the theme.

Thus the putative role of prefrontal cortex is to trigger and maintain switch-focusing by its action on the focusing mechanisms when the need to do so arises, but this specialized kind of focusing is maintained within the bounds of a subject matter by the latter being of itself able to command focus by its priority status, particularly if it has an emotional component, or by voluntary effort in response to some motive. The enormous selective value of such switch-focusing is in its effect of juxtaposing various aspects of a subject matter, leading to new and useful understandings. *This is the key to the explosive evolution of the human brain.*

For a theme to be kept in mind a motive must operate. A motive is "what induces a person to act" (Concise Oxford Dictionary). The motive for a particular action is therefore the reason for acting, or the explanation of why the action was undertaken. At this level of mental functioning motives are limitless in variety so it is not possible to implicate a particular area of the brain in motivation, but whatever the specifics of the reason for acting (the act in this case being thinking-to-understand) some type of emotional accompaniment, e.g. interest, curiosity, urgency, excitement or anxiety from anticipation of reward or distress, etc., may be an important factor restricting thinking to the theme, and such emotion may also operate on the prefrontal cortex to further activate or catalyse its neural apparatus to continue sending impulses to the focusing system directing it to undertake the characteristic switch-focusing.

There are known connections between prefrontal cortex and sensory cortices, between the latter and limbic structures, between the latter and the medio-dorsal nucleus of the thalamus, and between the latter reciprocally with prefrontal cortex. Such connections, in addition to those discussed in the following sections, support the plausibility of the above ideas.

1.21 RELATIONSHIP BETWEEN PREFRONTAL CORTEX AND LIMBIC SYSTEM

The limbic system is an ill-defined basal system of the brain that is in large measure concerned with emotionally driven behaviors and primitive appetitive responses (see Appendix C). It includes (according to one definition) principally the hypothalamus, hippocampus and surrounding cortex, amygdala, septum, mammillary bodies, epithalamus, anterior nuclei of thalamus, and parts of the basal ganglia. Intimately associated with and surrounding the limbic system, on the medial and ventral surfaces of each cerebral hemisphere, is an area of paleocortex which acts as a two-way communication linkage between neocortex and the limbic structures.

The anterior cingulate gyri and the subcallosal gyri are portions of the limbic cortex that communicate between the prefrontal cerebral cortex and the subcortical limbic structures. The principle target for fibres in the cingulum bundle from prefrontal cortex in the monkey is the retrosplenial cortex, which is considered part of the limbic system (Goldman-Rakic, 1981). However, it is not clear what the onward projections are from paleocortex to the emotion-generating elements of the limbic system, but it seems likely that these in part are via archicortices (hippocampus and amygdala) which are the principal gateways to the emotional system from cerebral cortex.

Destruction of certain of these communicating bundles and areas results in release of rage behavior in experimental animals. It seems reasonable to conclude that the erratic emotional behavior often shown by human subjects with frontal lobe lesions is due to impairment of normal modulating activity imposed on the limbic system by the prefrontal region. Higher level control over emotional responses has obvious advantages in proportion to the use of the mind in determining behavior, both because thinking requires minimum distraction and because responses based on understanding are to a certain degree essential for advanced cooperative social life in the artefactual niche and this is incompatible with facile emotionality: to the extent that man is a reasoning animal he is less an emotionally labile one, despite probably having a much richer emotional repertoire than any other species. See Fig.1.12(7)

1.22 RELATIONSHIP BETWEEN PREFRONTAL CORTEX AND THALAMUS

If specialized focusing of consciousness in thinking is under the higher control of prefrontal cortex we must expect to find important fibre connections with at least the thalamic component of the reticular activating system if, as speculated earlier, the generalized thalamocortical system has in man become specialized to function as the executive control system for the kind of versatile focusing which makes higher mental functioning possible. Anatomically it is known that the superior-medial part of the thalamus (medio-dorsal nucleus – MD) connects reciprocally with the prefrontal area of the frontal lobe. This nucleus receives connections from the hypothalamus and amygdala and sends a massive projection to the entire homotypical (six layered) frontal cortex rostral to areas 6 and 32 (Mountcastle,1980:274; Goldman-Rakic, 1981, Amaral et al.,1992). This suggests the means by which emotions generated in the limbic system in response to conscious experiences generated in the sensory cortices engage via the prefrontal mechanisms the focusing mechanisms on those conscious experiences; emotions very strongly engage the focusing apparatus on whatever situation causes the emotion, and this commonly involves engaging the specialized thinking-to-understand function proposed for prefrontal cortex. See Fig.1.12(8)

As discussed above if the prefrontal cortex acts as a cybernetic submechanism which instructs the focusing mechanisms to operate to produce specialized thinking, i.e. to undertake the kind of focusing required in thinking-to-understand, it itself must be subject to engagement by the need to think. Somehow the organism must 'recognize' situations in which such thinking is required, or such situations reflexly produce a thinking-to-understand response when aims, intentions, desires, ambitions, etc. are frustrated, i.e. when problems are encountered, or when an unfamiliar feature is present in the situation.

The prefrontal cortex receives no direct thalamic *sensory* input. That and other evidence indicate that this cortex probably does not generate consciousness. Yet a decision to act is said (Guyton,1987:225) to be 'conceived' in the frontal lobe, and this is a conscious act. These claims are contradictory. It seems probable that a pattern of consciousness generated in the sensory cortices may itself, on reconversion to neural energy, originate a pattern of neural signals acting on the specialized prefrontal cortical mechanisms to engage them in exerting their control over the specialized focusing that constitutes thinking and in modulating behaviors, especially by inhibition of more primitive responses. And the postulated mechanism in the prefrontal cortex for engagement and supervisory control of the specialized focusing required for thinking would achieve its function by activating specific components of the generalized thalamo-cortical system through the numerous connections as outlined earlier, but also via the mediodorsal nucleus which lies in close proximity to the intralaminar thalamic nuclei. There is also evidence that prefrontal cortex may suppress modality-specific sensory input to primary cortical regions via the thalamic reticular nucleus (Yingling and Skinner, 1977).; this mechanism may in part be responsible for the blocking out of sensory distractions during intense thinking.

However, the mechanism for activating prefrontal cortex may not be so straightforward. The sensory cortices are continually generating patterns of consciousness, most of which do not engender thinking. For a particular conscious experience to be 'recognized' as representing a problem, which we suggest is a prerequisite for engagement of the thinking mechanism, something like frustration or interest must be aroused in the individual. For frustration or interest to be aroused there must be an impediment to achieving some goal or a hint in the situation of possible reward.

Therefore, much must take place in the brain before the prefrontal cortex is involved. If the actual trigger is a feeling of frustration or a 'feeling' of interest this must presumably operate from the limbic system, where feelings are believed to be generated, via its connections with prefrontal cortex. Feelings act strongly to produce focus on situations causing the feelings – clearly a function that evolved because of its protective value – and such focus allows the brain's processing capabilities to bear exclusively on the situation as well as accessing whatever memories and response programs pertinent to the situation might exist through experience and learning. In man the highest processing capability is that of thinking-to-understand, the efficiency of which varies innately and by training over a wide range among individuals.

Note that, according to these ideas, emotional feelings generated by elements of the limbic system in response to patterns of consciousness in the sensory neocortex act directly on the proposed intralaminar thalamic and associated focusing mechanisms in *unthinking* situations, to cause preferential activation of the parts of the neocortex generating the particular patterns of consciousness , while, in addition, in situations requiring the specialized switch-focusing of thinking they act on these mechanisms indirectly by their catalysing effect on prefrontal activity.

A purely mental determination to think is the equivalent of any voluntary action – 'voluntary' because the effector organ (the prefrontal circuitry) is engaged from the cerebral cortex and not from lower reflexive systems or by emotional push. (Of course, it may be argued that every voluntary action is in response to *some* motive and is therefore, however obscurely, reflexive!)

Various studies have implicated the prefrontal cortex in other cognitive functions, e.g. judgement, self-control, discipline, working memory, to name a few. While it would be rash to propose that the sole function of prefrontal cortex is the specialized focusing of consciousness required for thinking, it is at least possible that many advanced cognitive functions spring from the ability to understand, and understandings are in part derived from thinking. Both distractability and its opposite, perseveration, seen in different instances of prefrontal damage, can be explained by disruption of different elements of the extremely delicate and highly sensitive micro-control mechanisms involved in productive thinking.

1.23 SLEEP, CONSCIOUSNESS, AND THE RETICULAR FORMATION

The relationships between the reticular formation of the brainstem, sleep, and consciousness have been much investigated and debated. It is now generally considered that no single neural system controls sleep (Legg,1989:181) and that it is at least in part a passive process resulting from removal of collateral activation of neural populations occupying the reticular formation of the brainstem (medulla, pons, and mesencephalon) and that 'this neural system by virtue of its upward projection *on the cerebrum, is thought to control the level of excitability of the forebrain and thus the state of consciousness*' (Mountcastle,1980:308, italics added).

This view clearly embraces the idea that consciousness is generated in the 'forebrain' (here presumably meaning telencephalon plus diencephalon) but is otherwise vague. There are, in fact, conflicting data: Large cerebral areas or even an entire hemisphere can be removed without evident loss of consciousness or of normal sleep-wakefulness patterns (op.cit.:309). This conflicts with the evidence that, for example, damage to an occipital pole results in regional blindness, i.e. partial loss of sight consciousness. There is obvious confusion as to what the word 'consciousness' means. On the other hand lesions involving the central core of the pontile and mesencephalic reticular formation (RF) may result in permanent loss of 'consciousness' (the terms 'somnolence' and 'coma' also being used in this context).

The RF of the brainstem is anatomically complex, consisting of many kinds of cells with large numbers of connections with other regions of the brain and within the system itself. When the brain of the cat was transected at the upper mesencephalic level (just caudal to the motor nucleus of the third cranial nerve) a permanent condition resembling sleep resulted, and strong olfactory and visual stimuli caused only limited and temporary activation of the EEG (Bremer, 1954). Present thinking is that input to the RF from various sources (sensory, emotional, mental, autonomic, hormonal) influences the level of activity of various parts of the RF which in turn activate the CNS generally and selectively. As stated by Mountcastle (1980:309) "How to untangle these complex and interconnecting control systems is a problem of major importance for which no ready solution is apparent".

There is both anatomical and electrophysiological evidence that neuronal systems of cortical origin project on the brainstem RF and that corticoreticulocortical systems may function as reentrant circuits (i.e. as control systems). The effects of cortical efferents on brainstem reticular neurons have been shown to be principally excitatory (Mountcastle, 1980:312-313), suggesting a positive feedback function resulting in increased receptivity of the involved cortical region.

These sparse data may be cited in support of the idea that the ascending RA system has become specialized, especially by elaboration at its thalamic level, for selective regional generation (focusing) of consciousness: those parts of the cerebral cortex involved in mental ('cognitive') functioning at any moment will need to be maximally activated, and signals from these areas to the parts of the RA system to which they are reciprocally connected will result in maintenance and strengthening of their conscious activity; and axonal branches from these ascending RA fibres will, through interneurons (probably mainly in the thalamus), inhibit other elements of the RA system responsible for modulating the generation of consciousness in other areas until priority is lost to another pattern of cortical activity constituting a different aspect of the cognition.

The enormous intricacy, sensitivity, and delicacy of control of this multifaceted focusing system would be a major challenge in any attempt at cybernetic modelling. Particularly difficult to model would be the manner by which neurons generating consciousness are selected for activity in an infinity of patterns, often changing with extreme rapidity, constituting representations of external reality and internal thoughts of every kind, these in turn eliciting memories, emotions, and responses of great variety.

The fact that the ascending reticular activating system is concerned with arousal and consciousness leads one to speculate on the evolutionary origin of this relationship. The primitive chordate Amphioxus (lancelet) has a poorly differentiated reticular formation (RF) which functions for multisynaptic transmission of signals from its primordial brain to its spinal cord (Sarnat and Netsky,1980:204). In vertebrate evolution (as inferred from comparative studies) the reticular formation became more organized and other transmission pathways between the brain and the cord appeared, with the RF at some stage taking on the role of a servomechanism in the responsiveness of the central nervous system to sensory input. It also developed a spontaneous (tonic) baseline activity which is responsible for influencing the activity of other neuronal systems of the CNS. Removal of this activity in higher animals leads to coma, while electrical stimulation of different parts may induce wakefulness or sleep, respiratory and cardiovascular activity or depression, etc.

It is evident that this whole system plays a major modulating role in the CNS, both by its spontaneous activity and in response to numerous influences. In its evolutionary history it may first have been a simple pathway in reflexivity between the rostral and caudal ends of the neural tube; later it took on the additional function of modulating reflexivity mediated by newly evolved transmission lines by-passing the multisynaptic reticular system; later still it extended this modulatory capability to establish the function of regulating the general responsiveness of the CNS according to environmental and physiological circumstances, probably operating spontaneously at a median level of activation, but, in response to different needs of the organism, at a higher level of alertness at one extreme and a state of sleep at the other; finally, specialization of its different parts, in particular the intralaminar thalamic nuclei, led to the capability of selectively activating increasingly narrow segments of the cerebrum concerned with the generation of consciousness, eventually to the point of extremely rapid shifts in the selective activation of different ensembles of consciousness-generating neurons or neuronal units which is the basis of thinking-to-understand, this last function being under the control of the most recently evolved circuitries of the prefrontal cortex.

Another direction of specialization is the capability of blocking, at the level of the dorsal horn grey matter of the spinal cord, signals originating in the peripheral nervous system. This is achieved by the raphe nuclei of the reticular formation, particularly the n.raphe magnus, and the associated periaqueductal grey matter, electrical stimulation of which results in loss of ability to experience pain from its sites of disease or injury (Barr and Kiernan,1988:157). Enkephalins (peptide neurotransmitters or neuromodulators) are released at synapses in the periaqueductal grey matter, the raphe nuclei, and the substantia gelatinosa of the dorsal horn of spinal grey matter. The enkephalins have analgesic effects similar to those of opiates which bind to the same postsynaptic receptor sites. Other opium-like peptides, the endorphins, have been found in several parts of the brain.

It is a common human experience, in the process of falling asleep or waking up, that discomforts, physical and emotional, present in the fully awake state are absent. On awakening there is a short period during which there is only visual and auditory consciousness after which various bodily sensations, memories, and emotional feelings intrude. Also it is well known that in physiological sleep the same bodily position can be maintained harmlessly for longer periods than in the awake condition. It seems highly probable that the enkephalin- and endorphin-producing neurons of the raphe nuclei and elsewhere are active in anaesthesizing the body and brain during sleep, thus blocking the generation and transmission of neural signals from body and brain to the consciousness-generating neurons.

1.24 VOLITION

The concept of freedom of will arises from our introspective analysis of the exercise of will which has an experiential sense of an uncaused cause – action that arises spontaneously in the ego in that it may be arbitrary or whimsical, and divorced from any external force, or so it seems. Is this an instance of the principle that when a system achieves a critical degree of complexity it may become something more than the sum of its parts; that is, that new *qualities* emerge? In the case of volition simple nervous systems do not display it, but sufficiently complex ones do. But what function does volition serve? For it to be retained and further evolved it must contribute to the organism's successful adaptation to its niche conditions. But volition is an instrument – it energises the effector systems to satisfy goals formulated by the thinking function or the body's physiological demands: it has in every instance an antecedent, arguably causal, circumstance.

To state that something is free we must immediately qualify this by revealing *from* what it is supposed to be free. Freedom of will must be freedom from control or influence by any force outside the mind. But what if the mind is deranged and delusions originating in the mind influence volition? We make another qualification and say that the concept only applies to normal minds. But obviously there is no end to this. We may simply say that we *define* volition or free will in a certain way, viz. that the subjective experience is that of the ego creating energy out of nothing.

It may be speculated that when the focusing mechanisms and their control systems evolved to a certain critical level the central nervous system was then preadapted for the emergence of the highest level of executive mental functioning: volition. We must remind ourselves that every biological system presently in existence is the result of (usually) very small incremental changes in pre-existing systems, the human faculty of volition no less than any other; the evolutionary roots of volition may go back a long way.

The site of initiation of voluntary motor or mental activity is unknown. This is hardly surprising as such an advanced and complex function of the brain must consist in the integrated functioning of several areas. Neuronal activity may be recorded in the sensory areas of the brain as early as one second before voluntary motor activity begins. Also, activity in the premotor cortex begins before that in the motor cortex, and the cerebellum and basal ganglia are activated at the same time of even earlier than the motor cortex. "Therefore, it is beginning to be believed that *cerebration* occurring in [the] 'integrative' portions of the brain, operating in association with the cerebellum, conceives and plans the complex sequence of movements that is to be executed" (Guyton, 1987:225).

As the brain evolves a greater capability for 'cerebration', behavior shifts from the immediate (reflexive) to the delayed (deliberative), during which motor activity is inhibited. When a plan of action is conceived it has to be undertaken, so a neural mechanism must exist to allow this to happen. The operation of this mechanism is what we call volition or willing, and it has an experiential component that, introspectively, has the characteristics of an 'uncaused cause'. Whether this conscious component, this feeling of will, is an incidental phenomenon – an epiphenomenon – or an evolved feature with an essential causal role is debatable, but its universal, albeit apparently variable, presence in humans strongly suggests that it has been selected, and if so it must be genetically based.

A voluntary act is one that is initiated in the cerebral cortex, but not all acts originating in the cerebral cortex are voluntary; e.g., random imagination may produce a scene that causes the individual to react involuntarily. It seems that our definition of voluntariness must include features like understanding, purpose, and intention. Even an act coming from an external command must include these features if it is to be classified as voluntary; otherwise it is an involuntary reflex.

Once the brain has evolved to the point where conscious experiences of causal relationships can be stored and subsequently used to affect the external world in a manner in keeping with an imagined outcome, a stage beyond simple reflexivity has been reached. It is true that the original source of the stored material is the stimulus from the external world and in this sense is the ultimate cause of the action, but the differences in the dimensions of causality involved in voluntary and involuntary reflexivity are so great that they are epistemologically distinct.

This subject is further discussed in Section 2.15.

1.25 THINKING AND UNDERSTANDING

> "By the mental process which is founded on (such) sensations we come to learn the conditions of these sensations, and to trace them to objects which are not part of ourselves, but in every case the fact that we learn is the mutual action between bodies" (James Clerk Maxwell, 1877).

Definitions

Human understanding is a biological function with an evolutionary history; that is, it is a faculty owing its existence to genetically based adaptations to niche conditions. It is the capacity to acquire and use knowledge of causal processes occurring in the natural, macroscopic world. Once this faculty had evolved to a certain critical level it allowed entry to the artefactual 'niche', and this proved so competitively advantageous that in the line leading to man it further evolved explosively, together with its associated faculties – memory, language, imagination, etc.

It is meaningless to speak of 'understanding' non-causal phenomena. One cannot 'understand' the colour green; but that mixing the colours yellow and blue gives green is an understanding. One has *knowledge* of green; it is a conscious quality stored in memory (in area V4 of visual cortex, according to experimental and clinical evidence – Zeki, 1993).

The dynamic events, or causal processes, occurring in the world, and above all those that occur between the organism and its environment, determine whether or not the organism survives. This is the ultimate imperative in biological evolution. Almost every structure and every function in every living organism exists because it is in harmony with the dynamics of the organism's world, the exceptions being those that although potentially harmful are genetically tied to others that confer overriding survivability.

The thinking function is merely the most sophisticated and recent utilization of consciousness by the evolving brain in its adaptation to the challenges of life. There is nothing esoteric about the functions of thinking and understanding. The principle underlying these functions is simple: the capacity to deal with physical causation. The faculties of thinking and understanding are the result of the capacity to evolve in a particular way in adaptation to the imperatives of physical causation. It is simple biological evolution.

The evolutionary viewpoint

In an effort to understand the mind as a product of evolution one arrives at the position of seeing the faculty of understanding as a logical (biological) end point of that process: it is the ultimate stage in the representation by means of consciousness of processes occurring in the environment and of the use of such representations to produce behaviors relevant to these environmental phenomena for the benefit of the individual.

This faculty has its greatest value through making possible the employment of the materials and forces of nature to alter the environment and the direction of events. Since this (by definition) artificial exploitation of nature is in a sense a domain within which behaviors can adapt through biological evolution I think of it as the *artefactual niche*.

The central adaptation allowing the *continued* exploitation of this niche after 'entry' has been achieved is the crossing of a critical threshold in the capacity to understand. Since understanding is a definite function of the brain carried on by evolved neural structures it is not a topic for semantic and philosophical debate but an area for scientific investigation. Nonetheless, since the word 'understanding' is so commonly used colloquially its scientific usage must be defined.

The nature of understanding

What constitutes an understanding? I have maintained that essentially it is the experiencing, the storage in memory, and retrievability as a whole into imagery of a causal relationship. But is this definition complete, and is it exclusive? It is incomplete in that the phenomenon of causation itself (i.e., what causation *is*) must be sensed by the individual, and this derives from innumerable personal experiences of its operation, which alter brain-body responses in subtle ways, especially in producing the mental-physiological state of expectation (anticipation), and most especially when volition is involved. So the phenomenon of understanding has a composite experiential side which must be part of its complete definition.

Is the definition exclusive? We speak of 'understanding' a language, but on analysis no causal relationships are revealed; we should instead say we recognize the meaning of the words and sentences. By my definition understanding a language would mean becoming acquainted with its evolution and the neuromental and neuromuscular processes involved in its acquisition and production, i.e., causal processes.

To take another example: As a result of hard thinking I come to understand that the earth moves around the sun in a clockwise direction as viewed from above their N poles. What is it that is understood here? What is involved is a mental picture or a sketched diagram in which one body is moving around another in a certain direction. Does this constitute an understanding? In itself I think it merely constitutes factual knowledge. Understanding here would come from 'seeing' that the circular motion is due to the effect of gravity of the sun accelerating the earth, i.e., a causal relationship, and from knowledge of the dynamics in the formation of the solar system, also a matter of causal processes.

Further, to understand that for the motion to be seen as either clockwise or anticlockwise depends on the viewing position, is a true act of understanding despite not being a physically causal process, because what is involved here is causal in the sense that one 'sees' that doing something (the act of imagination) has a particular result.

Thinking from presently available data may reveal a future state which may be non-dynamic; the thinking reveals a factual, not a causal state. In such a case one comes to 'realize' what the state will be, but one does not come to 'understand' it because it is not something that involves dynamics (although the process by which the thinking function operated would, if known, constitute understanding).

The mechanism of thinking

Thinking-to-understand is the process of specialized 'focusing' of consciousness, that is, its selective regional generation, which has two parts: the capacity for very narrow focusing and the ability to shift focus rapidly back and forth within the limits of a subject matter. As a consequence of the first of these activities retrieval of relevant material from memory strongly occurs, then the rapid switch-focusing allows various aspects of the subject matter to 'occupy' consciousness sufficiently closely for otherwise unsuspected causal relationships to be 'seen'. *These constitute new understandings*, which are representations of causal relationships existing, or expected to be found to exist, in the world of the subject matter. A subject matter requiring thinking may be of any form, but whether it is a situation to be understood, a problem to be solved, or a plan to be devised the brain has only one mechanism of thinking, the origin and evolutionary development of which will be briefly discussed in Part 2. (The specialized focusing mechanisms underlying the faculty of thinking-to-understand were discussed in earlier sections).

When an individual is confronted with a situation this may to a certain degree be recognized and understood, depending on prior experience. The recognition must take place in the consciousness-generating and their associated memory storage areas of the brain, presumably in the primary and secondary sensory areas of the cerebral cortex. The recognized elements of the subject matter retrieve from memory, through synaptic linkage, related understandings and factual material. These retrievals are from the memory stores of all the sensory modalities involved, each reconstituted image being composed of more-or-less large numbers of units of consciousness, each of which is generated by a specific type of neuron activated by its own memory neuron when the latter has been stimulated by a signal through synaptic linkage.

The specialized adaptation of imagery in the evolution of a thinking function

Is there any instance of thinking which is not carried on through imagery (of one sensory mode or another), or any understanding which is not composed of imagery? Are intuition, conceptualization, abstraction, insightfulness, and generalization forms of thinking or modes of understanding, and if so do they use imagery?

These are obviously all cognitive functions, meaning that they employ consciousness in their operations, and consciousness and imagery are synonymous terms in cognitive neuroscience. This does not mean that non-conscious mechanisms play no part in these functions; on the contrary, such mechanisms are intrinsic to all cognitive functions. In particular, a great deal of thinking employs acquired thought reflex packages established by repetition of sequences of thinking employing imagery. Such packages may be composed of entire sequences greatly speeded up or of short-cut jumps eliminating most of the intermediate stages of the original sequence, and as such they evoke at most only fleeting imagery.

Analysis of the above cognitive functions shows only that they are special cases. For example, conceptualization. In one of its common usages this term refers to the mental discovery and designation of a principle or process intrinsic to a number of phenomena in which its status as a common thread was hitherto unsuspected, e.g., the concepts of energy, evolution, justice. Take the concept of energy. Its history is obscure but probably very old, and it may have been widely sensed as some 'thing' that was always there when work was done, before being nailed down and brought into focus by the use of language. Even to modern physics the nature of that something remains a mystery, but when we think of it we invariably form images of specific situations. The crucial mental jump in this type of conceptualization is noticing for the first time something which is always before our eyes, and there is no unique mechanism involved in this or any of the other higher cognitive functions. They are variations of the basic thinking function (albeit historically providing a high rate of false understandings!)

If the CNS is a massive reflex arc then all of its functions must be reflexive

All mental activity is reflexive, although at the human level the complex interplay of subtle influences obscures this fact, and the subjective conviction that volition has no cause denies it. But even in volition every act is in obedience to some motive, and motives (at the highest level) spring from thought which in turn is an energy-consuming process. There is no self-starting in mental activity. Whatever activity is occurring has been started by a preceding activity. On awakening from dreamless sleep or general anaesthesia the nervous system is first activated at its periphery by external stimuli which start the flow of activity centrally. Consciousness generated will retrieve memories and engage various responses and cognitive functions, with each of these eliciting or activating others. The basic feature of the nervous system is *flow* of activity from input to output, and that flow continues through all the central processing structures, including the mechanisms that generate consciousness and support thought, and not withstanding the backflow in reentrant or reciprocal connections supporting modulatory control functions. (The flow-chart best captures the *raison d'etre* of the nervous system. Cartesian coordinate charts, widely employed in cognitive neuroscience, on the other hand record the relationships between parameters).

Thinking is reflexive in that a thought does not occur unless the images of which it is composed are retrieved from memory through synaptic linkage activity which is a function of neural reflex arcs. Through such retrievals some randomness in the sequential juxtaposition of images may occur which may allow a causal connection or a class relationship to be 'seen', constituting a new understanding.

Conscious recognition – its utilization in the evolution of an understanding faculty

Such 'seeing' is basically the operation of conscious recognition – a causal relationship between items in the thinking scenario is discovered because it is recognized, there being in memory a stockpile of similar or analogous causal relationships acquired through experience of the external world. Thus we may have had the experience that certain types of remark are offensive to people. On thinking we may 'suddenly realize' that a remark we had made might have offended someone. This realization occurs because we recognize in the thinking situation the stored experience; i.e. the present mental scenario is closely similar to material in memory. In other words the experience of the past is being approximately re-enacted in the current thought and the images of this re-enactment cause *direct* retrieval of the stored material back to consciousness where, it is hypothesized, it 'meshes' with the image already in consciousness to produce a sense of familiarity, or conscious recognition (see below and Section 2.3 for the basics of this process). This in turn retrieves linked material from memory, in this example the fact of people being offended. (The important distinction between direct and indirect memory retrievals and the essential role of the former in the faculty of recognition is discussed in the memory sections).

The core recognition is often embellished – the understanding is made more complete – by peripheral aspects of the thinking scenario being in turn recognized because there are in memory similar features; in other words the context in which the core understanding occurs has its equivalent in memory. Additional embellishment may come from the beginning engagement of response mechanisms and programs tied to the recognized item.

An act of thinking retrieves other items from memory. The items go back to memory where they tend to re-elicit themselves in a continuous cycle. So long as this is maintained each loop of neural impulses will reinforce the memory circuits involved. See Fig.1.7

From primitive neural mechanisms to thinking and understanding via conscious recognition

I have earlier suggested that loop-back (reentrant) signals from memory by reinforcing the sensory image, thereby altering the quality of the subjective experience, may be responsible for the sense of familiarity or recognition. The process would work like this: An external situation activates the sense organs, signals from which travel to the cerebral cortex where they generate consciousness; the consciousness is thus a representation of the external situation; the consciousness reconverts to neural energy to activate downline systems, including the memory system; in principle each consciousness-generating neuron (possibly a stellate cell in layer 4) is functionally connected to its own downline memory neuron (possibly a pyramidal cell in layer 5 or 6 of the same cortical column); when the consciousness neuron is activated by the sensory signal it sends streams of impulses which activate its memory neuron, which in turn sends streams of impulses not only onwards to other parts of the brain but also by special recurrent axonal branches back up the cortical column to produce a feed-back activation of the consciousness neuron, this being a servomechanism of ancient origin; the consciousness-generating neuron is thus doubly activated (by the sensory signal and by the return memory signal) producing a heightened conscious experience which, it is hypothesized, gives the experiential aura of familiarity. Up to this evolutionary stage this aura is an ineradicable epiphenomenon accompanying a vital function of ancient origin.

In the absence of incoming sensory signals if the memory neuron is activated by signals from some internal cerebral source it would by this loop-back arrangement activate its consciousness neuron to generate, somewhat weakly, i.e. of lower intensity, units of consciousness identical to those generated by sensory signals acting on this neuron; in this sense an incoming sensory signal would meet itself in consciousness by resurrecting its own memory; therefore a complex sensory input conveyed by thousands or millions of nerve fibres will, after traversing various processing way-stations, activate a pattern of thousands or millions of consciousness-generating neurons and through these their memory neurons which will *en masse*, by the above process, result in recognition of the pattern; the pattern will seem familiar in direct proportion as its precise design was experienced before – previous experience would have resulted in synaptic bonding between the individual memory neurons so that this particular pattern is 'in memory' and will be strongly recognized on reencounter because the constituent memory neurons on being activated would not only return signals directly to their own consciousness neurons but strongly activate one another for a massive return of signals, resulting in strong recognition and sense of familiarity. This whole mechanism explains why we often recognize situations and objects without at first being able to remember anything about them.

Serendipity and entrepreneurship in evolution

Assuming all this to be so we must make the attempt to surmise if and how it may have contributed to evolution of the mind, and to do this we must first ask what benefit may result from conscious recognition or a sense of familiarity. Of itself it is of no value, and may in fact have been an unavoidable, incidental feature in the loop-back reinforcement process for a very long period in the history of the lineage. It only becomes a target for selection if it is able to trigger or influence some newly evolved activity, and the most likely such activity would be the 'emotion' of interest or curiosity.

We may hypothesize that the subjective experience of recognition, or 'sense' of familiarity, by eliciting interest, however faintly, acts, through the agency of this 'emotion', to capture focus sufficiently long to allow any neural program or mechanism triggerable by the recognized event to be engaged. If such a program exists and has priority the focusing mechanism will continue to be engaged; if not some other item will capture focus. (Disinterest is commonly not an active process but simply absence of interest; but, as surmised elsewhere, it may, depending on circumstances, be due to active inhibition of response to the familiar).

From conscious recognition to understanding via the memory stores
In the function of thinking-to-understand the thought images which comprise the subject matter are switched from one to another, and if the fortuitous juxtaposition of such images happens to correspond with memory contents linked in a manner representing a causal relationship, that is, an understanding, these will tend to be directly elicited and mesh with the current thought image with resulting conscious recognition or familiarity, and this will engage the focusing mechanism on this aspect of the subject matter whereupon it comes to be 'seen' that the thought images represent a causal relationship, giving a new understanding.

This idea is fundamental, so must be clarified as fully as possible. Everyone has probably had the experience of thinking along certain lines and suddenly realizing that he or she has had a more-or-less similar thought before – suddenly the thought acquires familiarity. In this circumstance the current thought is being produced by more-or-less the same dynamic patterns of neuronal activation that have been used before, the memory neurons involved in these patterns being bound together by facilitated synaptic linkages. Each of the innumerable putative consciousness-generating neurons (or its functional equivalent) involved in the current thought activates its own memory neuron, but the whole package of such neurons acts as a unit, therefore there is a massive reactivation of the multineuronal unit in memory, resulting in the loop-back reinforcement of the current pattern giving rise (by 'meshing' or whatever the mechanism may be) to the sense of recognition or familiarity.

So in a sense the thought meets itself in memory and is recognized, the 'itself' being the memory either of a sensory experience or of a previous more-or-less similar thought. And this stirring up of the old memory results not only in direct loop-back retrieval for recognition but in signals being sent out from its boundaries via facilitated synaptic linkages to other memories associated with the subject matter, these in turn generating consciousness, that is, 'becoming' conscious images. And if the person is under the motivation of a need-to-understand this motivation activates the focusing mechanisms specialized for this most highly evolved intensity of thinking to produce rapid switch-focusing eliciting image after image within the confines of the subject matter (so long as the motive prevails).

It is evident from this that an act utilizing consciousness, e.g. thinking, may involve neurons which have been used in precisely this manner before, and therefore the memory neurons downline from the neurons supporting the conscious activity have already been 'imprinted' and bound by facilitated synaptic connections to constitute a memory congruent with that of the current thought. This is why the thought 'meets itself' in memory and is recognized.

We must attribute to the properties of synapses the extraordinary feat whereby a limited number of memory neurons can store a virtually unlimited number of memories: despite the enormous amount of overlapping that must occur a high degree of efficiency in functional compartmentalization is achieved. (Studies of the synaptic organization of the brain (e.g. Shepherd et al, 1990) have not yet revealed the essence of this evolutionary achievement.)

Since the similarity between the current thought and the memory of some previously acquired understanding is commonly that of analogy the understandings generated by thinking are of necessity provisional. (The essence of the scientific method, which, surprisingly, is a recently adopted discipline of the human intellect, is to try to verify such provisional understandings (hypotheses) by investigation of the physical world).

The images constituting an understanding are necessarily sequential

Items of understandings stored in memory, i.e. linked memories representing causal relationships, when elicited form sequential images in consciousness; that is, an understanding cannot be experienced as a single 'frame', but the close sequence of the 'frames' allows them to be experienced as a whole because of the finite fading time of images as well as (to put it somewhat vaguely) reverberation of the system, and because the neural mechanisms which are triggered by understandings to serve executive functions have evolved to be responsive to such stretched-out wholes. This allows the brain to function on contents of consciousness contained in segments of time greater than instants.

Thoughts on a subject matter may turn this way or that as different aspects are experienced through the senses or retrieved from memory. As discussed above if the subject matter contains a causal relationship unknown to the thinker this may be discovered if a fortuitous juxtaposition of elements of this relationship occurs in the thinking, provided analogous understandings are stored in memory. Put simply, the resemblance may strike the thinker. To repeat, the way this occurs may be as follows: First, some part of the present thinking experience, unknown to represent a part of a causal relationship, may be recognized by directly retrieving its equivalent or analogue from memory; second, this retrieved element will indirectly retrieve, via memory linkages, items representing the remainder of the equivalent or analogous understanding, which will be recognized to the extent that it is similar to the current experience. This translates to the sensation in the thinker of a 'feeling' of familiarity, and from this to the 'seeing' of a causal relationship in the current subject matter, the reality or accuracy of which will depend on the reliability of the analogy. Commonly, of course, the thinker does not realize the source of this 'flash of insight'.

Problem solving

In problem solving by use of the mind (as distinct from innate behaviors evolved to handle specific 'problems') novel difficulties are overcome. This capability is just within the reach of the highest level of non-human mental functioning in which information stored in memory is applied to the problem. At this level, although it is the pre-adaptive feature for the evolution of advanced human thinking capability, the process is in outline simple: the present problem, or some aspect of it, retrieves from memory, through recognition, similar or analogous situations and, by linkage, their outcomes. Whether or not the use of this is successful in overcoming the present problem, the mental process of applying stored information in this way is a major evolutionary advance.

Problem solving should then not be regarded as a specific capability of the mind distinct from the mind's general thinking capability. The mechanism of thinking-to-understand is what is employed in solving problems; it is only the nature of the task that is distinctive, and that depends largely on what one's definition of a problem happens to be, e.g., a set of circumstances requiring explanation, a plan to be devised, how to overcome difficulties on the way to achieving some goal, etc.

In practice the process may not be entirely mental, but may in part be determined by acquired behavior programs laid down in the CNS by earlier experience, possibly by a single experience of its kind. The degree of novelty of the present problem will determine the limits of the contribution from lower level reflexive activity. Conventional, retrievable ('declarative') memory (a function presumably of the cerebral sensory cortex) and corporeal, motor-control ('procedural') memory (a function presumably of cerebral premotor and cerebellar cortices) probably employ very similar neuronal properties of imprintability and linkage formation, and thinking and voluntary motor behavior may imprint these memory systems with equal facility. This would obviously be a highly adaptive capability in that it permits rapid learning, that is, acquisition of automatically performable mental and motor functions, thereby allowing the thinking function to operate more fully and freely on novel aspects of problems. Much of what we attribute to cogitation and problem solving may in large measure be engagement of acquired mental and physical behavior programs.

Obviously, problem solving ranges all the way from trial-and-error physical manipulations to the fullest use of accumulated understandings and factual knowledge in disciplined application of the mechanism of thinking-to-understand. It would be an exercise in triviality, except for specific practical purposes, to list in detail the individual steps taken in particular examples of problem solving.

Understandings beget understandings, but the process is fallible

As memory becomes more stocked with understandings derived from experience *and* from thinking it becomes easier for new thinking to form understandings (i.e. to reveal relationships) more remote from direct experience (i.e. less evident to the senses). This is because there are more opportunities for some degree of conscious recognition to occur resulting from partial correspondence between the imagery in thinking and stored material – causal relationships are apt to be 'seen' in the imagery of thinking through weak recognition of material in memory representing causal relationships (understandings) themselves of a provisional nature and already remote to some degree from sensory experience. To the extent that these recognitions have less correspondence with securely established, i.e. confirmed, understandings in memory, so will the new understandings they give rise to be less likely to be valid.

This analysis of the biology of thinking if correct means that its conclusions inevitably carry an indeterminate degree of inaccuracy! Thinking about thinking involves this peculiar circularity. The above ideas may of course be simply stated: In thinking we concentrate so that we can bring our accumulated knowledge to bear on the subject at hand. The thinking process can be made more efficient by frequent use and training, by discipline and logic in the ordering of thoughts, through experience in different ways of approaching subject matters, by avoidance of distractions, etc., but for the capturing of subtle or intricate understandings luck may play as great a part as anything else. Luck can sometimes be assisted by putting aside the problem from time to time so that current unprofitable eddies of thought in which we are momentarily trapped can be escaped from thus allowing the possibility of fortuitous juxtaposition of material retrieved from memory to give that satisfying flash of insight.

The imaginative function plays a large part in thinking of the speculative type, in which explanatory models are constructed from meagre material, and in planning, in which it is necessary to provide alternative scenarios for the achievement of some goal. In the latter case each plan is focused so that each of its parts and processes comes under scrutiny with resulting retrieval from memory of facts and understandings related to these, and the consequences of these are played out imaginatively to a position which can then be compared with the goal.

The mind has only one thinking mechanism which has only one way of functioning, but the range of understandings that can be achieved by it is limited only by the number and variety of causal processes in the world and by the strictures of logic.

1.26 SYMBOLISM IN THINKING

If the term 'thinking' is broadened to apply to all acts of memory retrieval then its range is from idle random linkage retrievals to the most intense focus within the narrow limits of a subject matter in thinking-to-understand. Most uses of the term are in reference to retrievals governed, however loosely, by some theme or motive. But no matter how idle the thinking there is always the possibility of it revealing new understandings by fortuitous juxtaposition of material.

The claim that all basic thinking is composed of imagery is challenged by those who maintain that they think verbally or abstractly and that mathematical thinking is non-pictorial. This is particularly true of those whose work involves much disputation or explanation, and who are therefore in the habit of voicing their thoughts as they occur. But although the evolution of language capability paralleled and was interwoven with that of the thinking function, and language use often clarifies and disciplines thinking, language is word symbolism employed in representing and conveying to other minds the 'contents' (i.e. the various forms) of consciousness: understandings, factual knowledge, feelings, intentions, etc., which are all experienced non-linguistically.

The two principal reasons for confusing language with thinking are, first, many people, for whatever reason, have developed the habit of closely expressing their thoughts so that introspectively they cannot separate the two processes, and second, much of thinking is of sequences that have been repeated and represented by language so often that they form more-or-less large thought packages wrapped in language representation and are simply 'taken as read' as components of wider thinking. Language itself is composed of meaningless sensory experiences – it has no significance beyond its sounds, etc. It acquires significance or meaning by being linked in memory to other memories representing primary experience.

In mathematics various symbols represent certain basic features of the sensory experience of natural phenomena and the relationships between these. By using the symbols for the relationships it proves possible to short-cut sensory experience to arrive, when retranslated, at a situation of nature with precision and relative ease (to those versed in the technique) often impossible or very difficult without this tool. This procedure appears open-ended and easily leads into realms where retranslation to sensory experience is difficult or possible only by analogy, but also it has historically led to predictions about reality that later, with new technology, proved correct (e.g. Maxwell's equations predicting forms of electro-magnetic radiation other than light and the speed of such radiation and Dirac's 'absurd' equation predicting (in effect) the existence of an antielectron, fulfilled later by the discovery of the positron).

As Adler (1972) put it: "The reality is the physical world. Mathematics allows great speculative freedom, but in the end each mathematical theory must be relevant to physical reality..."

The experiences symbolized in mathematics are of limited kinds and are related to the physical properties of the world: plurality, size, relation, function, correspondence, proportion, ratio, motion, change, categories, groups, etc. We should in principle be able to take any sample of mathematical symbolization and ask that it be retranslated into a physical model we can sensorially examine, but this is not possible with much of modern 'pure' mathematics in which the starting points are often not based on the 'real' world as revealed by the senses but on assumptions such as the existence of multidimensional space. According to Barrow (1991) Hilbert, with this in mind, "defined mathematics as nothing more than the manipulation of symbols according to specific rules. The resulting paper edifice has no special meaning at all. It should, if the manipulations were performed correctly, result in a vast collection of tautological statements: an embroidery of logical connections".

In principle mathematical representation and manipulation are applicable to biological systems, but in practice the variables are often too complex to represent. Biological systems evolved slowly over vast stretches of time, step by step, and such evolution guarantees the maintenance of stability of structure and reliability of function despite ever increasing complexity beyond the limits of mathematical representation.

1.27 THE LANGUAGE FUNCTION AND THINKING

The equivalence of speech vocalization and other voluntary activities

Vocalization is under voluntary control in the same degree and by the same mechanisms as other somatic muscular activities. We may speculate that voluntary limb movements, directed to achieving some goal, and voluntary vocalization for goal satisfaction employ essentially the same mechanisms; in voluntary vocalization speech sounds are used as instruments to effect a change in the environment (in this case the behavior and mental state of other persons). Essential for both these voluntary, goal-directed achievements is a critical level of thinking and understanding ability. It may be suggested that the extent to which voluntary vocalization is used to influence events closely parallels the equivalent use of limbs: if the early hominid understands on reflection that he can use his limbs to achieve an objective he must inevitably understand that he can also use vocalization to produce desired effects. The development of language is the inevitable consequence of the development of a thinking mind possessing voluntary executive capability.

The brain's language areas: (1) Broca's area
It is highly probable that Broca's area of cerebral cortex evolved through the selective advantages of converting thoughts to vocal language. One would expect it to have intimate connections with the sensory areas, the prefrontal areas, and the motor areas. A thought is composed of imagery. This is true whether it is a simple memory retrieval or an abstruse understanding, or whether the imagery is visual, auditory, somesthetic, etc.. That a thought may be represented, i.e. symbolized, in language is an immense aid in much of thinking, principally because frequently repeated thought sequences can be packaged in reflexly triggerable language programs, although true basic thinking is itself non-verbal.

Broca's area of premotor cortex is concerned with the production of speech. Damage restricted to this area results in loss of ability to speak whole words, but involuntary vocalization is not impaired – there is no paresis of the vocal apparatus, unless the damage involves the upper motor neurons controlling this. Unfortunately, data come mainly from stroke victims in whom the lesion invariably includes more of less of primary motor cortex and deep structures, including basal ganglia. The plight of the person with severe right hemiplegia and loss of all vocalization is that he has the same kind of difficulty with his vocal apparatus as with his limbs – he cannot get them to work because executive elements of his neocortex, the premotor and upper motor neurons, are damaged.

Broca's area of cortex belongs to the executive lobe of the brain. Its job is, in response to orders from the mental part of the brain, to select the appropriate combination of upper motor neurons for vocalization representing thoughts. Its circuitry is an evolutionary elaboration of prelinguistic vocal circuitry responsive to primitive volition, the

1.27 The Language Function and Thinking 159

primordium of which may be found well down the mammalian scale. It occupies the inferolateral part of premotor cortex (see Frontispiece 1) adjacent to and in intimate relationship with those parts of primary motor cortex controlling vocal musculatures. It evidently has the capacity to acquire and store speech programs representing thoughts, so while a voluntary trigger may be required to engage such a program much of the actual performance may be automatic.

In early phylogeny primitive articulation in response to conscious experiences would have operated directly from primary sensory areas to primary motor areas. With the evolution of thinking and understanding faculties more complex thoughts needed more complex articulation for representation, with resulting constant pressure for selection of circuitries in premotor cortex able to meet this demand.

Ancient pathways from the parts of the brain generating intention to produce primitive vocalization may therefore not go via the more recently evolved Broca's circuitry and may be spared in damage restricted to that circuitry, or, being simpler and more robust, may survive the stroke effects (many Broca's aphasics are capable of crude voluntary vocalizations).

Pure voluntary control of the vocal apparatus (larynx, lips, tongue, etc.), as with pure voluntary control of lower motor neurons controlling trunk and limb musculatures, probably operates via the upper motor neurons (Betz's giant pyramidal cells) of primary motor cortex (Brodman's area 4). By repetition of such movements the sequences this gives rise to come to be stored as motor programs outside primary motor cortex, principally in premotor cortex (Broca's area) but very likely also in cerebellar neocortex and possibly supplementary motor cortex, with the prototype in the retrievable memory system of sensory neocortex.

The brain's language areas: (2) Wernicke's area

Wernicke's area (Frontispiece 1) in the posterior part of the superior temporal gyrus is concerned with the interpretation of received language communication and probably the conversion of thoughts to their language symbols in the form of auditory or gesticulatory (somatosensory) imagery, which on reconversion to neural signals engages the vocal or gesticulatory mechanisms respectively.

Damage to Broca's area, but sparing Wernicke's area, should not prevent the congenital deaf-mute person from carrying out sign-language as no auditory and vocal pathways are involved in this form of communication. I am not aware of any reports on such cases, if indeed any deaf-mute has ever had a lesion restricted to Broca's area on the same side as used for sign-language. An intention to speak and an intention to perform a non-vocal muscular act presumably form in and operate through different cortical areas, but they are probably controlled by neural mechanisms involved in the formation of all intention.

Kimura (cited in Kolb and Whishaw,1990:593) on reviewing findings in brain-damaged patients and other evidence favoured the idea that gesture and speech depend on the same neural systems. But this idea is not in conformity with established anatomical facts. A thought that needs to be expressed is a non-linguistic conscious experience which must first be symbolized in the sensory cortices before physical expression can occur. The thought itself is prior to the elicitation of its language symbols, so whether the medium of expression is vocal or gestural the originating thought is produced by activity in the same neuronal ensembles. From these the language symbols are elicited into image form either in the auditory cortex (for most humans) or in the somatosensory cortex (for congenital deaf-mutes), via connections between the thought-generating ensembles of neurons and the chosen symbol modality. From these different cortical regions signals go to the motor cortex. If sound is employed the vocal apparatus is engaged from auditory cortex via somatosensory cortex to the regions of the motor cortex controlling tongue, lips, larynx, etc.. If sight is employed the hands and arms are engaged via motor cortex controlling these structures, and these two regions of motor cortex are anatomically distinct with little or no overlap, as demonstrated by pinpoint electrode stimulation studies.

A possible confusing factor in the Kimura studies is that deaf-mutes may also use their lips and face, and speakers may also use gestures.

The central mechanisms of language production and reception

The production and reception of language are separate neuro-mental processes. Reception is successful if the thoughts of the donor are reproduced in the recipient; this is an end process which occurs when the meaning of the communication is elicited from memory or when conditioned response programs are engaged. The production of language is preceded by the need to convey thoughts to other minds, and this need may arise from different circumstances. The word 'thought' is used here

1.27 The Language Function and Thinking   161

to refer to any pattern or process of consciousness, and 'language' to any means of communication using symbolism.

On vocalization the full import must be reproduced in the recipient, so the vocalization must be detailed and accurate enough to produce in the recipient a sufficiently vivid and complete replica for working success, but both the reception and production of language are, as with other skills, largely by means of the operation of acquired reflexes, and they are also both under voluntary control. As in learning any new skill the child (or adult learning a new language) has to make considerable (usually slow and clumsy) voluntary effort to form the correct sounds. With every repetition the motor program for the automatic production becomes more securely laid down in some structure(s) of the CNS, almost certainly Broca's premotor cortex, the cerebellar cortex, at least in part, and possibly the neostriatum and supplementary motor cortex. As a separate process the meaning of the word is established in conventional memory by inter-memory linkage achieved through long-term synaptic potentiation. These two processes occur simultaneously from the start and apply eventually not only to individual words but to whole sentences and linguistic styles.

A note on the structure of language

Grammar itself is a culturally evolved and culturally acquired set of protocols, its form and 'rules' being determined in their essential features by the nature of world reality. To the extent that reality in its fundamentals is the same for all linguistic groups all grammars must be basically similar. As with much else in the make-up of the organism the structures underlying the capacity to perform linguistically are the products of evolution and thus are genetically determined, while the use of such structures is to a greater or lesser degree a learning process which moulds the structures during the individual's lifetime.

Voluntary override of speech reception and production

When the received language is difficult *or its construction unusual or unfamiliar* the automatic processes partly fail and voluntary effort must be exercised to extract from conventional memory and by thinking the correct meaning. If this fails the received language is meaningless to the individual.

Similarly, with difficult thoughts voluntary effort must be exercised to find from memory and by thinking appropriate language representation, and further close voluntary effort may be required to produce the correct sentence vocally through the most direct mental control of the motor neurons involved in speech that the brain allows.

The lessons from aphasia

Clinical findings in aphasias (that is, defects in the interpretation or production of language due to brain damage or disease) are not always easy to interpret on the basis of theoretical ideas. There is much variation among patients with the same apparent lesions, and Broca's and Wernicke's aphasias have features in common. For example, some Broca's aphasics have comprehension as well as production deficits (Kolb and Whishaw,1990:571), a finding that may be due to unrecognized involvement of Wernicke's area; otherwise why should most Broca's aphasics *not* have comprehension deficits?

Interpreting the results of brain lesions is always a hazardous task, particularly as such a bewildering variety of deficits may be revealed by careful neuropsychological testing. This is no doubt due in large measure to general effects, such as confusion or impaired concentration, which even localized lesions may cause. Comprehension deficits found in some Broca's aphasics therefore may not mean that Broca's area has a role in the interpretation of language but that general mental disruption as caused by any brain lesion may be responsible, especially if testing is done with sentence constructions and word forms that the patient in his normal state had some difficulties or little acquaintance with. As for attributing, on the basis of such lesion findings, control of syntactic functions to specific neural mechanisms, a considerable degree of scepticism is to be expected; the existence of DNA for syntax is improbable not only because it would represent a hardly credible feat of genetic evolution over a relatively short period of perhaps 3-4 million years, but more significantly because it is not necessary, therefore not subject to selective pressure, due to the general learning capability of the evolving brain being fully able to acquire syntactic protocols.

Modern linguistic research: a story of misadventure?

Cognitive neuroscientists have been strongly advised to form their theories within the constraints of established principles of biological evolution (Cosmides and Tooby, 1995; Preuss, 1995). It is all too obvious that many have failed to do so: the field of linguistics is littered with abandoned theories; for example, those of Chomsky and his acolytes.

Much of modern research in linguistics seems to be concerned with correlating grammatical and phonetic structures with the activity of regional brain structures. That such correlation must exist is a *sine qua non*, but its significance is grossly misinterpreted. Every thought is produced by some part of the brain, different thoughts by different parts, and measurements of brain activity will vary with each. To suppose that different parts of brains are specialized for different linguistic functions – for example, one part or one type of brain activity for constructing past tense and another for a particular type of sentence construction – is bizarre. No known principle of biological evolution can be adduced to support such a notion; genetic bases for the symbolic representation of concepts emerging from experience is a biological impossibility; and in any case, as pointed out above, totally unnecessary as the *general* capabilities of human brains can fully account for the findings. Essentially no different is enlargement, through training, of structures of the brain in, for example, the musician who is able to fluently translate musical scores to auditory and manipulatory imagery and from the latter engage through his enlarged premotor circuitries the upper motor neurons controlling finger movements. One does not say that the brain evolved special structures for musical interpretation and performance. In general, preexistiing structures will be enlarged during the life of the individual through training and use, and if such use is continually adaptive *over evolutionary time* natural selection will result in genetically determined structural elaboration for greater efficiency, provided there is enough genetic variation for the selective process to be operative.

It is doubtful that Wernicke's area of cortex, or any other cortical area, is specialized for the interpretation of language any more than for other stimuli. Situated at the juncture of the major sensory modalities it is the main crossroads for fibre connections between them, and whether for accessing the properties of some sensory object or the meaning of words and sentences the process is that of engaging memory linkages within and across modality borders by subcortical, corticocortical fibre connections. A word or sentence heard or read will by this means elicit various images which constitute the meaning of the language. In turn a thought, which is composed of imagery in one or more sensory modalities, will, when the need arises for its conveyance to other minds, engage its language representation in auditory or somatosensory cortex, and from either of these signals originate for transmission to premotor cortex which contains the circuitry for selection of the appropriate upper motor neurons in primary motor cortex for vocalization or gesticulation.

So whatever 'innateness' there is for production and reception of speech in humans, that is, whatever specialized neural structures have evolved, it is evident that the highly *evolved* general human capabilities for concentrated voluntary effort, for the formation of intermodal memory linkages, and for the acquisition of automatic motor programs play major roles in the faculty of human language. Language has to be learned just as, or more painstakingly than, other skills, and no matter what the language, even one artificially constructed, to be successful it must symbolize the different categories of reality, and this imperative determines the structure of grammar.

The neural mechanisms of language

When language production is required it either happens automatically or by voluntary effort, usually some of each, and this is true of all performances of physical skills.

When speech is being rehearsed in the mind, or when in thinking we use language as a tool, a similar mix of *automatic* and voluntary contributions applies. In the case of the automatic part of such *internal* mental effort are we somehow accessing, i.e. tapping into, the putative premotor and/or cerebellar programs? Is it possible, in the closed mental process of thinking, to do so? Acquired programs for automatically performable motor acts (or 'procedural' memories) are not, in contrast to conventional memories, retrievable into consciousness directly; but possibly this may happen indirectly: The premotor, cerebellar, etc. program for the automatically performable motor speech act may operate in two stages. First, on being triggered by the thought that it expresses, it may send (in the case of the cerebellar program indirectly through brainstem connections and, via thalamic relays, through primary motor cortex) signals to all the motor neurons that are to be involved, and this is silent; then, for vocalization, inhibitory control is removed from the latter and sounds are produced. The problem is that although we can self-hear the vocalization, we presumably cannot 'hear' the silent part? Introspectively, our silent speech seems to be auditory imagery, therefore generated in the auditory sensory cortex, so that either the automatic program must be stored in the sensory cortex or a premotor or cerebellar program can automatically elicit auditory images, neither of which we believe, or the subvocal speech partially engages vocal musculature by some leakage through the inhibitory control and this is sensed somesthetically and from this transferred to the auditory cortex, which seems too roundabout even if neurotechnically possible.

While the retrievable memory system of cerebral sensory cortex undoubtedly stores the language, including knowledge of its construction and use, it almost certainly does not store the programs for the automatically performable motor speech acts. But what role may acquired *thought* reflexes play here? Why cannot a considerable amount of automatically performable *thinking* be a function of sensory neocortex, including automatically produced auditory language imagery? In fact, considerable amounts of thinking *are* highly automatic, an evolved capability which functions to allow the generation, through the speed factor and other advantages, of much fuller understandings by the mind. So just as when the need arises the merest beginning ('tip of the iceberg') of a complex thought can trigger automatically produced vocal language expressing the full import of the thought, so a mere thought may produce considerable auditory speech imagery automatically, in which case we seem to be thinking verbally.

If the cerebrum were to be disconnected from the cerebellum and from the lower motor neurons which innervate the vocalizing muscles we would therefore expect auditory language imagery to be possible, but without the faint somatic feed-back we normally experience which results from the leakage mentioned above.

While the voluntary production of speech, like other voluntary motor actions, is via the motor cortex, is all automatic speech triggered through this route? It has been reported that some aphasics with lesions of the frontal cortex (Broca'a aphasia) are able to produce snatches of fluent song or verse, which, after all, require the same vocal machinery, although confounding this is the possibility that the intact 'musical' right hemisphere is responsible for such performances (Barr and Kiernan,1988:242). In blood flow studies by Lassen et al (1978), cited in Kolb and Whishaw (1990:370), "repetition of what has been called "automatic" speech, such as naming the days of the week over and over again, fails to produce an increase in activity in Broca's area", a result that supports the idea that automatically performable actions, including speech, though they may be triggered reflexly from the cortex in response to an external cue, are largely controlled subcortically.

If this is so it offers support for the idea that automatic speech programs are located outside the cerebral cortex, presumably in the neocerebellum, but it also poses the problem of how such programs can bypass the motor cortex to activate lower motor neurons. The cerebellum is believed to coordinate and monitor the performance of motor skills; to do these things is must of course possess programs containing the ultimate details of the skills involved, but because of its lack of direct connections with the lower motor neurons it is not considered to be the executive agent for these skills.

If this is true some other region of the CNS must also possess the complete skill program, a seemingly unparsimonious duplication. It is probable that the ancient parts of the cerebellum possess hard-wired circuitry controlling primitive stereotyped movement and monitoring capabilities. Subsequent evolution gave memory capacity to the cerebral neocortex enabling it to store the general plan of higher level, voluntary performances operating via the primary motor cortex. But also evolving was access by acquired cerebellar skill programs to this primary motor neocortex; thus both voluntary and automatic activity would operate on the lower motor neurons via the pyramidal tract, so possibly in those few cases of Broca's aphasia producing fluent snatches of song the cerebellar access to primary motor cortex is not interrupted by the lesion.

In this scheme although the total program resides in the archi-, paleo-, and neocerebellar levels as an integrated whole it is largely concerned with the functions of monitoring and coordinating, though for these functions to be effective they must be able to influence signals from elsewhere to the lower motor neurons, which they may do via the cerebellothalamocortical pathway or via the brainstem extrapyramidal (reticulospinal,rubrospinal, vestibulospinal) pathways. Ivry and Keele (1989) have argued strongly for cerebellar timing and motor program storage functions.

It is undoubtedly significant that afferent input to the cerebellum "generated in virtually all kinds of receptors in all parts of the body" outnumber efferents by 40:1 (Carpenter, 1991:238), indicating that an enormous amount of information is required for the monitoring and coordinating functions.

The *appropriateness* (i.e. relevance to the current external situation) of the automatic skill performance is monitored by the cerebral cortex, in part automatically as we know from the fact that appropriateness is maintained 'with the mind elsewhere'. The prototype in retrievable memory also monitors the actual performance (as distinct from relevance to the external situation) so far as it is capable, that is, so far as it consists of detailed knowledge of the skill. When the performance is at odds with either the external situation or the cerebral prototype the higher functions of the mind are alerted and voluntary control takes over.

In aphasia voluntary speech production is blocked because the connection between the cortex producing the thought and the motor cortex is interrupted, so that while in the normal state the merest intention may act as a voluntary trigger for extensive automatic speech, in aphasia the strongest voluntary effort cannot engage the motor neurons. In the case of snatches of song and verse noted above it is uncertain what and where the trigger is, but the sensory cortices have substantial pathways to the basal ganglia and the cerebellum (via pontine nuclei) besides their connections with the frontal lobe (Guyton,1987:202). Also, parietal cortex contributes perhaps 40% of the corticofugal fibres of the pyramidal tract (Carpenter,1991:420), and whatever other roles these projections may have they possibly possess a limited capacity to transmit to *lower* motor neurons, by indirect connections, signals received from programs in basal ganglia/cerebellum (which as mentioned have no direct control over lower motor neurons but only indirectly via motor cortex by way of thalamic relays and brainstem extrapyramidal motor pathways).

The routes by which motor skill programs, including speech, are laid down in cerebellum and/or striatum during the course of voluntary motor performance have not been established, but on anatomical grounds must either be via collaterals from corticobulbar and cortiospinal pyramidal tract fibres, or more directly from the sensory cortices bypassing the motor cortex, or both.

The neural mechanism by which a thought is converted to, or triggers, action will be discussed later, but it may be noted here that the idea is that the consciousness-memory system evolved from the primordial reflex arc, and while this arc became enormously elaborated in advanced brains to support internal cognitive functions, its effector outlet to motor structures was maintained and specialized to respond to internally generated signals.

Final Words

It is evident that much remains to be discovered about skill acquisition and performance, including language: e.g., the routes by which voluntary effort operates, identification of structures able to store as programs voluntarily produced motor sequences, the routes by which these structures receive information, the mechanism(s) of program storage, the routes by which programs are reached for activation, the site and nature of the trigger and its method of activating the program, the routes by which the program acts on the motor systems, the details of the monitoring process, etc..

To naive introspection the 'self' experiences, thinks, and communicates, the last being a function essentially the same as any other voluntary action. What we discover about the mind and its functioning by introspection is what has evolved through natural selection. To understand the machinery of the brain as revealed by laboratory and clinical research we must interpret its functioning in terms of subjective experience, because it is in this arena that natural selection works. A particular type of feeling will be experienced by an animal because of its selective value in the evolutionary history of that animal's lineage, not because it is an incidental feature (an epiphenomenon) of its neural substrate; any other substrate producing the same feeling would have been selected. The type of brain man has may have been the only one able to give rise to his kind of mind, but it came into existence only because this mind enjoyed selective advantages over other varieties at each stage of its evolutionary history.

1.28   THE IMAGINATIVE FUNCTION

Its likely evolutionary origin

The imaginative function may have arisen out of the tendency for imagery to occur through random activation of memory neurons. Such random activation was an unavoidable consequence of the functioning of the retrieval and linkage systems of memory, and in itself had no useful function.

It is hypothesized that environmental and social cues of importance to an animal (e.g. alarm cries, particular odours, certain visual patterns, etc.) and to which it responded through evolved reflexive activity, also tended to elicit imagery through incidental activation of memories associated with the cues, and such imagery (e.g. of predator, prey, etc.) tended to augment the reflexive activity. Variations in the tendency to such image accompaniment, if genetically based, would offer material for the operation of natural selection if it affected performance, and it is suggested that to a limited degree this occurred, leading to an evolved capability for imagery that was richer and more easily elicited. To the extent that such imagery is constructed from memory elements from different experiences it would be synthetic, and because the linkage properties underlying the memory system permit only limited functional compartmentalization there is always a tendency for mixed elicitations to occur.

The tendency to such synthetic imagery accompanying environmental cues may have been present at the early mammalian stage and may then have increased slowly to the level of the pre-language hominids, possibly not very different from that experienced by present day apes. It is proposed that an enormous acceleration in the evolution of the imaginative function began with pre-man's entry to the artefactual niche, and proceeded hand-in-hand with the evolution of language, thinking, memory, etc. in accordance with the 'upward spiral' or 'leap-frog' principle which may be stated as follows: Improvement in any part of mental functioning by improving overall efficiency permits more versatile exploitation of the artefactual niche which in turn demands better minds for its utilization and further exploitation, so there is now stronger selective value in any improvement in other parts of the mental apparatus.

As an aside we may briefly note that the historical movement of behaviorism in psychology was a reaction to the apparently fruitless concern with mental experiences of animals, or even humans, and generally to the employment of speculation in science. Without going into the philosophy of the matter we may say that even the most committed behaviorist must acknowledge that everything basic about Homo sapiens, including all his mental properties and not excluding imagination, subjectivity, etc., is necessarily the result of the process of evolutionary change, and this implies that these properties were present in organisms more primitive than modern man.

The dependence of higher mental functioning on imagery

At some stage hominids entered the artefactual niche, for which they were pre-adapted. This entry consisted in the use of implements in the performance of activities where limbs and teeth were formerly solely used. The use of implements offered great advantages and was of open-ended potential, but the further exploitation of this niche was dependent on the understanding faculty of the mind (i.e. the ability to store in memory experienced causal relationships and subsequently to voluntarily use this knowledge with benefit), and even more on the thinking mechanism which made possible the internal generation of understandings, and on true language which allowed the communication of mental contents to other minds. And these functions are critically dependent on imagery, although this dependency may be obscured by the part played by acquired thought and language reflexes in handling much of routine thinking, communicating, and the utilization of stored understandings, in which only minimal imagery may occur.

The tendency of language to elicit composite imagery

Human language is possible because of that property of the brain which links separate memory circuits when they are imprinted or activated simultaneously or nearly so. This basic property allows any readily available sensory experience to act as a surrogate in conveying the contents of one mind to another, and the evolutionary process has mainly utilized the vocal and auditory systems for this. The surrogate item (a sound or a sight) is linked in the memories of the participants to the same primary experience. Subsequent reception of the surrogate will elicit through this linkage the image from memory of the primary experience, but this in practice will seldom if ever be identical to the image the donor is attempting to reproduce in the recipient, particularly when the contents become more elaborate and therefore impossible to represent in detail. Inevitably the recipient will produce composite images, i.e. images derived from different individual memories of the same class of experience, in part, as mentioned above, because the nature of the linkage system precludes rigid compartmentalization.

1.28 The Imaginative Function 171

As language capability evolves so will the richness of imagery experienced by individuals and the facility of image production as the neural machinery becomes more elaborate and efficient. Such imagery will also tend to occur spontaneously or by chance elicitation and to retrieve other sequences through memory linkages, but triggering factors besides language communication and random activation may occur, e.g. emotional and sensory experiences, and these will tend to produce sequential imagery along particular lines. Random sequential imagery may bring up material of relevance to the individual, that is, imagery tied to innate and acquired response programs and emotional mechanisms. These latter memory retrievals will be 'of interest' and this will reflexly engage conscious focus which will tend to keep subsequent retrievals within the boundaries of the interest. *This, finally, is basic imagination.*

Thinking and imagining

Where a sequence of linked memory retrievals is being activated within the focused context of a problem confronting the individual this may lead to imagery which may determine an appropriate response, particularly if the retrievals are of memories of past experiences of a similar kind together with appropriate outcomes achieved through trial. *This is basic thinking, and obviously thinking and imagining are closely related.* The small but important difference between basic thinking and basic imagination is that in the former the stimulus is a problem, while in the latter the stimulus has an element of curiosity and fascination; the former is biologically utilitarian, the latter mere titillation. How far back in hominid evolution we may find this divergence of function is open to speculation. The fully evolved thinking faculty in addition to employing switch-focusing on retrieved data from memory in the search for understandings also employs imagined scenarios as an aid to this process.

The development of voluntary control of imagination

From this level of basic imagination there gradually developed, in evolutionary adaptation to the artefactual niche, voluntary control of this faculty along with voluntary control of thinking and of physical manipulations. In reviewing the literature I have found no serious attempt to account in some detail for the operation of voluntary imagination. It may not have occurred to students of the mind that it requires or deserves explanation, possibly because it is performed with such facility that it is simply taken for granted. Yet that we are able in response to some motive or whim to voluntarily synthesize scenarios of endless variety far removed from reality and past experience, and to control the details of such syntheses in every phenomenal category (object, relation, size, motion, quality, etc.) within the sole constraints of logical possibility and the individual's spectrum or range in the variety of units of consciousness that can be generated, is a feat that is both remarkable and a challenge to explanatory ingenuity, and a moment's reflection will show that such explanation is not readily come by.

The following are possible mechanisms (Hale 1989:72-76):

1. Some neuronal mechanism can intercept retrieved signals from the memory circuits before they reach consciousness and alter them so that a distorted image appears in consciousness. The control of such a distorting mechanism would be guided by a motive (e.g. the curiosity of seeing what object x would look like with feature y altered). This implies that there is at least some preliminary knowledge of what is to be imagined; apparently something imagined before it is imagined. This apparent absurdity can perhaps be explained by the fact that the environment constantly presents us with rearrangements of its features, so we have no difficulty in wondering in a particular case what the result of a rearrangement would be like, and this engages the distorting neural mechanism; perhaps even prematurely, thus giving a glimpse of the transformation which may reinforce the curiosity and more strongly activate the distorting function. There presumably must also be a feedback from consciousness to maintain the distortion within the limits of the current motive.

2. There may he an inherent tendency for memory retrievals to 'drift'; i.e. for extraneous linkages to be activated, particularly in class retrievals as opposed to unique items. A class retrieval is a composite of many individuals within that class, e.g. of a dog composed of features from many dogs in memory. Part of the imaginative function may therefore simply be to inhibit whatever neural activity operates to dampen such drift, so as to permit such drifting to occur, perhaps with the additional capability of channeling the direction of drift. Thus a dog may be permitted to become larger or smaller; bark or howl, etc.

3. Our ability to imagine various possible outcomes for a particular situation depends on our store of experiences of numerous outcomes of

many kinds of situation. If a situation (or problem) is in mind and the need arises to determine the most appropriate outcome, given our ability to control events, we keep the elements of the situation in mind and we select (or are presented with) one category of outcome. We now allow the elements of the situation to change within the context of the outcome category as the stored details of the latter are retrieved from memory. During this unfolding and at its completion we are able to witness and review various relationships involving things, persons and events, thereby expanding our understanding, and perhaps also to experience relevant emotions.

4. To synthesize a fictional scenario of a subject performing an action, which is something we can very readily do, even for the most highly improbable scripts, a possible mechanism is that we have both the subject and the action 'in mind' An action cannot exist without an actor; so the action in mind, which is a memory retrieval, is focused so as to blur out any identifiable actor; the form of the action being concentrated on. We then refocus on the actor but substitute our subject who being in mind happens to be most readily available. We now have our subject performing an alien action.

However, we seem to need another explanation for the fact that a subject in full imagined focus can be made to perform any type of action, including truly bizarre creative ones that are certainly not in memory up to that point, at least in the complete form of the creation, although small individual components may be. A possibility is that any part of a retrieved scenario may be substituted by an extraneous item also retrieved from memory, and once the substitution is made the new item is maintained in its surrogate position by a certain mental effort during the 'first run', but with less effort on re-runs which are in fact retrievals of what is now a memory of an imagined scenario. (The elucidation of the neuro-dynamic mechanism of such substitution would be a fundamental revelation.).

5. That somewhat far-fetched theory of memory based on language structure, the so-called 'semantic network', can have at best only a remotely abstract correspondance with biological reality. One cannot even begin to guess how to fit it into a neuronal mechanism underlying imagination. The word 'dancing' has no significance in itself, and what it means, what it represents, is an image of action-reality which is inseparable from the actor. However, language can be altered without

considering meaning, and the altered form may have meaning, that is as symbolization it may be translatable within the constraints of reality. For example, suppose the meaning of the language sample 'John hit Mary' happens to correspond to reality. We may then randomly take the name of someone else we know and substitute it for John or Mary. Converting the new language item to image form we have a coherent fiction, an act of imagination. From this it would seem that language symbolization can be used as a means, or part of the process, of creating imagined (synthesized) scenarios.

6. Most retrievals tend to be composite. E.g. we may 'call up' images of our dog playing, and remember every type of behaviour. We are not trying to do more then idly remember; we are making no effort to introduce extraneous features, yet in fact no sequence of its actions we recall may ever have precisely occurred, and if asked to remember exactly yesterday's sequences it will be hard work. Therefore inherent in casual retrieval (and probably all retrieval) is an element of fiction, because the memory apparatus by the way it evolved is inherently incapable of precise faithfulness in recording and retrieving all experience. The thought now is that this fact was utilized in the evolution of the imaginative function to serve the new biological needs for communication and for thinking.

7. When we attempt to 'imagine' the outcome of some situation we utilize past experience, as outlined in No.3. The features of the situation as they enter consciousness elicit from memory facts and understandings to which they are linked, enabling expectations to arise. To the extent that the present type of situation has been previously experienced its outcome will be derivable from past experience, but where it has novel features a prediction of outcome depends upon past experience most closely related to these and of past experience of the closeness of outcomes of similar but nor identical situations. We may say that past experience makes it possible to have expectations in present circumstances, and these expectations diminish in confidence and reliability as similarity between past experience and present circumstances diminish. The scenario that enters consciousness when we try to imagine the outcome of some situation is derived therefore from pure memory, composite memories, and synthetic composites, there being in practice no definite dividing lines between these, the extreme ends of the spectrum being pure (true) memory and pure (maximally

fictitious or synthetic) imagination. In this type of case the synthetic images are derived from analogy between some past experience and the novel features of the present situation; that is, the things in memory most like the novel features. The more novel the features the more likely is such analogy to prove unreliable. Example: A group of savages meet some explorers in a hostile situation with conflict about to ensue. An outcome is imagined by both groups, and the imagery is accurate in many features, because of past experience (including vicariously derived facts and understandings). But the explorers draw handguns, a completely novel feature for the savages, whose expectation with regard to these is derived from whatever in their experience most closely resembles a handgun (perhaps small, oddly shaped pieces of wood). Their imagined scenario of the subsequent unfolding of the situation (i.e. their expectation) will therefore be very erroneous.

8. In the above example the images entering consciousness are derived from composite retrievals of events linked to hand-held stones and pieces of wood in hostile situations. Imagination here is automatic linkage retrieval of composite memories. Is purely fanciful imagination very different basically? Perhaps two phases should be distinguished:
(1) the selection of subject matter and (2) the synthesizing of scenarios.
(1) We encountered above (No.1) the apparent paradox of knowing beforehand what we want to imagine, so in a sense imagining it before we imagine it. This is probably illusory. We have from previous experience knowledge that we possess an imaginative faculty and can use it at will, and of the sorts of things it produces. So when we encounter a situation which interests us we may be impelled by some motive (curiosity, greed, jealousy, fear, its possible relation to something important to us, pure idleness, the way our minds and bodies happened to be disposed at that moment, the need to understand, etc.) to see how it may unfold in a manner governed by that motive (thus giving us our subject matter), but we do not know in advance what the coming exercise will produce, although brief, premature flashes of images may occur when the idea of the subject matter first enters consciousness. (2) We then proceed to allow free entry to consciousness of items in memory linked to various features of the subject matter and governed by the current motive, so the participants within the subject matter behave according to experiences in memory most closely analogous. As a result we get a show that we can vaguely anticipate, but now can see clearly, in its details, thus satisfying

the motive. When the motive is a need-to-understand, this unfolding imaginative scenario enables us to see relationships, patterns, points of significance we might not have been aware of before, which constitute new understandings that now become stored in memory.

The imagery of imagination is the result of activation of the consciousness-generating neurons of the brain, and so far as we know such activation can come from only two sources: 1/ The sensory receptors (and their centripetal pathways and relays), and 2/ the memory neurons by their loop-back (reentrant) axonal branches. The sensory pathways have no storage capacity, so while their stimulation may produce unorganized sensations such as flashes of light they cannot produce the rich imagery of imagination and dreaming, and we have no evidence that they can be played upon by some central mechanism to construct organized pseudo-sensory imagery; their function is purely for real-time responses to, and central representation of, the external world. The memory system on the other hand is a vast repository for organized conscious experiences, the elements of which can be accessed in infinite combinations for an infinite variety of imagery.

The operation of voluntary imagination

In voluntary imagination various memory segments are 'selected' for the synthesis. According to need the memory segments may be of any kind or size. Once selected and put together the product may be allowed to take a spontaneous course, but in this the tendency will be to stray from the theme that guided its construction.

Selecting a memory segment for a voluntary imaginative construction is dependent on some non-imaginative mechanism, otherwise one would be picturing (imagining) beforehand what is to be imagined. There must be present 'in mind' a theme which guides retrievals and a motive present in the system which activates and sustains the operation of the theme. Such a motive is a state of the organism which is a build-up of forces kept in check by inhibitory influences until time for release. Volition as it applies to the imaginative function is the same process that is operative in voluntary behavior generally and therefore yields to the same explanatory analysis.

The *motive* may be of many different kinds, e.g. curiosity, need to achieve a goal, vicarious pleasure, need to understand, etc.. A motive is a reason for constructing a synthetic scenario (or voluntarily doing anything else.) Commonly the 'motive' for thinking or imagining along certain lines is a situation or subject matter which involuntarily arises. There is always some trigger that starts the memory retrievals; dormant memories are not arbitrarily accessible, but by voluntarily keeping the theme in mind and by focusing on particular retrieved memories the ego can directly guide retrievals. (A reminder: Volition is specialized reflexivity and the 'ego' is an experiential composite).

The theme is determined by the motive. The distinction may be illustrated by this example: "The motive for his act of voluntary imagination was to achieve a vicarious thrill of heroism (a la Walter Mitty); the theme of this act of imagination was a rescue operation".

The causes of the motive and choice of theme in any instance of voluntary imagination are endless in their possibilities, ranging from simple instruction to innumerable variables of personality, temperament, culture, personal history, state of health, etc.

The operation of the theme in voluntary imagination

A retrieved memory segment will fade and disappear or become background to a new segment retrieved from memory by linkage operation of the theme in mind. The theme itself is a circumscribed memory sequence, for example of the category 'rescue operation' (commonly referred to as a 'concept'; but every concept, no matter how intellectually abstract, is no more than a memory sequence of some kind, which, when retrieved, materializes in the form of imagery). The theme is 'in mind' in the sense that there is constantly present more or less weak background consciousness (imagery) of the category prototype, or it may flit in and out of consciousness so long as the motive persists. The theme imagery may serve as a vague skeleton which is fleshed out by the detailed retrievals occurring in response to the requirements of the particular motive and sub-motives.

Dreaming and the imaginative function

The occurrence in dreaming of (apparently) instantaneously produced, highly elaborate scenarios with intricate detail which we 'know' we have never previously experienced is hard to explain. It suggests complete basic autonomy of the imaginative function, and from this that awake imagining consists in the control of this activity – guiding its direction by providing a theme, activating or suppressing inhibitory and augmentory controls, etc.. It also suggests that memory is far more richly stocked than awake retrievals can reach, but which the erratic retrievals occurring during dreaming may by accident flush out. It further suggests the possibility of some other process of scenario construction than put forward here. For example, the haphazard knitting together of items belonging to different categories of experience in ways that are incompatible with reality suggests the possibility that memory either stores categories separately or has distinct neural mechanisms which govern the assemblage of the categories according to the rules of reality which are ingrained in the brain by inheritance or learning. Therefore when we use our imagination in the awake state we have meaningful scenarios, but in dreaming because of the haphazard shutdown of different functions of the brain in partial sleep the linkages of memory may function erratically to produce bizarre scenarios.

During dreaming scenarios which are incompatible with reality are received with complete credulity, suggesting that the subjective 'feeling' of credulity is a semi-independent mental faculty which invests everyday life situations. (One may even speculate that the human readiness to believe (assertions, claims, the evidence of the senses, etc.) is an evolved faculty supporting social cohesion and is generally adaptive. This could be a large subject for investigation: e.g., the phases of trust and suspicion gone through by the developing infant are no doubt innate and therefore have been adaptive over evolutionary time; also the readiness with which the human herd accepts dogmas; and the difficulty, therefore late historical emergence, of exercising the essential scientific discipline of scepticism or distrust!)

The simplest, most straightforward, and probably correct explanation of the phenomenon of dreaming is that between wakefulness and deep sleep during which various nervous system functions are being shut down the normal controls of the imaginative function are erratically affected, with bizarre results. The actual sequence of shutdowns may be influenced by various factors, such as prevailing mood, states of the body, extraneous stimuli, etc., with the result that inhibitory and excitatory controls are unpredictably affected. An inspired analysis of the oddities of the dreaming state may therefore reveal the existence of control mechanisms governing normal cognitive functions which otherwise might not be suspected.

1.29 THE EMOTIONAL SYSTEM

In this section I offer a theoretical analysis of the emotional system in response to two main questions: Of what use is emotionalism and how could it have evolved? In the next section I attempt to support the theoretical construction with data from neuroanatomy and neurophysiology.

The employment of feeling in biological evolution

The position of feeling in biology has traditionally been that of an unwanted orphan: no one, until recently, has wanted to take responsibility for it. Yet feelings drive many organismic behaviors, natural selection having made use of the intrinsic property of feelings of being desirable or undesirable. To apply the patently metaphysical aphorism that "feelings are intrinsically important" to the workings of Darwinian evolution seems visionary, to be eschewed by every prudent academic. Yet it may be argued that without this principle the human mind as we know it could not have evolved, and it may have governed the evolution of nervous systems well down the phylogenetic scale.

'Emotion' is a word variously used in scientific literature, yet in most if not all such literature phrases like 'the expression of emotions', 'physiological changes accompanying emotions', 'central states of the organism [giving rises to behaviors ...]' etc. keep betraying the authors' ineradicable though often unacknowledged conviction of a category of subjectivity which manifests itself in various ways; which, in other words, is physically causal. In the present analysis the word 'emotion' refers to *the conscious subjective feeling* and to nothing else. The neural substrate of such feeling is as fully genetically based, therefore evolved through natural selection, as are physiological processes.

As organisms evolved in complexity new physical feelings appeared, increasing and improving conscious monitoring of the state of the body and acting as triggers or catalysts of new reflexive responses. But it is not clear that all are adaptive; it is possible that evolutionary elaboration to man's level while obviously adaptive on the whole has entailed acceptance of defects such as the generation of extreme pain which may cause circulatory collapse. This should remind us that although everything to be found in living organisms must be viewed first and foremost as products of evolution and *ipso facto* advantageous, exceptions exist which represent the price paid when it was profitable to do so when unavoidable.

Mentation vis-a-vis affect

The 'mental' processes of the brain – thinking, remembering, imagining, recognizing, willing, etc. – are not dependent on feeling, but much of the use of the mind is concerned with life situations involving feeling; and memory and the imaginative function commonly produce images which reflexly elicit emotional feelings of all types. Generally, the physical feelings (temperature, visceral sensations, pain, touch, etc.) are utilized in vegetative functions and in protecting the body from physical harm by triggering, augmenting, or catalysing protective responses.

The why and how of the evolution of the emotional system

The origin and evolution of the emotional system are clearly matters open to conjecture, yet much of such conjecture may be offered with some confidence if formed within the strict guidelines of orthodox evolutionary theory. The main thesis here is that the evolutionary process utilized emotions in forcing behaviors contributory to individual survival and genetic continuance. The behaviors, including expression of emotions, are controlled by neuro-muscular programs stored in the central nervous system. These are evolved, genetically determined programs and are engaged and/or catalysed by emotion consciousness. Baldly stated, the emotion has to be felt for the behavior to be optimally effected.

Emotions (when functioning normally, and when not affected by cross interference) are program specific, and an obvious question arising from this is what is the mechanism by which an emotion of a particular kind becomes causally linked to a particular type of behavior? Also, is there something intrinsic to an emotion which dictates the type of action response it is able to trigger or catalyse? These are deep questions which perhaps can only be answered speculatively, but if emotional feelings are derived from physical feelings, as will be suggested here, the questions get pushed back to that level.

Two hypotheses for the origin of emotions may be offered: A/ This may be called the 'echo' hypothesis. It postulates that the evolutionary process utilized pre-existing physical feelings to build behavioral responses to non-contact external situations. The pre-existing physical feelings, elicited centrally by neural signals from sensory nerve endings in various organs of the body, included pain, comfort, discomfort, temperature, and other feeling sensations that monitor the body's condition. The problem the evolutionary process had to solve was that of utilizing this system to generate mixtures or flavours of feelings in response to non-contact external information. The adaptive value of such a capability is obvious and the slightest heritable variation in this direction would tend to be selected.

The echo hypothesis supposes that neural signals in the course of their generation and transmission to central structures where they elicit physical feelings, are accompanied by a secondary disturbance in the transmitting neurons, a metaphorical 'vibration' of 'echo', which gives an aura or flavour to the pure physical feelings. If emotions were derived from such 'noise', then individual variations in which they were more prominent must have had significant selective value from the start. This would be so if an environmental situation which had been experienced as, e.g., painful, is re-encountered and 'recognized' and the recognition elicits the echo feelings which trigger the protective response which is normally triggered by the physical pain itself.

This subtle idea can be put this way: A contact encounter with an environmental event results in a physical feeling. The physical feeling may not be pure, but may be accompanied by inessential 'overtones' or 'background noise', more so in some individuals than in others. The source of such 'noise' may be incidental stimulation of unrelated sensory nerves, e.g. by spill-over impulses due to inadequate insulation or the presence of interconnections for other purposes, or incidental feedback from sensory endings in effector organs, or incidental stimulation of central neurons which process other physical feelings.

All such incidental sources of feeling may be termed 'echo' feelings. If they have a useful effect on the behavioral response they will tend to be selected. Thus if the echo feelings of pain are what we call 'fear' and if this contributes to more effective response in pain situations, then individuals with this phenomenon more developed (due to chance genetic variations) will be more survivable. Even more survivable will be those in whom echo feelings, hence the behavior responses, are elicited by exposure to the relevant environmental situation or event before the actual physical contact which elicits the primary feeling. Once such a functional separation of echo and primary feeling has occurred the way is open for great evolutionary development of emotions.

However, it is not immediately clear how such a separation could have come about. The problem has two parts: First the echo feelings must somehow be elicitable by recognition of the relevant component of the external situation. This means that neural pathways to the structures in which echo feelings arise must project from some recognition mechanism, so that an act of recognition can send signals which activate those structures. As it is highly unlikely that such pathways pre-adaptively existed in any significantly developed form, we must presume that natural selection acted powerfully on whatever variations existed in such pathways among individuals, so that even circuitous neural connections that served the purpose were selected.

As numerous environmental situations may elicit the same physical feeling, hence the same echo feelings, the recognition mechanism must be receptive to, or capable of experiencing, the core element common to all such situations. Obviously, in the primitive organisms in which emotions first emerged, such recognition mechanisms must have been very limited and genetically determined, forming a relatively simple reflex, yet proving capable of evolving to increasing levels of sophistication. Man's evolved faculty of thinking-to-understand greatly extends his ability to reveal in environmental situations core elements with emotional significance, which are then recognized by the innate ('hard-wired') mechanism, which reflexly elicits the emotion. While the understanding derived from thinking ultimately leads to the emotion, so that we may conveniently speak of 'core-understandings', it must be kept in mind that the actual trigger arises from activity in an evolved recognition circuitry.

The echo feelings may also in part be derived from partial excitation, 'in sympathy', of sensory neurons serving uninvolved parts of the body. If the response to the primary physical feeling involves bodily changes which secondarily generate other sensations, these too may come to be elicitable by recognition circuitries before physical stimulation occurs, further contributing to the flavour of the emotion. Thus from the primary physical feeling of pain may be derived the emotions of doubt, apprehension, uneasiness, anxiety, fear, and panic. From discomfort may come impatience, intolerance, irritation, and anger. And so on. Finally, some emotions may secondarily be derived from the primary emotions.

B/ A second possible origin of emotions is that of an evolved accessory to purely genetically determined behaviors. The maligned word 'instinct' is commonly used to refer to complex genetically determined behaviors, and all, or most, of the elaborate activities of primitive organisms are genetically based reflexive functions. Anthropomorphism may make it difficult to believe that the 'frantic' efforts of a lowly organism to escape danger are unaccompanied by fear and terror, so similar is such behavior to ours under similar conditions. Yet it is highly probable that such behaviors evolved to perfection long before the origin of emotions, and only in some lines did an emotional system evolve. In these lines various visceral and somatic structures involved in the instinctive activity may be the source of feelings through incidental stimulation of their sensory nerve endings during muscular contraction. Should such feelings secondarily augment the behavior they may contribute to differential survival and have selective value to the extent that they are genetically based. So an environmental situation relevant to an organism's well-being results first in prompt reflexive behavior which results in feelings that secondarily augment the behavior. By what mechanism feelings augment behavior is obscure, but it is one that has enormously evolved in higher animals to play a major part in the guidance of their behaviors.

The role of emotions

Emotions trigger or catalyse behaviors which are important for individual or group survival. Such behaviors are generally complex and socially relevant and would not occur, or only inadequately, without the emotional push. It seems most likely that the behaviors and their emotions evolved in concert, the improvement in one making possible further improvement in the other. For example, the need for prolonged parental care to capitalize on a more advanced learning capacity made parental care selectively beneficial, and as this evolved it was made more effective by the triggering and energising role of parental love, anxiety, etc.

Although it is not always easy to classify a particular feeling as emotional or physical, so that some feelings which are generated in response to purely physiological changes, e.g. sexual urge, may 'feel' emotional, it is generally the case that emotions are generated in response to external situations, either environmental or social. This means that there are neural recognition programs, almost certainly all evolved, therefore innate, which are activated by specific yet complex environmental and social situations and which in their turn activate other mechanisms resulting in the appropriate emotion.

This last point must be enlarged upon. There is abundant evidence, both from controlled experimentation on non-human animals and from human studies, that various deviations from normal patterns of life, such as parental deprivation in infancy and childhood, are followed in later life by abnormal emotional responses. To conclude from this that emotional behaviors are learned, and to demote or dismiss the innateness of emotionalism, is to misunderstand evolutionary biology, particularly as it applies to advanced mechanisms involved in social interaction. Essentially, what is observed under normal conditions is genetically determined, but the more complex the system the more indirect, though no less real, is that genetic determination, and the greater is the vulnerability to external interference and therefore the more fragile is the whole system. The huge number of delicate, subtle and vulnerable processes that must mature and interact with precision to successfully complete life cycles, the more so in 'higher' organisms, testifies to the extraordinary effectiveness of evolution by natural selection, in which every experiment is tested by 'trial to the death'.

One must of course distinguish between the innateness of emotional responses and the ability of novel experiences to tie into and to elicit those responses: the feeling of fear and the characteristic behavior triggered by that feeling induced by arbitrary circumstances such as electric shock and its associations are not learned. That is, the neural substrate generating the emotion is genetically provided; it is the capability of a situation to engage this substrate that may be acquired through experience.

The elicitation of emotional feelings at different levels (Figs.1.29(1-3))

The more primitive emotions may be elicited via recognition programs engageable by early sensory processing, although the eliciting sensory data may all continue to higher levels to generate perception (i.e. organized conscious representations) through which the recognition program may also be reached. In other words the sensory signals may, via neural pathways and circuitries that act as recognition programs, engage the emotional system before they go on to neocortex to generate

Fig.1.29(1) Emotional mechanism – first level elicitation
(From Hale, 1989)

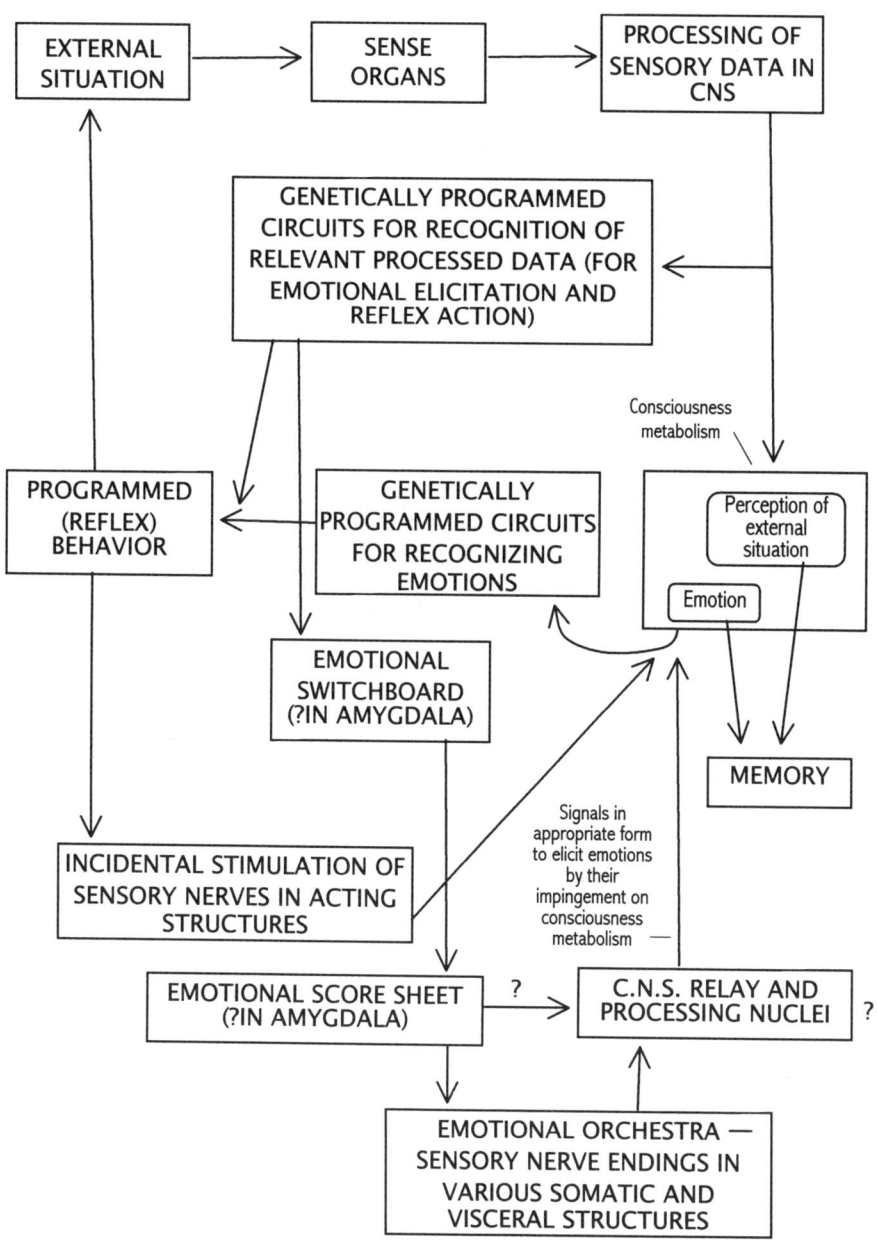

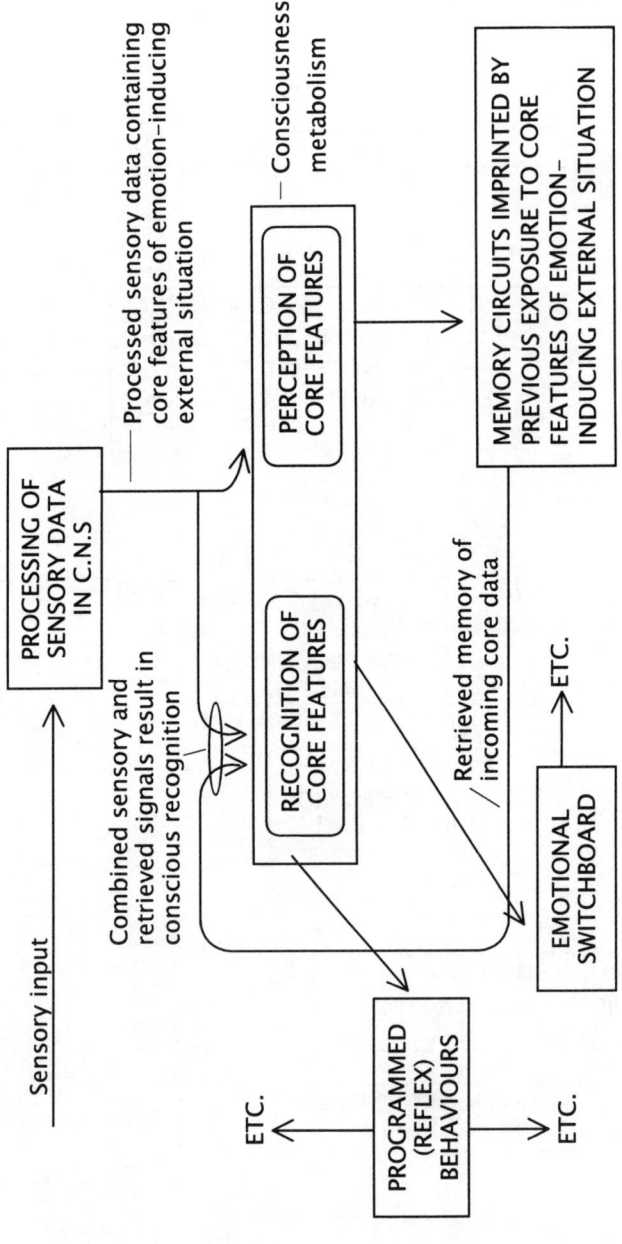

Fig.1.29 (2) **Emotional mechanism – second level elicitation** (From Hale, 1989)

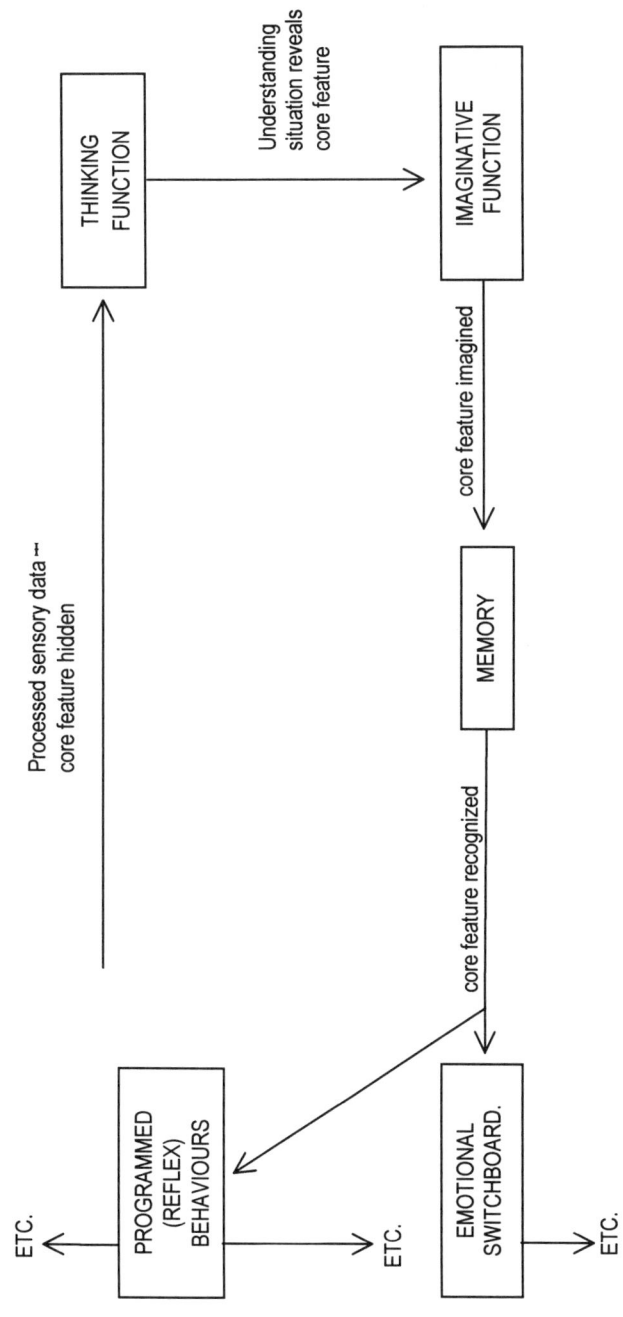

Fig. 1.29(3) Emotional mechanism – third level elicitation (From Hale, 1989)

sensory perception (LeDoux,1994). But, as noted below, very primitive reflex activity may be triggered by these sensory signals even before they elicit any emotion or generate any perception which may augment or elaborate the primitive reflex.

It is probable that when a new level of emotional responsiveness, or a new variety of emotion, evolves it does so *pari passu* with the evolution of additional circuitry able to recognize and respond to more of the information in the sensory input, which in turn provides selective advantages for elaboration of the transducing sense organ, which, to complete one cycle of the upward spiral, provides more information-packed input furthering the trend to higher emotionalism. The new mechanism has evolved to respond to more environmental or social specifics than the primitive structure was capable of, and for such additional information to be transduced and utilized new structures must evolve. Information reaching higher processing centres in advanced animals will therefore consist of the relatively sparse information able to elicit primitive responses, plus the more detailed information for more complete conscious representation. Again, as discussed in Section 1.8, there is difficulty in accounting for the more-or-less simultaneous evolutionary advance in structural and functional complexity and cooperative functioning in all parts of the system from sense organ through processing circuitries to behavior programs and their appropriate implementation.

Non-conscious and early emotional reflexivities

Certain stimuli (chemical vapours, physical vibrations, patterns of light, etc.) emanating from external features of vital importance to an organism in its early evolutionary history may be responded to by evolved non-conscious reflex activity. At the earliest stage of evolution of an emotional system the emotional feeling itself is elicited more or less simultaneously with the start of reflexive activity, and has the function of augmenting that activity. For such augmentation to occur the emotion consciousness must (by the so far unexplained process of reverse transduction) generate neural signals able to 'catalyse' the non-consciously induced reflexive activity. It should be noted that at this primitive level the emotional feeling is not generated via perception (i.e. higher, organized sensory consciousness); in theory the individual will experience the emotion (i.e., the emotional feeling will occur) even if the final sensory pathways to the primary cerebral cortices are blocked. In practise this may happen even at the human level, as subliminal stimuli (stimuli too weak to 'register' in perception) may yet have an emotional effect. This may explain Tranel and Damasio's (1993) finding in patient Boswell of acquired affective responses to environmental situations despite loss of the pathways from neocortex to limbic system.

The sites of generation of feelings

This raises the important point of where emotional feelings (therefore, of course, the primary physical feelings) are generated. 'Feeling' is a form or species of consciousness: to feel is to be conscious; 'unconscious feeling' is a contradiction in terms. (There is no such *thing* as consciousness per se, only feeling, seeing, hearing, etc.; these are kinds of consciousness, in the same sense that apples and oranges are kinds of fruit, there being no such *thing* as 'fruit'. When we speak of sensations 'entering' consciousness the erroneous concept arises of 'consciousness' being something separate from the sensations. This is an instance of the epistemological pitfalls attending conventional figures of speech; the sensation, of course, *is* the consciousness – it doesn't 'enter' anything, nor is it experienced 'by' anything, except by itself (unless it is part of a coalesced, composite consciousness in which the whole experiences all of its parts – the unitary mind.)) When certain specialized nervous tissues function (on being stimulated into activity) feelings occur. No one denies this, but there is a mental block among scientists in drawing the obvious, seemingly inescapable conclusion: specialized neuronal activity generates consciousness. Zeki, however (1993), cautiously speaks of "experiential cells".

It is possible that all feeling (i.e. that range of the consciousness spectrum we call feeling) is generated in elements of the brainstem reticular formation, the diencephalon, and the phylogenetically older parts of the telencephalon, in that feelings, including primitive emotional feelings, were probably being generated long before the evolution of the neocortex. This is supported by experimental and clinical data which show that interference with various limbic-diencephalic-brainstem structures produces a wide range of emotional effects – subjective, behavioral, and physiological. While it is true that neocortical lesions, especially prefrontal, may affect emotional and behavioral balance, the role of these recently evolved areas is probably inhibitory on the primitive centres to allow undisturbed functioning of higher mental activities and to override inappropriate primitive responses; in addition, in man, these higher cognitive functions so readily elicit emotions that disturbance of their neocortical substrate is likely to have abnormal emotional effects.

Some primitive physical feelings associated with basic homeostatic and reproductive functions, such as hunger, thirst, fatigue, sexual urge, etc., are elicited (or suppressed) by electrical stimulation of different elements of hypothalamus, supporting the claim of this ancient diencephalic structure to be involved, directly of indirectly, in the generation of these forms of feeling consciousness. Although pain is a much investigated phenomenon the precise localization of its generation is undetermined, possibly because it comes in so many varieties; but there is evidence that reticular elements of brainstem and thalamus may be responsible for this most primitive form of feeling consciousness (Guyton, 1987).

Emotions that are peculiar to man, and to a lesser degree to apes, have presumably evolved through some relationship between neocortex and limbic structures. Nostalgia, pity, compassion, thrill of beauty, ecstasy, subtle forms of humour, etc. are, so far as we know, uniquely human and largely evolved during the artefactual era. It seems at least plausible that they are composed of elements neocortically selected from the basic primitive limbic emotional system, and serve advanced human functions in the artefactual niche.

Processes theoretically required for emotionalism

It is proposed that an emotional feeling is compounded of sensory feelings derived from stimulation of sensory nerve endings in visceral, cardiovascular, and musculoskeletal systems, and perhaps central nuclear structures involved in the transmission and processing of these signals, the nerve endings being stimulated by muscular contraction in these organs (or the nuclear structures more directly from above). It is also proposed that the type of emotion is determined by the particular combination of the stimulated sensory nerve endings in the organs involved. It follows from this that some *switching* mechanism must exist to allow activation of the particular visceral and somatic components required for the building of each emotion, and this mechanism in its turn must obey instructions from *an executive centre* for the selection of particular components, and this, in its turn must receive information from a specific neural recognition program engageable by each of the various environmental and social situations the animal is genetically equipped to respond to emotionally.

To make it easier to understand this complex chain of mechanisms the metaphor of an orchestra may be employed. Each emotional species has an emotional orchestra composed of various instruments (the sensory endings in various visceral, cardiovascular, musculoskeletal organs). The executive centre has a score-sheet for each tune (emotion) in the species' repertoire, which determines via the control or switching mechanism which combination of 'instruments' will be played. The executive centre itself is reached by signals from each of the recognition programs for particular environmental and social situations, with activation of the relevant score-sheet. Alternatively, the same neural circuitry may combine both executive and switching functions, the 'score-sheet' directly engaging the individual organs.

Note that *recognizing* situations of emotional significance entails the *elicitation* of the emotion; the organism does not (figuratively) say to itself "I take cognisance of this situation, now let me consult my register of situations to find out if it has emotional significance, and if it does I will press button x to elicit the emotion."

Proposed structures and pathways required for an emotional system

The recognition program for the emotionally significant external situation must lie somewhere along the pathways of the special senses (visual, auditory, etc.). In the case of visual stimuli this would be the superior colliculus, the pulvinar complex, the lateral geniculate body, the primary visual cortex, the secondary visual cortex, and tertiary ('association') visual cortex – these having evolved to recognize progressively more complex patterns of light stimuli – and from each signals are sent to activate the emotional orchestra, either directly (which seems unlikely) or via one intermediate mechanism (which may well be the case) or via first an executive then a control (switching) mechanism (which would be the maximum chain of processing likely to be needed for the more advanced emotional programs).

The executive centre (if it exists) and the control (switching) mechanism (which, logically, must exist) are presumably circuitries situated between the recognition circuitry for each emotionally significant sensory input and structures of the limbic system, the brainstem reticular formation, and the autonomic nervous system. Amygdaloid nuclei have been determined to have prominent roles in these functions. The enormous number of interconnections between the various limbic structures and between these and higher and lower brain centres (see Appendix C) must presumably serve some vital functions, and as the emotional system obviously requires an elaborate neuronal basis it is highly probable that this is to be mainly found in the limbic system. See Fig.1.29(4)

When various instruments (visceral, cardiovascular, musculoskeletal, and central nuclear components) comprising this emotional orchestra have been activated in accordance with the scoresheet the sensory feedback signals from the muscular contraction of these organs will reach reticular elements of the brainstem and thalamus where, from the evidence of stimulation studies, primitive feeling consciousness is generated. Thus, if stimulation of some part of the hypothalamus results in hunger or thirst or sexual urge or anger, signals must first go from this hypothalamic area via the autonomic nervous system to the viscera, etc. and the muscular contractions of these result in sensory signals to the thalamus etc. where the particular feeling consciousness is generated.

Arguments for the theory

It is generally held that emotional feelings are generated in the 'limbic' system. We should therefore seek in the structures of this system the particular elements that generate feelings. We should then determine if these receive, directly *or indirectly*, activation originating from those upline circuitries which recognize emotionally-charged external situations. And, finally, from these feeling-generating elements we must trace their projections to structures containing hard-wired behavior programs, mainly the corpus striatum.

We must next try to account for the apparently non-adaptive, exuberant visceral, cardiovascular, and somatic activity that accompanies or even precedes emotional feelings and find an explanation in keeping with evolutionary principles. What we do find is that the prime candidate structure able to carry out the task of selecting the elements comprising the different emotional feelings is the amygdaloid nuclear complex. This has the internal connectivities which most logically serve the switching

Fig.1.29(4) Flow-chart of proposed mechanisms of the emotional system

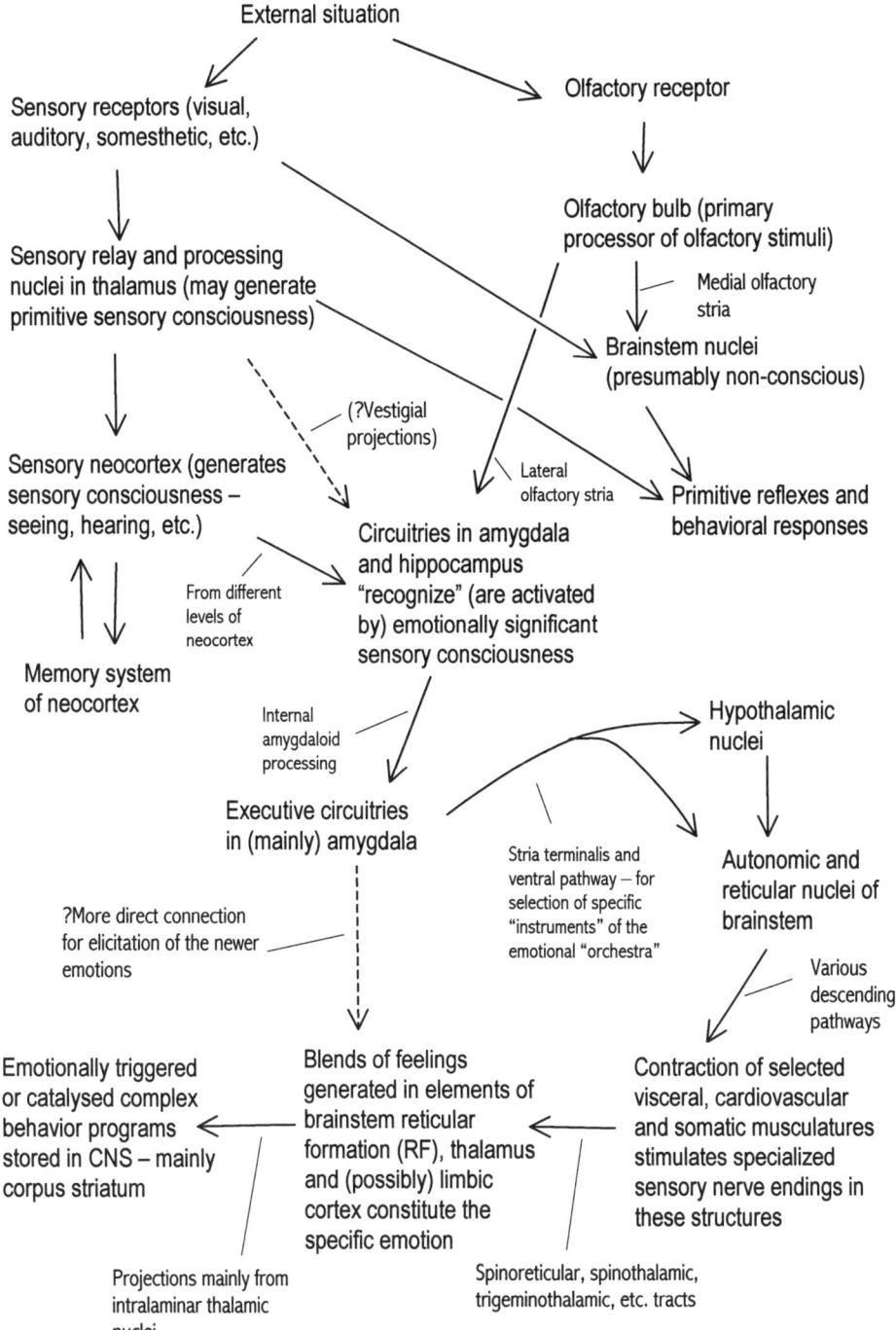

194 Features of the Mind

and selecting functions, but its output is mainly to structures that feed peripherally to visceral, cardiovascular, and somatic organs, and much less to reticular elements of brainstem and thalamus which we have grounds for believing generate feelings. "Targets of the descending projections from the amygdala are directly involved in the regulation of cardiovascular, respiratory, and gastric functions, all of which participate in the expression of fear and stress-related behavior" (Carpenter, 1991:379; and see Appendix C).

Direct connections from amygdala to feeling-generating neurons may possibly serve to elicit some of the newer 'human' emotions (such as interest and curiosity, compassion, pity, wonder, nostalgia, etc.) which appear not to be preceded or accompanied by strong involvement of structures outside the central nervous system.

Implications of the theory

There will obviously, therefore, be incidental physiological changes in the target organs before any emotion is felt, and these changes will tend to be non-adaptive ingredients of the complete emotional response package, not in functional harmony with other ingredients. However, preceding the evolutionary utilization of feeling consciousness primordial organ responses served vital behavioral requirements, any feelings arising from these being incidental and slight. Later, as increasing complexity in behavioral responses evolved, such feeling consciousness was conscripted to help drive the behaviors, leading to the evolution of specialized sensory nerve endings in the viscera, etc. for this function. In advanced mammals a good proportion of such sensory nerve endings may thus serve purely emotional functions. This, of course, poses a problem or involves a tradeoff for the evolutionary process: the benefits of emotional elicitation must outweigh the cost of unwanted, even harmful, organ stimulation: some of the physiological accompaniments seen in various emotional responses may be antiadaptive, especially in humans in whom the emotional system is so highly evolved. An example would be adverse gastro-intestinal effects in anxiety and anger; and in the emotion of embarrassment the *behavior* of seeking to hide or slink away may be adaptive, but not so the enormous autonomic and musculoskeletal changes that unavoidably occur in the production of the emotional *feeling* which is required to trigger the

1.29 The Emotional System 195

behavior. There are, of course, numerous other examples in biological evolution of this type of tradeoff.

From situation to response

In the reticular elements of the brainstem and thalamus (provisionally designated as the generators of feelings) the particular feeling consciousness evidently reconverts to neural energy to engage or catalyse some specific, innate behavior program. Innate, emotionally driven, behavior programs are probably built into the primitive cytoarchitecture of the basal ganglia-cerebellar systems, or into the structures of the limbic system in association with the basal ganglia, etc. Of course, situations eliciting particular emotional responses are seldom exactly the same on each occasion, so responses are variable to the extent that situational features vary.

Prodding an animal, invading its personal territory, stealing its food, and threatening it may all result in rage behavior very similar in each case. Although the aggravating stimuli are very different they must have a common element or a common significance for the animal which elicits the emotion and the behavior. This common element must be 'recognized' by some evolved central mechanism, or separate recognition mechanisms may have evolved to tie into the specific emotional behavior program. The process is obviously complex, and there must be an acutely sensitive facility for switching from one type of emotional elicitation to another in response to sudden changes in recognition, e.g. fear instead of rage if the aggravating source is suddenly recognized to be a superior adversary, or rage instead of fear if young are threatened.

Behavioral experiments and observations with various mammals, including humans, give relatively crude empirical data, and neurophysiological and anatomical data are often difficult to interpret in terms of emotional responses to particular life situations. The surface of knowledge has barely been scratched where the subject of inquiry is exactly what transpires in the central nervous system when an environmental or social situation leads to behavior mediated by emotional feeling.

From the subjective emotional feeling to behavioral response

It is a *sine qua non* that the emotional system exists because it serves some useful function. From this we conclude that there is something peculiar to emotional feelings that makes them employable in their biological role. That 'something' apparently is the unanalysable and unfathomable intrinsic property of being desirable or undesirable – of having intrinsic importance; and, most importantly, *this property is apparently causal in neural processes*. As discussed earlier such a seemingly metaphysical assessment may be unpalatable, but without it this particular phenomenon makes no sense at all; we simply have to accept as a fact of nature the physical causality of subjectivity, just as it has been 'accepted' and utilized by the blind evolutionary process.

Somehow, therefore, each kind of emotional feeling is functionally tied to a particular category of response, and one way of accounting for this is by supposing that the proposed limbic-diencephalic-brainstem neurons generating the particular range of visceral and somatic feelings comprising the emotion have evolved with functional connections to particular effector programs. Selectively activating elements of this neuronal ensemble results in a particular emotional feeling which results, on reconversion to downline neural energy, in the triggering, amplifying, or catalysing of a particular category of response. Note, for example, the dense connections between the caudal intralaminar thalamic nuclei and the pallidal and striatal nuclei.

Further, we may enquire into the process by which different but partly overlapping ensembles of limbic-diencephalic-reticular cellular elements responsible for the generation of feelings are functionally separated: emotions as different as fear and joy may have common feeling elements arising from activation of the same visceral and somatic sensory nerve endings, yet when these common elements are activated in *either* a fear or a joy situation they do not pull both ways but participate exclusively in the appropriate response. Such facile functional compartmentalization is presumably carried out by highly specialized switching properties of synaptic connections, employing essentially inhibitory and excitatory mechanisms. We may further speculate that when, for example, in a fear situation the cellular elements generating the fear emotion are activated they inhibit the elicitation of other emotions which share the common elements. This sort of facile compartmentalization is to be found in other parts of the central nervous system, notably the retrievable (declarative) memory system.

The very indirect, roundabout mechanisms suggested here for the elicitation of emotional feelings and for their role in behavioral responses attest both the powerful adaptive value of an emotional system and the ad hoc manner by which evolution often proceeds. It is another instance of the entrepreneurial opportunism of biological evolution.

If, as proposed in this analysis, emotional feelings are constructed from visceral and somatic sensory signals then one would expect quadriplegics to be emotionally impoverished. This is indeed the case, but not to the degree that one might expect. The vagus nerves which carry sensory information from much of the visceral and cardiovascular systems are spared in quadriplegia, as, of course, is all input from head and neck. Emotions such as exhilaration and excitement may in part depend on sympathetic input and may be grossly impaired, but others such as depression and embarrassment may be largely intact.

Three levels of emotional elicitation; recapulation. Figs.1.29(1-3)

In Section 1.1 attention was drawn to the finding that in dreamless (non-REM) sleep and under light barbituate anaesthesia, during which consciousness is presumably not being generated, evoked potentials to sensory stimuli may be recorded in the relevant sensory cortices, the obvious conclusion being that anaesthetics and sleep shut down the more sensitive neuronal metabolism responsible for generating sensory consciousness. It remains to be determined whether in the limbic-diencephalic areas where feeling consciousness is presumed to be generated the same two-level metabolic functioning occurs.

We do not know how ancient are the different forms of consciousness. The reticular elements of the brainstem and diencephalon are, from comparative studies (Sarnat and Netsky, 1981), believed to be phylogenetically older than elements associated with consciousness of the special senses, and the reticular system is thought to generate feeling consciousness. The 'minds' of primitive organisms may therefore consist largely of forms of feeling consciousness acting as servo-mechanisms on reflexive functions. Non-feeling (sensory) consciousness (seeing, hearing, etc.) if generated in such organisms would likely be very feeble with much weaker servo-functioning, but their great selective value would, in the line leading to vertebrates, have tended to the conversion of the reticular neurons supporting them to the modern neurons subserving the special sensory systems and the pyramidal motor system.

With the evolutionary elaboration of the reflexive systems utilizing sensory consciousness to represent the external world it became possible for complex environmental and social situations to be recognized and responded to well beyond the capability of the non-conscious reflexive systems. Numerous genetically determined behaviors, traditionally termed 'instinctive' because of their complexity, such as formation of social hierarchies, territorial ambitions, competition for mating, protection of privilege, etc., involve at the mammalian level (at least) the ability to 'recognize' within complex sensory input core elements which elicit specific emotions which in turn trigger or augment specific behaviors. The 'recognition' capability is an evolved mechanism: that is, there are genetically blueprinted circuitries in the CNS which are triggerable by certain essential (or core) elements of environmental and social situations via consciousness. This does not involve thinking or understanding or learning but only normal development and maturation.

The mechanism proposed here is that conscious representations of these situations, generated by and residing in the sensory neocortices, on reconversion to neural energy originate signals which flow to 'association' cortices to engage specific ensembles of synaptically connected neurons which constitute the recognition programs, and these circuitries in turn originate signals which flow principally to amygdala to engage particular circuitries there, which in turn originate signals to particular selections of diencephalic and brainstem centres for ultimate engagement of visceral, cardiovascular, and somatic musculatures for excitation of their sensory nerve endings.

We have now described two levels of emotional elicitation: one involving non-conscious (subcortical) and the other conscious (cortical) access to amygdala, etc.; the emotion finally generated is of course always a conscious experience: an 'unconscious' emotion is a contradiction in terms.

A third level of emotional elicitation occurs via thinking, understanding, and imagining. An environmental or social situation may have hidden elements of emotional significance which thinking or received information reveals, or may be pregnant with potential causal chains leading to situations with such elements which thinking discovers and anticipates. In either case the imaginative function or pure memory retrievals will then produce imagery of the emotionally significant feature, which will be recognized by the genetically provided recognition program as in the second level. Thus both real-time sensory perceptions and imagery internally generated from the memory stores have a common pathway to the emotional system. This is necessarily so if, as is proposed in this study and for which there is considerable evidence, the same consciousness-generating neurons are activated from both sources.

1.30 THE NEUROANATOMY OF THE EMOTIONAL SYSTEM

An attempt is made in this section to identify the neuronal substrates of the emotional system, with the dual aim of supporting the foregoing theoretical analysis and of making a contribution towards bringing functional order to the bewildering tangle of limbic-diencephalic connections. Such an attempt is considerably aided by taking an evolutionary approach. (Refer to Appendices C and E).

In summary, the theoretical plan is that emotion consciousness, i.e., subjective emotional feeling, is elicited indirectly via the following phylogenetic levels of circuitry: 1/ a subcortical, non-conscious pathway; 2/ cortical circuitries in which patterns of consciousness (organized sensory percepts) representing external features are generated, downline responses to such patterns thus being responses at secondhand to the external features; and 3/ imagery derived from memory and imagination.

Through downline pathways and control circuitries neural signals pass to visceral and somatic structures to stimulate their sensory nerve endings by muscular contractions, thereby originating centripetal signals to several brainstem and intralaminar thalamic elements of the reticular system, the activation of each resulting in the generation of a specific visceral, cardiovascular, or somatic feeling. The concomitant generation of several of these disparate bodily feelings gives an experiential mix which, through the arcane process of unification of consciousness, constitutes a specific emotion. Obviously, a huge number of combinations of bodily feelings, therefore of resulting emotions, is possible, but each species has evolved to elicit through hard-wired circuitries just a few for its adaptive needs. The simultaneous reconversion of all the elements of the emotion-consciousness to downline neural energy triggers, augments, or catalyses specific behavior program-circuitries in, it is suggested, the corpus striatum, this nuclear complex thereby functioning as the executive arm of the emotional system. The precise response will often be dependent on the effects of subfeatures of the external situation operating through ancillary neuronal circuitries.

A proposal for the anatomy of the visio-emotional system with some ideas about its evolution now follows.

In most submammalian vertebrates the optic tectum (homologue of the superior colliculus) is the main processing centre for light stimuli (Sarnat and Netsky,1981:275). In mammals this function is progressively taken over by the seeing geniculocortical system. Efferent projections from the superior colliculus of cat and monkey "support the hypothesis that the optic tectum is a correlative center capable of initiating or modifying reflexive motor functions..." (op.cit.:264); in other words, non-seeing visual functions.

The evolution of emotional elicitation by light stimuli would have started very simply, perhaps as a response to sudden changes in their intensity. The circuitry in the optic tectum would recognize this non-consciously and in turn transmit a pattern of signals to the brainstem reticular formation (RF) to engage autonomic and somatic nuclei controlling visceral and musculo-skeletal systems. This triggers simple innate physiological and behavioral responses. Sensory impulses from the nerve endings in the musculature of the acting structures ascend to the brainstem RF and the thalamus where they presumably activate whatever neural process is responsible for the generation of feeling consciousness. If this is so the animal may be considered to have an emotional response to light stimuli without sight consciousness, in that the mix of feelings of visceral and somatic origin is postulated to be the primordium of emotional feeling.

The function of the emotional feeling at this primitive level is presumably to accentuate 'higher' innate responses by acting as a servomechanism: Simple reflexes like eye-blink and head-turning would not benefit from an emotional fillip, but the more elaborate though still ancient 'instinctive' behavior programs, probably hardwired in the pallidum, would likely be; there seems to be no other reason for having an emotional system and it must have started evolving at some stage. Again, since so far as we know the optic tectum does not generate sight consciousness, the emotional feeling produced at this evolutionary level is presumed to be non-consciously elicited. That is, there is feeling but not necessarily seeing. Also note that the primordial pallidum (forerunner of the globus pallidus) which contains the primitive instinctive behavioral circuitries is probably derived from the rostral reticular formation.

As more, and more varied, responses to external circumstances evolved new varieties of emotions would have appeared, but non-conscious processing of incoming sensory data has inherent limitations for supporting such elaboration, so an emotional system at this level would necessarily remain primitive. An evolutionary breakthrough would have to come.

Non-feeling consciousness of the special senses (seeing, hearing, smelling, etc.) by enabling the formation of virtually limitless image representations of environmental particulars, and thereby of tailored responsiveness at secondhand to such particulars, allowed great expansion of the emotional system.

The locations in the central nervous system of transducing neuronal mechanisms where consciousness of the special senses was first generated are yet unknown. It is not improbable that before the evolution of the telencephalon thalamic elements served some of these functions, with a memory function for such consciousness being served by cells in the adjacent rostral part of the neural tube, one group of these cells providing retrievable (image) memory and later developing into archicortex (hippocampal formation), and another group that was to evolve into the archipallidum and/or archicerebellum serving motor 'memory'.

Although comparative anatomy texts suggest that thalamus was a purely 'integrative' centre without a motor function (e.g., Sarnat and Netsky, 1981:322), it must have had an effector outlet, and this was presumably the reticular nervous system which in a primitive organism like amphioxus acts as a multistage transmitter of impulses to spinal motor neurons. This system antidated the appearance of special sense organs in the head, and when these appeared the central cells receiving their input clustered around the rostral end of the reticular system, undoubtedly using it as a motor outlet; special senses without a motor outlet would be pointless.

What most likely happened next was a process of development that has apparently been standard in the evolution of increasing functional complexity in nervous systems: genetic variation would endow some individuals with a few extra cells, with more connections, in some nuclear group, boosting performance sufficiently to improve their chance of selection. This would continue, all conditions being favourable, and the new cells and their more elaborate connections would grow in number and either remain closely adjacent to the more primitive part (as extrastriate to striate cortex) or become physically separated from it by lengthening of fibre connections if forced by spatial constraints (as striate cortex from lateral geniculate body).

Evidently, parts of the wall of the neural tube rostral to the primordial thalamus and adjacent to the putative memory structure were invaded by cells expanding the function of the 'special' (nonfeeling) sensory cells of the thalamus (for seeing, hearing, etc.), taking some reticular motor output cells with them but also taking connections with archicortex and archipallidum (i.e., hippocampal and amygdaloid regions and primordium of the future corpus striatum respectively). These were the first cells of sensory neocortex.

Sensory neocortex would thus receive input from the special senses via thalamic relays and have three main outlets: motor, via elements of the reticular motor system which would gradually convert to the pyramidal motor system; to archicortex for some primordial memory function and for access to diencephalic structures for emotional and autonomic functions; and to archipallidum and archicerebellum for elicitation of innate behavior functions. With the further development of sensory neocortex cells subserving the primitive memory function proliferated to become the retrievable memory system, downline from, and in close association with, the putative consciousness-generating cells, and positioned between these and the archipallium (hippocampal formation and amygdaloid nuclear complex).

Accordingly, we find that in the modern mammalian plan external sensory input goes to thalamus, from this to sensory neocortex, and from sensory cortex by different routes to 1/ motor cortex, the projection cells of which we assume were taken from the reticular motor system and converted into more direct transmission lines to lower motor neurons of the entire neuraxis, 2/ archicortex (hippocampal formation) for some retained (and not yet fully understood) participation in memory function, 3/ amygdala, also part of archicortex, with connections to thalamic, hypothalamic, and brainstem elements of the emotional system, and 4/

1.30 The Neuroanatomy of the Emotional System

corpus striatum and cerebellum for engagement of innate motor programs and for the formation and storage of new ones.

The cells of the modern thalamus relaying signals from the special sense organs to neocortex may have given up some of their original functions while retaining others that are not at present fully understood. Cells in the thalamus and/or reticular formation subserving primitive *feeling* consciousness have presumably not totally relinquished this function nor migrated elsewhere, unless to limbic cortex (parahippocampal gyrus, cingulate gyrus). Since electrical stimulation of different parts of hypothalamus and brainstem reticular formation, in addition to parts of thalamus and limbic cortex, produces, in animals and humans, numerous observable responses and (in humans) verbal reports that we class as emotional, there remains uncertainty as to where feeling consciousness is generated.

Assuming this function to have originally been in the rostral reticular formation, it would there have had close anatomical and functional connections with the motor outlets of this formation, including that part which was the precursor of the pallidum, and with the primordial hypothalamus subserving emerging visceral and physiological functions, and through these routes primitive physical and emotional feelings (e.g., pain, fear, anger) could engage appropriate physiological and behavioral responses.

We may again note that the enormous pre-behavioral visceral, etc. involvement in emotional *elicitation* in humans and animals cannot be adequately explained solely on the basis of its adaptive needs for fight, flight, etc. Part of this investment in visceral activity may be explained on the basis of its usage as a source of internally generated sensory input to the thalamus (or whatever limbic-diencephalic-RF elements generate feeling consciousness) to be experienced as a particular emotion which then helps drive behaviors.

When the different kinds of sensory consciousness of the special senses (seeing, hearing, etc.), by virtue of their potential for representing external reality in greater detail, came increasingly to be used to elicit emotional feelings they presumably did so through elaboration of the amygdaloid outlets already in place to hypothalamus and the brainstem RF for visceral and somatic muscular contractions giving the particular mix of sensory impulses from these structures back to the evolving limbic system for construction of the required emotional feeling.

Similarly, the cells of archipallium presumed to be supporting a primitive memory function for the early thalamus, elaborated to become the hippocampal formation, and became the principal gateway to diencephalic and brainstem structures which may be important for the consolidation of memories in neocortex.

The proliferating (consciousness-generating?) thalamic cells receiving input of the special senses expanded the neural tube to form neocortex, taking most of the thalamic projections to amygdala and hippocampus with them. Now input from the special sense organs (eyes, ears, etc.) to thalamus became increasingly relayed to amygdala and hippocampus via neocortex. Any retained capability at the thalamic level to generate primitive consciousness of the special senses (seeing, hearing, etc.) would presumably still engage the most primitive consciously-mediated emotional responses via primordial elements of the amygdala and the even more ancient direct thalamic relays to hypothalamus and RF, but more elaborate conscious representations of the external world, generated in the new extension (neocortex), would operate via concomitantly evolved, more complex amygdaloid circuitries.

In a parallel development the olfactory bulb and nuclei, which may have generated primitive olfactory consciousness, may have had an extension of this function by cellular proliferation into the rostral wall of the neural tube to eventually become the piriform cortex, with connections to amygdala and via this to the emotional-behavioral systems. Thus the special sense of smell has never been directly associated with the thalamus, the olfactory bulb and nuclei possibly being the phylogenetic and functional equivalent of the latter. (See Appendices B and E.)

Recapitulating, the proliferation of the thalamic cells serving the special senses extended into the wall of the neural tube rostral to the thalamus, eventually to become a separate neuronal mass, the neocortex, by lengthening of the connections with the original special sensory neurons of the thalamus, taking with them (in addition to their motor outlets) their richer connections with the primitive hippocampal and amygdaloid processing and relay circuitries. As a result the connections from the special sensory receptors to amygdaloid and hippocampal structures (for emotional elicitations and memory and vegetative functions respectively) increasingly came from neocortex. These routes would additionally allow the elicitation of newly evolved emotions by

1.30 The Neuroanatomy of the Emotional System 205

more elaborate sensory perceptions and internally generated imagery. (Primitive emotions may still be elicited in the round-about manner by whatever special sensory consciousness the thalamus itself may continue to generate).

The increasing adaptive benefits gained by continued elaboration and extension of thalamic function into the rostral wall of the neural tube resulted in the enlargement of this area by evagination to form the cerebral hemisphere on each side, comprising cortical and subcortical (striatal and parts of amygdaloid) elements. (Appendix E.)

With the continued evolution of neocortex, induced by the adaptive value of more elaborate percepts (forms of consciousness representing in greater detail the external world), more versatile and appropriate (i.e., more successful) behaviors became possible, and new emotional feelings which assist in the driving of these behaviors would have tended to be selected.

Does the diencephalon (and brainstem RF) continue to be the generator of all emotional feeling? Or has part of this function, as with other functions, shifted to telencephalon? We must first ask what structures other than thalamus receive sensory information of the feeling kind from visceral and somatic sources? If visceral and somatic feeling sensations are handled by the same system as pain sensation then a major destination is the brainstem reticular formation; Guyton (1987:171) states that three-quarters to nine-tenths of pain fibres terminate there. Other pain fibres go on to intralaminar thalamic nuclei, and some to the ventrobasal and posterior thalamic nuclear groups, from which signals go to other areas of thalamus and some to somatic sensory cortex (probably only for localizing the pain, not for feeling it – the cortex is pain insensitive to electrical and mechanical stimulation). Somatic sensation travels in the dorsal spinal column (lemniscal) pathway, visceral and cutaneous in the spinoreticulothalamic and spinothalamic pathways (Barr and Kiernan, 1988:278).

There are ascending visceral pathways distinct from the pathway for pain (Barr and Kiernan,1988:351). One originates in the nucleus of the tractus solitarius in the medulla, which receives general visceral afferents mainly from the vagus nerve. Another originates in spinal cord segments T1 – L3 and S2 – S4. These ascending fibres are included in the spinoreticular and spinothalamic tracts. By these routes impulses of visceral origin reach the reticular formation of the brainstem, the hypothalamus, and the ventral posterior nuclei of the thalamus. According to the above authors a thalamocortical projection provides for a feeling of fullness or emptiness in stomach, bowel, and bladder, but this implies that the neocortex generates feeling consciousness which is almost certainly erroneous.

The spinoreticular tract, originating in spinal laminae v through viii, includes crossed and uncrossed fibers terminating in the pontine and medullary reticular formations respectively, which "may be involved in the *perception* of pain *and various sensations originating in internal organs*" (Barr and Kierman, 1988:77, italics added). Also, the intralaminar group of thalamic nuclei receive sensory data through the extralemniscal route that involves the reticular formation, and these nuclei are involved in the awareness of pain (op.cit.:96).

There is therefore some evidence that the neurons and neuronal circuitries concerned with the generation of visceral consciousness reside in the brainstem and thalamic reticular systems. Although some specific pain pathways have been identified it is very doubtful that pain consciousness has a unique anatomic system for itself – numerous sensations when mild to moderate are not experienced as painful, but on strengthening gradually become uncomfortable, then distressful, then actually painful.

Pain itself should not be considered an emotion but a physical feeling. The *cause* of pain is local damage, disease, or dysfunction resulting in intense sensory stimulation; the *cause* of emotional feeling is instructions from above to contract a widespread pattern of smooth and skeletal musculature thus producing a mix of sensations.

At some stage in the evolution of special sensory receptors (which occurred somewhere, as deduced from comparative anatomy, between the phylogenetic levels of Amphioxus and the most primitive extant vertebrates, e.g., cyclostomes) a conscious function associated with these receptors appeared. At present there is no way of telling when consciousness of any kind appeared in phylogenesis. Whether the optic tectum ever generated consciousness is therefore unknown; its mammalian homologue, the superior colliculus, mediates primitive, presumably non-conscious, reflex responses to light stimuli (head turning, eye movements, etc.). So far as I know there are no reports of visual consciousness being generated by electrical stimulation of the superior colliculi or of lateral geniculate bodies in human patients who have lost their striate cortices (but see Beckers and Zeki,1995); if these organs do generate consciousness it is evidently not included in the global unitary consciousness of the mind.

While consciousness, functioning as a servomechanism, may be employed in the entire neuraxis, including the optic tectum, without being a part of the global unitary consciousness of the mind, consciousness as a representational instrument may first have appeared at the thalamic level. This function would be an evolutionary breakthrough allowing a rapid spurt in brain evolution through, e.g., expansion of the memory system and elaboration of behavioral and emotional mechanisms. The crucial difference is that these systems and mechanisms *respond to consciousness* and therefore only indirectly to events in the outside world: consciousness on this level *represents* (is the agent or surrogate of) the outside world, and such representation is of necessity a unified whole – it constitutes, or is the defining feature of, 'mind'.

The early thalamus may have functioned as a relatively simple reflexive system employing consciousness in some manner as a servomechanism, engaging innate motor behaviors via the upper reticular network and simple autonomic functions via the primitive hypothalamus. Representational consciousness may have appeared in phylogenesis when a critical level in complexity of this conscious-reflexive system had been reached, where further increase in complexity of circuitry handling the incoming data was no longer able to significantly improve performance; there could be little or no further elaboration of genetically determined (innate) emotional and behavioral responses at the reflexive, non-representational level.

It may be suggested that a genetic change in the constitution of consciousness-generating neurons allowed the realization of a natural tendency for units of conscious energy to coalesce, with two main effects: crude conscious facsimiles of the external world could be produced in the brain, and these, acting as surrogates, could engage increasingly complex and potentially more appropriate, therefore more adaptive, emotional and behavioral responses.

It may further be proposed that this change in neuronal properties occurred in some of the neuroblasts producing those thalamic sensory cells serving the special senses, with the result that (as proposed earlier) a new tier of sensory thalamic cells appeared. These at first would have had the same connections to motor elements in the upper reticular formation, but elaboration of the latter allowed more comprehensive motor responses and this became a target for selection, resulting in the conversion of some reticular motor pathways to the primordial corticospinal pathways for more direct control of lower motor neurons.

Similarly, an increasing range of emotional elicitations would be made possible by representational consciousness, requiring some means of selecting, via hypothalamic and brainstem nuclei, the particular mix of visceral and musculo-skeletal activation for the generation of emotional feeling. New circuitries able to recognize and respond to more elaborate conscious experiences were 'needed', and the slightest genetic variations in this direction would have been strongly selected, leading to the appearance of tertiary neocortex and elaboration of the amygdala. At first the primordial amygdala would handle information of the special senses directly from the original thalamic relays (and separately from the olfactory bulb and nucleus), then, later, from the new thalamic extensions dealing with the special senses, and eventually mostly from these as they became neocortex.

In like manner the primordial hippocampus, presumed to serve the beginnings of retrievable memory, may in addition have acted as a gateway for representational consciousness to gain access to other aspects of emotionalism, such as the evolving 'feelings' of interest and curiosity, as well as to the autonomic nervous system, perhaps for secretion of adrenaline, all of which (in addition to possibly several other factors) may be contributory to the formation and consolidation of memories in the sensory neocortices.

With these proposals in mind we may now briefly look at the principal features of the human limbic-diencephalic-brainstem anatomy which are thought to be involved in emotionalism.

Hypothalamus has reciprocal connections with spinal and brainstem nuclei of the autonomic nervous system. It receives visceral information which it may transmit to anterior thalamic nuclei and thence to cingulate cortex via the mammillo-thalamic tract. "...the anterior thalamic nuclei and the cingulate cortex share with the other components of the limbic system responsibility for those emotions and aspects of behavior related to preservation of the individual and the species. The hypothalamus contributes to the subjective experience of these emotions ...." (Barr and Kiernan, 1988).

1.30 The Neuroanatomy of the Emotional System

There are three main routes by which the functioning cerebral cortex may gain access to the emotional system:

1/ The amygdaloid nuclear complex has several recognized subdivisions with specific connections, receiving input from pyriform, frontal, temporal, and occipital cortices (Aggleton et al, 1980; Herzog and van Hoesen, 1976; Iwai and Yukie, 1987). "It has become increasingly evident that amygdala ... is involved in complex cognitive functions that influence emotion and behavior in a global fashion. These functions appear to involve virtually all regions of the cerebral cortex and all sensory modalities .... [including] modality-specific association areas" (Carpenter, 1991:381).

There are numerous interconnections within the amygdaloid complex which may allow a 'switchboard' and possibly also a 'scoresheet' function for selection of limbic-diencephalic-brainstem pathways to visceral, cardiovascular, and somatic structures.

The downline amygdalofugal pathways (Carpenter,1991:376-381) include the stria terminalis to nuclei of the same name; the medial forebrain bundle to several hypothalamic nuclei and to several brainstem centres; a ventral projection to septal region, hypothalamic nuclei, and nucleus of the diagonal band; the inferior thalamic peduncle to periventricular nuclei and mediodorsal nuclei of thalamus; and projections to neostriatum, substantia innominata, hippocampal formation, subiculum, entorhinal cortex, parabrachial nuclei, and dorsal motor nucleus of vagus. (See Appendix C).

Onward projections from these numerous amygdaloid targets affect potentially all systems of the body involved in emotionalism. The connections may also allow direct activation of the central neurons generating feeling consciousness, thereby short-circuiting their roundabout activation via visceral, cardiovascular, and somatic structures, but this remains to be determined.

Many of the amygdaloid afferent and efferent connections are reciprocated, presumably for modulation in maintaining balance and precision in the extremely complex and delicate cognitive-emotional processes. M.P. Young (1995) writes: "...almost nothing is known concerning the function of .... backward projections which constitute a substantial proportion of the connections of the [occipitotemporal visual] system. Backward projections appear to terminate in wider cortical domains than those of forward projections ...".

2/ The mediodorsal (MD) nucleus of the thalamus has a large reciprocal connection with 'association' cortex of frontal lobe (prefrontal cortex), and various emotional and behavioral abnormalities result from cutting this connection (prefrontal leucotomy), suggestive of the removal of higher level inhibitory control over crude behaviors and emotional reactions. This nucleus also receives input from olfactory cortex and from amygdala, thereby probably mediating emotional-behavioral responses to olfactory stimuli via its extensive connections with intralaminar and lateral thalamic nuclear groups. That MD may itself be a generator of feeling consciousness cannot at present be ruled out.

3/ According to Squire and Zola-Morgan (cited by Squire, 1992) the hippocampus is in reciprocal, multi-stage connection (via entorhinal, perirhinal, and parahippocampal cortices) with 'unimodal' and 'polymodal' association areas of frontal, temporal, and parietal lobes. The hippocampus proper and its adjacent cortical areas (subiculum, dentate gyrus, parahippocampal gyrus), referred to *in toto* as the hippocampal formation, have reciprocal connections with the lateral olfactory area, anterior thalamic nuclei, posterior hypothalamus, mammillary bodies, septal area, substantia innominata, ventral tegmental area, raphe nuclei, and the parabrachial nucleus (Barr and Kiernan, 1988:268). The fornix is the largest discrete two-way fibre system between the hippocampal formation and limbic-diencephalic-brainstem centres.

Although research has largely been concerned with the role of the hippocampal formation in memory, it is probable from its connections and its strategic position that it has a significant role in emotional-behavioral elicitations by neocortical (mental) activities. Furthermore, its participation in the establishment of new memories may in part be by involving the emotional system and through this the focusing mechanisms in the ongoing mental processes; 'paying attention' may in part be essential for new memory formation and the hippocampus may play a significant role in this, especially, in association with amygdala, in the elicitation of interest and curiosity which act to increase focus on the relevant item in consciousness.

1.31 RECOGNITION CIRCUITRIES FOR THE NEWER EMOTIONS

Neural recognition circuitries must necessarily exist to enable particular conscious experiences to activate the emotional system.

1.31 Recognition Circuitries for the Newer Emotions

'Recognition' here means that each conscious experience of emotional significance for the organism is able to activate a particular neuronal complex (or 'module') which, therefore, 'recognizes' the conscious experience.

A major contribution to the size of the human brain may be from circuits responsible for emotional elicitations. Evidently, in evolutionary adaptation to the artefactual niche, interpersonal and social relationships played an increasingly important role, and among the strategies evolved to foster and control appropriate responses was the employment of emotional feelings.

It may not be possible to determine what proportion of the normal human's almost continuous emotionalism is an artefact of the imaginative function or is psychophysiologically adaptive, but it is generally agreed that humans have a much richer basic emotional repertoire than other animals. This being the case we must try to determine what neural structures support this newer functioning.

Phylogenetically older structures have more stable genetic underpinnings than more recent ones, this being a basic evolutionary principle, therefore there is less opportunity for the older structures to internally evolve the complexity we believe is required for the human level of emotionalism.

Among structures in the limbic-diencephalic regions which are relatively more developed in man are basolateral amygdala, entorhinal cortex, posterior hypothalamic nuclei (including mammillary bodies), intralaminar thalamic nuclei, neostriatum, subthalamic nucleus, zona incerta, and various 'non-specific' thalamic nuclei. But most of these differences are relatively minor compared to the huge development of neocortex in primates and especially man. We may therefore expect to find in neocortex neuronal circuitries responding to elaborate patterns of consciousness which represent particular environmental and social situations, such responding circuitries engaging the downline emotional system via amygdala, etc.. These evolved neocortical circuitries therefore 'recognize', via surrogate consciousness, external situations that 'need' an emotional fillip for adequate response.

Inasmuch as only the vaguest notions exist about the functions of 'association' cortex, and as these areas are evidently the most recently evolved, we may look here for the circuitries able to recognize the situations associated with the more recently evolved emotions.

And, as with much of the organization of the central nervous system, we may expect to find different levels of reflexive emotional elicitation operating in closely adjacent areas. For example a fairly primitive neocortical reflex circuit for the elicitation of fear may be revealed by bilateral ablation of amygdalas in cats resulting in apparent loss of fear in hostile situations. What is interrupted by this damage is presumably a primitive reflex circuit employing consciousness generated in neocortex and which in turn engages recognition circuitry in the cortex or the amygdala itself, although we cannot rule out the possibility that interrupting primitive pathways from thalamus to amygdala in the cat is responsible for the Kluver-Bucy syndrome.

The more recently evolved emotions such as compassion, pity, thrill of beauty, and many others presumably have their recognition circuitries in neocortex adjacent to the more primitive ones and consisting of more elaborate architectonics. It is doubtful that amygdala can have evolved sufficiently to fill such complex recognition roles, but it may remain the main route by which cortical recognition networks gain access to the emotional system and it almost certainly evolved more complex internal circuits for selecting the appropriate downline elements for construction of the relevant emotional feeling.

1.32 CORTICAL CYTOARCHITECTURE AND MENTAL-COGNITIVE FUNCTIONS.

Not nearly enough is known about the organization and properties of cortical neurons to enable us to do much more than to say they must be such as to perform our cognitive functions. The great morphological diversity of these neurons implies functional diversity; for example, specialization in linkage characteristics may be contributory to 'higher' cognitive functions: circuitries that specifically respond to complex patterns of consciousness representing specific events in the outside world may depend for their functional integrity and reliability on presently unknown synaptic properties.

Cortical features most distinctive in man include : 1/ the populations of neurons, mainly stellates in layer 4, increase in density; 2/ increasing amounts of 'association' cortex; 3/ increasingly abundant connections between association cortices of the sensory lobes and frontal cortex (Barr and Kierman,1988); 4/ the entorhinal area, which relates the hippocampus to the cingulate gyrus, is largest in man (Sarnat and

1.32 Cortical Cytoarchitecture and Mental-Cognitive Functions 213

Netsky,1981); 5/ the anterior temporal lobe, prefrontal cortex, and occipital poles are most developed in man (op.cit.); 6/ there is marked increase in size of motor cortex and in direct (monosynaptic) control of lower motor neurons by motor cortex from monkey to chimpanzee to man (Evarts,1981); 7/ layer 4B of visual cortex and its reciprocal relationship to the distal visual association area in the superior temporal sulcus (ST1) is apparently a special feature of primate cortex – there is no direct homologue in the cat (Lund,1981); 8/ somatosensory area S1 in rats, squirrel, tree-shrew, and other non-primates is the homologue of 3b in primates – the additional somatosensory cortical areas in primates presumably being evolutionary developments to support higher mental functions (Kass et al,1981); 9/ the basolateral amygdaloid nucleus is most developed in man and is thought to have 'association' functions (Sarnat and Netsky,1981).

Given the present level of knowledge of cortical cytoarchitecture any attempt to assign specific cognitive functions to particular neurons must largely be conjectural. It is one thing to measure the electrical responses of individual cortical cells to sensory stimuli, but quite another, of a higher order of difficulty, to establish the connections and the flow of neural signals among the huge numbers of specialized cells in even a single cortical column, and a yet higher order of difficulty to assign specific cognitive functions to these.

Yet there must exist in the brain neural bases for consciousness, for memory, and for all cognitive functions. By the same token the neuronal elements of the cerebral cortex must serve cognitive functions; when we look at a cortical neuron we see a cell that is a participant in some cognitive function, directly or indirectly involving consciousness.

It would seem reasonable, therefore, to make the attempt to provisionally assign specific functions to specific neurons, guided by the available data and some principles of procedure such as parsimony, prima facie evidence, the known cognitive tasks that must have neural substrates, etc.. The principal benefit of such an exercise would not be in directly advancing knowledge, which would be almost nil, but in posing a challenge for future research. Ultimately we want to know how every aspect of mental functioning is produced in terms of the working of the specialized neurons composing the brain. This may be the unspoken agenda of all neuroscientific research, but the necessary ultraspecialization is paradoxically tending to obscure that goal. Refer to Figs.1.32(1-3)

Fig. 1.32(1) **Cortical cytoarchitecture: layers and columns of cells**

   A cortical column extends from the pial surface to the white matter and is 0.2 - 0.5 mm in diameter. It contains a complete complement of specialized neurons subserving the functions of that area of cortex. The following sketch is a distillate of several cytoarchetectonic schemes from various sources, some of which are contradictory; e.g., that one sensory axon from the thalamus serves each cortical column (Barr and Kiernan, 1988:230), or that a large number do so (Carpenter, 1991:410).
   Cortical layers are semiartificial divisions based on a preponderance of particular cell bodies.
   Note: Throughout this book axons and their terminal butons are represented as arrows (⤳), dendrites as cusps (⋗), and cell bodies either as circles (○) or triangles (△).

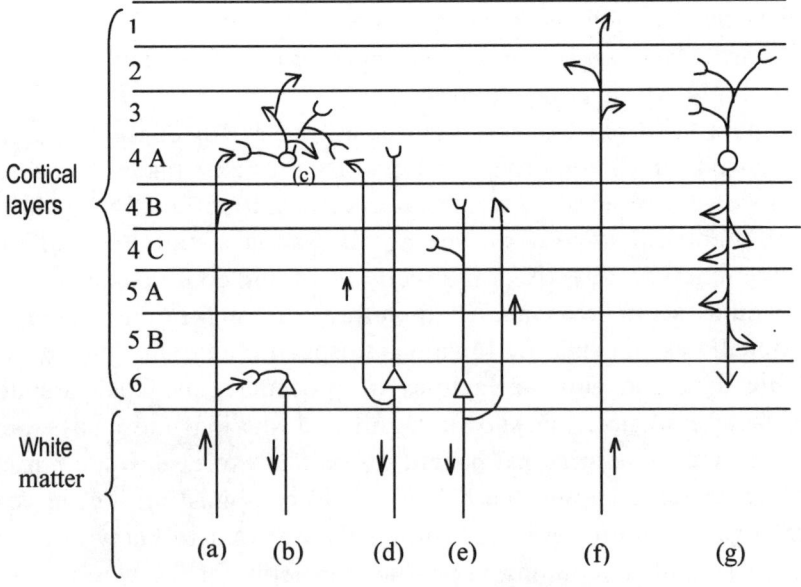

Fig. 1.32(1) **Symbols**

(a) Axon from sensory relay neuron in thalamus (visual, auditory, somatosensory, gustatory, or vestibular).
(b) Pyramidal cell in layer 6 receiving sensory input and immediately exiting the cortex, probably subserving a higher-level, non-conscious function.
(c) Spiny stellate interneuron in layer 4. In the human neocortex these are greatly increased in numbers and are possible candidates as generators of consciousness; that is, as transducers of neural energy to conscious energy.
(d) A pyramidal in layer 6, with dendritic roots in layer 4 which are well positioned to receive input from (c). Its axon exits the cortex but sends a recurrent branch to layer 4 where it is in a position to activate (c) thus acting as a servo-assisting mechanism and inducing further generation of consciousness. This pyramidal may therefore be a memory cell.
(e) A pyramidal similar to (d).
(f) An axon of an intralaminar thalamic cell of the ascending reticular activating system (RAS.) It arborizes in the superficial cortical layers and is presumed to have a modulatory function on all cortical cells with dendritic roots in these layers. It is the principal candidate for the selective regional control of the generation of consciousness; that is, for the 'focusing' of consciousness.
(g) This radially distributed interneuron carries the vasoactive intestinal polypeptide (VIP) neurotransmitter which controls vascular activity in the cortical column and thereby cortical activity. It may be under partial control of (f) and therefore be one of the submechanisms by which consciousness is regulated.

Fig. 1.32(2) Cortical Columns and intermemory connections

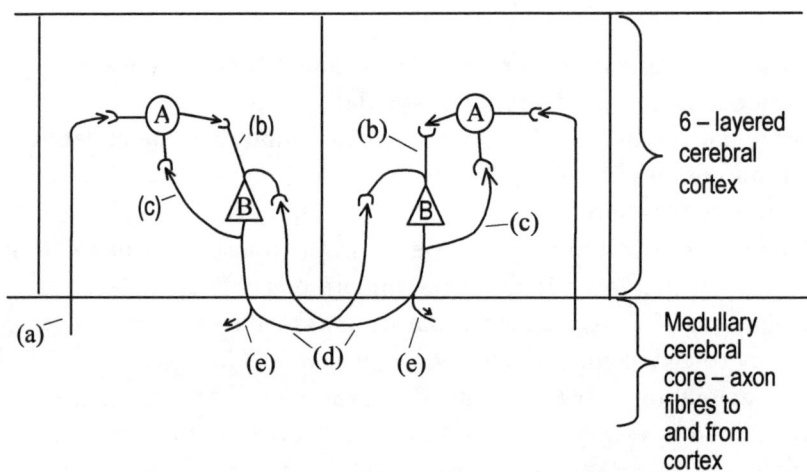

Sensory input axon (a) synapses with candidate consciousness-generating neuron (A). Each putative unit of consciousness (the 'menton') converts to neural energy received by dendrite (b) of candidate memory pyramidal cell (B) in a deeper cortical layer. B gives rise to an axon with the following branches: c, back to the consciousness-generating cell; d, to memory cells in other columns in same or another sensory modality; and e, to downline effector mechanisms (if this pathway has not become vestigial as a result of memory specialization — see text).

Fig. 1.32(3) Alternative arrangement — letter symbols as in Fig.1.32(2)

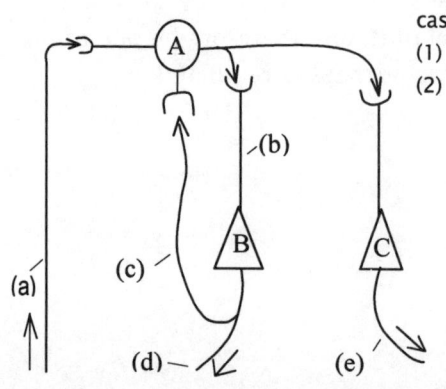

The following arrangement may be the case:
(1) B serves a memory function exclusively.
(2) A's conscious energy on reconversion to neural activity innervates its memory function (B) and, by a separate axonal branch, neuron (C) for a downline effector function (see text). Note that since a conscious experience may activate one or more of several downline mechanisms it must have access to their circuitries by separate axonal projections.

1.32 Cortical Cytoarchitecture and Mental-Cognitive Functions

Our attempt should start with the generation of consciousness. Consciousness is the core element of cognitive functions, and the major part of the cerebral cortex has evolved to provide these functions. The position adopted in this study is that consciousness may be regarded as a unique form of energy, convertible to conventional forms of energy, generated by specialized neurons in the cerebral cortex and, in the case of primordial forms of consciousness, in limbic-diencephalic structures.

Consciousness is initially sensory, meaning that it is first produced by input from sensory receptors acting on consciousness-generating cells – it has a real-time relationship to environmental and corporeal events. Except for olfaction all sensory signals of external origin relay in the thalamus before proceeding to the sensory cortices. Primitive forms of consciousness may be generated in the reticular (non-specific) elements of the thalamus and brainstem. There is behavioral evidence from decorticate animals that this is probably so.

In the cortices sensory projections from the thalamus terminate principally in layer 4, "but the identity of those cortical neurons which directly receive thalamic input is largely unknown" (White, 1981). White then gives an account of the "successful efforts to identify neurons involved in the thalamocortical synapses in two primary receptive areas of the mammalian cortex" – the somatosensory and visual cortices of the rat.

In layer 4 of mammalian primary sensory cortex there are numerous small spiny stellate cells whose dendrites mostly remain in this layer, and a dense axonal plexus containing large numbers of thalamocortical afferents, these facts suggesting that layer 4 stellate cells are the principal recipients of thalamic sensory input.

However, it has been shown (in rat and mouse) that numerous dendrites in layer 4 which receive thalamocortical axon terminals belong to a variety of cell types whose cell bodies reside in cortical layers 3 through 6. According to White (1981) experimental results indicate that every neuron with dendrites in layer 4 (of mouse SM1 cortex) receives input from thalamocortical afferents. In addition, the data indicate that interneurons (nonspiny stellates) receiving thalamic projections themselves synapse on other cortical cells also receiving thalamic input, presumably functioning to boost input as servomechanisms.

But although many cortical cell types may receive thalamic input, the preponderance is to spiny stellates whose cell bodies and dendritic roots are in layer 4.

The general flow of neural signals in the cortex is input to upper (superficial) layers, through to lower (deeper) layers, then out via the white matter to various destinations, with some of the deeper cells sending axonal branches back to the more superficial layers.

We know from introspection that the conscious experience must in some manner convert to a non-conscious form or effect which becomes stored and later can reconvert to the conscious form, and in the present speculations we make the assumption that this is achieved by the energy of consciousness reconverting to neural energy to contribute to depolarization and chemo-structural alteration of downline memory neurons.

If a downline neuron has a memory function it must, theoretically, possess certain features. First, its repeated excitation by conscious sensory input must result in synaptic potentiation at both its input and output ends; secondly, it must have a loop-back branch axon to synapse with its upline consciousness-generating neuron; thirdly, its axon must exit the cortex to synapse directly or indirectly with other memory neurons of the same or other sensory modalities. In addition it may have access, directly or indirectly, to various cognitive, emotional, and motor mechanisms.

The putative memory neuron must be accessible to input from potentially all other memory neurons of the cortex, and if it has not become specialized purely for memory functions but retains output functions its exit pathways to these must be under inhibitory control to allow mental operations to proceed without unwanted motor and other responses; and, obviously, the anatomical point of such inhibition would have to be beyond the system of intermemory connections.

It is at this point that theoretical construction becomes complicated. For example, does the axon of every memory neuron have access to downline systems, or does it contribute to some narrow collecting neuronal system, at which point inhibition can be applied and from which instructions go to the downline systems? Or does each cortical column have specialized neurons, distinct from the memory neurons, with access to motor, emotional, and physiological functions, so that unwanted responses during internal mental processing is achieved by inhibiting these neurons? Or does inhibition operate at various levels of the effector systems through the entire neuraxis?

Whichever of these or other possibilities is actually the case – and we know that such an inhibitory control must exist from the fact that we suspend physical action when thinking intensively, yet sometimes our thoughts break through that inhibition to cause involuntary responses – we must, at some stage of our theoretical construction, propose a neuronal system of inhibitory control employing the anatomical and physiological data of cortical cytology available to us. And we must face the possibility that such data, collected largely from lower mammalian orders, may, in important respects, not correspond to the cortex of man, which is enormously specialized for advanced cognitive functions.

A further point to consider is that neurons in the primary sensory areas participate in reflexive functions via primitive consciousness. Therefore much of our knowledge of detailed cortical cytoarchitecture, which has largely been obtained from studies of the primary visual cortex, may be of elements not serving higher cognitive functions. Ultradetails of the cytology and functional connectivities of *human* cortical areas outside the primary sensory areas are only slowly becoming available, and such information from the cat (e.g., Graybiel and Berson,1981) may represent either a different evolutionary specialization or a stage of evolution which has been superseded and become vestigial in man: considerably more visual competence remains in the cat after loss of its primary visual cortices than in man, indicating that man relies more than the cat on sight consciousness.

Assuming that some cortical neurons are specialized to generate consciousness, which would be the most likely? Lund's (1981) finding is that the bulk of sensory input to primary visual area 17 of macaque monkey from the thalamic lateral geniculate nucleus (LGN) goes to subdivisions of layer 4. There are numerous spiny stellate cells in these layers which presumably absorb much of that input. Do these cells generate consciousness? If so they must have connections, directly or indirectly, with all other consciousness-generating cells of the cortex to give the global unified conscious experience. Individually, that hardly seems possible, but if all the spiny stellates in layer 4 of each cortical column acted as a unit then logistically it would become more manageable. Do spiny stellates in layer 4 have access to candidate memory cells? Such cells would have to be downline in signal flow (in a deeper cortical layer) and would have to show means of returning impulses back to the consciousness-generating cells for which they provide the memory function. This may be by recurrent axonal branches, and there are pyramidal cells in layer 6 with such branches in the cat (Gilbert and Wiesel,1981:182), or indirectly by interneurons, of which the cortex is richly endowed.

Other theorists in this guessing game, e.g. Crick (1994), suggest that pyramidals in the deeper layers are more likely candidates for the generation of consciousness, in that some processing of the raw sensory data must occur before the stage of consciousness. Other schemes are possible, but all can be shown to have flaws, perhaps inevitably so since primitive mammalian cortices are mostly used to explain human cognitive functions. The best we can do at this stage is to construct a provisional wiring diagram (e.g. Gilbert and Wiesel,1981:182) to fit one's particular theory of cognitive functions and wait for new anatomical data, preferably from the higher primates.

We are guided by the histological information provided by Lund, Jones, Gilbert and Wiesel, and others in forming our speculations. Stellates in layer 4 have clear access to corticocortical pyramidals in layers 3 and 4. If some of these stellates are consciousness-generating neurons their activity can drive not only the deep pyramidals (the putative memory cells with loop-back axons) but also pyramidals exiting the cortex to other cortical areas possibly to fulfil some of the linking and effector functions we need to account for. In this way consciousness would not only be remembered but would be executive, with these functions being separately achieved through different pyramidal outlets. Such a separation of mnemonic and executive functions, apparently forced by histological data, would not be incompatible with introspective experience, in which our voluntary behavior seems to come directly from consciousness.

But the problem of memory linkages remains. Memory neurons need to be interconnectable in a manner that does not involve consciousness-generating neurons, and the charts of cortical histology that are available do not reveal any straight-forward way that this can be achieved. Input to striate cortex from other cortical areas, e.g., extrastriate and visual association cortex of temporal lobe, arborize mainly in the superficial cortical layers where they have some chance of meeting dendritic roots of some layer 6 pyramidals with putative memory function. They also

1.32 Cortical Cytoarchitecture and Mental-Cognitive Functions 221

have a strong opportunity to innervate pyramidals in superficial layers destined for extrastriate areas, and these on their way out supply layer 5 with axonal collaterals which have the opportunity of synapsing with pyramidals destined for pulvinar and superior colliculus. These pyramidals give loop-back axonal branches before leaving their cortical columns and may possess some memory function.

We may also appeal to the vast number of interneurons known to exist in cerebral cortex for transfer of information between different classes of output pyramidals – after all, these interneurons must support various cognitive functions.

It has been estimated that only 10-20 percent of synapses on spiny stellates in primary sensory cortices are of thalamic origin (Colonnier,1981:142). The majority input to these nominal generators of consciousness must come from other sources, e.g., loop-back axonal collaterals from layer 6 pyramidals; excitatory interneurons responding to the need to generate more consciousness in their area as determined by the consciousness priority mechanism; inhibitory interneurons to shut down the generation of consciousness when some other area gains priority; and connections allowing integrated functioning with other areas for the generation of coherent, structured forms of consciousness, commonly referred to as 'percepts'. The percentage of input to spiny stellates in layer 4 of *secondary* sensory areas coming from thalamic relays via the primary cortices has probably not been determined, but one would expect the range of inputs to be similar since not only must the 'experiential' cell, wherever it is in the sensory cortex, generate consciousness but it must be under the above influences and controls.

A percept may be formed from current sensory input or from memory. In either case it is formed by the functional integration of large numbers of consciousness-generating units. These units may be individual neurons or an entire cortical column to which such neurons belong or some other neuronal assemblage. Their collective, simultaneous activity gives the conscious experience of distinct phenominal features. This must be achieved by a very elaborate network of corticocortical connections with extremely efficient synaptic transmissions between the parts, and also by highly specialized receptive-field characteristics of the participating modules in the case of sensory input.

But the percept is a purely subjective experience – the cytology has evolved to generate percepts, but percepts are not discoverable in the cytology. The percept is at the heart of higher order cognitive and behavioral functioning of the organism, and the percept together with all other aspects of consciousness at any moment is unitary. Somehow the individual units of consciousness must coalesce into a unitary whole, and this coalescence is dependent on the integrity of the (structural) connectivities of the cortex, as shown by the dissociation of consciousness in commissurotomized (split-brain) subjects; different items of consciousness, whether generated by individual, specialized neurons or by 'patterns' of neural activity, must have access to one another via intact neuronal fibres.

Such unity is evidently necessary to enable the organism to perform one task at a time, this linear application presumably having proven the most effective way of utilizing consciousness in mammalian evolution.

To the majority of cellular elements of the cortex no clear functions have been assigned. In the words of E.G. Jones (1981) in reference to the several classes of cortical interneurons described "it is not yet possible to weld them into any particular connectional scheme of the cortex". Of course, each *serves* some function of cognition, and, conversely, every aspect of mentality open to introspection is produced by some set of cortical neurons.

1.33 AI, CONSCIOUSNESS, AND THINKING

Among artificial intelligence (AI) workers and science-fiction writers the questions as to whether machines can be conscious, think, etc. used to be, and perhaps still are, debated. Since consciousness almost certainly is a product of organic biochemistry its production by simple inorganic materials can be confidently rejected. Animal thinking utilizes consciousness and evolved because the inherent properties of consciousness made bio-technological breakthroughs in nature possible, but the goal of animal thinking, that is, the useful application of such thinking, may also in theory be achievable by non-biological systems. Animal thinking, primitively present in higher mammals but appreciably developed only in man, is dependent first on there being in memory a stockpile of sensorially acquired environmental causal relationships and factual knowledge. In dealing with novel situations the thinking mechanism elicits from the stockpile analogous information, which enables a provisional causal explanation to be assigned to the present situation, the next step being (if necessary – or if one is being scientific) testing the new understanding for validity.

There is no theoretical reason why machines cannot be designed to do the same sort of thing, substituting some other procedure for conscious recognition. Animal thinking and understanding mechanisms are among the evolved, technical 'solutions' to problems posed by the vulnerability of life – they are solutions resulting from the winnowing of genetic variations by natural selection. At the highest level these mechanisms function to generate (or reveal) provisional understandings (i.e. possible causal relationships) which are not immediately evident to ordinary sensory experience. If the word 'thinking' is being used in this sense in AI research the technological difficulties may be very difficult to overcome; and, of course, impossible if our definition of thinking includes the imaginative function.

Of much greater interest to biologists is light that engineering knowledge can throw on logistic and control mechanisms in advanced brains. These technical problems have been 'solved' by biological evolution utilizing living tissue. So far we have not been bright enough to more than dimly grasp what these problems are, but they include: the operation of the linkage systems in memory; the control systems involved in determining priority among incoming information and amplifying (or facilitating) the higher and inhibiting the lower; in adjusting response to input in the most precise manner with the greatest speed when that input is from several sources simultaneously; in coordinating several independent mechanisms acting to produce a particular effect, as in the focusing of consciousness; in the precise and instantaneous responses of the various muscular systems, including the vocal, to rapidly changing thoughts; and so on. These technical problems are in principle amenable to mathematical, mechanical, and computational simulation. They are strictly speaking not all mental problems, but must nevertheless form part of any comprehensive evaluation of the mind.

It might be thought that the 'neural network' models so much in vogue these days among 'connectionists', and which are apparently so promising for understanding the workings of the brain, would be particularly applicable here. But it is my conviction that this whole discipline is tackling the wrong problems, or tackling the problems from the wrong end. First there is the completely hopeless idea that such networks through successive stages of processing can end up with thoughts, intentions, understandings, imaginings and other purely mental functions, all of which are non-existent in the absence of subjective consciousness. Second, these computer networks are designed to see what they can do, not to see how the brain carries out its mental functions. What is first needed is a model of the mind centred on consciousness with several neural sub-systems existing to carry out the functions of consciousness. Engineering theory may then try to model (mathematically, mechanically, electronically) how these functions are in fact carried out.

Among the more recent network ideas is that of Edelman (1989) who is able to envisage the emergence of consciousness from the back-and-forth passage of neural signals between neuronal groups; but the mere movement of neural signals, however intricate the patterns of such movement or whatever converging, diverging, switching, or reentering may take place, cannot generate consciousness any more than electrical signals in copper wires. Edelman's scholarship is impressive, but ambiguities rob his ideas of conviction, e.g., that perception and memory precede consciousness (p.11), whereas to everyone else a percept is *composed* of consciousness (an unconscious percept is a contradiction in terms) and memory is a recording of consciousness so obviously succeeds it.

The guiding principle in attempting to reconstruct the evolution of the mind is never to lose sight of the fact that the system at any stage is the result of small inheritable changes in the genome of the preceding stage which happened to confer greater survival advantages on those individuals possessing them. *The mind evolved from the simplest stage at which consciousness can reasonably be supposed to have emerged and become functionally incorporated in the biological system.* Mind is in existence from that point on, there being no fundamental qualitative difference between it and the mind of modern man, any more than between seedling and mature plant.

PART 2

STAGES IN EVOLUTION

OF THE MIND

INTRODUCTION

Mind is the totality of those functions of the central nervous system utilizing consciousness in dealing with the challenges and opportunities of life. It began with the emergence of consciousness in some unknown, presumably simple, and probably very ancient, life form. As the lineages utilizing this property evolved, certain lines did so in the direction of increasing complexity and sophistication through the development of various subfunctions, the appearance of each heralding a major phase in the evolution of mind.

Our ultimate interest is in the 'finished' product, the mind of man. The function of the major part of man's large brain is the function of mind, and this brain achieved its present size because of the success of each subfunction in contributing to the main exercise. Although most studies deal with the mind as it now is, and enormous gains in understanding have been achieved, it is virtually impossible to properly understand so intricate an organ system at this level of approach.

In order to thoroughly understand any complex system it is necessary to start at its elementary beginnings and work up through the history of its development. In the case of the mind this approach is no less desirable, but is thwarted by the unavailability of an historical record. From the comparative anatomy of extant nervous systems we may speculate more-or-less confidently on their evolutionary histories, but thoughts on the evolution of mental functioning of nervous systems are themselves based on such speculation, making them very speculative indeed.

The method used here is to take each component of human mental functioning and applying what knowledge we have of evolutionary principles, as well as data from the neuro-mental sciences and self-knowledge of our own minds, attempt to reconstruct what 'must have' taken place from the earliest stage onwards in order to result in what we have today.

We therefore have to conjecture on (1) how consciousness, once it appeared, could have contributed to more effective functioning of the organism; (2) the origin of a memory function permitting learning; (3) the origin of memory retrieval and therefore of imagery; (4) the linkage of memory neurons permitting indirect retrieval, that is, retrieval of another memory by the one now in retrieved (image) form; (5) the

Introduction 227

elaboration of consciousness and memory functions; (6) the origin of the emotional system; (7) the origin of the imaginative function; (8) the development of anticipatory ability; (9) volition; (10) thinking and understanding; (11) the increasing ability to store automatically performable learned motor programs; and (12) the origin and development of language capability.

Although the principles of organic evolution are now well understood, the application of this knowledge in accounting for particular organs and functions is largely conjectural.

There are no absolutes in organic nature. There is always the chance of exceptions being found to the principles we formulate, because these principles were derived by sampling nature and nature can never be more than partially seen. We may infer, we may judge and balance, we may imagine and invent, but we must do so under the guidance of the following principles:

(1) Until shown otherwise any property found in all members of a species may be presumed to exist because it contributed to the survival and/or reproductive success of that species' ancestral line.

(2) Such properties are therefore genetically based.

(3) All organs and functions had the simplest of beginnings.

(4) From these simple origins they evolved to their present level of complexity by very small steps, each increase in complexity providing enough difference for the forces of selection to be operative.

(5) A confined population within an unchanging niche will evolve toward maximum fitness for that niche.

(6) A niche change, or isolation of part of a population in a slightly different niche, will offer an opportunity for some variations to confer selective advantages. In particular this applies to variations in specific structures and functions which allow these to be more effective under the new niche conditions. This may lead to explosive evolutionary change.

(7) Ineradicable epiphenomena (obligate side-effects) may, under changed niche conditions, contribute to differential survival and become targets for (indirect) selection. This principle may underlie many of the major breakthroughs in evolution, including some features of the mind (for which it is invoked in this study in attempting to explain some of the most crucial breakthroughs leading to the mind of man). Such breakthroughs may also lead to extremely rapid evolutionary development.

(8) Where a new adjustment of structure or function

offers very strong survival and competitive advantages any variations in that direction, even those that are roundabout or involve costs not otherwise sustainable, will tend to be selected.

(9) In complex, multifaceted systems with much inter-dependence of constituent elements, and therefore having elaborate control mechanisms ensuring coherent performance, the elements commonly participate in different functions, i.e., show versatile responses to different kinds and sources of input, and variations in these allow nature to respond to changed niche conditions with faster rates of evolution than is possible with simpler, more uniform systems. For example, a complex behavior may be supported and carried by several anatomical, physiological, and hormonal elements each of which will be under its own genetic control and therefore exhibit individual variations; the whole package is therefore much more able to adjust to changed niche conditions than simpler systems.

(10) The 'upward-spiral' (or 'leap-frog') principle may be stated as follows: Improvement in any part of a complex system by conferring greater efficiency on the system may open up new avenues of functioning which will confer greater selective value on improvements in other parts of the system.

(11) The level of genetic variability is a limiting factor on the rate of evolutionary adaptation.

(12) Parsimony – "that no more causes or forces should be assumed than are necessary to account for the facts" (Concise Oxford Dictionary) – requires the committal of the least amount of genetic material to evolutionary adaptation.

(13) Pragmatism: Success (in individual survival and genetic continuance) is the only criterion for selection of a phenotypic variation.

(14) Conservatism (conservation): As a system evolves in complexity it retains its simpler stages, both in structure and function, with a minimum of modification. But:

(15) Usurpation of function: As a new, more complex structure evolves, first by elaboration of, then separation from, its primitive antecedent to provide greater sophistication of function, the latter may cease to provide its simple version of that function. (This contrasts with the conservation principle).

(16) A multifaceted system may be under an overall genetic control in addition to the numerous genetic controls over its individual parts. This

may allow duplication 'in one go' of the whole system, i.e., from sense organ to central processing mechanisms; e.g., most visual systems are composed of large numbers of single, complete systems in parallel, the numbers varying among individuals in each species.

(17) Interconnections for cooperative functioning between systems are less likely to form de novo the more highly evolved the systems: if interconnections are not present at the preceding stage of a newly complex system they may never subsequently be possible. In addition, various factors may constrain the elaboration of existing interconnections as the evolution of complexity proceeds.

(18) Contingent factors may influence the entire direction of evolutionary development; e.g., the rostral positioning of sense organs in the neuraxis (adaptive in food seekers) constrained their central pathways and synaptic relays to be in close proximity, giving rise to the thalamic conglomerate and allowing the multiplication of sensory and reticular interconnections leading to advanced brains.

(19) Phylogenetically older parts of structures are generally simpler in cytoarchitecture and more resistant to adverse conditions than superstructures added to them by later evolution.

(20) 'Paragenesis': The genome will allow randomness in final neuronal configurations in foetal and postnatal development if the serendipitous results are sufficiently often beneficial.

(21) In various systems during ontogeny (e.g., cerebral cortex, retina (Chalupa, 1995:45)), foetal features disappear, or are reduced, or stop functioning. These may be phylogenetically ancient features that have become vestigial or redundant in the adult.

There is still much controversy among evolutionary biologists, palaeontologists, and others on how speciation comes about (Mayr, 1988). The details need not concern us here, but two main ideas, which are not mutually exclusive, are (1) *sympatric* speciation, also know as vertical evolution, whereby a whole population changes within itself (as would be seen by snapshots taken at long intervals of time) in response to changed conditions, various mechanisms being proposed to account for this, and (2) *allopatric* speciation, also know as horizontal evolution, in which from a parent population *small* breeding groups become geographically separated then evolve divergently from the parental group in adaptation to different conditions (e.g. Darwin's Galapagos finches).

2.1 THE ORIGIN OF CONSCIOUSNESS AND MEMORY

(1) At some period in the evolution of living forms at least one line developed the ability to generate consciousness. This marked the origin of mind. Inasmuch as mental functioning is performed by neural structures of the brain with consciousness being central to the process, and inasmuch as this complex apparatus evolved from the simplest of beginnings, we can consider as arbitrary any placing of the origin of 'mind' at some stage between the first appearance of consciousness and the emergence of man.

(2) Consciousness is generated in specialized nervous tissue, presumably by a particular type of metabolic process within that tissue. This metabolism must have become greatly elaborated in the course of its evolution, but it may still retain the basic structure that generated the first unit of consciousness.

(3) We must attribute to the genetic base underlying those primitive cellular properties which led to conductivity and nervous function the potential for change resulting in the generation of consciousness. For such a change in the genetic constitution to be retained and further developed in descendant generations it must have been of value to the individual.

(4) We may presume that the benefit conferred by consciousness was that it permitted the organism to respond more appropriately to, or to finer details of, environmental situations. One possibility of how this was achieved is that environmental agencies (light, heat, etc) acting on the organism stimulated the nascent consciousness metabolism to generate units of consciousness which on reconversion to neural energy *augmented* contractile responses (Sherrington, 1947, expressed a similar view). It may have had this effect *by acting as an amplifier* in one of two ways: by adding its energy to the more primitive non-conscious reflex trigger, resulting in faster and more definite response, or by magnifying slight differences in non-conscious impulse energy by virtue of major differences in the consciousness produced, these differences in turn being more reliably applicable in producing discriminating responses.

(5) At this first stage consciousness helps in triggering genetically determined reflexive responses. It is simply part of an inherited reflexive system, the contribution it makes resulting in greater effectiveness and discrimination of response. *It acts as a servomechanism.*

In the most advanced nervous systems the external world is represented in consciousness, and so is the organism itself: the global unitary consciousness consists both of elements representing an external world and a self, and in this world of consciousness when the surrogate self acts upon the surrogate world effects are produced within the corporeal organism which direct its actions upon the external world. It is in the surrogate world of consciousness and its associated cognitive functions that protocols for more effective relations between the corporeal self and the external world are established. The representative conscious system therefore acts as a highly complex reflex circuit piggyback on, and therefore parallel to, the non-conscious reflexive system − it interacts with the external world at second hand. Sperry (1977) enlarged upon this idea.

(6) It must be hypothesized (in order to account for the origin of a memory function) that subsequent genetic changes resulted in a certain degree of plasticity in the biochemistry of the primitive consciousness-assisted reflex arc, allowing the response to the triggering to become more sensitive with repetition (Levitan and Kaczmarek,1991:160). Further development along these lines would then have resulted in a process in which the first exposure to the pertinent environmental property primes but does not yet trigger the reflex circuit, the consciousness generated by this first exposure doing the priming, and subsequent exposure both strengthens the priming (or imprinting) and triggers the response, also via the energetic servomechanism of generated consciousness.

(7) Such circuits, 'imprintable' and triggerable in part by conscious experience, being of selective value increased in number and range. They were, it is hypothezised, the origin of the acquired memory function, which later became specialized to serve two separate functions: that of motor skill acquisition and that of image memory.

At this stage three reflexive systems may be present in the same organism: (a) Non-conscious reflexes, which though limited in versatility are potentially capable of evolving increasing complexity; (b) the latter augmented by conscious activity, requiring only simple maturation of the daughter organism to become operative; and (c) the reflex that requires priming by conscious experience before it can become responsive on subsequent exposure to the same experience, thus constituting the primordium of memory function.

(8) The formation of a memory is an energetic process. The fact that conscious experience invariably precedes the establishment of memory is therefore *prima facie* evidence that consciousness is energetic. However, since there are always measurable neural impulses associated with consciousness we may be justified, as a practical matter, in ignoring consciousness and taking note only of neural impulses. But there is evidence that in advanced brains neural impulses activate two cortical systems, one that is suppressed by light barbiturate anaesthesia with loss of consciousness and behavioral response, and the other unaffected by this agent and presumably supportive of primitive, non-conscious reflexive functions. From this it may be argued that in the former case impulses instigate the generation of consciousness through physico-chemical means (Jasper, 1981).

Johnson (1990) discussed the development of cortical anatomy in relation to visual performance in early infancy. Layers 5 and 6 of primary visual cortex have been shown to mature first. At this stage, before other cortical layers appear, they respond to geniculate input by engaging primitive visual reflexes via connections to superior colliculi and brainstem centres. Layer 4 and other superficial layers mature later with connections to the middle temporal area and frontal eye fields.

In my scheme these upper cortical layers are largely concerned with functions associated with consciousness and have many other connections for cognitive functions besides voluntary eye movements, such as memory, the 'focusing' (or selective generation) of consciousness, innate and acquired recognition-responses, emotional elicitations, thinking, etc. These later-maturing upper layers are of more recent evolutionary origin and may be expected to be more intricate and delicate and sensitive to adverse conditions such as anoxia and anaesthesia than the more ancient deeper layers.

Although neurophysiology can say much about the brain without mentioning consciousness it may eventually reach the point where it ceases to give worthwhile answers, further progress then depending on working with consciousness and its unique properties.

Fig. 2.1(1) **The prototypical reflex circuit**

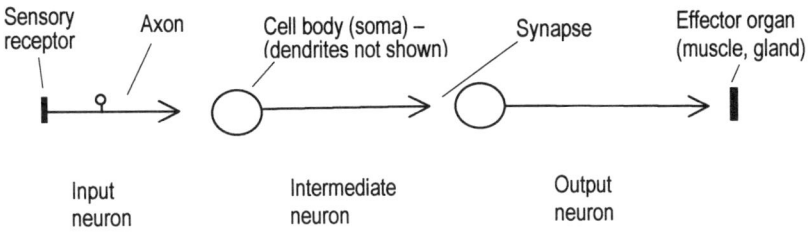

Fig. 2.1(2) **Servo-assisted reflex circuit (origin of recognition-memory)**

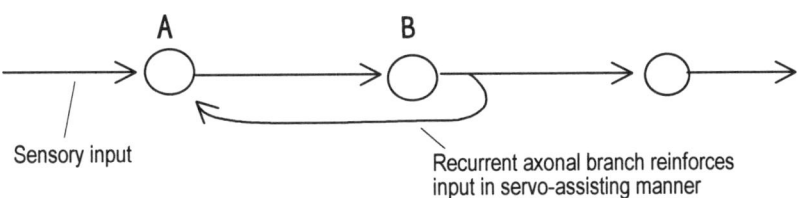

At some evolutionary stage neuron A (in the rostral part of the primordial nervous system) became specialized to generate consciousness, and neuron B to be altered by impulse energy from A, in part due (as proposed in this work) to reverse transduction of consciousness. This alteration of B is the memory 'trace', and is no more than a heightened sensitivity, or lowering of firing threshold, to input energy.

Thus the consciousness-memory system derives from the basic reflex arc. It is further proposed that chance genetic variations produced branches of B's axon growing toward A, resulting in additional impulse energy to A when B fires, thereby reinforcing in a servo-assisting manner A's effect on B, with resulting improvement in performance sufficient to become a target for selection. Subsequent activation of B (from any source) would result not only in reflex action but also reactivation of A. The combined effect of sensory input and recurrent activation equates to 'recognition' of the stimulus.

In advanced central nervous systems the sensory cortex is the only structure with this type of recurrent axonal branch back to a putative consciousness-generating neuron. It may be noted that axons of mitral and tufted cells of the olfactory bulb have similar recurrent branches, providing additional evidence that the bulb is the earliest sensory cortex and very likely where primary olfactory consciousness is generated.

Fig. 2.1(3) **Origin of inter-memory retrievability**

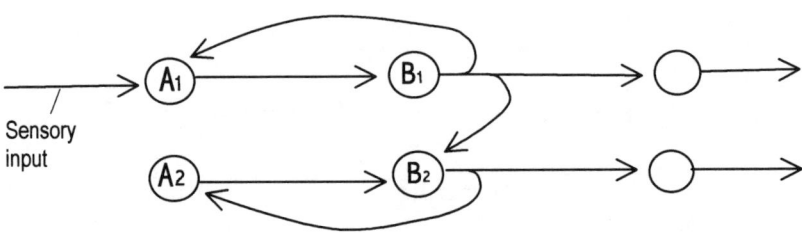

Memory neuron B1 sends a branch axon to memory neuron B2 which in turn, via its recurrent axonal branch, activates its own consciousness-generating neuron A2. Thus, sensory activation of A1 will result in indirect memory retrieval from B2 to image consciousness in A2.

Fig. 2.1(4) **Conversion of memory system at stage in above figure to a specialized system**

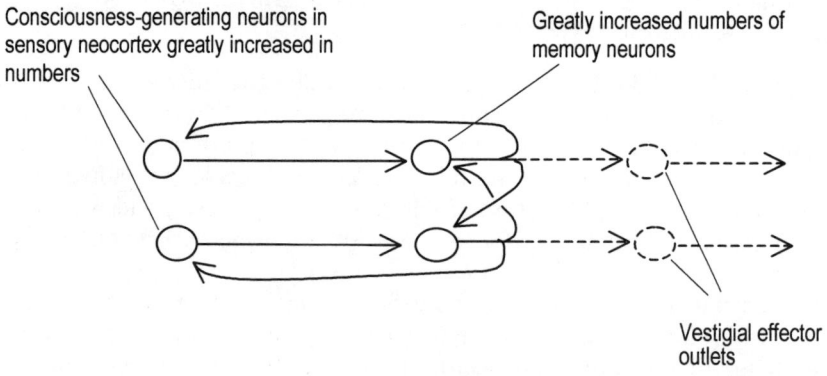

Due to the high value of an advanced memory system in a species set on the evolutionary course of reliance on cognitive mechanisms (i.e., its mind) in niche adaptation, it is hypothesized that genetic variations coding for proliferation of semifunctional, supernumerary consciousness-driven reflex circuits tended to be selected, and the output (effector) neurons of these became increasingly non-functional, underdeveloped, or uncoded for in proportion to the expansion of the memory function, to the point of becoming vestigial and disappearing.

It must be noted, however, that primitive reflexive circuits including those in cortex driven or augmented by consciousness, continued to be fully functional, particularly those mediating innate responses to vital cues.

Fig.2.1(5) **The origin of separate, consciousness–driven effector outlets**

It is further hypothesized that there was concomitant divergent specialization from the stage in fig. 2.1(3) giving the consciousness-generating neurons separate access to downline effector systems:

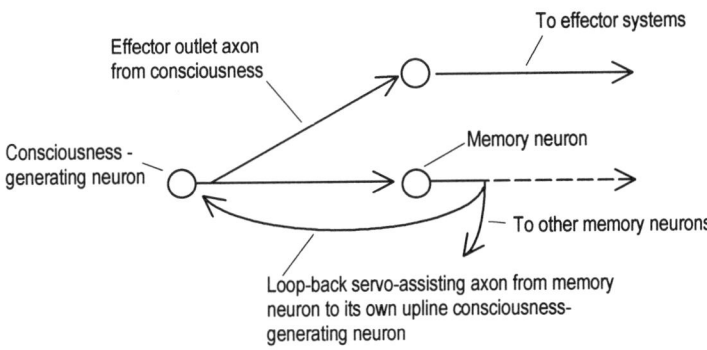

Thus, from the stage of the primordial reflex arc various primitive reflexes were retained; then came more complex non-conscious reflexive systems without memory function; then out of these a primitive servo-assisted feed-back mechanism, at which stage the reflex arc functioned both as an effector outlet and a (conscious) recognition-memory system. Next came wider connections, direct and indirect, between memory neurons permitting memory retrievability; and, finally, conversion to a dual system, one specialized for internal functions with loss of effector outlets, the other specialized to access and activate downline effector mechanisms from the consciousness-generating neurons.

Fig.2.1(6) **The neural basis of intermemory associations**

(a)

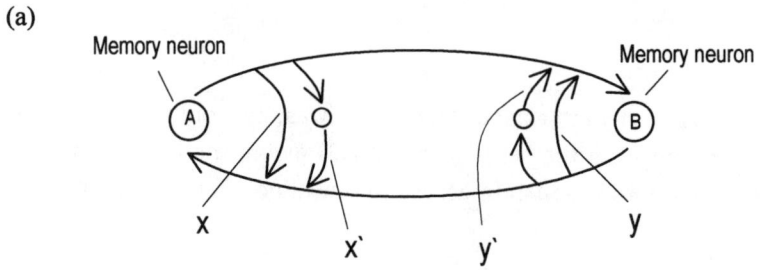

Memory neurons A and B are nearly simultaneously active. They reinforce one another's signals either by impulses through axon branches x and y, or interneurons x` and y`

(b)

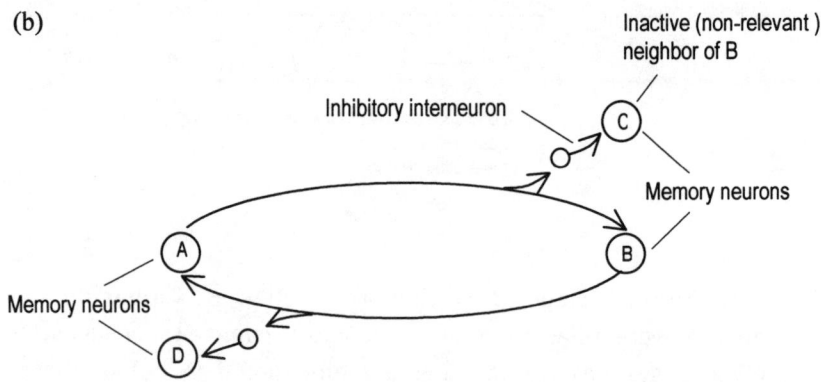

A and B are nearly simultaneously active with mutual strengthening of their synaptic bonds. Neighboring inactive memory neurons C and D 'holding' non-relevant memories may be specifically inhibited from incidental activation ('noise') to sharpen the clarity of the relevant memory elicitation.

Note that in this set-up A and B had previously become 'associated' as in (a), so that activation of either would now tend to elicit the other, but more sharply so if stray (irrelevant) elicitations are prevented or reduced.

Fig. 2.1(7)   'Internal' and 'external' memory linkages

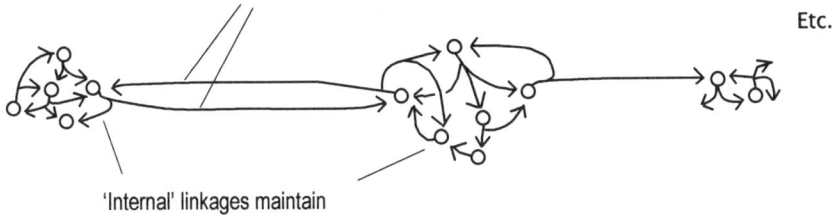

'External' linkages allow mutual retrieval of discrete memories in same or other modalities.

Etc.

'Internal' linkages maintain discrete (object/event) memories.

Activation of any neuron belonging to a group holding a discrete memory will strongly tend to activate all other members of that group via their strongly facilitated ('internal') mutual synaptic linkages. Activation of such a group may or may not elicit other memories via their weak ('external') linkages. Inter-modality linkages are all 'external'.

Fig. 2.1(8)   The final evolutionary configuration of the consciousness-generating and memory storage systems: their cooperative and separate functions

Consciousness-generating neurons: neuronal bridge supports consciousness syncytium (i.e., the unity of consciousness)

To effector systems

To other consciousness-generating neurons or to effector systems

Memory neuron and its servo-assisting axonal branch back to its consciousness-generating neuron

Memory neuron

To other memory neurons

2.2 ORIGIN OF THE LINKAGE SYSTEMS OF MEMORY

(1) Mutations resulting in the functional linkage of adjacent reflex circuits would allow several simultaneously occurring stimuli to have a single response, in effect constituting pattern recognition. All three reflexive systems may benefit from such linkage. Environmental features or events which have significance for the members of a lineage may, over evolutionary time, become 'recognizable', such recognition being evidenced by appropriate reflexive activity.

Functional linkages between individual reflex circuits may have taken several forms and have had several consequences (see Shepherd, 1990, for a full treatment of this subject): 1/ The exit pathways of adjacent reflex circuits merge so that two inputs produce one output (Fig.2.2(a)).

This may have the effect of allowing weaker stimuli through summation to produce the same response as a previously stronger stimulus. Also slightly dissimilar stimuli occurring together may trigger a response, widening the range of pattern recognition. 2/ Branching of the input segment with connections to adjacent units (Fig.2.2(b)).

This may allow a single input to have a wider response, especially in proportion to strength of input. 3/ The basic structural unit, the individual cell, was maintained in the evolution of the linkage systems, its association with other cellular units remaining essentially functional. The functional unit, the reflex arc, came to be composed of multiple structural units, prototypically three: the input, the intermediate, and the output. Subsequent multiplication of intermediate units permitted greater versatility of response.

(2) At about this stage some *inter-circuit linkages* may as a result of genetic changes have displayed 'openness' ('imprintability','plasticity'), in that priming by exposure to the relevant environmental features is required before pattern recognition can begin to occur. Signal passage through and between such circuits brings about lasting changes in molecular configurations, leading to both easier signal passage and to increased sensitivity of response.

Some randomness in the configuration and imprintability of such open linkages in the conscious reflexive system would allow an increased range and therefore some uniqueness in pattern recognition to occur, at first of a very limited nature but capable of elaboration to encompass more dissimilar environmental features if such randomness is genetically

Fig.2.2 The origin of inter-arc connectivities

(a)

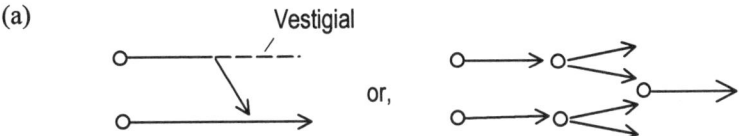

In these arrangements two separate reflex arcs, by genetic mutation, channel their energy to a single outlet, with the result that sensory stimuli that were formerly too weak to produce a response may now do so.

(b)

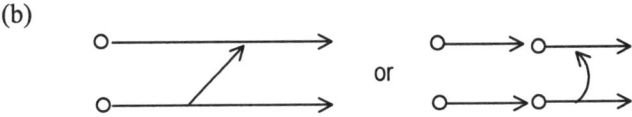

And is these arrangements a single arc, strongly activated, may spread its activation to provide a wider response.

These examples, which may well have been the primordia of reflex circuit interaction, illustrate one of the two most fundamental principles of nervous system functioning and evolution: variations in connectivities between reflex circuits are potentially limitless, providing equally limitless varieties of function available to the winnowing process of natural selection. This principle, together with the other of the two most fundamental principles, viz. that neuronal interaction is either excitatory or inhibitory, accounts for all control functions of nervous systems. Between them they determine how the organism's metabolic energy is utilized in responding to the challenges of life.

determined (i.e. if genetic determination *allows* such randomness) and is of selective value.

(3) The organism now has the ability to learn, i.e. to acquire responses to unique patterns of environmental stimuli during its lifetime. To what extent a species is able to learn is dependent on the number and variety of its 'open' reflex circuits (or 'arcs') and 'open' linkages between such circuits. These are genetically determined, with some allowable randomness during final maturation, and are constrained in their expression and further development by their degree of compatibility with other phenotypic features contributing to niche fitness and by inherent limits in genetic variability.

(4) Species may now be classified as (a) those with purely non-conscious reflex systems, (b) those with the latter plus consciousness-mediated but genetically fixed reflexes, (c) those with these two systems plus circuits that require priming by specific conscious experience to become operational, and (d) those with these three systems plus an 'open' system permitting limited learning; that is, the ability to be primed by unique patterns of stimuli.

While in theory all levels of reflexivity utilizing consciousness may be present in the same organism we have evidence through introspection and verbal report of only that involving a memory system. If the energy of consciousness helps drive some lower level reflexive activity we cannot demonstrate or attest its existence as it is not part of the global, unitary consciousness, has no access to retrievable memory storage (as the reflex it serves has not been converted to this function but remains purely effector), and has no access to verbal witness. Only the elucidation of the biochemistry of consciousness generation would be able to settle this matter.

Genetic variability and expression are dependent on many factors, and among the different species these factors vary. It is genetic variability that permits evolutionary change, and the nature of the variability will in part determine the direction of such changes. In the line that led to organisms with highly developed minds there was presumably much variability in the genetic material coding for the metabolism of consciousness, as well as for the imprintability or synaptic plasticity of reflex circuits, and for the connectivity between circuits. There must also have been niche factors favouring the continued elaboration of primitive learning capabilities. (The linkage systems of memory are more fully discussed in Section 2.8).

2.3 ORIGIN OF RECOGNITION MEMORY AND MEMORY RETRIEVAL

(1) It is postulated that at some stage a mutational breakthrough occurred which was to prove crucial for the further development of the mind. This led to the evolution of a loop-back connection from a downline section of the consciousness-assisted reflex arc to the more proximal consciousness-generating section, creating a mechanism which, it is hypothesized, improved the appropriateness and sensitivity of response of the reflex. *We are forced to postulate some such mechanism in order to account for memory retrieval.* And the idea for the origin of *conscious recognition* from the operation of this mechanism follows naturally – and conveniently, as otherwise we would have difficulty in accounting for the evolution of higher mental functioning.

We hypothesize that some loop-back connection developed out of a side effect of consciousness-mediated reflexive activity, in that at this primitive level with perhaps poor insulation of the operating parts stray or 'echo' electro-chemical activity during operation of the reflex might seep back to minimally activate the consciousness metabolism, sufficiently so to augment the impulses still coming in from the external stimuli, with the result that the now enhanced consciousness energy (i.e. more units of consciousness per unit of time) would more powerfully activate the reflex. (In modern nervous systems astrocytes "may serve to restrain ... the spread of electrical disturbances through the neuropil" – Barr and Kiernan, 1988:30). See Fig.2.1(2)

This feedback 'servo-mechanism' would have two possible benefits: The more nearly identical the current external stimulus to the original one which 'fixed' the open reflex the more likely that the reflex threshold would be overcome and the stronger would be the echo or loop-back activity to augment the reflex, so in effect it makes the response more appropriate to the external event; and secondly, relevant stimuli that may be too weak to overcome the reflex threshold may yet by partial activation of the unit result in the echo feedback and reinforcement – sufficient now to overcome the firing threshold.

It may be argued that because of the all-or-none principle applying to action potentials due to depolarization of nerve cells there could not be any grading in the postulated loop-back impulse. But impulses of low frequency through a few synapses may yet by temporal summation cause depolarization.

It may further be argued that the sensory receptor for a reflex arc can only be sensitive to one type of stimulus and dissimilar stimuli cannot have an effect on the arc. However, even for the simple single reflex arc slightly dissimilar stimuli may be able to overcome the firing threshold though perhaps at a lower firing rate, but with several dissimilar stimuli comprising some environmental feature, of which each individual stimulus is able to activate only one kind of receptor and its specific reflex arc, somewhat dissimilar *patterns* of that feature will produce graded responses due to different degrees of activation of the individual arcs.

(2) To the extent that loop-back reinforcement was beneficial and to the extent that it had a genetic basis, it would have tended to evolve through natural selection. It is not difficult to envisage the gradual evolutionary development of a physical structure with an increasingly efficient feedback function, and such may have been the origin of the recurrent collateral axonal branches from pyramidal cells in the deep neocortical layers back to the superficial.

Whether recognition memory or retrievable memory existed in archi- and paleocortex prior to the evolution of neocortex is not known, nor for sensory thalamus prior to the origin of cerebral hemispheres. Recognition memory for odours is well-developed in many species and thought to be carried out by paleocortex of the rhinencephalon. Whether an axonal loop-back function exists in paleocortex has apparently not been determined, but it is doubtful that true retrievable memory exists for odours, even in humans – we cannot *re-experience* odours from memory, although we can readily *recognize* odours previously experienced.

It seems that when we try to remember odours we retrieve the context of odours mainly in the form of visual imagery, in the same manner as we remember specific pains without *feeling* pain, although we can readily *recognize* a particular type of pain when re-experienced, which again may be a function of recognizing the context. When we re-experience an odour numerous memory associations may be activated, which can only be the case if the cells generating the odour consciousness have facilitated synaptic linkages with other sensory modalities, but the reverse activation does not occur: we may easily retrieve the memories associated with an odour (its name, source, etc.) but these never result in the actual experience of the odour.

Odour hallucinations occur in 'uncinate' fits and are known to rival sensory olfaction in strength and to carry conviction of sensory reality. If these are centrally generated they must come either from direct stimulation of experiential cells (or of afferent fibres to these) or from a memory source, and only by means of reentrant connections can the latter occur.

(3) The loop-back activation of the consciousness-generating neuronal metabolism would generate the same consciousness as the sensory stimulus. It would be the same basic kind or variety or quality of consciousness – blue if blue, red if red, etc.

(4) It is hypothesized that this process of reinforcement by its effect on the consciousness-generating metabolism may give an additional quality to the combined consciousness, which is experienced as a 'feeling' of familiarity and is thus an embellishment of recognition memory. This heightened recognition would therefore be a subtle alteration in the quality of consciousness which occurs when the servomechanism of loop-back reinforcement takes place. This is distinct from vegetative 'recognition' which is the engagement of a reflex function (innate or acquired) without the participation of consciousness and which is evidenced by the occurrence of some response; feedback circuits in such reflexive systems have other functions, for example the monitoring and controlling of the performance through non-conscious mechanisms.

(5) Such an alteration in the *quality* of consciousness (giving the 'aura' of familiarity) would be a by-product of a useful function: an ineradicable epiphenomenon in that it does not have a separate genetic basis. It would probably have remained of no value for tens of millions of years before the evolutionary process was able to use it (indirectly) in the higher development of the mind.

(6) It may seem far-fetched to assign the subjective property of familiarity, which is the characteristic element of human conscious recognition, to the proposed loop-back reinforcement of the consciousness-mediated reflex circuit, but it must have had a start somewhere. Although at the human level the act of recognition, consisting of a 'feeling' of familiarity, is commonly embroidered by

various memory retrievals and emotional and motor elicitations, it is proposed that the essential act itself does not involve these but is the result of interaction between *each one* of the great number of consciousness-generating neurons making up even simple perceptions and *its own* memory unit.

It is an alternative possibility that the sense of familiarity which accompanies recognition memory at the human level is elicited downline in the limbic system, evolved through its effectiveness in alerting the mind to the recognized object or situation; that is, the basic loop-back reinforcement which originally evolved to servo-assist the reflex arc allowed the evolution of retrievable memory and was ipso facto a recognition memory system, without additional functions that a later evolved sense or 'feeling' of familiarity, elicited in the limbic system, eventually led to.

Whether the percept is complex or very simple the process underlying recognition memory is the same, in theory down to the unit level. Recognition of complex perceptual objects as wholes rather than their parts may be due to the strong 'internal' memory linkages combining the parts into a whole so that when the complex object is re-experienced it retrieves its complete memory image with a resulting massive recognition due to coalescence of individual units of consciousness into a composite, unitary consciousness. (See M.E.Smith,1993, for an experimental investigation of this topic).

This may explain why objects, composed of features separately experienced in other contexts, may fail to elicit any recognition when encountered for the first time: the subfeatures will be recognized but they elicit only a mild sense of familiarity in comparison with that elicited by a complete object which is present in memory as such; that is, with its subelements combined by strong 'internal' synaptic linkages.

The 'internal' linkages (potentiated synapses) which hold an object in memory may not be engaged if the features of the object are camouflaged, as too many irrelevant linkages are engaged by the camouflaging material. Once a sufficient number of the object's constituent parts are recognized, perhaps by chance, there usually follows a massive engagement of the remainder by the recognition process. The camouflaging set-up now becomes part of the memory store and is itself recognized on re-encounter with easy recognition of the object.

2.3 Origin of Recognition Memory and Memory Retrieval

(7) *It is this loop-back servo-mechanism, together with inter-memory linkages, that makes memory retrieval possible.* A long-term memory is a molecular change (potentiation) in a specialized downline neuron and its synaptic connections caused by (as inferred from prima facie evidence) the energy of consciousness – no consciousness, no memory. This neuron on subsequent activation sends impulses via its axon and axonal branches (1) back to the consciousness-generating neuron upline from it with which it is developmentally and functionally associated, (2) via synaptic linkages to other memory neurons which in their turn may be activated, and (3) to effector mechanisms if access to these is present and not inhibited. Therefore the only way that a dormant memory can be indirectly retrieved (as opposed to direct retrieval by reexposure to the original sensory experience) is by activation of its neuronal base by other currently active memory neurons via previously enhanced (potentiated) synaptic linkages. Each memory neuron indirectly activated in this way will, via its own loop-back connection, cause specific units of consciousness – the memory image – to be generated.

(8) These ideas seem incontrovertible. It cannot be denied that what is remembered are the details of conscious experience: we can briefly see an object and much later, from memory, draw or paint it with accuracy, or hear a musical piece and replay it from memory. Neurons in the brain must somehow, from the sensory input, generate the conscious experience and other neurons must in some manner store this experience and be able to recreate the conscious experience, albeit rather faintly. Furthermore, the conscious experience that is thus stored and reproduced need not be a primary sensory experience, but may be an act of imagination or a dream. Some neural mechanisms must exist for all this and must function along lines essentially no different from what is put forward here.

One problem, touched on in (2) above, concerns the memory of physical feelings: the memory does not reproduce the actual feeling, as one might expect it should if the theory is valid. We can certainly remember having a pain, or even something of the quality of the pain, but that memory is not a re-experience of the pain. If the pain we feel is generated by consciousness-generating neurons, that is, if certain specialized neurons on being activated generate pain consciousness and these neurons are activated by loop-back impulses from their memory neurons we should experience the same pain, albeit more faintly, but evidently we do not. A possible explanation is that primitive physical feelings are generated in phylogenetically older parts of the brain and their reflex downline neurons have no memory function, therefore no loop-back mechanism, so the feeling experienced cannot be re-experienced via activation of context memories in the retrievable memory system. However, the feeling experienced is part of the global unitary consciousness of the moment and the entire *context* of the feeling experience is established in retrievable memory. When we recollect a painful incident, e.g. a toothache, we re-experience everything except the actual pain, but something of the quality of the pain is re-experienced, perhaps because it was selectively advantageous that the subsequently evolved consciousness-memory system was able to produce variations in the consciousness spectrum that represented pain. We can therefore remember everything about a painful experience, including the pain, without feeling the pain. Likewise with emotional feelings: we can remember the characteristics of the emotion without feeling it, but this must be distinguished from reeliciting the emotion through imagination or recollection of the type of situation that causes it, in which case the actual emotional feeling is re-generated in the limbic-diencephalic emotional system.

(9) "The study of the circuitry of the cortex has been extremely difficult and seemingly hopeless" (Colonnier, 1981:145). "It has long been known that the thalamus projects to mammalian sensory cortex but the identity of those cortical neurons which directly receive thalamic input is largely unknown" (White, 1981:153). However, new labelling techniques have greatly increased knowledge of the fine structure of the cerebral cortex, and enough detail is established to allow some conjecture at correlating the functions of consciousness and memory with particular cortical elements. It should hardly be necessary to argue that neuronal elements of sensory neocortex are concerned in some way with consciousness and memory, and that those of 'association' and motor cortex with orchestrating in some manner these functions or serving as executive agents in various cognitive acts.

Briefly, sensory projections to primary cortical areas from the thalamus synapse largely in layer 4 on stellate cells, of which there are several varieties, although there are relatively few morphological types of synapses. Layer 4 of mammalian primary sensory cortex is characterized by (1) a high concentration of small stellate cells whose

2.3 Origin of Recognition Memory and Memory Retrieval

dendrites are mostly spiny and mostly have their arborization in this layer, and (2) by a dense axonal plexus containing large numbers of thalamic cortical afferents. Although cells in other layers have dendritic roots in layer 4 and probably receive direct thalamic input (White 1981:154) we may provisionally assume, on face value, and as an exercise in heuristics, that specialized stellate cells generate consciousness. (The fact that we cannot begin to guess how they might do so is beside the point; we are simply attempting to narrow the locality of consciousness generation from somewhere inside the skull, and from somewhere in the cerebrum, to particular neurons in the cerebral cortex).

Axonal output of the stellate cells of layer 4 project to other layers and synapse with dendritic roots belonging to pyramidal cells mainly residing in the deeper layers. Axons of these pyramidal cells leave the cortex for ipsilateral and contralateral cortical destinations, for reciprocation with the thalamus, and for deeper cerebral and brainstem centres. We may provisionally assign memory function to some unknown subclass of pyramidal cells, probably in layer 6, which typically have recurrent axonal branches arborizing in more superficial layers, especially layers 4 and 5 (Lund 1981:107). We may tentatively assign memory retrieval and recognition functions to such loop-back axonal branches.

According to Gilbert and Wiesel (1981:184): "The rich projection from layer 6 to layer 4 suggests that some properties manifested by layer 4 cells may not depend solely on convergence of geniculate input onto layer 4 cells or on connections made by those cells within the layer". Although Gilbert and Wiesel then suggest a role for this loop-back projection in terms of "orientation specificity, preference for direction of stimulus movement", its possible role in memory retrieval is very striking, and it is the strongest candidate for such a function among all the cortical cells.

According to Colonnier (1981:145) it can be concluded from the evidence that the incoming thalamocortical afferents terminate directly on (1) output cells, (2) excitatory interneurons, and (3) inhibitory interneurons, and that some of the excitatory interneurons with long vertical axons containing the powerful vasoactive intestinal polypeptide (VIP) would spread the focus of excitation in a columnar fashion through the layers of the cortex. Concerning these (VIP) interneurons, however, it is not clear which thalamic cells are involved: if these belong to the ascending reticular activating (the generalized thalamocortical) system it would represent further evidence for the role of the latter in the modulation of consciousness.

In support of the hypothesis that memory is served by neurons in the same cortical columns as those generating consciousness may be cited the report (Zeki, 1992) that bilateral destruction of prestriate cortical area V4 results not only in loss of colour vision but also of the ability to remember or even imagine colour.

It may also be noted, apropos Colonnier's conclusions, that these support the idea that sensory cortex may function at two levels of reflexivity: non-consciously via the deeper layers, and consciously via layer 4. As mentioned in section 2.1(8) this idea receives further support from the finding that under light barbituate anaesthesia and in synchronized sleep, during which all forms of consciousness as well as organized behavioral responses are absent, evoked potentials from sensory stimulation are recordable in the cortical sensory receiving areas (Jasper, 1981), the inference from this being that non-conscious neural activity being more primitive and robust is able to continue, while the metabolism supporting consciousness being more highly evolved is more delicate and vulnerable.

2.4   THE ORIGIN OF MENTAL PROCESSING MECHANISMS

(1) A crucial breakthrough in the early evolution of mind may have been the introduction of a delay in effector triggering so that the firing threshold may be overcome by the combined input of diverse stimuli. This represents a gathering of information so that action when it occurs is likely to be more appropriate. In theory any of the four reflexive systems may be involved but increasingly it would tend to be the consciousness-mediated systems and particularly the learning system. As organisms evolve to be able to recognize (innately or through learning) more complex environmental situations more 'processing' of sensory information is required. This takes time during which action must be delayed. In the course of the evolution of mental processing mechanisms there will be in operation two conflicting selection pressures: that demanding speed of processing for rapid response, and that demanding maximum extraction of information for more appropriate response.

(2) Mental processing requires that certain operations be performed on incoming data so that the eventual form action takes is more

appropriate to the individual's interests in a wider context than is achievable by sub-mental reflexive systems. In earlier evolutionary stages this processing operates solely on real-time sensory input, but further evolutionary development enabled the individual's past experience to be a guide in the handling of the current data. This at the highest mammalian level is the exercise of the thinking function in the generation of understandings. This is an internal process of the brain which proceeds isolated from the effector systems indefinitely, this isolation presumably being achieved by a highly evolved inhibitory mechanism on the motor pathways from the mind.

(3) The early stage in the evolution of processing by the central nervous system was perhaps that at which the beginning of very elaborate neuronal mechanisms may have occurred, such as inhibitory influences among the different reflexive systems, the coordination of responses to input from the different sensory systems, the focusing mechanisms of consciousness, the development of increasing cerebral control of more specific motor activities, and the increasing ability to acquire, through learning, reflexly triggerable, automatically performable neuro-muscular programs, all or most of which made possible, much later, the evolution of the functions of thinking, intending, willing, understanding, etc.

The position at this stage must be considered as being important for experimental neuroscience, for here begins the elaboration towards that complexity which in advanced brains is almost impossible to penetrate when tackled without the aid of a simple, correct theoretical model of the mind. It is also therefore important for neurology and neuropsychology which labour under great difficulties in attempting to satisfactorily explain many of the cognitive defects accompanying brain damage and disease.

As mentioned earlier (Section 1·33) functional complexity of brain mechanisms may be amenable to modelling by mathematical, mechanical, or electronic techniques. Such complexity is in detail beyond the grasp of unaided visualization, and our thinking and understanding powers cannot keep pace with more than two or three interacting influences each of which may be continually varying in response to outside factors as well as feed-back from the interactions with one another and from the varying effects the resultant output of the system has on related systems. If functional complexity has a unitary correspondence with anatomical complexity the task of simulation by any means may be beyond achievement, when one considers the up to one hundred thousand synaptic connections that each of the brain's estimated one hundred billion neurons has with other neurons, but the beginnings at least should be understandable by the methods of mathematical and cybernetic engineering of the right kind, and this should be able to take us into some detail.

2.5 THE BEGINNING OF HIGHER MENTAL FUNCTIONING

(1) Mind at this level – i.e. a conscious system capable of limited learning, with an emerging ability to discriminate between some environmental particulars, a slight increase in the versatility of responses, and a limited ability to delay response while information is gathered – may have persisted relatively unchanged for tens of millions of years with slow elaboration to the level of the advanced pre-mammalian vertebrates.

(2) From this point evolutionary development to a higher level of mental functioning begins. The pre-adaptations are all in place. What now occurred was typical evolutionary progression and was presumably in response to the challenges of new niche conditions. Further elaboration of these pre-adaptations would allow the animal to establish through learning specific responses to an increasing range of environmental situations.

The general 'teleonomic' (McNaughton,1989) rationale governing the evolution of mind is that the fashioning of neural mechanisms able to cope with and utilize more specifically the processes and properties of nature is advantageous. The modern human mind triumphed over other minds because the genetic basis of its neural mechanisms varied sufficiently for natural selection to operate to fashion a system capable of open-ended exploitation of the artefactual niche. What we find when we delve deeper and deeper into the ultrastructure of the brain is simply nature's solution to this challenge, a salutary thought for neurobiologists.

(3) From the very beginning of the establishment of the loop-back axonal connections from the deep pyramidals to the putative consciousness-generating neurons in layer 4 it must have happened, if the evolutionary development occurred along the lines so far proposed, that random activation of these (memory) pyramidals resulted in haphazard generation of imagery. With increasing adaptive elaboration

2.5 The Beginning of Higher Mental Functioning 251

of the consciousness-memory system such random imagery would tend to occur more frequently and to be more organized and complex. In the absence of sensory input the imagery would not be masked and would tend to be experienced as distinctly as its strength allows. To clarify this idea: An experience stored in memory may be randomly recollected – it 'comes to mind' by chance – and it does so in the form of mental imagery (of a picture, a sound, etc.) which is a faint but definite experience. If the original sensory experience, of which the image is a weak copy, were occurring at that moment it would elicit the image but this would not be separately experienced, because the same consciousness-generating neurons are involved, although it would have the effect of conferring a sense of familiarity or conscious recognition. In general the strength of sensory input will force the generation of consciousness which will tend to mask all other internally induced imagery, although on occasion focusing on the latter may be sufficiently strong to largely inhibit the generation of consciousness by sensory stimuli. (Any doubt or disbelief that the imagery of recollection, imagination, or dreaming is identical to sensory imagery should be dispelled by considering the strength of imagery of hallucinations and dreams which of course are internally generated and which may rival or exceed that of sensory experience and have identical behavioral effects).

Such imagery would reconvert to neural energy to reactivate the originating group of linked memory neurons, in principle each unit of consciousness to its own downline memory neuron, restimulating these to repeat the cycle but also, as a group, sending impulses to other groups with which it has linkages formed by previous co-experience, causing these to discharge impulses to their own consciousness neurons with the consequent tendency to generate new imagery which may or may not be sustained. Random imagery (which is an unavoidable consequence of the functioning of the mind so far evolved) would tend to produce unwanted motor activity. *It is hypothesized that natural selection acted on variations in exit pathway firing thresholds or inhibitory influences to evolve the system to be minimally susceptible to motor triggering by random imagery,* and this inhibitory system would have tended to evolve *pari passu* with the increasing tendency to random imagery.

(4) In addition, recognition now becomes a stronger conscious experience, and as most of the recognitions are of aspects of the environment not at that moment relevant to the animal's interests some

Fig. 2.5 **Linkage retrievals** (From Hale, 1989)

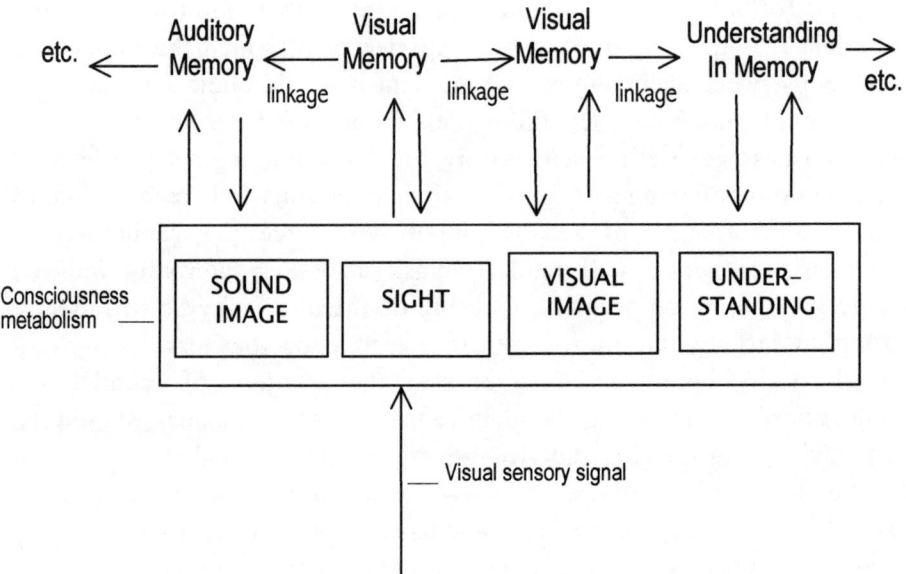

When a previously experienced item (which is now in memory) is re-encountered, not only does it stimulate its memory circuit to send a loop-back replica to consciousness, but such stimulation may activate linkages the circuit has with other memory circuits, causing these to discharge their particular impulse patterns back to consciousness through their loop-back connections, with resulting image production. Furthermore, such a new image in consciousness will pass back to its circuit in memory and, if strong enough, may activate linkages to yet other memory circuits, causing these to become imaged, and so on.

form of inhibition must operate on the response systems. When the organism is still very primitive there will be relatively few recognition-response circuits and these will tend to fully operate on exposure to the stimulus. When the system has evolved to the complexity so far described there will, in addition to retained and strongly active primitive vital recognition-responses, be many recognitions whose reflexive pathways to effector organs are poorly developed, degenerate, or non-existent as expressions of genetic variations. These conscious recognitions will tend not to translate into action.

(5) But if a non-executive recognition becomes linked through co-experience to a strongly reactive recognition-response circuit, renewed exposure to the former will tend through this linkage to engage the latter, and the more often co-experience occurs the stronger will this become.

To understand this and its important implications it should be recollected that when consciousness is generated it promptly reconverts to neural energy which activates downline elements of the reflex pathway with three possible effects: the triggering of some effector function; loop-back re-stimulation of the consciousness-generating element to generate new 'units' of the same consciousness; and, through facilitated synaptic connections with parallel reflex pathways to activate these which in turn may trigger *their* own effector functions, activate *their* own areas of consciousness, and activate *other* reflex units.

It should further be recollected that when different cortical areas generating consciousness are activated sufficiently closely in time linkages form between their respective downline (memory) cells through the 'imprinting' or 'potentiation' of synaptic connections between these, presumably through the operation of some facilitating biochemical process which alters the conductivity of structures that directly, indirectly, or potentially connect all parallel reflex pathways. We presume that when separate reflex pathways, or separate groups of these, are being activated simultaneously or nearly so the biochemical or electrochemical changes radiating through the axonal-dendritic networks emanating from each will, when they encounter one another, result in a more-or-less long-lasting facilitation of signal passage between the two by altering the bio-structures connecting them, however circuitous these may be. (See Figs. 2.1(6 – a and b).

The bio-structures connecting reflex pathways are synaptic junctions. The evocation of one memory by another can only occur via *preferential* passage of signals across synapses connecting memory stores. Experimental neurophysiologists working on memory generally favour the idea that permanent synaptic changes induced by the passage of neural signals are at least part of the basis of the memory 'trace'. This is of course a safe enough supposition, as there is hardly any place else to look (Kandel and Hawkins, 1992; Wu and Black, 1989).

Such physical changes are in principle demonstrable, but the difficulties of this are still largely beyond present technology. A discharging neuron, A, sends its action potential to all of its synaptic junctions with other neurons. If one of these other neurons, B, is separately activated near enough in time to A it may *through those of its own axonal terminals which lie on the axonal fibrils it receives from A* strengthen the impulses coming to itself, with resulting use-hypertrophy of the interconnections between these neurons. It is even possible, in keeping with the principles of evolutionary theory, that natural selection favoured concomitant inhibitory activity, via inhibitory interneurons, on axonal fibrils from A impinging on B's neighbouring, non-active neurons, as in theory such an arrangement would improve the accuracy and specificity of later memory retrieval. (Figs. 2.1(6 – a and b).

These properties are basic – the evolution of mind is impossible without them. What is proposed here is an underlying mechanism which would allow simultaneous or closely succeeding conscious experiences to form memory associations so that subsequently the occurrence of one will tend to recall the other. Modern neural network hypotheses of one sort or another, some of which are supported by impressive histological and histochemical detail (e.g., Edelman's 'Neural Darwinism') or ingenious computer simulations, are obviously groping in this direction, but until they put consciousness as a unique energetic phenomenon into their systems they will never be more than marginally, perhaps even trivially, successful. To exclude subjective, energetic consciousness from the model is to model something which is not the mind.

The gradual evolutionary elaboration of the mind at this stage led to more efficient and versatile functioning in part due, as mentioned above, to the provision of many memory units with poor or inhibited pathways to effector structures, permitting wider recordings and recognitions of environmental features but with little or no executive functions of their own. Such recognitions may, however, as mentioned above, become linked through co-experience to more primitive, powerfully acting recognition-response circuit complexes thus broadening the range of relevant environmental features the organism can incorporate into its recognition-response repertoire. Alternatively, with proliferation of memory components, all, or many, memory neurons may have access to effector structures but with strong inhibition of exit pathways, thus allowing internal mental functioning to proceed without effector triggering until the inhibitory control is relaxed by a need or decision to act.

A final alternative (Figs. 2.1(5 and 8)) is that the retrievable ('declarative') memory system is largely or entirely isolated from the effector systems and serves purely internal mental functions. If this is the case the consciousness-generating neurons must have separate access to the skill ('procedural') memory system, to the emotional system, to various acquired and innate behavior programs, and to the pyramidal motor pathway for voluntary action, each being under more of less inhibitory control to permit undisturbed internal mental functioning, least so perhaps for the emotional system since stray thoughts readily elicit emotions. There is evidence for this separation in patients after bilateral hippocampectomy who display anterograde amnesia but are otherwise behaviorally normal.

2.6 THE ORIGIN OF ANTICIPATORY ABILITY

(1) Increase in the range of the basic consciousness spectrum (e.g., to include colour consciousness) with concomitant increase in memory circuits, will continue to evolve if of value. Genetic variations in this will offer material for natural selection, but the *ability* to store and recognize items and patterns of experience which have no immediate relevance are unlikely to be genetically retained over many generations unless some benefit accrues to the individual, such as a slight capability for anticipation.

(2) *The ability to anticipate opened up a wide avenue for the further development of the mind.* It seems very likely that it became functional at this stage and may have resulted in a very rapid spurt in the development of the neuronal substrate of other mental properties, in particular the proliferation and conversion of many of the consciousness-mediated reflex circuits, especially those with loop-back connections, for specialization in memory functions and great elaboration of the synaptic linkage systems. Indeed, these were probably

already at a high level of pre-adaptation for contribution to higher mental functioning.

(3) Anticipation occurs when some situation being experienced prepares the individual, through various memory linkages, physiological adjustments, and motor programs, for some future situation. This is more than the Pavlovian conditioned reflex, which it incorporates, because, at least minimally, image formation is an essential element. Exposure to particular sequential environmental events, if sufficiently often and if the events occur sufficiently closely, will result in linkages being formed between their respective memories if the properties of synaptic physiology permit this. Subsequent exposure to the first event will, through these linkages, elicit image formation of the second event. If this second event has relevance for the animal the image experience will begin to engage reflexive functions before the actual event appears, assuming that effector connections are present and functional.

It should be clearly understood that this is distinct from the vegetative Pavlovian reflex response. The latter conditioned response may be formed via the non-conscious reflexive system or via the conscious reflexive systems, and it tends to form with multiple repetitions of the stimulus and its surrogate, and this function is a property of neuronal physiology (Kandel and Hawkins, 1992) that the evolutionary process has utilized in the elaboration of habit programs which play a major role in niche adaptations. In *mental* anticipation there is *in addition* the image preview of the coming event which acts as a surrogate of the latter and may elicit emotions, other relevant images, and bodily preparations with feed-back sensations. These are in large measure conscious experiences. At this primitive level they may be very slight yet with a strong tendency towards functional elaboration if there is enough genetically based variation for natural selection to be operative, which evidently was the case in the line leading to man.

(4) This gives us five levels of reflexivity: (a) Non-conscious, genetically provided (innate) reflexes. (b) Genetically provided reflexes utilizing consciousness. (c), (d) Genetically provided circuits and inter-circuit linkages functionally modifiable by conscious experience and not operative on simple maturation, so sensory deprivation from birth may result in atrophy of the system. In its early evolution the functional range of such modifiable circuits was closely determined genetically; although the 'openness' allowed natural selection to evolve responses to more

complex aspects of the environment, the reflexes being operative following priming by repeated exposure to these aspects, genetic control remained tight thus limiting what could be 'learned'. Later, resulting from some degree of *genetically allowed* randomness ('paragenesis') in the final neuronal maturation of the 'open' circuits and linkages, an increasing diversity of environmental events and patterns could imprint circuits, thus increasing the range of learning ability among individuals. (e) Finally, out of the above there evolved anticipation, which is a two-stage or indirect reflex utilizing imagery.

It is worth reiterating, to dispel a common misunderstanding, that the enormous amount of developmental randomness in the determination of the final configuration of neurons and neuronal connections in neocortex is a process (which may be termed 'paragenesis') which is *allowed* by the genome; the degree of such randomness is an *evolved* feature of development which exists because of its benefits – randomness per se can hardly be adaptive, but in this instance it is adaptive because it permits, within broad limits, a wider range of experiencing and learning than full genetic determination could possibly achieve. This arrangement may also carry costs to the population outweighed by the benefits, such costs possibly including tendencies to various psychoses, personality oddities, criminality, homosexuality, and antisocial forms of genius, tendencies more or less influencable by the vagaries of social and psychological experience.

Thus the characteristics of the individual are not only due to Nature (genetic determination) and Nurture (environmental influences), but also to Chance (the biological uncertainty principle).

2.7 THE EXPANSION OF MEMORY CAPACITY

(1) There is much apparent opportunism in evolution. Often when a dead-end seems to have been reached some mutation or niche change or entrepreneurial opportunity presents itself and a whole new enterprise starts up. This, it is suggested, was the case with memory specialization. Abruptly, as evolutionary time is considered, there was a wholesale conversion of the more recently diversified 'open' (imprintable) reflex circuits with their relatively weak reflexivity (as opposed to the more primitive and more powerfully reflexive system at an earlier stage) to specialized memory functioning. *Memory became big business, now that it could be used to anticipate the future and 'plan' for it.* This use of

memory would obviously have been a very feeble function at first, but its usefulness was such that any genetic variations that tended to further it would have been strongly selected. Chief among these, it may be conjectured, were widening of the consciousness spectrum, increased facility in the modifiability of molecular mechanisms in downline neurons and their synaptic linkages by conscious experience, increase in the number, variety, and functional characteristics of these synapses, better image formation through improvements in the physiology of the loop-back axonal connections to the consciousness-generating neurons, *and the development of control over exit pathways to effector structures.*

We can of course only speculate on how this 'conversion' could have come about. If the retrievable ('declarative') memory system consists of neurons isolated from the effector systems, and if these at a more primitive stage were part of the reflexive systems, therefore with motor outlets, then mutational changes would have to have eliminated such outlets. On the face of it this seems unlikely, considering the astronomical numbers that would have to be eliminated, but it remains possible that there may have been relatively simple genomic control over such exit pathways, so that alteration of only one or a few genes might have been sufficient to eliminate the outlets. There is no evidence that the human retrievable memory system can drive behaviors without the participation of consciousness, so its effector outlets, if ever they existed, have probably been lost rather than remaining under inhibitory control; the precise opposite applies to the skill ('procedural') memory system, which evolved to function automatically with only superficial supervisory conscious control.

(2) This stage in the evolution of mind may have coincided with the appearance of mammals, and the changes taking place and the appearance of mammalian characteristics may have been mutually influential in many subtle ways, e.g., in thermogenesis, but it would be carrying speculation too far to explore this topic here.

The increasing ability to store in memory environmental particulars and to link these memories when significant relationships between them have been experienced, and subsequently to use such stored information with benefit, allows the animal to enjoy increasingly versatile interactions with its environment. Its sphere of interests is widened; it profits from being alert to more happenings; it takes in more information which requires more processing to determine relevance. There is an increasing reliance on the mind in coping with the challenges of life. But the animals were living in natural niches for which they were generally well adapted, so their new mental capabilities were selectively advantageous up to a point, allowing rapid neuronal changes only up to that point. Only slow consolidation and elaboration may have taken place over the following tens of millions of years. In the primate line this elaboration comprised the pre-adaptations leading to pongid and early hominid minds.

(3) Apart from only limited and inconstant benefit accruing from elaboration of the new mental capabilities beyond a certain point (this 'law of diminishing returns' thereby effectively constraining evolution in that direction), there are constraints on such elaboration imposed by the limitations of genetic variability, particularly where the preservation of vital pre-existing complex neural systems is incompatible with the new tendencies.

(4) While 'paragenetic' (chance in development) factors are prominent in determining many of the details of the mature individual, paragenesis, as mentioned before, may in certain areas of operation have been selected (that is, in these areas the genetic blueprint *allows* freedom from genetic control, with benefit); some randomness in the final stages of maturation of memory and consciousness neurons may allow greater versatility in behaviour and learning capacities which, up to a point, may be selectively beneficial.

2.8 THE LINKAGE SYSTEMS OF MEMORY

Gradual improvement, through genetic 'fine-tuning', in synaptic physiology and connectivity would tend to continue even under stable niche conditions and would enable inter-memory linkages to form more readily, but also genetic variations in synaptic physiology and anatomy would result in the evolution of different linkage properties if of selective value. Note that the thrust of the analysis in this section (and, indeed, throughout this book) is first to establish the features of the mind, that is, what may be discerned by introspection, then to conjecture on their anatomical bases, and finally to seek these in the empirical findings of neuroanatomy and neurophysiology. The reverse process is hardly ever to be found; for example, apropos the present section, the publications of Levitan and Kaczmarek (1991) and Shepherd (1990) contain exhaustive details of neuronal and synaptic properties but with little or no attempt at relating these to the entity they evolved to provide, their very raison d'être: the mind.

The following classes of linkage functions may be postulated (See Fig.2.1(7)):

(a) Strong or 'internal' linkages which permit environmental entities to be recorded as such. A perception of an environmental entity is 'composed' of elements of the same sensory modality, although the same object may be experienced through different modalities each having its own memory system. Each unit of consciousness 'imprints' its own memory circuit, and when an environmental entity on being encountered results in the generation of large numbers of units of consciousness units simultaneously, not only will their individual memory circuits be imprinted but these will be tightly bound by mutual linkages. *External, objective reality shapes the functional structure of the brain* – the brain evolves to support those mental properties which represent those features of the external world which have vital relevance for the well-being of the animal.

Since the world consists of distinct objects behavior must be consonant with this reality. In organisms which have evolved representative consciousness the representations of reality must unequivocally be of distinct objects in that the behaviors driven by conscious representation must be appropriate to reality, and the memories of such representations must have strong internal cohesiveness for the same reason. This biological imperative exerts strong selective pressure for the accumulation of synaptic properties that maintain perceptual and mnemonic object identity.

As object delineation becomes more selectively beneficial with increasing mental capabilities, so will genetic improvements in internal linkage properties. (In the higher forms of mind other factors come into play in consolidating object identity, particularly understandings and factual knowledge relating to the object and the use of language which fosters preoccupation with the object).

There must obviously be elaborate and sophisticated neural mechanisms in addition to mere linkage properties that allow objects in the world to retain their identity in conscious representation despite being seen, felt, etc. in varying positions. But even this capability (which is an intractable problem for robotics) may in part be dependent on memory linkages through experience providing the individual with

2.8 The Linkage Systems of Memory 261

object identity composed of numerous aspects – if the individual sees and handles an object often enough the different aspects experienced will become linked in memory, so subsequently experiencing one of these aspects will tend to retrieve the other aspects, including properties, uses, name, contexts, etc., thus contributing to knowledge of object continuity. Even so, it is not an uncommon happening to come upon a familiar object from an unusual angle and not recognize it immediately.

The secondary (more recently evolved) sensory areas of the cerebral cortex are where, from experimental and clinical evidence, percepts are formed (a 'percept' being a coherent or structured item of consciousness – Kolb and Whishaw, 1990:223). There can be little doubt that the specifics of neuronal connectivity in these neocortical areas underlie the generation of percepts such as object identity; and synaptic properties and arrangements, in addition to other neuronal specializations, must constitute this neural substrate. It is probable, however, that percept formation involves all levels of the relevant sensory modality, with cooperative functioning between the older and newer regions; functionally there probably does not exist rigid compartmentalization between sensation and perception as implied in neuropsychology texts.

The ability to form percepts is advantageous through the influence these have on behaviors, either through more-or-less direct triggering of motor programs or indirectly by contributing to more sophisticated internal mental operations. Specialized synaptic and neuronal properties and connectivities for percept formation are complemented by equally specialized memory structures, and these are what is meant here by 'internal' linkages. It is evident that maintaining the permanence and integrity of such memories is of major functional importance, and we can predict that internal linkages will have evolved particular strength.

(b) Weak or 'external' linkages (Fig.2.1(7)) connect the memory circuits recording different objects and events, including those of different modalities, when they are imprinted or activated simultaneously or nearly so. Such linkages although of early evolutionary origin and therefore at this primitive level robust and reliable, were greatly elaborated in later advanced development of the mind in a crash undertaking which utilized material not perfectly pre-adapted for the new tasks, with the consequence that although of enormously increased capacity and efficiency it has failure tendencies that are apparent at the highest level.

But a major logistics problem must be considered: How to connect each one of the astronomical number of memory neurons to every other memory neuron; since we know that every conscious experience is linkable through memory to every other conscious experience the evolutionary process must somehow have solved this problem. The most plausible explanation may be found in the distinction between 'internal' and 'external' synaptic linkages: The numerous memory neurons storing a perceptual object are strongly bound together by 'internal' linkages. The activation of any one of these neurons will tend to activate the remainder as a unit, therefore in principle only one connecting line each way is needed to link different memories.

Many if not most of the ipsilateral, intersensory corticocortical fibre tracts in man are probably concerned with 'external' memory linkages. For a sensory event, or a thought, to become linked to particular memories, whether of the same or another sensory mode, of necessity requires a physical connection between memory stores, and the only means of such connectivity we know of in the CNS is via synaptic junctions between neurons. We also know that any memory is linkable to any other memory, no matter how remote from one another they may be located in the brain. Therefore, directly or indirectly, every neuron subserving a memory function must be accessible to every other memory neuron via synaptic junctions. And since we also know from anatomical studies, in addition to merely logistical considerations, that individual neurons have limited targets for their axonal projections, most memory linkages must be via interneurons in a manner such as suggested above.

Obviously, intermodal neuronal connections exist prior to the establishment of memory associations – synapses cannot instantaneously appear or change position; but whether new synaptic connections form over time between strongly associated memory substrates must be determined by future research; we know that such sprouting does occur in the cortex in certain circumstances, for example to invade adjacent cortical areas deprived of their sensory input.

The cerebral cortex contains large numbers of neurons of several different types, each type presumably evolved in serving some specific function. The principal functions of the cerebral cortex are increasingly sophisticated conscious representations of the external world, the storage of these in memory, and the use of these memories in mental functioning, all directed to producing the most effective behaviors. These functions are carried out by the cooperative activity of cortical cells, with intermemory 'external' linkage capability being one of the most important ingredients.

(c) Time-sequential linkages permit memory storage of dynamic events. There is no satisfactory theory of how this is achieved, as the neural basis required would seem to be horrendously complex. At this stage in the evolution of the mind – the level of the earliest mammals – time-sequential linkages may not exist, or, if they do, they may be extremely primitive. It is possible that at the hominid level the problem was solved not by neural complexity but by supplementing the primitive system with the aid of the imaginative function. On the other hand it is generally believed that some non-human animals dream (REM sleep has been demonstrated in several species – see Sarnat and Netsky,1981:94-6), and as the imagery in dreaming can hardly be static we must suppose that their memories can store and reproduce dynamic events.

(d) Context linkages: Being able to remember the co-occurrence of separate features of an experience and their environmental context requires that diversely stored memories, commonly representing different fundamental categories of experience, be linked in the brain. The evolutionary origin of this type of linkage capability must be relatively ancient, as primitive animals are able to relate particular experiences, e.g. food sources or danger episodes, to particular environments. In man this capacity is highly developed, yet as everyone knows it is very prone to failure. It is very doubtful that any specialized linkage property other than the general 'external' linkage mechanism is involved. It seems highly improbable that the evolutionary process could have evolved yet another type of linkage property, if only on the basis of the law of parsimony.

Dissociations in context remembering occur not only in normal humans as a not uncommon happening but permanently in monkeys and humans with particular lesions of prefrontal cortex (Squire 1987 – see summary), suggesting that this cortex has a role in establishing functional correlation between widely scattered storage sites (Goldman-Rakic, 1992). In other words elaboration of the 'external' linkage system to permit more advanced feats of memory was selectively beneficial and may have been achieved, at least in part, via connections through prefrontal cortex (Shimamura, 1995), but so far we have no plausible theories of how prefrontal cortex may carry out this and other control functions.

(e) If two items of consciousness are 'in mind' together or in very close temporal relationship they are both part of the global unitary consciousness at that time, and each activates its own downline memory neurons, these separate groups of memory neurons therefore being simultaneously engaged, thus facilitating (potentiating) the synaptic connections between them, as previously suggested. But what if *within the consciousness-generating system itself* energy can pass from one item of consciousness to another with mutual strengthening, bypassing the memory system? Such energy passage must be along fibres but these will connect the consciousness-generating neurons and not the memory neurons. When one aspect of the current global consciousness thus activates another *at the conscious level* each will not only strengthen the imprinting of its own memory system, but also result in facilitation (potentiation) of the interconsciousness fibre connections. So perhaps the peculiar properties of the consciousness system permit memory connections at two levels (Fig.2.1(8)).

If, suppose, stellates in layer 4 are the consciousness-generating neurons then stellates in all the sensory modalities must be connectable to allow the unity of consciousness, a kind of energy syncytium, bypassing the memory system. But stellates have only limited connections across cortical columns and no direct subcortical connections with one another, so the logistical constraints make it difficult to see how the unity is achieved, particularly as the evidence from commissurotomy subjects indicates that the neuronal bridge is essential for unity.

Note that in this scheme energy does not influence energy directly but only indirectly via matter: either consciousness generated in area A first reconverts to neural energy to influence the generation of consciousness in area B via the memory system, or, still as a conscious state, it coalesces along neuronal bridges with near and distant contemporaneous consciousness, either by multisynaptic transcortical connections through cortical columns or by some other cortical architectonics not yet revealed by anatomical research. It is a tenet of the theory of consciousness in this study that no part of the energy 'syncytium' of consciousness can directly influence any other part. By analogy, in physics, electric and magnetic fields do not affect electromagnetic waves (Muncaster, 1985:423).

One of the major unanswered questions concerning the memory system is why bilateral removal of the anterior temporal lobes, including the hippocampi, results in inability to form new memories. There is an extensive clinical literature on this subject, much of it on the patient H.M. (e.g. Milner et al., 1968) whose anterior temporal lobes were removed in an effort to relieve his epilepsy, and numerous experimental studies on animals (e.g. Squire, 1992). It is important to note that established memories are not obliterated, supporting the claim that permanent memories are stored in the sensory cortices in close association with consciousness-generating neurons.

Of course, it is not surprising that massive interference with the brain should have major cognitive effects – removing major parts of lobes bilaterally is no minor assault – but numerous studies support a specific role for the hippocampus in memory formation, for which there must be a simple explanation not yet forthcoming.

Damasio (1989) sees the entorhinal cortex and the parts of the hippocampus to which it projects as constituting a unique subsystem in that "it is the only brain region in which signals originally triggered by neural activity in all sensory cortices and in centers for autonomic control can actually co-occur over the same neuron ensembles". He considers this "the appropriate substrate for a detection of temporal coincidences", which is a function he proposes for this system and which he believes to be lost in amnesia following hippocampal damage.

One must welcome all attempts at explanation of the role of hippocampus in the establishment of permanent memories. However, Damasio's ideas in their present form do not yet constitute explanation. The limbic cortex, including hippocampus and corticomedial amygdala, is an ancient region and at one stage of evolution presumably would have been the highest cerebral region. Evolutionary expansion of cortex would of necessity leave this in some way as a functional centre through which the newer areas would have to operate, particularly in the elicitation by neocortex of emotional and autonomic functions, but also, evidently, in connection with the consolidation of memories.

According to Kandel and Hawkins (1992) neural input travels from the sensory (in their discussion, visual) cortex to the hippocampus where it is stored for several weeks before it is transferred back to the cortex for permanent storage. For these and other researchers this is what the experimental and clinical evidence tells us. But if the hippocampus stores conscious experiences which are readily retrievable (we can remember them) during the "several weeks" before sending them to a permanent home in the neocortex why is this latter transfer necessary? After all, such memories are perfectly retrievable before they become "permanent", so why not continue to use the hippocampus for permanent storage? But can the small, ancient hippocampus, little evolved in millions of years, even temporarily store the vast amounts of information the normal human is capable of remembering in short periods of time? Their explanation of the role of hippocampus is clearly unsatisfactory.

It must first be asked, before trying to determine the role of hippocampus, what processes may possibly be involved in the acquisition and the consolidation of a memory, and as a corollary what conditions may affect these processes. These questions turn out not to have simple answers because of the number of possible stages and processes in memory functioning: 1/ The conscious experience, i.e. the generation of consciousness – no consciousness, no memory. 2/ The reconversion (of the energy) of consciousness to downline neural energy, thereby increasing the efficiency of subsequent signal passage through target neurons, including memory neurons. 3/ This activation of memory neurons by input from consciousness resulting in synaptic and other changes leads to their subsequent increase in responsiveness to impulses from their upline consciousness neurons as well as from other memory neurons, this responsiveness translating to increased activity on effector mechanisms and on loop-back reactivation of their consciousness neurons. 4/ The process of conscious recognition (sense of familiarity) from the presumed 'meshing' of the returned memory image with incoming sensory data, results in reinforcement of the consciousness-memory loop. 5/ The efficiency of intermodal signal passage and intermemory linkage mechanisms may be subtly affected by distant brain damage. 6/ Little understood influences may modify the efficiency of the various linkage mechanisms of memory. 7/ The strength and narrowness of the focusing (i.e., the selective regional generation) of consciousness during experiencing determine the strength of signals reaching memory neurons, and the elements of the focusing mechanisms are so intricate and sensitive that virtually any damage to the brain may adversely affect their functioning. 8/ The efficiency of cellular

2.8 The Linkage Systems of Memory 267

metabolism, or functioning of this metabolism, may be influenced indirectly, e.g. through hormonal disturbances. 9/ The elicitation of emotions, especially interest and curiosity, which strengthen focus and thereby memory formation may be curtailed or distorted by distant brain damage.

In what ways can the anterior temporal lobes, including the hippocampi, play a part in any of these processes? Does short-term (working) memory depend on any of these processes or is it simply a reverberation of activity in the consciousness-memory loop lasting a few seconds? Obviously, impairment of any of the above listed mechanisms may affect the establishment of memories. It seems most probable that the hippocampi have an indirect role, e.g. by acting as a gateway to the limbic system in stimulating interest or eliciting emotions sufficiently for some minimal degree of situational attention to occur, or recruiting the autonomic system to increase metabolic activity in the focused areas, or inhibition of other brain activities which may otherwise have a distracting effect. Even with intact brains we sometimes live through situations without remembering them, and even more often fail to link in memory one experience to another.

The hippocampal formation is believed on grounds of histology and comparative anatomy to be the oldest part of the cerebral cortex. This cortex is believed to have evolved as lateral outpouchings of the rostral end of the neural tube to supplement thalamic activity, possibly by serving a memory function or by elaboration of thalamic influences on hypothalamic and other limbic responses.

Sensory neocortex evolved by extension of thalamic sensory nuclei, in effect becoming a way-station between these nuclei and primordial (limbic, hippocampal, amygdaloid, etc.) cortex. (How the neocortical motor outlet evolved is unknown, but presumably by taking over whatever motor outlet the primitive thalamus must have had; thalamus does not now have a direct motor outlet). The sensory neocortex developed its own memory function through specialization of neurons downline from its consciousness-generating neurons: it must be kept in mind that the brain is a set of massive reflex arcs of different levels of complexity operating in parallel, with the neocortex being the most recently evolved and the most elaborate. (See Fig.(5) Appendix E).

Where then does the participation of hippocampus in the memory function of neocortex come in? Which of the many possible factors contributing to memory 'consolidation' is influenced by hippocampus? It is not even conclusively known that the process of memory 'consolidation' really exists, apart from the consolidation that results from re-experiencing and from memory retrievals; the experimental and clinical data on which the idea that hippocampus is required for memory consolidation is based are open to alternative interpretation.

My guess is that for an experience to become established in memory it must engage more than superficial focusing: it must command a critical strength of focus by involving subcortical mechanisms which have built-in access to the focusing mechanisms of consciousness, as discussed earlier, and hippocampus may be one of the gateways to these mechanisms. In mammalian brains input to hippocampus is mainly from cortex, so presumably when thalamus extended into neocortex its projections to hippocampus shifted and became largely indirect, via neocortex.

Shortly after many routine activities the events occurring cannot be recalled. This is presumably because the nature of the activities is such that it is unnecessary to memorize the details, therefore eventually the habit develops of not doing so. Somehow, under these conditions, there is failure to do something extra which would store the material – the mind is undoubtedly otherwise engaged and the actions are largely automatic. In hippocampal anterograde amnesia something of the sort may happen. My impression is that there is, in the case of routine actions, failure not only to focus the mind on the sensory input to the exclusion of other stimuli but failure also to take an additional mental step, which normally happens automatically with focusing, of allowing the details to engage associations and form new ones; there is a failure of the sensory experience to establish synaptic linkages outside its own cortical columns to allow it to become retrievable. If this is so it implies that mere focusing may be insufficient for the normal establishment of memories and the extra ingredient may be a function akin to interest, an almost visceral involvement, which may well be generated in the hippocampal formation or other regions of the limbic system via the hippocampus.

I have earlier suggested that hippocampus may be the gateway for certain experiences to elicit the 'emotions' of interest and curiosity in the limbic system, and that these 'intellectual' emotions act on the focusing mechanisms (rostral intralaminar thalamic nuclei, reticular nucleus, locus ceruleus, etc.) to activate the areas of cerebral cortex generating these conscious experiences, thereby increasing the chance of memories of them forming. The role of the hippocampal formation is further discussed in Appendix C.

2.9 THE FURTHER EVOLUTION OF HIGHER MENTAL FUNCTIONING

In Section 2.5 the origin and early evolution of higher mental functioning were considered. This section explores the further expansion of mental functioning to the pre-hominid level.

(1) Higher mental functioning includes the tendency to focus attention on more environmental and social particulars, the ability to store such material in memory, and the ability to use this knowledge (factual material and causal relationships) in modifying behavior with benefit. Every genetic variation contributing to improvement in these capabilities must have had strong selective value in the line that led to primates, and there must have been a relative abundance of such variations. Random exploratory behavior would have to be harnessed and directed by mechanisms serving these higher mental functions.

Exploratory behavior is undoubtedly very ancient and probably remains largely stereotyped below a relatively high development of mind. It presumably evolved because of its success in bringing the organism to new supplies of nourishment. Various recognition-response programs must be operative to take advantage of opportunities and to avoid dangers. In non-conscious and early conscious reflexive systems these are simple and few. In conscious systems capable of learning there is selective advantage gained by an ability to discriminate among environmental details as this allows the acquisition of more appropriate response programs.

A crucial breakthrough to higher mental functioning occurs with the evolved ability (or tendency) to focus on novel (i.e. miscellaneous) features of the environment for which there are no inborn recognition-responses and before any linkage has formed to those that exist through co-experience. For the evolution of such a focusing tendency to have occurred it must have been of significant value, and this probably could only have been the case by virtue of the brain at this stage being able to store and utilize experiences of environmental causal relationships, i.e. to understand, and to modify behavior accordingly.

(2) The understanding function enables the organism to profit from whatever tendency it has for inquisitive behavior, which exposes it to more environmental particulars that may be relevant. These two capabilities are dependent on one another for some of their usefulness, so presumably originated independently and had other functions before becoming associated in higher mental development. The understanding capability no doubt arose from the more primitive mechanism of expectation, which is based on the formation, through co-experience, of linkage between the memories of incidental features and biologically relevant features of the environment (Section 2.7.(2)). The elaboration of this for more efficient function would increase the ease and frequency with which linkages formed between the memories of co-experienced features; and concomitant improvement in the neurophysiology of time-sequential linkage properties would as a consequence tend to place in memory increasing numbers of environmental causal relationships.

(3) As memory becomes more stocked with information linked to biologically relevant situations, greater areas of the environment are now of 'interest' to the animal. Exploration brings it into contact with situations which formerly were irrelevant but now, due to improved storage and linkage capabilities, have relevance because they have become connected in memory to important environmental features momentarily out of sensory range.

Environmental particulars which in this way have become relevant, i.e. have 'acquired' relevance, will of course vary in their true objective relationship to the primarily relevant aspects of the environment, i.e. those which precipitate innate reflexive actions. The relationship may be a short-term, chance positional one, or a fixed property one, or a true causal one.

In the earlier stages of the development of this capability the linkages of incidental features will be to innate recognition-responses. In the more advanced stage which we are now considering linkages will also be to acquired reflexes, giving wider behavioral options. Also, variations in the genetic basis of all this may produce some individuals with advanced memory linkage capabilities allowing more remote environmental particulars to acquire relevance, as well as revealing indirect causal relationships, and this represents a significant advance in mental development.

(4) All mental functioning at this stage is clearly reflexive and consciousness is a functional, essentially mechanical, part of the process. The unique self-experiencing nature of consciousness, including physical and emotional feeling, is utilized biologically in this process. In advanced brains innumerable acquired responses greatly extend the versatility of behaviors serving increasingly wide mental formulations, to the point where it may be doubted that the elemental consciousness-mediated reflex arc is the fundamental basis of it all, particularly where voluntariness, purposefulness, and intentionality are concerned. But in any system, no matter what functionally new feature emerges, complexity remains dependent on, and can only be explained in terms of, the elementary processes.

(5) Experiences are more securely stored in memory if consciousness is focused, i.e., the more strongly sensory input emanating from such experiences generate consciousness. The neurophysiological mechanisms underlying focusing are subject to genetic variation and the operation of natural selection. It follows that as the ability to employ the contents of memory in useful ways improves as suggested above the more advantageous will be improved focusing as well as any increased tendency to use it on randomly encountered situations.

2.10 THE ORIGIN OF CURIOSITY AND 'PURPOSEFUL' BEHAVIORS

(1) At some stage in mammalian evolution there appeared curiosity behavior. Certain environmental situations elicited the 'emotions' of interest and curiosity. These then directed or heightened exploratory behavior towards the eliciting situations. For the guiding of behavior by curiosity and interest to evolve it must be of selective value; it must make exploratory behavior more profitable, presumably by acting as a mechanism that selects from the environment the sorts of data that may serve higher mental processing, in particular the processing that incorporates the new data into the memory system controlling behavior in that area; for example, new details about the environment and other circumstances in relation to a food source will become added to the memory of that area and this expanded knowledge may modify activity with benefit.

This ability will function most profitably on certain types of environmental data and this will be the determinant of which genetic variations of exploratory behavior will tend to be selected; the kinds of things an animal is found to take an interest in will, due to the evolutionary process, be those that proved of greatest benefit to its ancestors; biological evolution is totally pragmatic.

For all this to come about exploratory behavior must have reached the stage at which it was pre-adapted for elevation to the fundamentally new level of curiosity behavior; relatively minor genetic changes would then allow some control by mechanisms activated by the 'feelings' of interest and curiosity. At this new level behavior is more opportunistic, less stereotyped.

There must already have been considerable development in this direction, requiring enormous sophistication in the neuro-muscular coordinating mechanisms. For example, rapidly changing input from the senses must be responded to by changes in behavior which must keep pace. At one and the same time the sensory inputs may activate inborn (genetic) reflexes, consciousness-mediated acquired reflexes, and behaviors influenced by knowledge accumulated through experience. All of these must have reciprocal inhibitory and augmentory connections which make possible the instantaneous implementation of priorities under the conditions of each moment. (This is currently a busy area of neurobiological research. See Section IV: 'Strategies and Planning: Motor Systems' in 'The Cognitive Neurosciences', M.I.T. Press 1995).

(2) Purposeful behavior at the human level is usually considered to be voluntarily controlled behavior directed to achieving some goal, and therefore involving the highest mental processes, but many behaviors considered to be purposeful in this sense are largely reflexive, of both the acquired and innate kinds.

(3) Stereotyped exploratory behavior is probably programmed in the basal ganglia-cerebellar motor systems, geared to respond in particular ways to particular stimuli, mostly related to food sources. The more primitive the organism the fewer the stimuli that it is able to 'recognize' and respond to, but at the stage at which interest and curiosity appeared the neostriatum and the neocerebellum were probably beginning to develop to support more elaborate acquired behaviors. (It is salutary to ponder, however, the enormous storage capacity of the pinhead-sized brains of insects for elaborate innate behavior programs).

We may suppose that the neural substrate for the generation of the 'emotions' of interest and curiosity evolved to be responsive to certain life situations after these are recognized and processed to a critical cognitive level, the 'emotions' then acting to catalyse exploratory behavior towards these situations.

2.11 THE EVOLUTION OF MENTAL CONTROL OF FINE PERIPHERAL MOVEMENTS

(1) It seems probable that at about this stage – the early development of versatile and opportunistic exploratory behavior propelled by curiosity and interest – the mental control of more narrowly delimited muscular activity began to develop. This presumably had selective value in that it allowed opportunistic exploratory behavior to be more adaptive, and there must obviously have been sufficient richness and variability in the underlying genetic material.

(2) Innate behavior programs are made up of components consisting of specific, limited movements not normally separately activable. We may suppose that the master program for every complex instinctive behavior evolved to control the activity of different numbers and combinations of lower motor neurons, potentially down to the individual ones. We may further speculate that mental control of fine movements evolved through, at least in part, being able to tap into different levels of inborn program sequences. When the nervous system began evolving from the stage of simple reflexes hierarchies of control developed, each level in turn coming under the control or influence of a newly evolved higher level. The control program at each level, when activated, is thus able to activate every level beneath it to which it is functionally tied. (Hierarchies of control in the major domains of life – nutrition, defense, and reproduction – may have evolved in parallel and semi-independently of one another from the earliest stages).

(3) The view held in this analysis is that the earliest mind was a reflex arc driven or amplified (servo-assisted) by the energy of generated consciousness. As the nervous system evolved its conscious and non-conscious reflexive systems did so in parallel, each to perform increasingly complex functions but with inhibitory influences on one another. Both systems operated through the same motor outlets (with some exceptions) and each developed its own complexity of organization, but the ability of the conscious system, via collaterals from pyramidal tract fibres (which arise in both motor and sensory cortices) to project on the non-conscious system at different levels of the latter (in

basal ganglia, brainstem reticular formation, cerebellum, and lower motor neuron pools) is presumably what makes possible the establishment of complex behavior and skill program circuitries in these motor-control centres.

More specifically: Voluntary engagement of lower motor neurons via the pyramidal tract results in peripheral movements which satisfy mentally conceived objectives. This relatively recently evolved capability is slow and clumsy, but axonal branches from pyramidal tract fibres carry copies of the signal sequences to structures, mainly cerebellum and basal ganglia, which house innate ('hard-wired') behavior programs; and in addition, and more directly, the supplementary and premotor cortices receive and store the sequences. These various structures, evolving *pari passu* with voluntary systems, increasingly developed the capacity to be imprinted with the voluntary sequences: the synaptic and cellular properties of their 'neo' parts became capable of learning or 'memorizing' the sequences (hence the designation 'skill acquisition', or 'procedural memory'). Since these imprintable (malleable, plastic) 'neo' circuitries are elaborations of the ancient ones they remain interconnected with the latter, and by this means can access elements of the innate programs, so that when the learned program is subsequently activated there is automatic, fast, non-conscious execution of the original voluntary movement sequence.

This clearly was a major evolutionary advance, with such great selective benefit that natural selection acted powerfully to develop it in genealogical lines in which other essential pre-adaptations were in place, most effectively in the hominid line. As with other highly adaptive advanced functions it is noteworthy that several structures were recruited for service by the evolutionary process.

(4) The voluntary control of finer peripheral muscle movements very likely evolved in step with opportunistic exploratory behavior as the latter proved selectively beneficial. This was at least partly achieved by improvement in the focusing of consciousness which allowed narrowing of the range of lower motor neurons which may be activated by the mind, but perhaps mainly by increasing the number of consciousness-memory neurons with relatively direct connections to upper motor neurons in primary motor cortex controlling particular moving parts.

Two neuroanatomical facts have relevance here: One, the pyramidal tract is a late evolutionary development, its size and functional

2.11 The Evolution of Mental Control of Fine Peripheral Movements

importance increasing from non-primate mammals through monkeys and apes to man, the obvious conclusion from this being that it permits the latter organisms to have more precise cerebral control of lower motor neurons than is possible with the primitive 'extra-pyramidal' system. The other fact is that although most corticospinal (pyramidal) fibres synapse on interneurons in the lateral grey matter of the spinal cord thus activating, via these, relatively large groups of muscle fibres, in man and much less in the higher primates but not in lower mammals a significant number synapse directly on the lower motor neurons of the anterior grey matter thus allowing control of much finer muscle movements from the brain.

2.12 THE INITIATION OF MENTALLY DETERMINED MOVEMENTS

(1) If a novel action happens to prove profitable for an animal its repetition is dependent on the operation of memory. The repetition is guided by memory but for the memory to be operative one of two processes must apply: it must either be retrieved into consciousness through activation of the memory neurons, in which case the consciousness has an executive role in the behavior, or the activated memory subconsciously drives the motor system, in which case fibre connections must lead directly from the memory neurons to the motor control mechanisms.

Whichever of these modes of action is actually the case the effector pathways must be under inhibitory control to prevent continuous, unwanted motor activity resulting from memory activation and imagery, and this inhibitory system must become increasingly sophisticated as the brain evolves to perform increasingly complex internal mental operations.

It follows that there must be a mechanism which allows action to occur through this inhibitory barrier when this is appropriate, that is, when as a result of internal operations a 'decision' to act has been made. (At the early mammalian level all of this is still primitive, and memory images, if they occur, may tend to be promptly operative).

In the case of the conscious route the image of the action to be repeated must somehow activate the same muscular sequences that occurred originally. This idea is fundamental. An image of moving a finger moves the finger because such an image is the generation of

276 Stages in Evolution of the Mind

consciousness in those consciousness neurons which are indirectly but functionally connected, either through their memory neurons or by an exit pathway independent of these, to the upper motor neurons that control the finger musculature. These connections date back to the origin of consciousness in the primordial reflex arc. The consciousness-generating neuron, its downline signal-transmitting neuron (later converted to specialized functions, including memory), and the elemental effector structure (usually muscle) thereafter remain functionally connected through all the elaborations and morphological distortions brought about by subsequent evolution. A thought in the form of a complex image of movement is composed of numerous units of generated consciousness, each of which is functional on its own muscle entity.

(2) There are two points that seem to argue against this idea. First, we can imagine a movement as vividly as we like without anything happening; and second, we can will a movement without any definite image formation.

In the first case we must do something extra for movement to occur: we must 'let go'. It has already been put forward that in the evolution of an advanced, specialized consciousness-memory system for higher mental functioning strong inhibitory control over effector triggering is essential. At the human level such control is very complete, allowing strong action images, whether remembered or synthesized, to occur in the course of thinking without unwanted movement. It follows that when action is required the inhibition must be released, and the way this operates seems to be a 'let it happen' frame of mind. In the course of the thinking a need or motive for action arises, either revealed or engendered by the thinking itself or indicated by external information, and inhibitions are automatically released. Identical or very similar neural mechanisms may be involved in the control of micturition, in which by composing oneself to 'let it happen' the inhibitory control is released.

In the second case there is often in active willing no clear-cut participation of image formation. Certainly the part being willed to act must be 'in mind' in some sense; we must be 'thinking' of moving the finger if it and not some other part of the body is to be moved. What may well be the case here is that frequently employed movements come under the control of acquired, automatically performable subconscious neuromuscular programs for most of their applications, and that extremely

2.12 The Initiation of Menatlly Determined Movements

sensitive neural control and feed-back mechanisms have evolved to be instantly receptive and responsive to rapidly changing incoming data. It may therefore require the merest thought, with image formation so faint as to be virtually unintrospectable, for appropriate movement to occur.

It follows from the above that specific elements of sensory cortex are tied anatomically and functionally to specific elements of motor cortex and subcortical motor systems. When we think we employ large numbers of cortical consciousness-memory neuronal units in the ever changing combinations that make up the imagery of which the thoughts are composed, and when we think of performing some action the consciousness-memory neurons involved in such thinking are the ones anatomically and functionally connected directly, or indirectly via previously established automatically performable motor programs, to the upper motor neurons to be employed.

There is somatotopic representation (localization) in motor cortex of the different musculoskeletal systems of the body. There is also somotosensory representation in parietal sensory cortex of different areas of the body. But do we think somatosensorially? When I 'think' of moving my finger is the thought visual or somatosensory? If I have a pure visual image of moving my finger then decide to move it in strict accordance with the visual image by what route does this translate to action – directly to motor cortex, or via somatosensory cortex? So far as we know although close connections, part-to-appropriate-part, exist between parietal somatosensory cortex and motor somatotopic cortex, there are no such connections between visual cortex and motor cortex, so no obvious means by which a visual image can guide physical action directly. But how does it manage to do so indirectly, as evidently it must? When we have a visual image of a finger movement does that image engage the cells of parietal cortex which represent the finger, so that when intention to move the finger forms and precipitates action the parietal cortex activates the motor cortex? We do not know, but intention to perform a movement and carrying out that intention must occur in and operate from parietal somatosensory cortex in congenitally blind persons.

Adding to the uncertainty is the finding that during mental rehearsal of a finger movement increased cerebral blood flow occurred only in the supplementary motor area, but with actual movement both this area and the primary motor cortex were active (Kolb and Whishaw, 1990:271).

2.13 THE CONVERSION OF THOUGHTS INTO ACTION

(1) In the conversion of a mental image to appropriate action the basic principle is simple, but the actual process so complex that its psychoneurophysiological elucidation is still very incomplete.

Consciousness, whether a sensory perception, a feeling (physical or emotional), or an image retrieved from memory, we infer (through our reliance on basic scientific principles) to be generated by the activity of specialized neurons. Now most perceptions, feelings, or images would be created by the simultaneous activation of large numbers of individual consciousness-generating neurons, but as each neuron may have only one specific effect the complex behavior caused by the image is the sum of these individual specific effects (ignoring for the purpose of this analysis the intricate, evolved synaptic features permitting spread or constriction of signals through the neural networks which add refinement and delicacy of control to complex neural systems).

It was suggested in the previous section that the thought or image of moving a finger moves that finger and not another because the image of that finger is composed of units of consciousness each of which is directly or indirectly functional on a specific motor unit which is developmentally and functionally connected to a muscle fibre in one of the muscles controlling the particular finger movement. But in the evolution of control of fine-movements by mental activity the point was never reached where individual muscle fibres were activable, as this would have been non-adaptive. The finest muscle response to mental activity probably involves fairly large numbers of consciousness-generating neurons, possibly as contained in several cortical columns. With the strongest focusing this would be the limit of fine movement. It is unlikely that activation can be limited to a single giant pyramidal Betz cell in motor cortex, much less a single alpha motor neuron in the spinal cord and through this the smallest motor unit of three or four skeletal muscle fibres (Guyton,1987:183,211).

Again as discussed earlier, this mechanism has evolved to such a level of efficiency that (on introspection) the appropriate movements almost seem to occur by themselves when they are parts of frequently used sequences (Section 2.12(2)). This presumably happens because in these instances the inhibitory activity on such movement is totally removed so the slightest activation of the consciousness-memory neurons results in action. At other times, in attempting new patterns of movement, the strongest possible image formation produced by full conscious focusing is required to guide the appropriate movement.

(2) At the human level thoughts do not often in themselves generate action even when inhibitory control on the effector connections from the mind is not being consciously maintained. It is generally when a need or motive for action arises that another mechanism comes into play. The body's neuro-muscular and neuro-secretory systems are susceptible to engagement by a variety of cues which may appear in thinking, feeling, or perceiving. Such cues in addition to engaging specific innate or acquired recognition-response programs elicit a non-specific urge feeling which acts as a catalyst to boost action. (Such an urge feeling is, like other vital mental functions, knowable only to introspection. The experimental neurophysiologist must be told, when measuring brain activity, what is being subjectively experienced. Investigating the structure of the mind is the realm of introspective analysis; experimental neurophysiology attempts to discover how the brain, and what parts of it, may produce these effects. The minds of less encephalized related species are no doubt largely homologous to the more primitive parts of the human mind, and therefore to a degree may be understood by careful introspective analysis by the human).

But internally generated thought images may on occasion precipitate acquired and innate behaviors, much as vital cue sensory experiences do via the lower level conscious reflexive system, most notably by way of emotional arousal, in the apparent absence of any additional propelling mechanism. This is the basis of so-called lie-detector tests. In the abnormal states of hallucinating, sleep-walking, and sleep-talking this is exaggerated.

(3) Ilinsky, Jouandet, and Goldman-Rakic (1985) and other workers have traced the neural connections of subcortical motor systems with frontal cortex. Obviously, in some way, these connected areas must be part of the substrate responsible for conversion of thoughts to action, but Ilinsky et al only allow themselves to conclude that "it is tempting to relate them [the neural pathways] to the cognitive functions of these areas, in particular, in the capacity to initiate and sustain sequences of motor behavior toward anticipated goals".

Fig. 2.13(1) **Sensory and motor areas of cortex and flow of activation – left lateral side of brain**

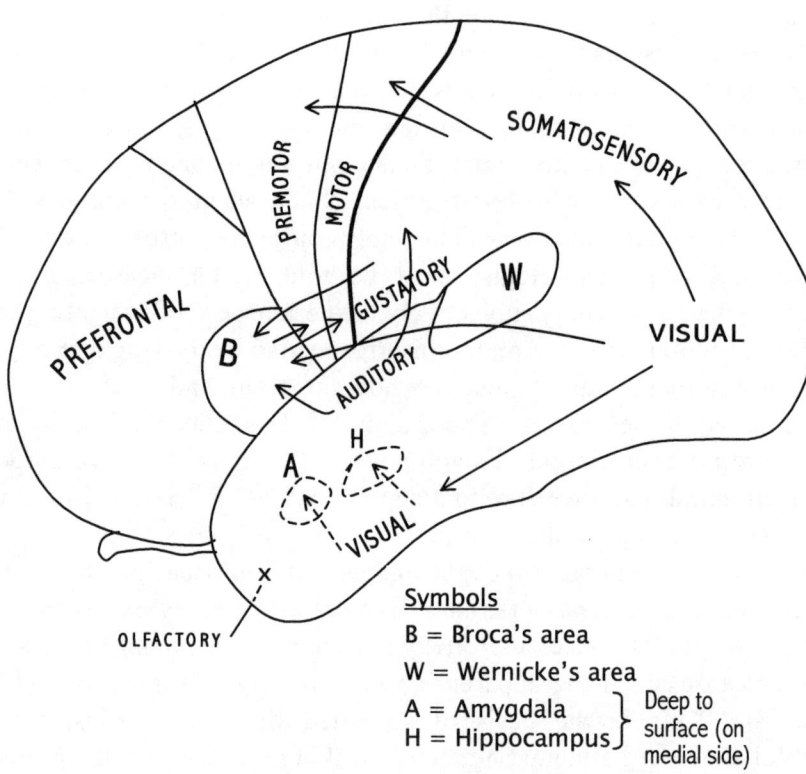

Symbols
B = Broca's area
W = Wernicke's area
A = Amygdala ⎫ Deep to
H = Hippocampus ⎬ surface (on medial side)

Thoughts, in the form of sequences of imagery, occur in the sensory cortices. They translate to physical action via different parts of the motor cortices. For example, a thought of moving a finger forms in visual and somatosensory cortices and acts on upper motor neurons controlling finger movements. Similarly, thoughts of speaking form in auditory and somatosensory cortices and activate upper motor neurons of vocal apparatus via Broca's area (or more directly for primitive vocalizations.)

It should be noted, however, that most motor actions precipitated by thoughts are engaged automatically from motor programs stored in one or another of the following structures: cerebellum, basal ganglia, supplementary motor cortex, and premotor cortex.

Fig. 2.13(2) Voluntary and automatic control of motor function

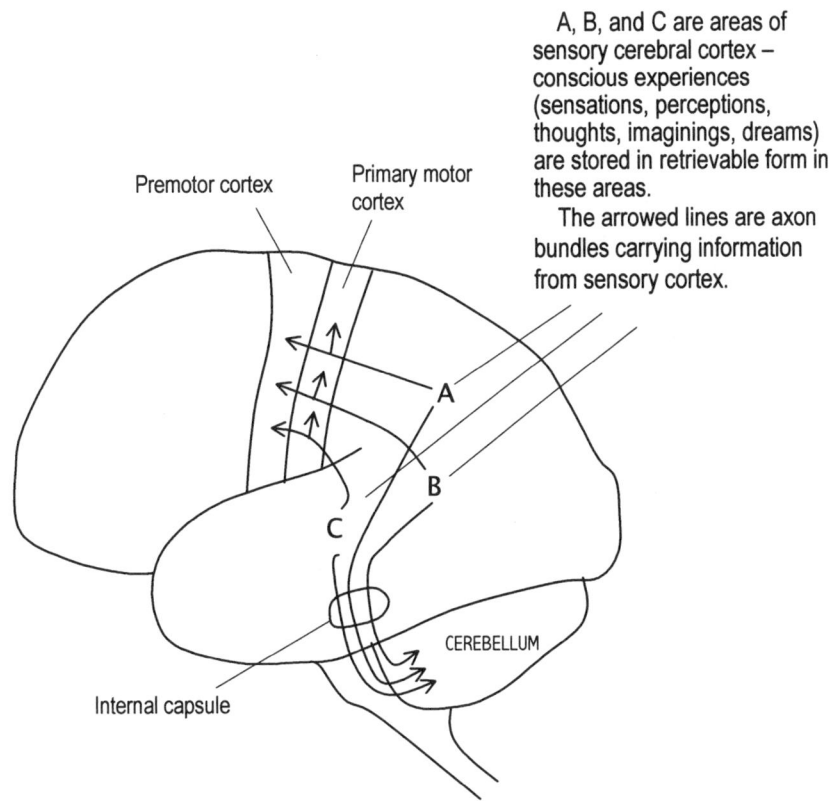

Voluntary movements spring from the workings of consciousness. The conscious experience, which is a species of energy, reconverts to neural activity and activates upper motor neurons, principally the Betz cells, in primary motor cortex, which in the human have direct synaptic connections with lower motor neurons of the neuraxis.

At other times A, B, C, etc. trigger motor programs, simple to complex, stored in cerebellum, basal ganglia, supplementary and premotor cortices, which act automatically and independently of voluntary control, except for some degree of guidance by the latter or full override if necessary. By various routes these programs engage and monitor sequences of movements constituting adaptive behavior, freeing the mind for processing current matters.

2.14 THE FACULTY OF INTENTION

(1) The evolution of the faculty of intention was 'necessary' to complement the thinking and understanding functions which would be impotent without it. The subjective aspect of intention is private to the mind and cannot be sensed, detected, or measured by any independent agency. However one may characterize or describe the subjective qualities of intention its essential function is that of predisposing the individual to the implementation of mentally conceived action-plans. Once the subjective experience we recognize as intention arises, various mental, emotional, and physiological changes begin to occur. These may include preparing or readying in some manner the neural pathways through which the neurons involved in conceiving the plan or which hold the plan in the conscious state are able to engage the appropriate motor function. Intention is therefore as strictly biological (that is, genetically based) as any bodily function, and is obviously closely related functionally to the faculty of volition, with which it undoubtedly coevolved. Biological intention must of course be distinguished from its fraudulent namesake, but even the latter may harden into resolve in which case pyhsiological changes begin to occur.

(2) The neural substrate of the faculty of intention is not likely any time soon to become precisely known. In the first place we can only guess what parts of the central nervous system are involved when an intention forms. An intention to perform an action in accordance with some closely conceived plan may involve much of the sensory cortices; imagining, thinking, understanding, etc. required for conceiving the plan depend on widespread cortical areas as well as on diencephalic focusing mechanisms. In addition, emotional concomitants, urges, and drives may involve the limbic system, the brainstem reticular formation, the autonomic nervous system, and hormonal influences.

Introspectively, there is a difference between doing something by habit and doing it with concentrated purpose. In the latter case the understanding of what the effort will achieve if successful is a propelling factor, therefore only the advanced brain of man, and possible of the higher primates, is capable of this level of intention. An understanding, as defined in this study, is a conscious experience of a causal relationship which is stored in memory and is subsequently usable in determining behavior. A particular understanding may include elements from several of the senses, so its parts will be widely stored in various sensory areas of the cortex, its integrity being maintained by intermodality synaptic linkages. For such an understanding to contribute to the formation and execution of an intention it must be retrieved into consciousness, and if the consequences of the causal process that the understanding represents is sufficiently desired the faculty of intention is engaged and the conscious image of the activity will convert to efferent signals which engage the appropriate neuro-muscular program: if an understanding is that an action will have a particular result then when that result is sufficiently desired the faculty of intention is engaged and all inhibitions removed the image of the action guides the action, and the more novel the action the closer the guidance.

An understanding may lead to an intention entailing complex action, so vast numbers of widely distributed neurons must be bound into functional packages for storage and to allow retrieval into accurate conscious representations to produce relevant behavior patterns, these huge packages functioning as effective units. We may wonder at the versatility of the linkage systems which allows the formation of innumerable such complex packages each having many of its parts shared with others yet with functional discreteness being maintained. This is one of the most dramatic examples of the power of biological evolution.

(3) According to the ideas in this study when memory neurons or, more likely, other pyramidals downline from the consciousness-generating neurons, have their effector outlets released from inhibition impulses pass from them to activate, via motor cortex, the particular muscles they are anatomically and functionally associated with. This idea is derived from considering the evolution of the nervous system from the level of the elementary reflex arc. The receptor at that level is anatomically and functionally linked to the effector, and this relationship is presumed to remain all through subsequent evolution, although in advanced brains it is greatly obscured by the complex network of connections within and between the reflex arcs which developed as they became more specialized for sophisticated internal functioning, and by the serpentine morphological changes forced by spatial constraints.

(4) When an intention is forming the content of the intended act is in image form, presumably in the sensory areas of the cerebral cortex. This image reconverts to neural energy to activate the memory and other outlet neurons, in principle each consciousness-generating neuron

activating its own downline memory and outlet neurons. If the action to be performed is novel, therefore is not stored as a motor program in the cerebellum, etc., then when the inhibition has been removed from the effector outlets signals pass to the premotor and motor areas with activation of the corticospinal (pyramidal) motor system in obedience to the image of this intention, and propelled by the energy of volition. It may be presumed that the same signals simultaneously pass, either via collaterals from the pyramidal pathways or more directly via the connections from the sensory cortices mentioned earlier, or both, to the basal ganglia, cerebellum, and other structures concerned with acquiring automatically performable motor programs (so-called 'procedural' memory). These structures immediately start storing the pattern of the voluntarily produced or mentally rehearsed novel action so that the next occasion the same intention is implemented some degree of automatic participation occurs.

Eventually, in man, large numbers of motor programs, including those for language expression, become established and automatically performable, requiring only the faintest trace of intention to set them off along appropriate lines, with minimal monitoring of feedback from the performances to keep them on track. *This delegation of duty is one of the major pillars on which the mind of man is built.*

2.15 THE ORIGIN AND NATURE OF VOLITION

(1) Volition (or 'free exercise of will') has never been satisfactorily explained and is evidently much misunderstood. It is a mental-experiential phenomenon with which every normal person is fully familiar, and every literate person knows what is meant by the concepts of 'free will' and 'personal responsibility'.

The full-blown voluntary capability of modern man is an evolved function: accounting for it in biological terms requires the assumption that it evolved through natural selection of favourable genetic variations from the earliest stage of *mental* processing capability, where a 'choice' of reflexive responses involving consciousness is delayed by inhibition or high threshold until overcome by the effects of one of two or more competing stimuli. The response is still reflexive, but now a delayed and 'directed' one, and if this process is genetically based and improves survival chances it will be selected and become established in succeeding generations.

2.15 The Origin and Nature of Volition 285

(2) This, I suggest, is the origin of volition. The evolution of mental processing capability is a progressive elaboration from this stage, eventually culminating in the highest capabilities of thinking, understanding, remembering, imagining, etc.. Such elaborate processing (or internal mental activity) is so obscurely reflexive that its reflexivity is commonly denied. When such processing eventually culminates in action the latter may be so remote from the stimulus, and the intervening machinations so involved, that the suggestion of a causal relationship or that the entire process is based on neural reflexivity is generally considered too simplistic to have explanatory value.

(3) Neocortical processing is in part a transducing operation on sensory information to generate an internal (conscious) representation of some aspect of external reality. At the preliminary stage of such processing the representation (which is the limit of simpler brains) is defined as a sensation; at a further stage of processing (achievable by more advanced brains) percepts are generated, and these may range from simple to complex; and, finally, the most advanced brains acquire and generate understandings, which are conscious representations of causal relationships existing (or provisionally accepted as existing) in external reality, and which are stored in memory and used in guiding behavior or as fodder for further thinking.

The point to bear in mind is that every conscious representation may act as a stimulus within the brain to produce a behavior, and since that behavior must be appropriate and relevant to external reality the conscious experience (sensation, percept, understanding) must be a reliable and sufficiently comprehensive representation of that aspect of external reality with which the behavior is concerned. (What the putative external world is 'really like' is, of course, a metaphysical matter and therefore undeterminable; except, it seems, in so far as it can be known mathematically).

The mental operations performed upon sensory input have the function of providing a response that is more appropriate to the general interests of the individual than an immediate reflexive response, or of supplementing the latter with benefit.

The form of action will vary from the simplest to the most complex, from that which can immediately be completed to that which is drawn out, in stages, etc., but there is no qualitative difference between an action based on the most careful deliberation and one hastily implemented after the briefest reflection, although the first may seem fully voluntary and non-reflexive and the latter impulsive and reflexive.

(4) The implementation of the kinds of complex action-plans that advanced minds can devise requires some mechanism beyond simple reflex triggering. The faculty of intention is part of such a mechanism, and so is that of volition. The action plans may ultimately derive from external circumstances but the internal processes of thought are, introspectively, the origin of such plans which therefore are seen as the free creations of self.

Plans resulting from thinking and understanding are of no avail unless translatable to action on the physical and social environments. As discussed earlier, this capability evolved hand-in-hand with the mind. It functions with such facility under habitual circumstances that thoughts and intentions so faint and fleeting as to be almost introspectively undetectable bring about major actions which seem to occur by themselves, as under these circumstances the faculty of volition is hardly brought into play.

(5) Self in relation to environment constitutes a fundamental dichotomy. Much of a lineage's evolutionary history is concerned with the development of mechanisms which interact most effectively with the external world. In advanced animals these mechanisms include those that come under the broad term 'self-awareness', and among these at the highest level is an evolved subjective experience of 'will' which accompanies and facilitates voluntary (i.e. highest level reflexive) action, presumably by its effect on harnessing, channeling, or catalysing energy utilization, on augmenting (strengthening) the focusing of consciousness, and on removing inhibitory influences from the action to be performed.

For energy to be released for the performance of a voluntary act the sympathetic nervous system must be activated. At lower CNS levels and in primitive organisms mechanisms exist which automatically precipitate action when certain environmental cues appear, probably operative through the hypothalamus and centres in the reticular formation and catalysed by the release of adrenaline. Presumably these structures have been tapped into by the evolving mental processes or such connections with them were already in place from earlier times and became more established as the evolving brain needed increasing executive capability to serve advancing cognitive functions, eventually those of thinking and understanding.

(6) These experiences of self and will are forms of consciousness which in the pre-linguistic state are unlikely to become objects of much introspective notice. With the evolution of language one of its earliest applications may have been in communicating thoughts and feelings and intentions reflecting the dichotomy of self and world with the inevitable result of increasing awareness of will and self; The use of language has an enormous influence on directing the brain's mental processes.

(7) In discussing will and self one has to be careful to avoid semantic pitfalls and metaphysical dead-ends. 'Free will' is a figure of speech which is perfectly intelligible in daily life in connection with the practical ramifications of personal responsibility, regardless of whether will is 'really' free or not, or even what being 'free' really means.

Selfhood is the property of consciousness: it is *intrinsic* to each putative unit of consciousness (the 'menton') and therefore to the global, unitary consciousness of the mind. The integrity of the body which generates this consciousness is assured in part by the utilization of the properties of consciousness, in increasingly sophisticated ways, culminating in the faculties of thinking and understanding which linguistically identify the body and its conscious content as the self.

(8) The mental activity of willing is most evident under certain conditions, such as when trying to get a semi-paralysed muscle to perform: the mental force of concentrated willing may become so strong as to spill over to activate much of the musculature of the body. The intriguing question is, and has always been, what is the neural basis of this mental activity? It is clearly an energetic process, for not only may the body become exhausted from the spill-over muscular contractions in the case above but there are also subjective sensations of brain fatigue. I suggest that a possible explanation is that feed-back from failure to move the part with normal willing results in compensatory over-activation of the co-ordinated mechanisms controlling focusing of consciousness, to achieve maximum activation of the motor neurons concerned, and this is so energy-demanding when it is strained to the limit that neural and haemodynamic mechanisms are overworked.

(9) It seems evident that higher mental functioning, in particular at the level of man, requires an equally highly evolved executive capability. Natural selection would be under continuous inducement to evolve such a capability, and the mechanism of volition would seem to be one of the principal results.

(10) The selection of the parts to be willed into action is determined by some motive. In man the capriciousness of thinking may produce motives which are so far removed from biological relevance that we may doubt that their influence operates at a biological level. But a need or an urge to act, whether produced by ratiocination, caprice, or physiological processes, is still a need or an urge, and has a primitive, reflexive propelling effect. Decisions to act, however trivial or whimsical or arbitrary, convert to action only when all inhibitory influences cease and all competing or opposing notions lose access to consciousness, thus allowing the prevailing need or urge to precipitate action.

The sense that action originates in the psychic self may be purely epiphenomenal to the recruitment of energy in the performance of physical and mental tasks, and this experiential epiphenomenon may be quite ancient; in the end the sense of volition may be a purely experiential by-product of energy utilization in a conscious being, in no way causal, its vividness thus being directly proportional to the degree of physical (and mental) energy being recruited.

Melzack (1997) has argued from an extensive study of phantom limb phenomena that the brain contains a genetically coded neuromatrix distributed among sensory and limbic systems that internally generates the percept of the body and its parts and sensations. On evolutionary grounds there is justification for this idea, but his anatomical proposal is still too vague. Self as opposed to environment is the most fundamental of all biological principles, so any genetic variations contributing to self-awareness would tend to be strongly selected, and the parietal lobe (as Melzack suggests, based on clinical evidence) is a very likely candidate structure contributing to this function inasmuch as it generates somesthetic consciousness. But many innate behaviors in newborn animals, controlled by programs in basal ganglia, cerebellum, premotor cortex, and supplementary motor cortex, are 'released' by visual, auditory, olfactory, etc. cues, and their feedback sensations contribute to self-awareness independently of any internally generated corporeal self-awareness.

2.16 EVOLUTION OF THE CAPACITY FOR MOTOR PROGRAM FORMATION AND STORAGE

The storage structures

(1) The volitional activation of lower motor neurons via the pyramidal tract provides the most direct control of movement by the mind, and is essential for the successful management of novel situations and for the implementation of plans for manipulating the environment. The *pure* volitional control of movement, especially complex movement, is slow, tedious, and clumsy. But repetition rapidly results in the sequence of movements being stored as a program in the vegetative motor control system, probably in the cerebellar cortex but possibly also in premotor cortex, supplementary motor cortex, and the neostriatum. It must be assumed that cerebellar, etc. cortices contain 'open, imprintable' neurons and synaptic linkages (i.e., a neuronal system with the property of storing sequences of neural signals) and that during volitional activation of the lower motor neurons via the pyramidal tract axonal branches carry copies of such activation to the cerebellum, etc. for storage, and that subsequent triggering of such programs results, either indirectly via thalamus and motor cortex, or more directly via the reticulospinal system, in largely automatic yet appropriate movement. Thus the cerebellum is a memory system, but unlike the memory system of the cerebral cortex its contents are not retrievable into consciousness and can only be consciously experienced through observation of automatic performances. It should be noted that even if its role were purely monitorial and non-executive this would still require storage of the motor program. (See Kolb and Whishaw, 1990:533, for the many terms employed by different authors to distinguish between conventional memory and motor 'memory').

(2) Encephalization is most advanced in man, with enormous development of neocortex of both cerebrum and cerebellum. The latter fact proclaims loudly that man's highly evolved mind requires for its effectiveness a highly evolved motor control system. The thinking function of the cerebrum can devise numerous plans of action, and the memory function of the cerebral cortex can store these plans as prototypes for action, but their execution requires motor movements of different levels of complexity. The mind is able to initiate these by voluntary effort in a slow, tedious, and inefficient manner through the

recently evolved pyramidal system; it is therefore able to translate to action a mentally created prototype, a product itself of the recently evolved thinking capability, but the slowness and clumsiness of this limits its usefulness. It is the probable function of the cerebellar cortex, in probable association with the neostriatum and premotor and supplementary motor cortices, to store the motor control program for such action, and to automatically undertake and supervise its subsequent execution with speed and precision free from interference from above. The neocortex of the cerebellum is part of the executive bureaucracy of the evolved mind, which explains why it evolved *pari passu* with the cerebral neocortex: "The lateral portion of the cerebellar hemispheres appears in mammals. The most lateral part is associated with fine coordination of the fingers. It is present only in primates, and is best developed in man" (Sarnat and Netsky, 1981:215).

Supporting the idea that movement programs are stored in cerebellum and striatum are the findings that "cerebellar neurons discharged well in advance of visually triggered volitional movement" and "basal-ganglia-cell discharge occurs in advance of volitional movements" (Evarts,1981:280, citing various sources). These findings indicate that motor cortex (Brodman's area 4) is a conduit for signals originating elsewhere (cerebellum and/or basal ganglia) and that these may be preconsciously generated in response to sensory cues, or reflexly generated in response to such cues via consciousness, giving automatic behavior, while pure voluntary movement is fully dependent on consciousness-cum-cognitive processes restricted to neocortex for the implementation of new movement-plans. During such pure voluntary movements the cerebellum and basal ganglia are silent, having nothing to contribute, although in practise this may seldom be fully so.

(3) There is an inclination among neuroscientists to place motor programs in the cerebral premotor cortex. This region probably has a limited program-storage capacity for controlling the sequential recruitment of upper motor neurons in area 4 and may have a role in voluntary initiation of action in conformity with the prototype stored in memory, probably in sensory cortices. But it is hardly credible that the premotor cortex is also able to store the vast number of automatically performable motor programs that the higher primates, and especially man, acquire in their lives.

The cerebellum does not have direct motor connections with the lower motor neurons; that is, it has no direct capability for causing muscle contraction. However: "Particularly potent drives on the motor cortical areas are derived from all divisions of the ventral lateral and the ventral posterolateral, pars oralis (VPLO) thalamic nuclei", which, especially VPLO, receive their input principally from the deep cerebellar nuclei (Carpenter, 1991:424). This supports the contention that the cerebellum stores complex learned motor programs and executes these, via thalamic relays to the motor cortex, on being triggered by thoughts or various other cues. Its function in motor control is in association with motor activities initiated elsewhere – in the spinal cord, the reticular formation, the basal ganglia, or in areas of the cerebral cortex. It is especially involved in the control of very rapid muscle activities such as talking, athletics, music making, etc. The standard explanation of how it makes its contribution is that it "both helps plan the motor activities and also monitors and makes corrective adjustments in the motor activities elicited by other parts of the brain" (Guyton,1987:215).

(4) Obviously, to perform these monitorial and regulatory functions at least a copy of the finest details of the skill program must reside in the cerebellum, but if it is executed from elsewhere it must also reside in such an executive centre. But which? Since we do not believe that the cerebral motor areas control the automatic performance of complex learned skills the most likely other system is the corpus striatum complex. However, this system does not seem sufficiently evolved to accomodate the large numbers of complex motor programs the human is capable of acquiring, but perhaps the larger motor system comprised of the corpus striatum (caudate nucleus, putamen, globus pallidus), n. accumbens, the substantia nigra, subthalamus, parts of the thalamus, reticular formation, and red nucleus may as a whole have this function.

But from various evidence, in particular its close association with the limbic system, it seems more probable that the older parts of the corpus striatum store the innate motor programs for emotionally driven expressions and behaviors, while the neostriatum stores acquired programs controlling emotionally driven behaviors, and the cerebellum may have a participatory role in ensuring the smoothness of the response. Furthermore, the nucleus accumbens, which is ontogenetically closely related to caudate and putamen (Carpenter,1991: 328; Gray, 1995), is also more closely related to hippocampal formation and amygdala than other parts of corpus striatum (Sarnat and Netsky, 1981: 353) and may have a prime function in emotionally driven behaviors or in their acquisition.

The premotor ('association') area of frontal cortex has abundant direct and indirect connections with the basal ganglia and cerebellum. Also, roughly as many pathways connect the sensory areas of cerebral cortex with the basal ganglia as with the motor cortex (Guyton,1987:202). Through these various connections it seems at least likely that automatically performable motor skills may be partially established in lower centres by mental rehearsal and voluntary effort and their performance monitored by the general prototype in conventional memory. (For charts illustrating the evolution and structure of the motor control systems see Sarnat and Netsky,1981:40-1, and Kolb and Whishaw,1990:278)

(5) Experiments by Roland and coworkers (cited in Kolb and Whishaw, 1990:271) in measuring cerebral blood flow in human subjects showed that during mental rehearsal of a finger movement only the supplementary motor area (the medial part of Brodman's area 6) was active, but with actual movement both this area and primary motor cortex were active. The supplementary motor area has profuse connections with parts of the caudate nucleus and putamen and through this route may play a part in the establishment of motor programs, while other evidence indicates a possible role in the initiation of voluntary movements (Carpenter,1991:424).

(6) But no matter how thoroughly learned and automatically performable a motor program may be the performance requires both intact lower centres and motor cortices. Passingham and coworkers (1983:675) unilaterally removed sensorimotor cortices (areas 4,3,2,1) from Rhesus monkeys and found temporary impairment of all movements and permanent impairment or loss of ability for individual finger movements and other skilled hand movements in the contralateral limb. In general the corticospinal pathways provide speed, strength, and dexterity to limb movements, especially discrete finger movements, while of the lower motor centres the rubrospinal system controls gross arm movements and the ventromedial (reticulospinal and vestibulospinal) system controls gross body movements (Lawrence and Kuypers, 1968; Beck and Chambers, 1970).

We may conclude from all this that when we are playing the piano, knitting, political speech-making, etc., and at the same time thinking of other things, the automatic performance is controlled not only from programs in lower centres but also from or via program-circuitries in the cerebral neocortex, because the lower centres do not have direct access to lower motor neurons controlling distal fine movements. We may also conclude that neocortex, neocerebellum, and neostriatum evolved together to provide an increased capability for acquiring automatically performable motor skills, involving all skeletal muscle groups. At a more general level we conclude that these changes came about because in an organism relying on the mind for exploiting the artefactual niche they had greatest selective value; in other words, they are niche adaptations.

Origin and evolution of the system

(7) The fundamental problem is how the capacity for the acquisition and storage of motor skills arose. The enormous advantage of such a function is obvious; once its primordial basis was in place there would be constant selective pressure to evolve it further. But how did it begin?

Innate behavior programs are 'hard-wired' in the archi- and paleocerebellar and pallidal circuitries, requiring simple maturation to become operational. From a very early stage of evolution of nervous systems behavior programs began to evolve, in principle from the first cooperative functioning of adjacent reflex arcs, eventually to achieve enormous complexity in a wide variety of 'instinctive' behaviors. These innate programs are of different levels of complexity; they consist of circuitries situated between the sensory receptors and the motor and glandular organs. As they grow more complex they may be discerned as macroscopic structures; for example, in myxinoids (hagfish), a primordial cerebellum consists of "a medial cellular extension of the acousticolateral area toward the fourth ventricle" (Sarnat and Netsky, 1981:214).

(8) The primitive parts of the CNS where programs for instinctive behaviors are hard-wired are presumably the parts that were added to which enabled learned skill programs to be laid down: "New cerebellar structures, such as the lateral hemisphere of mammals, are characterized microscopically by repetition of the architecture of the phylogenetically oldest parts of the cerebellar cortex" (Sarnat and Netsky, 1981:216). We may hypothesize that the evolving periphery of these hard-wired

circuitries were slightly modifiable by sensory input; the genome would allow some imprintability, with resulting responsiveness to slightly different cues or slightly more elaborate responses to the same cues.

This function of imprintability may have appeared at a very early evolutionary stage out of properties already in place. The more often a reflex circuit is engaged the more efficient it becomes up to a natural limit. This may apply even to the most primitive reflex arcs, thus constituting the most elemental form of learning. Molecular readjustments forced by signal passage would allow subsequent signals to pass more easily. This, it may be suggested, is the beginning of motor program learning; one may have to go back this far to account for the origin of skill acquisition.

(9) The next stage may be considered to be inherent in the first. Enlarging circuitries allow more versatility of response, and this is furthered if the newer circuit elements also show greater molecular plasticity. Newer and older circuits may be able to function at least semi-independently (e.g., fine finger skills can be employed in isolation) but the close interconnectedness between the different levels allows them to function cooperatively in the performance of many skills. In general, although parallel circuits, representing successive phylogenetic levels of reflexivity, may in theory operate independently of one another this may seldom be purely so; the older circuits may more often operate in isolation, but the newer circuits, which may be considered to consist of the older and newer parts, may tend to involve all levels in their operation.

(10) Elaboration of circuitries allows more complex responses, in part by accomodating the sequential ordering of the elements of such responses. No study has shown how neuronal systems accomplish this feat. Somehow, when one part of an automatically performable complex movement has been completed the next subprogram must be triggered (released) by some standard mechanism. Therefore, in the voluntary establishment of a new motor sequence, when the cerebellar cortex is being imprinted with the first part the trigger for the second must be inserted. The possible mechanism may consist of interneurons working on one another and on the subprograms: the first subprogram on being laid down includes the imprinting of inhibitory interneurons which are active when the subprogram is active; when this subprogram has been

Fig. 2.16(1) Stages in evolution of advanced motor control systems

The reflex arc is the basic mechanism of nervous systems and has remained so through all of evolutionary history — every structure/function of even the most advanced nervous systems is progressive elaboration of the reflex arc. Successive levels may be seen in comparative anatomy studies and in individual nervous systems. In advanced brains the evolutionary process has utilized the properties of consciousness — the human mind is simply the latest, most intricate elaboration of the basic reflex arc.

The following sequences depict the stages of evolution of the outlet (motor) part of the reflex arc:

(a) Thalamus → motor elements of rostral reticular nervous system → multisynaptic pathways to lower motor neurons of neuraxis.

(b) Thalamus → sensory neocortex → motor elements of rostral reticular nervous system

(c) Sensory neocortex → conversion of some multisynaptic motor pathways to more direct transmission lines to lower neuraxis (the early pyramidal tract.)

(d) Sensory neocortex → new relay cells which allow greater control of motor system appear and are strongly selected, giving rise to motor cortex → pyramidal tract.

(e) At stage (a), or even earlier, elements of the rostral reticular motor system evolved into circuitries controlling simple stereotyped motor movements in response to particular stimuli, these circuitries being precursors of basal ganglia and cerebellum.

Fig. 2.16(2) The penultimate stage in evolution of motor control systems

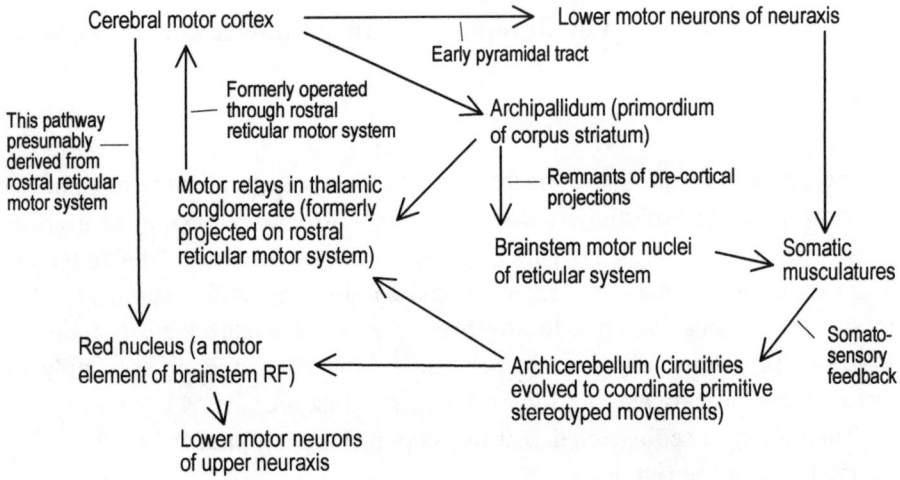

Fig. 2.16(3) The latest stage: the capacity to acquire advanced, automatically performable motor skills and behavioral responses

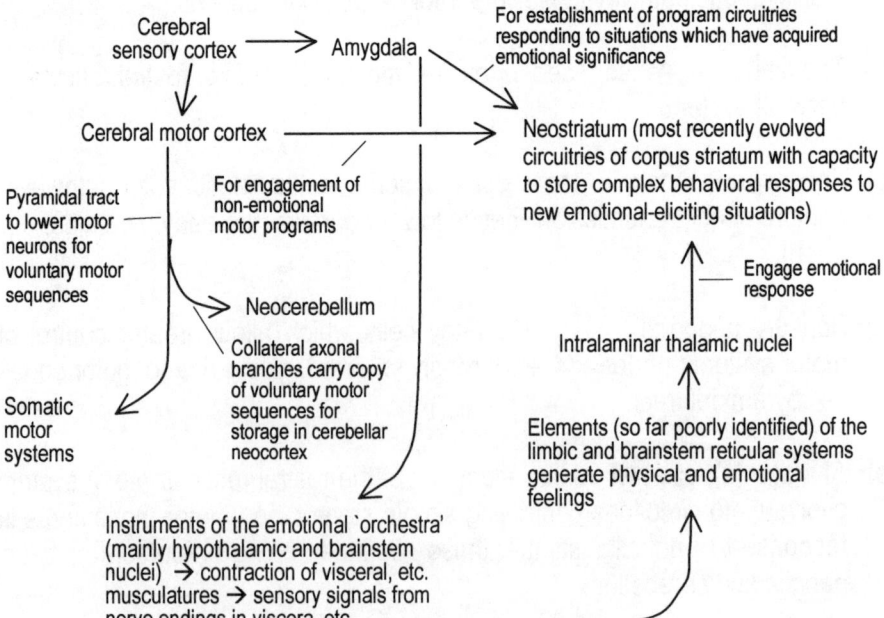

played out the inhibitory interneurons cease activity, releasing excitatory interneurons which trigger the second subprogram, and so on.

(11) The phylogenetically newer elements will mature later than the older and simpler reflex arcs of which they are elaborations and may require more repetitive activation for facilitation to set. Furthermore, the more elaborate the system the more varied are the patterns and sequences of stimuli that can find pathways for the establishment of recognition-response circuitries, and the more frequently these stimuli are encountered the more responsive the system becomes to them, so that increasingly weak input can set off the full response. Such motor programs will always require a trigger in order to be 'released', and in the early stages of evolution this will be an external trigger, but with evolution of a forebrain internally generated signals may act as triggers.

Even at advanced stages of evolution a good portion of circuitries are responsive to stimuli of ancient and enduring relevance to the species. They are largely 'hard-wired' and remain so in many phyla no matter how complex they become. In many instances the elaboration is in the response program, the triggering stimulus (e.g., a pheromone or a seasonal hormone) remaining relatively simple. But, in vertebrates, complexity of motor program formation is increasingly acquired through learning, through the ability of more complex stimuli to set behavioral responses to themselves. At first this is a matter of trial and error. The animal faces a situation to which it must respond. It will react tentatively with a single movement. If this produces a result in the right direction it will react with an additional movement, otherwise it will start over again with a different first simple movement. Failed efforts are not repeated either because they are inhibited by punishment or because an alternative effort is rewarded. A connected series of pathways become facilitated thus becoming in effect a program governing a successful complex behavior which becomes more established with each execution.

(12) In the prepyramidal motor system of early vertebrates these motor programs were contained in and operated through the reticular formation (RF). The special sensory receptors situated rostrally relayed in the rostral RF, necessarily close to one another, for onward transmission of signals, the physical proximity of these relays leading to the evolution of the thalamus. (Such proximity forced by spatial constraints may have had serendipitous results by allowing more connections between different systems, leading eventually to the modern

human cerebrum and higher mental functioning). The downline part of the RF, the motor RF, contained the circuitries that comprised the behavior programs, with different parallel lines to the lower neuraxis, mediating responses ranging from simple reflexes to complex behaviors.

As the thalamic relay nuclei of the special senses evolved in complexity this was accomplished by adding new tiers of cells which invaded the rostral part of the neural tube which then evaginated to form the hemispheres, carrying many of the RF motor fibres with them. Those left behind mostly innervated the circuitries constituting behavior programs in the primordial globus pallidus in the upper part of the RF motor pathways. These controlled different behaviors from those controlled by the primordial cerebellum, principally behaviors responsive to physical and emotional feelings.

The primordial cerebellar pathways to motor outlets went via different levels of the RF motor system, e.g., the cerebellopontine, the cerebellorubrospinal, and the cerebellothalamic.

But it may be surmised that the effectiveness of the developing cerebral sensory neocortex was enhanced by the concomitant development of more direct lines to the neuraxis; its RF motor outlet presumably became adapted for this function by conversion of multisynaptic pathways to those with fewer synapses, and this conversion also involved the cerebellar-thalamic-RF pathways so that they operated via the new cerebrospinal (pyramidal) transmission system. (See Appendix E)

(13) The ability of the cerebral sensory neocortex to generate conscious representations of the external world (i.e. 'percepts') was of such strong adaptive value, in that it allowed more comprehensive and appropriate behavioral responses, that it led to a large increase in the size of this cortex. And with the development of understanding and thinking functions even more effective behaviors could be devised. This required the ability to directly control individual joint movements, and this led to the rapid development of the pyramidal motor system projecting on lower motor neurons.

Sensory input now not only triggered innate and unthinkingly acquired behavior programs but also provided the raw material which the thinking function used to develop a new level of triggering. But the new control, exercised through the equally new voluntary capability with imperfectly evolved access to motor function, is slow, clumsy, and tedious.

2.16 Evolution of Capacity for Motor Program Formation and Storage

Cortically conceived motor plans, voluntarily implemented with difficulty via the corticospinal tract, become with repetition automatically performable motor programs in the neocerebellum and operate with speed and efficiency via the cerebellothalamocortical pyramidal system and other motor outlets (rubrospinal via the red nucleus, olivospinal via red nucleus and olive, and the lateral vestibulospinal via the lateral vestibular nucleus).

(14) The function of the supplementary motor cortex (area M2 or medial part of area 6 of Brodman) is not fully known but "There appears to be general agreement that neurons in M2 modify the activities of cells in the primary motor area [M1 or Brodman's area 4] and probably are involved in the programming of skilled motor sequences" (Carpenter,1991:424). Among the main projections of M2 are those to the primary and premotor areas and to the caudate and putamen motor structures. It receives input from parietal cortical areas 5 and 7 and from thalamic nuclei "which show increased activity prior to any movement" (op.cit.:425). The supplementary motor area, like the primary motor area, has a somatotopic organization.

The 'pure' voluntary implementation of mentally conceived motor sequences is by action on lower motor neurons via the pyramidal tract for immediate movement, but these signals are simultaneously stored as motor programs ('procedural' memory) via parallel pathways or axonal branches to one or more of the cerebellum, basal ganglia, supplementary motor area, and possibly the premotor area, while the conventional ('declarative') memory system of the sensory neocortex stores the prototype which is retrievable back to imagery to participate in cognitive functions, and through sensory feedback from the performing structures to monitor any subsequent automatic performance of the motor sequences.

(15) It is arguable that the cooperative interconnections between the various sensory modalities of the nervous system must have arisen at the very earliest stage, in that had they evolved separately to any degree of complexity it would have been difficult if not impossible for such connections to then become established – if the chance is not taken extremely early it may be lost forever. Perhaps all the genetically determined (hard-wired) connectivities of advanced brains were *potentially* in place primordially – the whole brain evolved from the one-celled amoeboid stage of life in which every part is connected to every

other part directly or indirectly. For a new structure to evolve it must do so ultimately from the primordial form of life.

Responsivity of the single-celled organism to external agencies is the primordium of the neural reflex function, potentially to all physical and chemical stimuli that can affect the organism. Inherent in the molecular structure of the cell is the propensity to be affected by radiation, chemical reactivity, temperature, pressure, etc.. All the sensory transducers of such stimuli are the structural consequences of such propensities. So also, we may surmise, is the transducer of neural energy to consciousness. Can the genome mutate to code for a completely new morphological feature, one that is not in any way a variation of a preexisting structure or function?

2.17 THE DEVELOPMENT OF MONITORING BY THE MIND

(1) As is so often pointed out the mind can at any moment override automatic performances and reassert direct control over the lower motor neurons, though under most such circumstances this is only partial, being just sufficient for current needs. Here we have a major neurophysiological mechanism of great complexity and efficiency of functioning: that of the mind's monitoring of learned automatic performances, including language production.

The origin of mental monitoring may date back to shortly after the origin of consciously mediated acquired reflexes, and at first must have been a very simple operation. One may speculate that the first reflex acquired via consciousness (i.e. the primordial mind) although beneficial enough and reliable enough to provide survival advantages (so that natural selection could operate on genetic variations to evolve it further) yet failed at times either by acquiring an inappropriate reflex, or failure of the reflex to function normally, or through the reflex no longer being relevant to changed circumstances. Individuals unlucky in these ways would fail to survive unless resulting danger situations promptly triggered evasive reflexes. Furthermore, genetic variations in which such emergency evasive reflexes had an inhibitory side effect on the acquired reflex might have been the origin of neural inhibition and of the mutual inhibitory controls between the separately evolving reflexive systems.

(2) Animals at the early mammalian level of opportunistic exploratory behavior, with an evolving ability to acquire automatically performable behaviors, may already have a well-developed monitoring system for

such behaviors, principally operating at the cerebellar and brainstem levels, with feed-back information from the performing structures somehow being matched to the programs in these areas, thus allowing continuous readjustments. But the further evolution of internal mental processes (thinking, remembering, imagining, etc.) and thus the ability to formulate and store plans of action, however primitively, and to execute these, led to the elaboration of monitoring by the mind. The prototype is in conventional (retrievable) memory and when the performance takes place (largely automatically on triggering the motor program) feed-back information is gathered by the senses and elicits recognition if the performance corresponds to the prototype in memory, in which case it is allowed to continue, but if there is failure of recognition an alarm mechanism interrupts the performance and direct volitional control is re-established.

(3) There has been much controversy over this topic, mostly I think due to failure to notice and appreciate the general principle underlying the mechanisms involved: The effectiveness of the mind is greatly enhanced by mechanisms which allow it to delegate duties. This 'law of the mind' explains the powerful action of natural selection in evolving the automatic functioning of learned behaviors and skills.

(4) Here again two opposing biological needs must be accommodated: that of allowing maximum automation for speed of action and to free the mind for thinking, and that of monitoring the automatic behavior to avoid disaster. Mental monitoring can only occur via consciousness, because only through consciousness can the memory store of the prototype be reached by feed-back information from the performance for recognition if correct or failure of recognition if incorrect. But this mechanism has evolved to such a high level of efficiency that the faintest generation of consciousness by the action of the feed-back signals is able to maintain the monitoring – a level of sensitivity equivalent to that of innate and acquired alarm mechanisms when their cues appear.

When this system is working at full efficiency the individual's mind may be 'so far away' that he is 'quite unaware' of the automatic behavior and its environmental context, and as a consequence is able to remember little if any of it. In effect monitoring via marginal consciousness of the performance may occur, yet with this weak consciousness being unable to imprint new memory circuits, or so faintly that subsequent retrieval is very unlikely. At the same time other areas of

302 Stages in Evolution of the Mind

consciousness-generation involved in thinking, imagining, remembering, or sensing may be very active. And, as is well known, if such mental preoccupation is too strong the monitoring of a current automatic behavior will fail and if some flaw in performance develops accident is the likely result; in fact, if internal focusing is very strong there may be reflex inhibition of all body movements (an evolved mechanism which minimizes distraction) so even the automatic behavior may abruptly stop.

2.18 THE EVOLUTION OF RESPONSE TO UNFAMILIAR ITEMS IN FAMILIAR CONTEXTS

(1) It is a common experience that an unfamiliar item in otherwise familiar surroundings immediately captures attention and elicits interest and curiosity. There can be little doubt that this is a primitive response and that it primarily served the purpose of alerting the animal to possible dangers and opportunities. When we try to unravel the underlying neural mechanism we soon realize that this is a nice example of the intricate workings of natural selection.

Becoming familiar with its surroundings means that the animal stores in memory numerous details (possibly supplemented by acquired behavior programs) which are linked to form complex patterns (or 'maps') reinforced by repeated exposures. Such memory storage may be limited in accuracy and detail but so long as the same surroundings are being repeatedly experienced a certain level of representation will be established, and what matters from the point of view of natural selection is that this representation is sufficiently accurate for the mechanism of conscious recognition to operate, since out of this can evolve a system which is responsive to the difference between the familiar and the unfamiliar and mechanisms which utilize this distinction with benefit. (Figs. 2.18(1-3)

Conscious recognition occurs when an item or event being experienced is already in memory and this results in a sense of familiarity. We must presume that the elicitation of this sense of familiarity is an evolved process serving some useful biological function. The neural mechanism of its production is unknown but it was hypothesized earlier in this study that when an item already in memory is re-encountered the memory neurons serving the involved consciousness-generating neurons become activated and send impulses back to the latter to generate image consciousness which, when this reinforces the sensory

2.18 The Evolution of Response to Unfamiliar Items in Familiar Contexts

percept or when both sets of impulses act on the involved consciousness neurons simultaneously or nearly so, there results a sense of familiarity.

That this is not merely a cognitive artefact is attested by the serious and distressing nature of subjective unreality effects from the loss of sense of familiarity which some neurological and psychiatric disorders may produce.

A possible effect of this sense of the familiar may be to allow the individual to safely ignore most of the sensory data coming in, as the occasional recognized data representing vital interests instantly engage genetic or acquired responses (even, in the case of some primitive responses, preconsciously, therefore well before conscious recognition may occur). Although it is possible that the site of engenderment of the sense of familiarity may be other than at the juncture of action of sensory input and retrieved memory impulses on the consciousness-generating neurons – for example, via the limbic system – this seems unlikely as the neural circuitry required would be enormously complex; but some mechanism must exist which either actively inhibits response to the familiar, or actively elicits response (e.g. investigatory behavior) when failure of recognition occurs in the midst of a set of recognitions. If the former is the case then the unrecognized will fail to inhibit the response which will then occur, this response being, at least in some more advanced mammalian species, the elicitation of the feelings of interest and curiosity which heighten investigatory behavior.

(3) Unrecognized environmental items should have no influence on the animal – there are no genetic or acquired programs responsive to them: if over evolutionary time certain aspects of the environment are of no significance for a species no mechanism will evolve to respond to them. Yet animals with advanced minds have evolved a capability for 'noticing' novel features, as this has proven selectively beneficial in association with opportunistic exploratory behavior and with improvements in mental capabilities.

How did the neural mechanism underlying a noticing capability evolve? There must have been some pre-adaptation for this, and it may have been the presence and operation of primitive focusing mechanisms: perhaps it is unavoidable in the functioning of the latter that irrelevant items may receive some incidental focus, so that well before there evolved any priority for the mental processing of novel features these were able to incidentally capture some attention and to be stored in memory and subsequently to be recognized, although no response mechanism existed for them; i.e. they had no behavioral effect. But with evolutionary elaboration of the linkage mechanisms of the memory system there was an increasing accumulation of memory linkages between such incidentally acquired memories and those tied into the reflexive system, and this in turn resulted in a tendency to respond to wider environmental details, which proved generally profitable thereby itself becoming a target for further evolutionary elaboration in keeping with the 'upward spiral' or 'leap-frog' principle governing evolution of the mind. (See Figs.2.18(2) and (3)).

(4) So the evolving mind increasingly 'notices' the environment and its details, but this also has a disadvantage in that there is a tendency to be continually distracted by irrelevancies. Such distraction is anti-adaptive, therefore any mechanism protecting against it would tend to be selected from an early stage of the noticing capability, this mechanism subsequently evolving to keep pace with the other. It was suggested above that this protective mechanism may be a system of inhibition on reflexive response to familiar stimuli, this inhibitory system failing to be engaged by stimuli which are unfamiliar or when preempted by 'vital' cue responses or when a familiar item has become associated with some function important to the individual. The response we are discussing here is investigatory behavior; other responses concerned with routine activities may occur readily when their familiar cues appear, as in much of daily habit behavior.

Le Doux (1997) reports that cells in the lateral nucleus of the amygdala responded to auditory stimuli in one of two ways: Consistently or by habituating. In the latter case the animal learned to ignore – eventually did not respond to – unimportant sensory stimuli. This may have some bearing on the fact that familiar surroundings do not excite but out-of-place new features do. There seems to be an alarm mechanism which kicks in when this occurs, but where is this mechanism and how does it work? Amygdala is the gateway to the emotional system so may be an essential element in this evolved behavior; and its basolateral nuclei are most developed in humans, less so in lower primates, and hardly in primitive mammals.

Fig. 2.18(1) **Preservation of correspondence with environmental patterns in consciousness and memory** (from Hale, 1989)

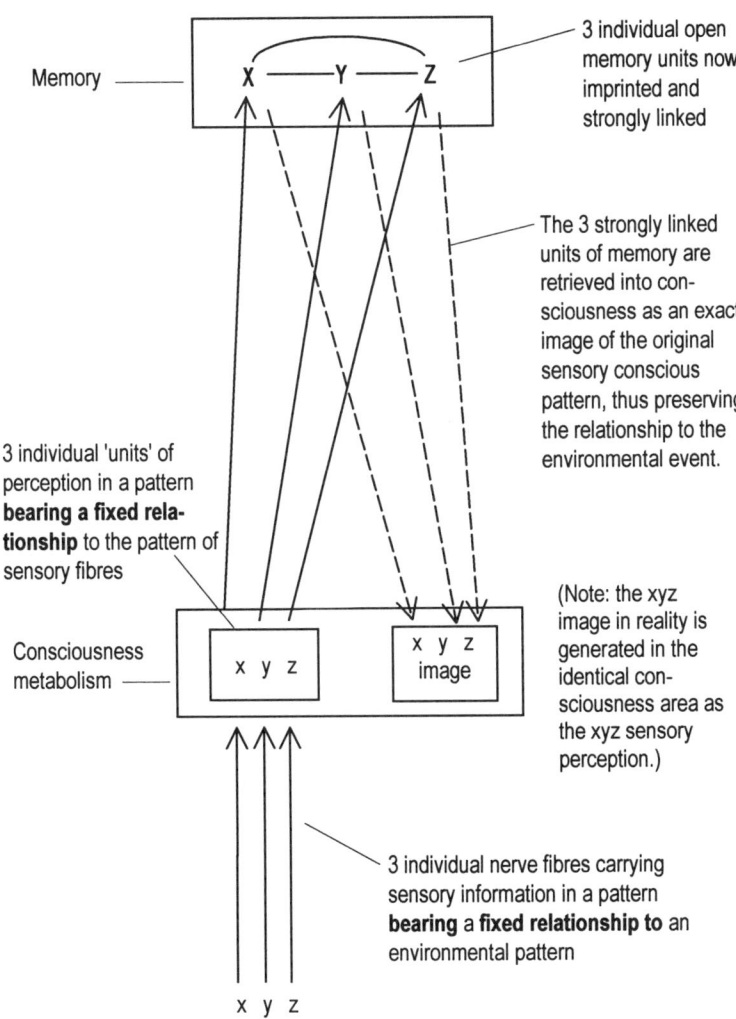

Note: Different organisms will have different perceptions of the same environmental event, but in each the pattern correspondences will hold in the whole system, thus ensuring reliable interactions with the environment.

Fig.2.18(2) **Hierarchial processing of, and responses to, environmental information** (From Hale, 1989)

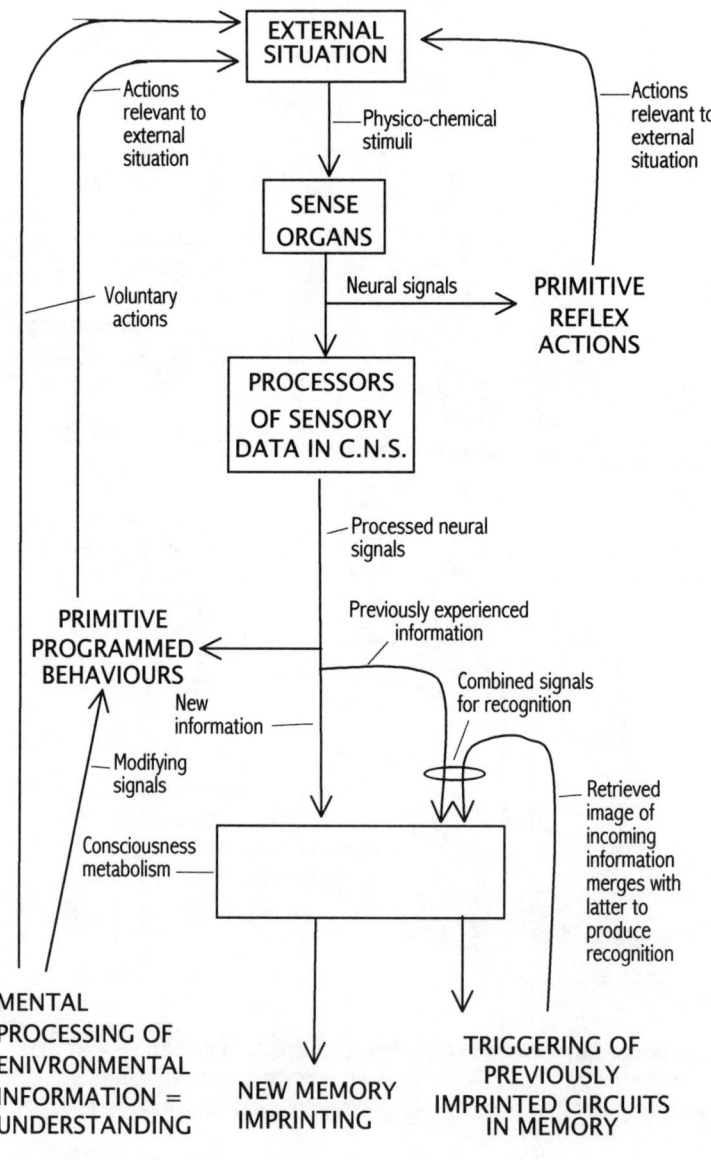

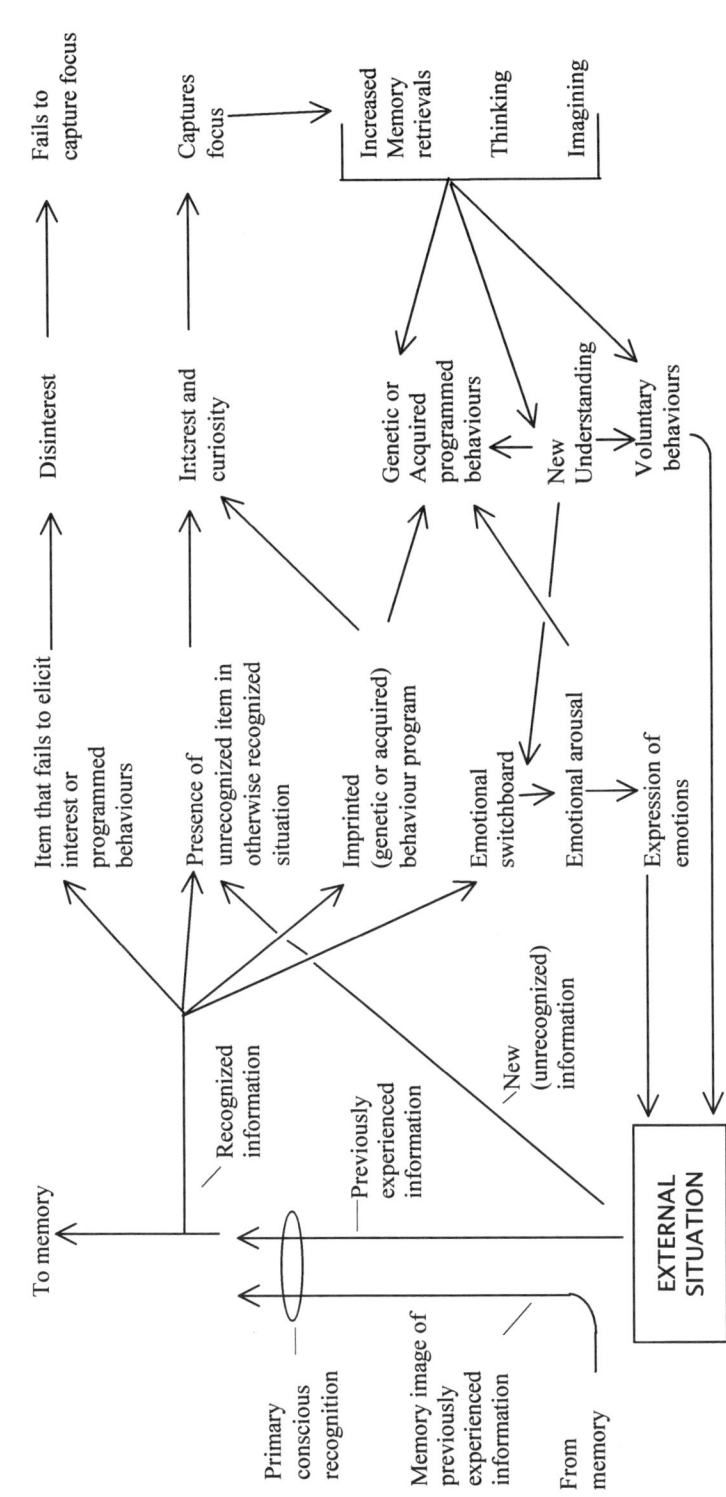

Fig.2.18(3) **Processing of recognized and unrecognized environmental information** (From Hale, 1989)

2.19 THINKING AND UNDERSTANDING

The highly specialized mental functions of thinking and understanding probably begin at the level of the more recent common ancestor of hominids and anthropoid apes. The mammalian line leading to these groups was slowly evolving in a direction towards becoming pre-adapted, perhaps over a period of tens of millions of years, for the emergence of a specialized thinking function and the capacity to formulate and execute action plans.

Perhaps the reason this break-through took so long in coming was three-fold: the general pre-adaptive features had to reach a sufficiently high level of efficiency in their functioning; the inhibitory mechanisms acting on the motor outlets of the memory and other neuronal systems supporting internal mental functioning had to achieve a critical level of efficiency; and the focusing mechanisms of consciousness likewise had to reach a critical level of efficiency. In none of these on its own would improvement have been strongly adaptive, i.e. of much selective value, yet, evidently, sufficiently so for slow evolutionary development. Eventually, possibly in the most recent common ancestor of man and apes, the first acts of thinking-to-understand began to occur through the combined action of these pre-adaptations, and such thinking capability must have been of sufficient selective value for it to be retained and further evolved to the level which was pre-adaptive for the emergence of man.

The earliest benefit in the evolution of a mechanism of controlled shift-focusing on different aspects of a situation results from increase in the likelihood of retrieval of understandings relevant to the situation, thereby increasing the chance of the most appropriate behavior being engaged. A fairly large store of understandings and factual knowledge must be present in retrievable memory for much benefit to be derived, so this function is not likely to be operative in immature individuals or in species which have not evolved an advanced memory capacity. Possible mechanisms were discussed in Section 1.25.

2.20 MENTAL PROCESSING AND BEHAVIOR

(1) We have reached the stage where relatively prolonged mental activity may occur without reflexive physical activity. The animal is processing complex information at the conscious level. Information stored in memory is being used to help determine action. Previous experience of similar or analogous situations or elements of such

situations and their outcomes are in memory, and the present situation retrieves more or less of these through the loop-back mechanism described earlier, providing conscious recognition or sense of familiarity (Section 2.3). Secondary retrievals of related understandings may then occur, and these may prepare the individual for action appropriate to the outcome of the present situation, through anticipatory mechanisms (Section 2.6).

When a situation has been met with several times, and appropriate responses developed through trial and error or by thinking, the whole process becomes speeded up as neuromuscular programs are established. The process will still operate via consciousness, but now the thinking function will largely be bypassed. The rapidity with which such 'learning from experience' can occur is, as has been suggested earlier, an important evolutionary development contributing to greater effectiveness of the mind. Therefore, in much of behavior casual introspection may fail to show any definite mental component consisting of imagery; but when a situation is novel the deepest thinking may be required to determine appropriate behavior, and the clearer the imagery the better. This is partly achieved by blocking sensory distractions, e.g., by closing the eyes or through central inhibition of sensory transmissions.

By 'toying' mentally with the situation or problem, more retrievals are likely to occur. This behavior may be an evolutionary extension into the mental arena of opportunistic exploratory behavior through being selectively beneficial in conjunction with improved focusing and memory capacity and retrievability.

(2) Attributing all of this to non-human animals may be suggestive of anthropomorphism, but human mental faculties did not arise full-blown. As one goes 'down' the phylogenetic scale there is less likely to be imagery and consequently there is less influence on behavior by imagery, and at the evolutionary point at which imagery first plays a part it may do so by being only slightly contributory to the triggering of behaviors. At this level imagery is likely to be very weak, but it was an essential element of the early pre-adaptations that led to the mind of man.

We may give as an example of this the following: An animal sees a fruit and eats it, no internal mental processing occurring here apart from consciousness being a link in the reflexive behavior; it may smell the fruit which is out of sight or hear sounds from other individuals associated with the finding and eating of fruit and this triggers an acquired behavior program of movement towards these cues; this behavior is likely to be more definite if the cues also elicit images of the fruit, this constituting an elementary level of internal mental processing; a more advanced level would be operative if some indirect cue, such as secretive behavior of another which had been discovered in the past to signify fruit, and which had become stored in memory as an understanding, retrieves from memory the understanding, thus revealing the probable existence of nearby fruit. This may be construed as the operation of a Pavlovian conditioned reflex, but unlike the latter such an association may be strongly established by one experience; and in any case the neural processes involved may have much in common.

On innumerable occasions in daily life we respond appropriately to sensory information without having to visualize the response; such responses have become habitual, but not uncommonly the most detailed visualization may be employed, e.g. when we require something and try to visualize where and how we might obtain it.

(3) As the cognitively advanced primate explores and 'thinks' its behavior tends to be more fine-tuned, versatile, and appropriate. It is using its knowledge (memory stores of causal relationships and factual material) for this purpose. Until its thinking turns up information demanding action the parade of retrievals will continue, with conscious focus shifting between such retrievals and sensory data.

Whether a thought image precipitates an action or not, assuming there is a motor program triggerable by it, will depend on the sensitivity to triggering of the program and competition from other programs. In dealing with the environment the nervous system is on a knife-edge: the proposed inhibitory mechanism which prevents imagery from engaging unwanted effector activity during mental procedures is probably extremely sensitive to disengagement by alarm and vital cue information as well as some classes of imagery; some thoughts, for example, readily elicit emotions and their somatic and autonomic effects.

2.21 THE EVOLUTION OF THE HUMAN MIND

The ability to generate understandings through thinking is evidently of limited value in the natural niches; there is probably little selective advantage in acquiring long chains of understanding. A 2-unit chain, i.e. A is causally related to C through B, is probably the best that any non-human mind can acquire through thinking.

The evolution of the human mind from this level of pre-adaptation was the result of entering and adapting to the artefactual 'niche', the essence of which is that environmental material and forces can be manipulated in various ways to improve success in life.

The artefactual niche is there for any organism to enter and exploit, and many have done so in various ways and degrees by means of genetically determined behaviors. Man, however, is the only animal to have extensively entered and exploited this niche because its exploitation requires, as is the case of other niches, advanced development of certain functions, in this case the faculty of thinking-to-understand.

Once the capability of thinking-to-understand had evolved the qualitative level of man had been reached. Subsequent transformation to the modern human mind was largely a matter of elaboration of structures already present. Except for the ability to communicate knowledge no new evolutionary breakthrough occurred. The difference in power between the mind of modern man and pre-man is such, however, that the levels of understanding we can reach delude us into believing we possess a unique apparatus. It is in the *products* resulting from the exercise of greater power that qualitative difference exists, e.g. new kinds of understanding, symbolic communication, artificial means of recording knowledge, etc.

Original thoughts may be relatively rare happenings, but if acquired by the entire population through language each individual in time comes to possess wide knowledge, and when this becomes too much for natural memory artificial storage greatly aids mental efforts, increasing the likelihood of more original thoughts occurring.

We can only conjecture (e.g., Hale,1989) on how genetic variations leading to the human mind actually took root in human societies – how the 'upward spiral' in fact played out. A reasonable scenario is that early hominids lived in small groups in territorial competition with one another and, in the early exploitation of the artefactual niche, and more generally in the evolutionary commitment to relying on the mind as an instrument of survival, every improvement of intelligence gave a competitive edge, 'intelligence' being the functioning of the numerous faculties of mind analysed in this study.

Throughout the text structures of the central nervous system more highly developed in the human than in other primates and in less encephalized mammals were noted, most of which were presumed to be substrates supporting man's advanced cognitive capabilities.

Also of considerable interest are the various maladaptive morphological, physiological, and functional features found in man which represent the price paid for the advantage of evolving an advanced mental apparatus able to exploit the artefactual niche. Some of these have been previously mentioned such as of the difficult parturition due to the large foetal cranium, the tendency to choke on food due to anatomical readjustments of pharynx and glottis for speech, and frequent low back and hip-joint problems due to assuming and erect posture.

Concerning the last item of erect posture there have been several conjectures offered as to its relevance to the development of human intelligence, either as a contributing factor (e.g., in freeing the forelimbs for specialized applications) or as a compensatory factor (e.g., minimizing the build-up of heat in the brain), but little or no mention on the effect it had on the performance of coitus, and the secondary effects of this on 'humanization'.

At some stage front-to-front coitus became as equally possible as the heretofore obligatory front-to-back, and this drastically changed the nature of the encounter. The distal part of the anterior mucosal wall of the human vagina is firmly corrugated, and the ventral skin of the penis is richly supplied with sensory nerve-endings tied to the ejaculatory reflex. These factors allow rapid ejaculation of semen, and since the chance for copulation in primitive groups is often fleeting these anatomical features being adaptive were established through the process of natural selection. But in front-to-front coitus the ventral penile surface is in contact with the smooth posterior vaginal mucosa and ejaculation is consequently slower, so not only do the participants experience a more interpersonal encounter but a new dimension of physical pleasure. (Note that the rugae-like folds of the posterior vaginal wall are soft and elastic thus allowing a great distension without tearing during parturition.)

The conjecture from all this that I wish to make is that the new situation appealed to the more sophisticated and intelligent individuals of both sexes, attracting them to one another with the consequence of more rapid evolution of intelligence in such subgroups and more rapid development of erect posture.

Erect posture, encephalization, and 'humanization' proceeded apace in the hominid line, influencing one another, no doubt in numerous ways, obvious and subtle, in keeping with the 'upward spiral' or 'leap-frog' evolutionary principle.

APPENDICES

APPENDIX A

AN HEURISTIC MODEL OF CONSCIOUSNESS

"From the standpoint of the search for truths, it is noteworthy that Ptolemy, like Eudoxus, fully realized that his theory was just a convenient mathematical description that fit the observations and was not necessarily the true design of nature" (Kline 1985:66).

"When some natural fact strikes us as strange, it means that we are looking at it from the wrong point of view" (Sawyer, 1943).

The following model of consciousness is developed from the points raised in the previous sections. To my knowledge no other published author subscribes to these straightforward (many would call them naive) views (but Darwin is quoted as saying that there is nothing wonderful about the brain secreting thoughts any more than gravity being a property of matter (Eccles and Robinson, 1985:177), and Penfield (1979) pleaded for a scientific search for the special energy of mind). The ideas put forward here tend to be rejected out of hand as being simplistic, unsupported by evidence, and above all going beyond legitimate rules of inference. But I have already argued that the various other approaches reviewed in Section 1.1 are defective, which possibly leaves the following or similar ideas the only ones separating us from total incomprehension.

That functioning nervous tissue generates consciousness is almost universally accepted – the evidence for this is overwhelming. Yet almost no one believes that neurophysiological investigation will reveal the mechanism involved. What does this apparent impasse tell us about the nature of explanation? And is there any principle of epistemology that may offer guidance in this type of situation? Surely if the first part (the generation of consciousness by nervous tissue) is true the second part (the belief that the process is beyond elucidation) must be false? There must surely be something in the behavior of neurons open to investigation that holds the key to understanding this phenomenon, perhaps something we may clearly see without realizing its significance.

There is no denying that neural signals from the sense organs acting on cells of primary sensory areas of cerebral cortex 'result in' or 'cause' or 'engender' consciousness, or else 'correlate' precisely with consciousness. The essential question here is whether or not the energy of neural signals is an absolute prerequisite for consciousness to appear. If the answer is in the affirmative then we can with certainty say that consciousness is a form of energy transduced from neural energy by some mechanism in the cortical cells. The argument for correlation is that since no such transducing mechanism has been identified the energy theory fails by default. But correlation, which is the only possible alternative to the energy theory, involves an asymptotic relationship between consciousness and the neural signals, in that it must be exact but cannot in any way involve causation: consciousness must at the same time be totally dependent on and totally independent of the neural signals. Correlation theory (or parallelism) is logically untenable and is herinafter dismissed as a *non sequitur*.

The briefest thought-image may be followed by profound bodily changes. If the thought is a remembered incident the concerned memory neurons have been activated. This process is energetic – it is metabolic activity utilizing oxygen, glucose, ATP, etc.. It results in the conscious experience, the thought image. The bodily changes that follow are energetic – they utilize energy in the same way – and no one doubts that they are triggered by the thought image. But every trigger, no matter how delicate, is an energetic process, and since energy cannot be created the energy of the triggering must be derived from the immediately preceding state, in this case the subjective conscious state. If the conscious state is composed of units, the postulated 'mentons', we may conclude that like photons these are forms of energy, convertible to more 'standard' forms of energy.

When neural activity is generating consciousness we obviously cannot determine this by instrumentation since consciousness is inviolately private. The causal relationship would have to be established by the behavioral effects of the consciousness, preferably verbal report; that is, if when the ultimate biological process that transduces neural energy to consciousness is activated there is on every occasion immediate confirmation that consciousness occurs. We can then legitimately propose that *this* biological process is the transducer, converting energy of one form to energy of another. The fact that this demonstration is at present beyond our technical skills simply means that final proof is lacking. At the gross level we have, of course, proof that the activity of brains, and even certain parts of brains, generates consciousness. By analogy, an electric current generates a magnetic force which in turn can reconvert to electric energy (as in the voltage transformer); and the magnetic flux is unknowable by an observer except by its effects, just as is consciousness.

Concerning the unity of consciousness, different elements of consciousness are generated in different parts of the brain, but if there is one global consciousness, as we all seem to attest, these different elements are conjoined in some manner. But how? Is there some central mechanism to which they all report, this central mechanism then being conscious of all the other consciousnesses simultaneously? This would mean a secondary generation of the consciousnesses or a consciousness of consciousness (an apparent absurdity) and the problem of unity would have to be explained here and remains unsolved; furthermore there is no evidence that such a centre exists (Zeki,1993:296).

An alternative view elaborated by Edelman (1989) and supported by Zeki (1993) that somehow signal passage back and forth between areas of sensory cortex defines or creates the percept and maintains its integrity is very appealing until looked at closely. Mere signal passage cannot create consciousness so the concept of re-entry as a generator of consciousness is logically invalid. However, the maintenance of the unity of consciousness depends on intact neuronal connections, as is well demonstrated by dividing the corpus callosum and by numerous dissociations described in the clinical literature. Somehow, therefore, consciousness 'a' and consciousness 'b' generated simultaneously in areas A and B become a composite unitary consciousness, 'ab', by virtue of the intact physical connections between these areas, but not by virtue of signal passage between them *unless* the signals in some manner act as 'tentacles' of consciousness 'a' and consciousness 'b' which meet one another to form a syncytium; otherwise 'a' and 'b' use the neuronal bridge to join one another, which, presumably, could only be the case if consciousness *per se* is a form of energy existing separately from the brain producing it and if its energy field is conducted by intact neurites.

How else can we account for the unity of consciousness and the fact that this unity is lost by destroying the physical connection between the different cortical areas 'associated' with subjective conscious experience? Not, it must be emphasized, by mere signal passage back and forth – such reentrant signaling serves important functions but the nerve impulse cannot be regarded as a carrier of consciousness from one area to another, although it may conceivably serve to put units being generated in different areas in touch with one another.

Gilbert (1995:73) suggests that "perceptual integration" may be mediated by "a plexus of long-range horizontal connections, running parallel to the cortical surface". Geniculate input is more restricted in receptive field responses than these horizontal arbors would indicate; geniculate projection fibres to the primary visual cortex activate consciousness-generating cells, while the horizontal arbors may integrate the activity of these (op.cit.:76).

It certainly cannot be claimed that the characterization of consciousness offered here sheds any light on how common-or-garden physico-chemical energy can give rise to consciousness. Ultimately, the existence of consciousness is a mystery, just as is the existence of gravity and the other fundamental forces of nature, but despite this it is incontrovertible that it has been used as a tool by the processes of biological evolution – blind natural selection has gone about its business of utilizing consciousness untroubled by philosophical doubts about the possibility of doing so.

Phenomenal transduction occurs at two borders: The body surface, between the environment and the sense organs, and the cortical layer, between cortical cells and consciousness. That we can follow the former transduction instrumentally, and the latter only by a combination of instrumentation and introspection has been the traditional and universal reason for avoiding consideration of the latter transduction – it is simply not scientifically legitimate to do so. Therefore in seeking to achieve a breakthrough in understanding we must abandon strict scientific procedure in the hope that by doing so we may open up a new field where science may safely enter.

So, allowing free rein to conjectural interpretation of empirical data from various sources we may say that consciousness behaves *as if* its role in the central nervous system requires it to have the following properties:

(1) It exists only so long as it is being produced. More specifically, it exists for only the briefest moment after being produced, almost immediately reconverting to neural energy or dissipating as heat.

(2) It is generated by the metabolic activity of specialized neurons.

(3) This metabolic process utilizes available cellular energy in generating consciousness.

(4) The utilized energy is now, partly at least, in the form of consciousness. Consciousness must therefore be energetic. *It is, we seem forced to accept, a form of energy.*

(5) Neural impulses impinging on the specialized consciousness-generating neuron activate its metabolism.

(6) Consciousness is postulated to be particulate: it is assumed to come in quanta of energy, which may be called 'mentons'.

(7) There is a consciousness (sensorioemotic) spectrum: a range of variation in the metabolism allows a range of distinct 'kinds' or 'qualities' of consciousness. This variation is genetically based and is analogous to the electromagnetic energy spectrum.

(8) Each menton is 'pure experience' – it is self-experiencing. For example, a blue menton *is* seeing blue; a pain menton is feeling pain. *There is nothing extrinsic to the menton which does the seeing or the feeling.* Conscious individuality, or essential selfhood, inheres in each menton. The menton is the unit of self. An animal's corporeal entity, its biological or vegetative self, is not what sees and feels, except by courtesy of linguistic usage; it generates or manufactures units of consciousness which are then separate from the body in the same sense that manufactured products are separate from their factory, or quanta of electromagnetic energy are separate from their source. It is the manufactured product which is the experiencing self.

(9) Neighbouring mentons, whose 'energy fields' meet via intact neuronal connections, integrate. They form a composite unit. This unit is, e.g., seeing blue and feeling pain: it is a single, complex self: a global unitary consciousness. It is not a new consciousness; not something separate which is 'conscious of' the individual mentons. It consists solely of mentons, which unite into one selfhood – an energy syncytium.

(10) It is not possible for consciousnesses which are not joined in this way to 'know' what is 'in' one another, except indirectly, by report or by inference. The conscious 'I' of human self-awareness, i.e. human mental individuality, is the compound unitary consciousness; it is not some entity outside this.

(11) Damage to, or functional disturbances of, the central nervous system may, according to some evidence, result in divided or separate

consciousnesses which, from the evidence, know nothing of one another: within the corporeal individual, as between individuals, the same inscrutability results.

(12) The ability of mentons to coalesce into larger units while still retaining their individual anatomical and phyiological points of action is an inherent property of consciousness *which made possible the evolution of advanced brains.* In particular it allowed natural selection to accumulate genetic variations resulting in complex machinery for processing conscious experience by making such processing linear: that the whole machinery can be concentrated on one task at a time allows a much higher quality of treatment.

(13) It may also be suggested that an umbrella effect over widely separated neurological processes may, by helping to coordinate their functions, have contributed to making complexity possible, whereas a non-conscious system could not evolve sufficiently efficient reciprocity between its parts to reach such a level of complexity.

How could such an umbrella effect, if it exists, operate? The compound, unitary consciousness self-experiences all of its constituent parts simultaneously. But each menton is restricted to its own anatomical position and has its own neural effects on reconversion – it presumably cannot, except very locally, influence the behavior of other mentons directly. It may be suggested that the unitariness of compound consciousness makes possible a much more efficient level of focusing of consciousness and thus of serial mental processing than non-conscious mechanisms alone can achieve. The various kinds of information from all sources materialize as various kinds of consciousness – sensations, emotions, images, etc. – structured more-or-less complexly. The central nervous system must have a mechanism, or, rather, it operates as if it has a mechanism, which decides continually which of these inputs will receive preferential treatment. In relatively simple systems genetically programmed hierarchy channels operate successfully, but these may be unable to handle the increasing range of situations competing for focus that evolving mental functioning demands. But although introspectively it seems that by virtue of the unitariness of consciousness, in which the whole is experienced all at once, this or that aspect may be directly selected for focusing, this cannot be so. There is no mechanism *within consciousness* allowing this to happen: no part of global consciousness can *directly* (that is, horizontally) control any other part and through it its associated neural mechanisms. It therefore seems that the idea of an umbrella effect cannot be sustained.

(14) What seems more probable is that the coalescence of separately generated units of consciousness allows the brain to *represent* discrete, complex objects and subject matters, and this representation by acting as a surrogate for the external world can influence behaviors in more advanced ways than non-conscious processing, particularly through the mechanism of instant conscious recognition of environmental entities and processes which were previously experienced and which are now in memory.

In simple systems various response mechanisms in the central nervous system are able to cope with a relatively small selection of incoming data, mainly in the vital domains of nutrition, safety, and reproduction. In advanced brains responses may be to the products of thought, which is only possible if an internal replica of the external world is constructed, and only through integrated consciousness may this be achieved. We may say that the tendency to coalesce is an intrinsic property of mentons which allows more elaborate internal representation of the external world, both in real time and as imagery from memory, which in turn allows natural selection to evolve more sophisticated machinery for dealing with the world at secondhand.

At any moment different parts of global sensory consciousness represent different environmental and corporeal situations of varying degrees of relevance to the organism. Such relevance may be through ties to innate and acquired recognition-response mechanisms and programs. Discrete parts of the integrated consciousness gain access to these mechanisms and programs though their specific neural connections which have evolved (and are thus genetically based) or which have been established through learning.

Each such recognition-response mechanism or program when engaged (triggered, released) will compete with others for sole use of the serial processing and executive capabilities of the brain's mental apparatus. If successful this will result in the part or parts of consciousness representing the relevant situation being more strongly generated at the cost of other parts.

(15) Mental functioning is impossible without consciousness, since by definition mind is a function of the brain in which consciousness is used to represent the external world for more elaborate, and thus more

appropriate, responses than is achievable by a non-conscious system. It is therefore meaningless to speak of a non-conscious mind, except in the sense that there are numerous subconscious brain functions that are part of the total apparatus supporting mental functioning, e.g., intermemory linkage functions, priority processing for the selective generation of consciousness, etc. And, of course, numerous non-conscious physiological processes may influence the generation of consciousness. Similarly, non-conscious thinking cannot occur; the apparent solving of problems during *dreamless* sleep is almost certainly due to the fading away of interfering eddies of useless thought, e.g. in the common circumstance of being unable to remember a name or a situation because some other name or situation keeps intruding.

Non-conscious neuronal networks cannot display intention, understanding, belief, preference, value judgement, physical and emotional feeling, thoughts, etc. As cited earlier, under light barbituate anaesthesia or in dreamless sleep neuronal activity may still be recorded in the sensory cortices in response to sensory input, but consciousness is absent and there are no behavioral responses, nor, so far as has been reliably determined, any memory recordings. (At least, neither I nor anyone else with whom I have spoken have formed memories under such conditions!)

(16) The neural processes determine the patterns of consciousness generated, but once generated such consciousness enjoys, momentarily, an independent existence of some sort. However, each unit of consciousness maintains an association with the neuronal structure producing it and with the downline elements which it activates on reconversion. We may attribute the momentary mental confusion following minor head injury in part to dislocation of this menton/neuron association. Immediate disturbances of consciousness following minor head injury have never been adequately explained, except in a general way (Kolb and Whishaw, 1990:137,817). Instantaneous but momentary loss of consciousness with no sequelae is obviously not due to massive structural damage of the sorts described in neuropathology texts: shearing of nerve fibres, raised intracranial pressure from haemorrhage and edema, anoxia from major vascular blockage, etc. The most likely explanation is momentary interruption of blood supply due to some sort of haemodynamic effect from the mechanical jarring, but this would be

difficult to demonstrate. A direct mechanical effect on neuronal metabolism *per se* is unlikely to result from minor head injury.

(17) The number of patterns of consciousness that can occur, even in relatively primitive conscious organisms, may be virtually limitless. This is because at any moment the mentons being generated are the result of activity of any combination of the specialized neurons and therefore any part of that animal's potential spectrum. But an organism can only generate the kinds of mentons its metabolism permits, and this depends on its evolutionary history. Also the operation of the neural mechanisms underlying mental processes determines what patterns are produced. The consciousness-generating neuronal system is dependent on the genome, the conscious representation on the pattern of activation of the neurons, the behavior on the conscious representation, and the effectiveness of the organism (and thus the operation of natural selection) on the behavior.

(18) As evolution proceeded along the line that led to man these underlying mechanisms became more complex and the range of the consciousness metabolism widened. New forms or 'flavours' of consciousness able to control (trigger, release) more sophisticated behaviors evolved. While certain forms such as the sense of a separate external world, depth perception, and conscious recognition (sense of familiarity) may be relatively primitive, others such as sense of self and will, aesthetic sense, guilt, shame, nostalgia, the sense of enlightenment involved in understanding, etc. if not of recent origin at least have been much developed in the evolution of man.

Some forms of consciousness are clearly emotional, such as compassion or remorse, others purely perceptual, such as sense of spatial depth or of solidity, while others are difficult to classify, such as a sense of familiarity or a sense of conviction. Some, such as a feeling of indignation, may be shown to be composed of several subelements which may vary somewhat according to circumstances; others, such as wonder, may be less divisible. It seems very probable that the more advanced or recently evolved forms of consciousness, those that we tend to consider as uniquely human, are composed of elements of more primitive forms.

(19) It must be emphasized again that all forms of consciousness are self-experiencing; linguistic usage such as "I am feeling (some emotion)" implies that some independent entity experiences the experience, which is impossible. In primitive organisms, and pre-linguistic infants the 'I' resides only in the feeling. In mature, linguistic man, largely for the

purpose of communication, there develops the concept of self as independent of its experiences; the language communicates that it is *this* individual organism that is generating the feeling. This self-concept emerges from the sea of experience and is equated with the corporeal self; it is the illusion, within the global unitary consciousness, of the corporeal self being conscious of all aspects of consciousness, including itself. It must be noted that this experiential edifice is the consequence of the property of individual 'mentons' being able to merge to form a complex unit via intact neuronal connections.

(20) All forms of consciousness serve two functions: as raw material for internal mental operations, i.e., thinking, and as triggers for various forms of behavior, acquired or innate. The behavioral effect is triggered by the reconversion of the constituent units of some part of the contemporary global consciousness to neural energy to engage a downline response program. There may first be convergence on some relatively simple neural mechanism which acts as a trigger for the final behavior program in the cerebellum, basal ganglia, or supplementary motor cortex, as the case may be, but we are far from being able to verify experimentally the validity of such ideas.

It remains to be determined whether the first-stage downline effector (outlet) neuron serving each consciousness-generating neuron is also the latter's memory neuron or whether these functions are served by different neurons: there is theoretical and experimental support for each possibility. (For 'neuron' one should perhaps read 'functionally unified group of neurons' – the cortical column may be the smallest functional unit).

(21) It was noted above that the anesthesized animal may be used in tracing impulses from the sense organ to the cortex, and in recording cortical cellular responses (e.g. Gilbert and Wiesel, 1981, using the primary visual cortex of the cat). Intracellular electrodes in the cortex of the anesthesized animal, which, presumably, is unconscious, respond to visual stimuli. These cells are functioning even though the animal is unconscious, and, by extrapolation from human experience, no cognitive functions are occurring and no memories are being established.

If the anesthetic does not stop the passage of neural signals in the cortex yet stops the generation of consciousness and all cognitive functions, how are we to explain this? Possible explanations include: 1/ The generation of consciousness is a specialized cellular process activated by signal passage and this process is blocked by the anesthetic which does not block the signal passage, presumably because sensory input branches to different cortical layers, with the deeper layers serving more primitive and robust functions.   2/ Consciousness and cognitive functions are generated by more elaborate, therefore more vulnerable, metabolic and intercellular processes which are easily abolished by anesthetics without stopping elementary cellular processes.   3/ Both of these mechanisms may be operative, with the more recently evolved uses of consciousness and intercellular connections for advanced cognitive functions being the most susceptible to adverse conditions and the first to be disrupted by anesthetics, anoxia, etc..   4/ A greater depth of anesthesia would, by the above reasoning, be expected to abolish all neural activity in the cortex.

Ruminations on the model

An objection to the above model of consciousness may be put as follows: Consciousness is private; it is isolated. No external agent can measure or experience or directly know or be influenced by it. Therefore natural selection should not be able to accumulate particular kinds of consciousness married to particular types of response. Nor can consciousness select what kind of reflex to activate, so whether a reflexive response is an attraction or an aversion cannot be determined by the nature of the associated consciousness. Yet this is what happens with feeling consciousness, if not with non-feeling consciousness. We can perhaps imagine visual and auditory consciousness cross-operating with their respective responses, but hardly so for pleasant and unpleasant feelings.

Somehow the feeling must have a determining influence on the nature of the behavior. One possibility is that the stability of integrated (composite) consciousness is destroyed by unpleasant feelings if these accumulate, this being an elemental property of the energy 'force fields' of consciousness; a high content of unpleasant feeling may disrupt the whole consciousness apparatus resulting in erratic reconversions to neural activity, distorted neural functioning, and perhaps vegetative damage. We know of course from common experience that this happens, so the attribution of these properties to hypothesized units of consciousness (mentons) and the postulated energy syncytium they form while highly speculative is perhaps not illegitimate.

If these ideas seem forced consider the alternative, traditional view. In this the sensory encounter triggers (or releases) autonomic, musculo-skeletal, and hormonal responses which comprise the behavior. At the same time these responses are said to be accompanied by a 'central state' (a non-committal reference to emotional feeling – McNaughton, 1989), if indeed this is mentioned at all. For the physiologist the subjective conscious experience is an irrelevancy. At most it is considered to be epiphenominal since there is no way it can be investigated physiologically and may be safely ignored. But it has earlier been argued that consciousness as an epiphenomenon is logically untenable if our premises include the principles of evolutionary theory; it must be physiologically causal at least at the higher levels of brain function, and very probably at lower levels and in primitive organisms.

So the 'self' that suffers, enjoys, understands, hears, sees, feels, etc. is the population of mentons united into a compound consciousness being continually but varyingly generated by specialized neuronal metabolism in response to the coordinated functioning of the complex neural systems underlying the mental apparatus of the brain. And this apparatus exists because the evolutionary process was able to fashion and/or utilize neuronal properties to take advantage of the unique properties of consciousness. The so-called 'continuity' of self, i.e. the subjective and objective persistence of uniqueness of individual personalities, is due to the relative permanence of the organism's structural organization, to its acquired reflexive programs (controlling complex behaviors, thinking processes, habits, emotional responses, etc.), and to its store of memories. The incomprehensible complexity of all this must function with orderliness for subjective and objective continuity of self to be maintained; and there are many functional and organic pathological conditions which impair, alter, or destroy 'self'.

Our everyday, non-analytic experiences of mind, self, and consciousness have the status of empirical validity. It is our theories (from psychology, philosophy, theology) that tend to lead us astray. It is suggested that the 'menton' theory of consciousness may resolve traditional difficulties. By treating consciousness as a form of energy generated in units by transducing metabolic activity traditional lines of debate on the mind-body problem are rendered vacuous. By assigning subjectivity, privacy, etc. to these units together with a propensity to coalesce into a composite unitary whole and to reconvert to neural energy *we are doing no more than accounting for the facts in a particular way which has the advantage of being specific*, in contrast to the extremely vague and improbable ideas such as emergence from complexity or attachments from ethereal emanations. Certainly consciousness is an emergent phenomenon, meaning that it could not have been predicted from its antecedents. It is as weird and improbable as some of the phenomena of the quantum mechanical world. But that it is generated by some kind of organic process is an inference with almost the strength of scientific fact that many people refuse to accept, a not uncommon type of psychological resistance found in the history of science.

The most difficult question is how the various forms of consciousness generated in widely separated areas of the brain become a single conscious experience. If in the intact brain units of consciousness in existence at any moment are coalesced into a composite unitary whole then such coalescence must operate over several centimetres, presumably via axonal-synaptic connections. While a strong chain of argument sustains the hypothesis of generated units of consciousness and their coalescence into a composite, global unitary consciousness, any attempt at this time to formulate detailed explanation would be pure speculation.

Even so there is the cardinal failure to see, amounting almost to wilful blindness, that consciousness has a down-to-earth biological function, and failure to accept that this is so because in the process of evolution its genetically based properties proved selectively advantageous.

Analogical arguments for the model: Legitimate or specious?

From analogy with the concept of energy in physics can we derive any support for the idea that consciousness is composed of energetic 'mentons'? If a biological process can produce photons, and we know this to the case, then, logically, a biological process may produce mentons. However, we do not know that this is the case; we only know that a biological process produces consciousness, although perhaps we do not 'know' this with the same order of certitude of knowing as with the photon.

Bioluminescence is common in nature: atoms of substances (luciferins) emit photons (quanta of electromagnetic energy) when they return to the ground state after having been elevated to the excited state by biochemical processes involving oxidation, ATP, the enzyme luciferase and several intermediate stages (McElroy and Seliger).

The photon generated by any process travels at constant speed (in vacuo) from the moment of its creation, and if undisturbed will continue to do so. In this state it is invisible; there can be no knowledge of its existence except what may be inferred from detecting the process that in the past always gave rise to photons. When we detect the existence of a photon we do so by reconverting its energy, thus annihilating it, to some form we can sensorially experience, e.g. a moving dial, the feeling of heat, the seeing of light, etc. The photon is produced by a mechanism we can inspect and has a result we can inspect, but in between we can only infer its existence: A -> (?B) -> C.

In the case of consciousness we *infer* that A -> B, B being the subjective conscious experience (which is direct, absolute knowing) and A an activity of nervous tissue requiring oxygen, glucose, ATP, enzymes, etc. It may justifiably be claimed that we also know that B -> C, C being the causal effects of consciousness, in that by introspection we observe that under certain conditions only when we see (or hear, feel, smell, etc.) do we react.

By analogy, consciousness has the position of the photon in its state of existence in that it is unknowable to an observer. And from this, as a working hypothesis, we may say that consciousness is made up of basic units analogous to photons, which we may call 'mentons', and that specialized nervous tissue, when active, generates mentons in a continuous stream, these mentons almost immediately reconverting to neural energy by a process of reverse transduction, thereby disappearing; the unit of consciousness thus lasts for the briefest moment after its production.

Bioluminescence is a ubiquitous phenomenon, having evolved in numerous classes of animals. There is no reason to suppose that consciousness is any less ubiquitous, although we cannot know this until its biochemistry has been established. Consciousness may be generated in parts of the nervous system other than those that support the mind. It may in these other parts have a primitive function, for example as a servomechanism, with no access to memory or language and no coalescence to form a complex unitary structure.

What is the epistemological and cosmological significance of the menton being the unit of conscious self-hood, if the menton theory is correct? By this I mean what does it say about the nature of the world? In the theory the characteristics of the menton serve purely biological functions, involving a form of energy that is convertible to other forms of energy and governed by the universal law of the conservation of energy. The subjectivity of consciousness is thus a tool used by the evolutionary process, and the existence of subjectivity is no more explicable than the existence of the elementary forces of nature. Nor explicable is why it should first appear in living organisms, virtually at the end-stage of the unfolding of the universe, but we must remember that complex organic molecules, from which consciousness apparently emerges, can be traced step by emergent step from primal undifferentiated energy at the beginning of the universe, each emergent step being a fact beyond explanation.

The menton is presumably generated by metabolic activity within the soma of the neuron. Where then does it go? Does it somehow leave the cell, as the photon obviously does in bioluminescence? Since its effects are on downline neurons, either memory neurons or effector neurons, and since so far as we know all effects are via synapses, the menton's effects must be along axons and via synapses. It presumably accompanies and influences neural signals along these axons, but if it acts as a servomechanism why is this necessary or in what way helpful? After all, the non-conscious nerve impulse does not seem to need any help. Why consciousness? It is there, it is genetically determined, so it must perform a vital function, and presumably this function must at least be partially explicable on the basis of subjectivity itself, and subjectivity is an unanalysable, irreducible given of nature.

Is the answer to be found in the property of unified consciousness being able to represent external reality and to drive behaviors relevant to that reality? If so then at what stage of evolution did such representation appear? Did consciousness first have another function, e.g. as a servomechanism, only later being utilized for representation? If so then inherent in the menton is the ability to merge and make contact with other mentons to give a panoramic, unitary, multi-detailed subjective experience, in which the whole experiences all of its parts, or, rather, in which the conscious experience is now multifaceted. But would it not be extraordinarily fortuitous, intuitively to the point of extreme improbability, that the property of coalescence should be inherent, lying dormant for the chance that multicellular organisms should evolve? Is it not more likely that some mundane characteristic of non-conscious neuronal functioning should underlie the unity of consciousness? Unfortunately, pursuing such thoughts leads nowhere, as has been shown earlier.

I have so far eschewed the temptation to speculate on the mechanism of transduction from cellular metabolic activity to consciousness and the reverse transduction to neural energy. In the final analysis it is an article of faith that such transduction is explicable in terms of fundamental physics, but we may be missing the point if we look to what we currently know of fundamental physics for answers. We may simply be failing to realize that the existence and transactions of units of consciousness (mentons) are fundamental physics in their own right; that just as electrons, photons, etc. are unanalysable and indivisible givens of nature so are mentons. But we should not bar ourselves from looking to traditional fundamental physics for ideas; no analogy, however far-fetched, should be rejected out of hand. For example, physicists tell us, on what basis I do not know, that electrons on their orbits around the atomic nucleus emit and absorb virtual photons, this process somehow altering the energy characteristics of the atom (Weinberg, 1993). Does some analogous process emit and reabsorb virtual mentons? If consciousness and its place in the central nervous system are natural phenomena we may only reach final understanding by keeping our minds open to all suggestions that do not violate scientific logic.

APPENDIX B

THE OLFACTORY SYSTEM

Each of the special senses of advanced vertebrates projects through parallel levels of processing, ranging from simple reflexes to higher cognitive functions. The differing morphological arrangements displayed by the various sensory systems reflect mainly the contingencies of evolutionary history.

That the olfactory system does not relay in the thalamic conglomerate is probably in part due to its earlier evolutionary history: "The olfactory epithelium was probably the first receptor of distant information" (Sarnat and Netsky, 1981:337.) Following the conversion of epithelial cells in the rostral orifice to specialized detectors of odours its earliest application would have been to trigger the simplest of reflexes: away from danger and towards reward. The reflex would be carried by primordial nerve fibres in the wall of the neural tube to the lower neuraxis via synaptic relays, the first of such relays being only a short distance from the sensory neuro-epithelium. The short axons of the latter constitute the *olfactory nerve* (Barr and Kiernan, 1988:262).

These first synaptic relays gradually underwent evolutionary elaboration and specialization to form the olfactory bulb able to discriminate more odours and guide more specific behaviors in concert with the complementary development of other central nervous system structures, especially hypothalamic, autonomic, and brainstem reticular nuclei.

It seems reasonable to speculate that the origin of the lateral ventricles was to accomodate the crowd of new olfactory cells in the rostral wall of the neural tube by the process of outpouching, so there came to exist a multilayered bulb with a cavity – the first telencephalic structure (Sarnat and Netsky, 1981:337, write of " the early phylogenetic appearance of these [olfactory] structures in the telencephalon..").

If this chronology is correct it was somewhat later that the other forward situated special sense organs evolved out of the primordial propensity for undifferentiated ectodermal tissue to be sensitive to several kinds of external stimuli. Because of the constraints of space some of the relays of these, at that stage mediating the most advanced level of reflexivity of each system, were in close proximity to one another and to the upper elements of the reticular formation at the site that was to become that of the neuronal conglomerate known as the thalamus. Further elaboration of both sensory input and motor output relays at the thalamic level was only possible by expansion into the adjacent wall of the neural tube, and the proliferation of cells bulged the wall outwards to form the cerebral hemispheres. This bulging of the neural tube was continuous with the rostral olfactory bulge, the contained cavity being the lateral ventricle.

Later, in many vertebrate species, the elongated olfactory extension of the lateral ventricle narrowed to form a tube or hollow stalk in the wall of which ran nerve fibres constituting the olfactory tract, from and to the olfactory bulb (Carpenter, 1991:362). The region of cerebral cortex with which the base of the stalk is continuous is generally called the piriform (or pyriform) cortex.

Olfactory tract fibres not only continued to have primitive relays to hypothalamus, habenula, and other brainstem centres for primitive reflexes, but multiplication and branching of tract fibres relayed in archipallium (hippocampus and amygdala) and paleopallium (parahippocampal gyrus, uncus, etc.) as these regions developed.

At some stage olfactory consciousness became integrated with consciousness of the other special senses and with physical and emotional feeling consciousness of the limbic system, to become part of the global unitary consciousness of the mind. It is mostly guesswork when it comes to answering the question of where olfactory consciousness is generated. The bulb may correspond in function to the primary visual, auditory, and somatosensory neocortices, and the piriform cortex to the secondary sensory cortices, but in man the olfactory brain remains primitive in contrast to the visual brain and is paleocortex in structure (Barr and Kiernan,1988:263).

The fact that we can recognize odours previously experienced means that there is a system for acquiring odour memories. But we cannot reproduce the odour experience from memory any more than we can re-experience physical feelings through memory. When we try to remember odours it seems that we retrieve the context of the odours mainly in the form of visual imagery. But what is involved in the process of recognizing an odour? Are we recognizing the retrieved context or does the odour which is being re-experienced 'meet itself' in non-retrievable memory causing a neural interaction that manifests itself as a sense of familiarity?

If odour recognition occurs in the olfactory bulb, then it follows that odour consciousness is generated there and non-retrievable odour memory resides there. Piriform cortex would then serve 'associative' functions with other sensory systems, principally for intersensory memory linkages and for integration into the unitary consciousness of the mind. In addition, being an ancient structure, piriform cortex would transmit information from bulb to lower vegetative structures and via amygdala to the limbic system for emotional elicitations.

Granular and small stellate neurons of the upper (i.e., outer) layers of the bulb increase in phylogeny "to integrate olfactory impulses with afferent impulses from other structures of the basal forebrain... Association fibres confined to the olfactory bulb, particularly recurrent collaterals of mitral cells, increase progressively in phylogeny" (Sarnat and Netsky, 1981:331). Many vertebrate lines show regressive olfactory systems, including primates, but in others "lamination of the olfactory bulb ... is ... remarkably well differentiated" (op.cit.:331). Also, the olfactory bulb receives direct reciprocal feedback from virtually all parts of the brain to which it projects (op.cit.:335).

The flow-chart Fig.B(1) illustrates the essentials of what we currently know of the distribution of olfactory information.

Fig. B(1) The Distribution of Olfactory Information

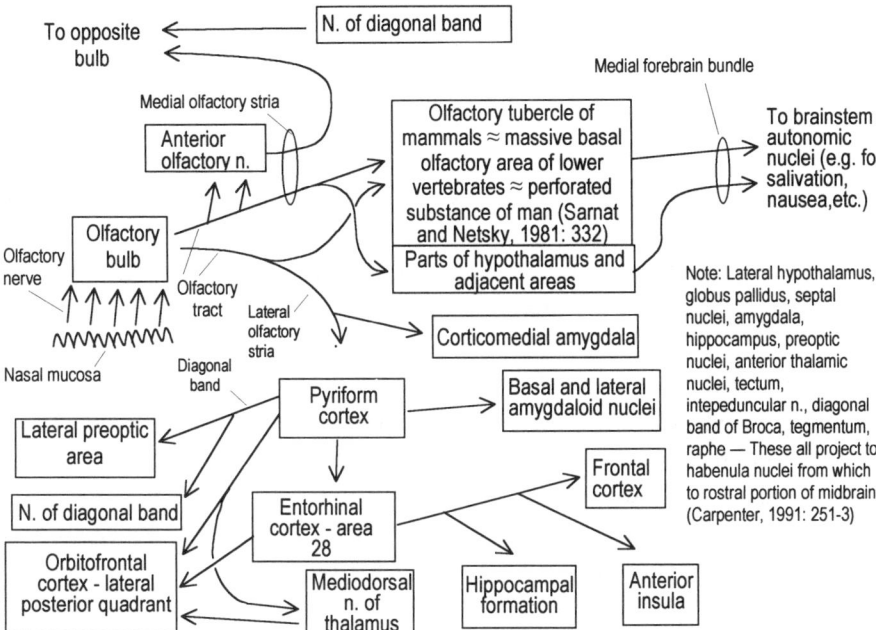

Note: There is much uncertainly and disagreement in nomenclature, connectivities, and functioning of the various structures believed to be directly or indirectly involved in olfaction. E.g., in Barr and Kiernan (1988) the "lateral olfactory area" is composed of paleocortex of uncus, entorhinal area, and cortex in region of limen insulae, whilst Carpenter (1991) has pyriform cortex as primary olfactory cortex and separate from entorhinal cortex, and Guyton (1987) has pyriform cortex and corticomedial amygdaloid region as primary olfactory cortex. But evidence from comparative anatomy and embryology indicates that the olfactory bulb is telencephalic archicortex — it is multilayered and contains an extension of the fourth ventricle.

Note also that "complete removal of the lateral olfactory area [supplied by the lateral stria] hardly affects the primitive responses to olfaction" (Guyton, 1987:327.) Obviously, the medial olfactory stria is the route by which most of these functions are carried out and is the more primitive route comparable to the retinotectal route in vision which mediates primitive visual responses after decortication.

APPENDIX C

THE LIMBIC SYSTEM

There is no coherent set of structures with a specific function comprising a limbic 'system'. The structures generally lumped together under this rubric in fact serve two distinct functions: emotional and homeostatic.

Different functions may employ some limbic structures in common. For example, various elements of the hypothalamus may be engaged in both vegetative functions (such as flushing of skin in temperature regulation) and in emotional elicitations (as in embarrassment).

In evolution of the emotional system nature employed whatever *in situ* structures and systems suited its 'purpose', prominently among these the hypothalamic and autonomic nervous systems. The consequence is that many emotions feel vegetative and many vegetative functions have effects that have something of an emotional feel to them.

There is a vast difference between vegetative regulative mechanisms which operate to keep the internal environment stable and complex behaviors appropriate to external events driven or catalysed by emotional feelings, but there are areas of overlap between these systems in that the more primitive emotions may have evolved because they assisted the vegetative responses in elemental life situations beyond the strictly internal stabilizing needs.

Structures generally included in the limbic 'system' are: cingulate gyrus, parahippocampal gyrus, entorhinal cortex, paraolfactory area (anterior perforated substance), subcallosal gyrus, orbitofrontal cortex, uncus, hippocampal formation, amygdaloid nuclear complex, hypothalamus, anterior nuclei of the thalamus, mediodorsal thalamic nuclei, thalamic elements of the reticular activating system, parts of corpus striatum, septal area, and elements of the mesencephalic tegmentum. (The last five are treated elsewhere in this book).

To achieve a degree of conceptual clarity in face of the enormous complexity of the limbic system we may appeal to the broad outline of the evolutionary history of this region of the brain.

Originally, even at the unicellular stage of life, the organism exhibited four principal functions: energy acquisition, self-protection, internal stabilization, and reproduction. These remain the principal functions of all organisms. Every part of the nervous system contributes to (that is, evolved in the performance of) one or another of these functions.

If we list the subdivisions of these main functions we find specific structures responsible for carrying them out, and their fibre connections serve either as parts of the input-to-output reflex process which is the *raison d'être* of a nervous system, or for cooperative functioning, including monitorial and modulatory, between and within systems and subsystems.

Therefore, when looking at any part of the limbic system we must ask (1) which of the four major functions it participates in, (2) which subsystem it is a part of, and (3) which of its connections with other structures are for effector responses and which for cooperative modulatory functions. We must also judge how far into detail we need to go for conceptual clarity.

The reader is referred to the frontispiece illustrations and to neuroanatomy atlases for a feeling for the gross anatomy of this and other systems.

The Limbic 'Lobe'

The limbic cortices are transitional in histology to neocortex: Archicortex (hippocampus, dentate gyrus, and amygdaloid cortex), paleocortex (pyriform region and parahippocampal gyrus), and mesocortex (cingulate gyrus). These structures appear early in vertebrate phylogenesis and "possess a certain constancy in gross and microscopical structure" (Carpenter, 1991:384). The functions of these structures "are not yet fully understood" (op.cit.), but almost certainly have to do with early encephalization: more tailored behavioral responses to sensory input, early memory functions, the elicitation of primitive emotions, and control mechanisms to balance the increasingly complex cooperative and competing functions. There will therefore be numerous connections between these cortices and between them and subcortical structures such as amygdala, thalamus, hypothalamus, corpus striatum, septum, brainstem nuclei, etc..

The general principle that new additions to older structures continue, in part, to operate through established routes may be invoked to support the contention that the more recently evolved regions of the cerebral hemispheres, the neocortical lobes, considered to be elaborations of the primitive structures (Sarnat and Netsky, 1981:325), funnel the results of their internal activities through such routes, in the case of the limbic system principally those activities that involve emotional elicitations.

The Cingulate Gyrus

Many of the connections of the cingulate gyrus and their functional significance are uncertain. Electrical stimulation of different parts of cingulate and orbito-insula-temporal cortices produces effects similar to stimulation of different parts of amygdala (Carpenter, 1991:385).

As mesocortex one would expect the cingulate gyrus to have been the highest cerebral cortex prior to evolution of neocortex, and in the modern brain to funnel some neocortical activity to the more primitive structures. To what extent this is the case is apparently unknown – neocortical projections to archicortex (hippocampus) and amygdala appear to largely bypass mesocortex, but the large expanse of cingulate and parahippocampal cortices suggest important functions not yet fully elucidated.

The cingulum is an association fasciculus (band of axonal transmission lines in the white matter) running the length of the cingulate gyrus connecting medial regions of frontal and parietal lobes with parahippocampal and adjacent cortical regions, and no doubt between these and cingulate cortex (Carpenter, 1991:35). The medulla (white matter) of the cerebral hemispheres is composed of vast numbers of axons, including a large number of short and long bundles interconnecting all parts of the cortical mantle. The neocortical connections of cingulate cortex appear to be principally with the orbitofrontal lobe and its other connections with older limbic structures. Since cutting this connection with frontal cortex results in the syndrome of distractability, facile emotionalism, sexual indiscrimination, etc. it is a likely hypothesis that it is, at least in part, through the cingulate cortex that neocortex exercises restraint on primitive reactive behaviors to permit the operation of higher cognitive functions. The effects of lobotomy are usually attributed to disconnecting the mediodorsal thalamic nuclei from the prefrontal region, but such lesions also probably involve the cingulum (Kolb and Whishaw, 1990:635).

Fig. C(1)   **Connections to the cingulate gyrus**

(A) Afferents

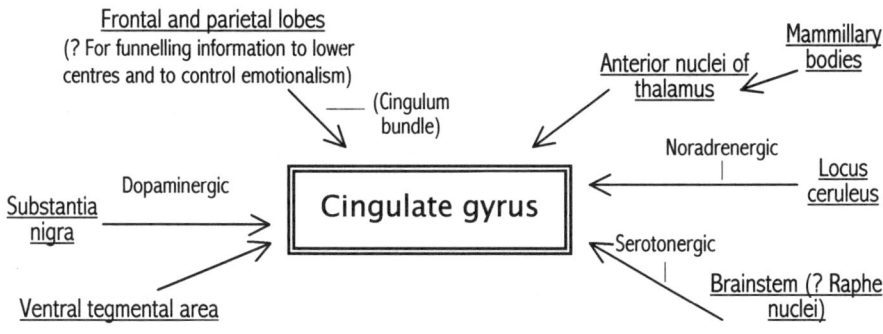

(B) Efferents

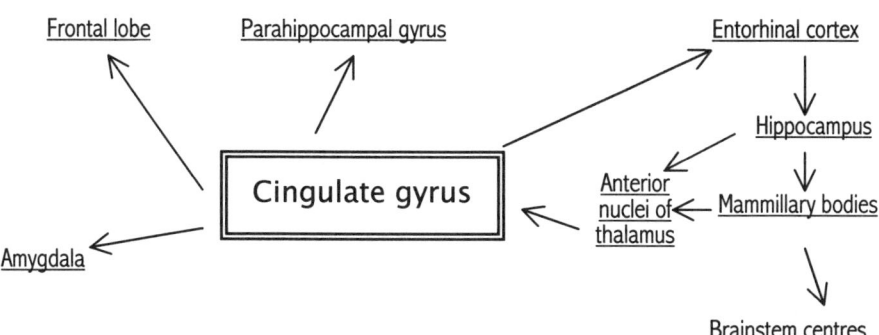

The Parahippocampal Gyrus

It is probable that this large gyrus has important functions exclusive of those of its anterior portion (entorhinal cortex, etc.). Various studies (e.g., Halgren, 1992) have shown EEG responses in posterior parts of parahippocampal gyrus to stimulation of, e.g., the primary visual areas. Again, on evolutionary grounds, we must suppose that paleocortex served primitive cognitive functions before the appearance of meso- and neocortices, and that these primitive functions may still operate and be the foundation upon which the superstructures of higher cognitive functions are based. Therefore, responses to sensory input via thalamic relay nuclei, including the generation of primitive representational consciousness, some narrowing of cortical activity (focusing, attending), some memory function, some access to emotional mechanisms, etc. may have occured in paleocortex when it was the most advanced cortex, and may still primitively occur.

Improvement in the various functions could occur either by internal elaboration of in situ structures, an unlikely happening due to the resistance to internal changes in extant structures, or by structural elaboration at the periphery, giving rise to new structures able to perform more elaborate functions.

Also, elaboration of existing structures for greater efficiency of functioning may, serendipitously, provide the preadaptations for the emergence of qualitatively new functions. For example, the function of thinking-to-understand arose out of the increasing ability to narrow the regional generation of consciousness through elaboration (mainly by structural extension) of old structure/functions, in conjunction with the elaboration of other subfunctions which already cooperated at a lower level of efficiency. Whatever exists grew out of what previously existed, and this includes interconnections for cooperative functioning – no connections between advanced organ systems can arise *de novo*, but only by elaboration of preexisting simpler connections, presumably going all the way back to the ancestral unicellular stage.

The Entorhinal Cortex

As with the cingulate gyrus many of the pathways connecting entorhinal cortex with other structures (Fig.C(3)) have not been clearly defined, nor their respective functions. For example, Carpenter (1991) designates pyriform cortex as the primary olfactory cortex, and

Fig. C(2)   **Connections of parahippocampal gyrus**

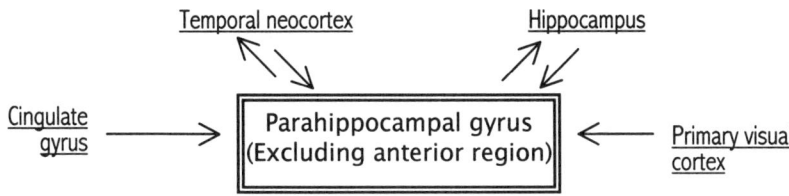

Fig. C(3)   **Connections of entorhinal cortex**

(A) Afferents

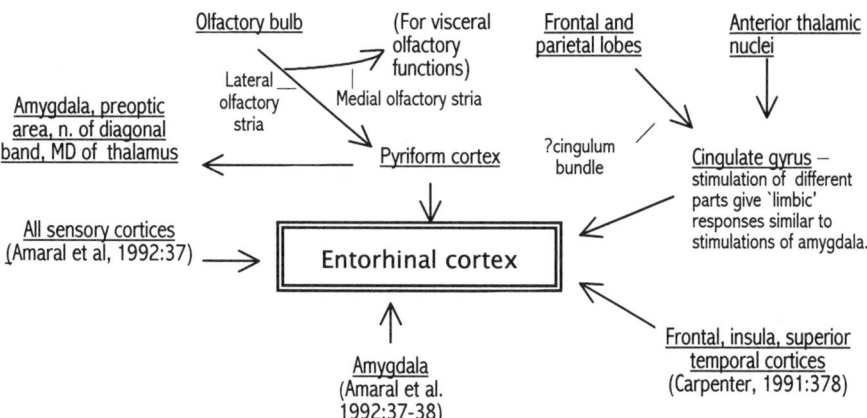

(B) Efferents

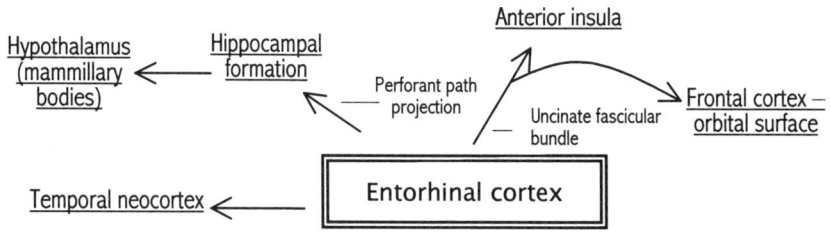

entorhinal cortex as secondary olfactory cortex, but this may be disputed: histology, embryology, and phylogeny implicate the olfactory bulb as primary olfactory cortex. Barr and Kiernan (1988) have entorhinal cortex, uncus, and limen insulae as *part* of the pyriform cortex.

The principal *effector* connections of entorhinal cortex are probably concerned with aspects of emotionalism and memory consolidation via the hippocampal formation in response to perceptions formed in the sensory neocortices.

The Hippocampal Formation

Experimental and clinical data implicate the hippocampus in the consolidation of memories in the cerebral sensory cortices, but *the modus operandi* of this is in dispute.

If a memory function existed for exteroceptive sensory experiences before the appearance of neocortex it was presumably sited in cerebral paleo- and archicortices, receiving input via the thalamic relay cells (Sarnat and Netsky, 1981:325). In the modern mammalian plan such a memory function is for conscious experiences, with the consciousness being generated in sensory neocortices and the retrieved memory consisting of imagery. Did the early thalamus generate sensory consciousness? Did paleo- and archicortices store such experiences? And if so did they return these back to thalamus for recreation in the form of imagery? If so, what functions did such imagery serve? Was the evolutionary development of neocortex an elaboration of these functions? Is its consciousness-generating function an extension of a primitive form of this in the thalamus, and its memory function an extension of a primitive form of this in archi- and paleocortices?

If a sensory function of early thalamus utilized archicortex for a memory function and if the memory function was greatly extended by proliferation of cells into the adjacent neural tube to form neocortex, wouldn't the latter supplement the thalamic connection to archicortex? Similarly, whatever function archicortex exhibited as receptor of processed sensory information from thalamus may have been elaborated by development of paleo then mesocortices, so now access to hippocampus from thalamus is mainly via neocortex and intermediate cortices. In the modern primate brain there is very little direct connection from sensory relay cells in thalamus to hippocampus, but profuse connections to sensory neocortex and from the latter, via paleocortex (principally entorhinal cortex), to hippocampal formation.

341

Fig. C(4) Vertical, transverse section through hippocampal formation (see also frontispieces)

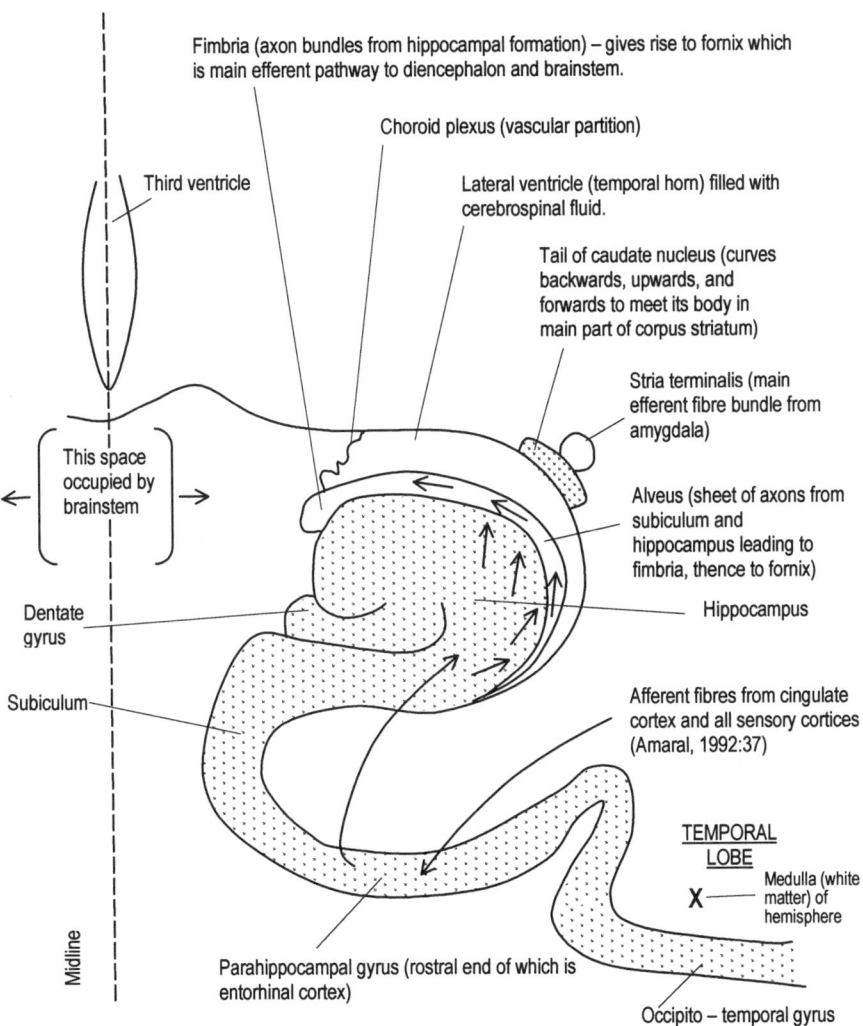

(References: Barr and Kiernan, 1988:267; Carpenter, 1991:374; Kolb and Whishaw, 1990: 537. Note that Carpenter (p.374, fig.12.12) refers to hippocampal 'formation' as separate from dentate gyrus and subiculum, whilst deGroot's (1991: 184) definition includes dentate gyrus, supracallosal gyrus (indusium griseum), fornix, and " a primitive precommissural area known as the septal area".)

Fig.C(5) **Connections of the hippocampal formation**

Note: Boxed structures participate in effector functions, the unboxed in control functions.

(A) Afferents

"Through these connections, as well as others involving the parahippocampal cortex generally, the hippocampal formation can be informed of the higher activities of the brain" (Barr and Kiernan, 1988:268.)

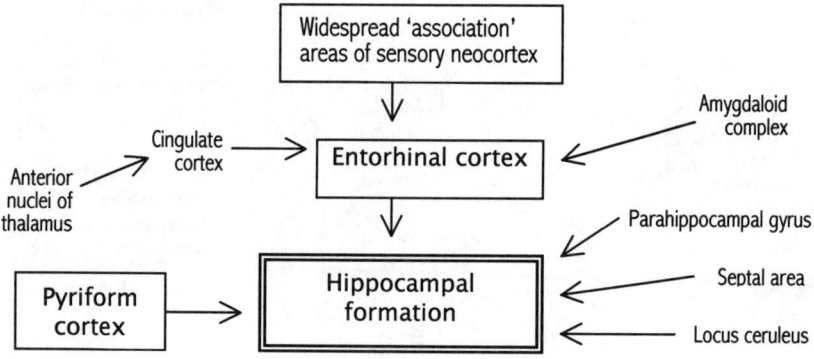

(B) Efferents

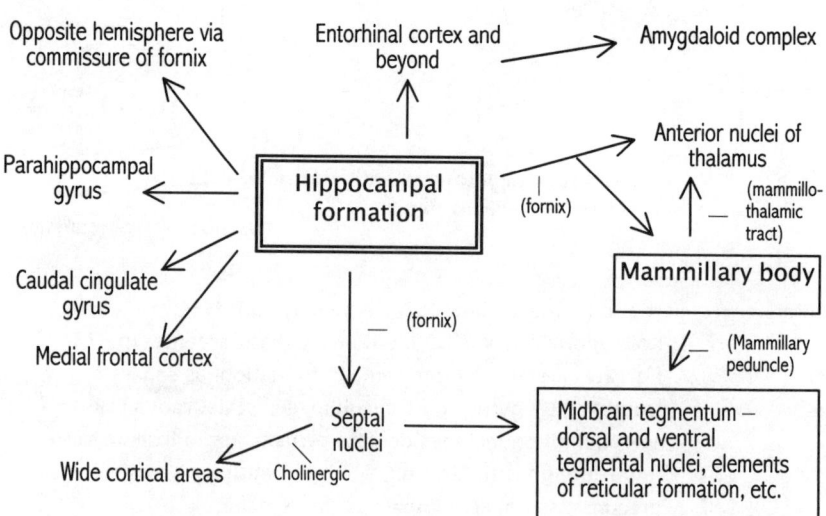

In a parallel manner the projections of early thalamus to the amygdaloid part of archicortex (for emotional elicitations) now operate largely through neocortex to amygdala via 'association' temporal cortex with few connections via paleo- and mesocortices.

Several questions relating to memory remain unanswered. For example, some permanent memories form instantly, while others require much recycling through the retrieval loop. If hippocampus is involved does it act as a gateway to the sympathetic nervous system and the focusing mechanisms for these to act on the neocortical consciousness-memory system by 'potentiating' relevant axonal-dendritic linkages? Its projection on mammillary bodies gives it access to brainstem autonomic centres, and on anterior thalamic nuclei access to emotionalism which may direct the focusing mechanisms. It also acts on septal nuclei and locus ceruleus which have excitatory effects on cerebral cortex.

Beracochea and Jaffard (1990) found that lesioning the mammillary bodies in mice induced memory deficits in "spontaneous spatial alternation (SA) tasks", but not tasks involving motivation. These findings support the above ideas: mammillary projections on the brainstem recruit non-emotional centres, while projections on anterior nuclei of thalamus eliciting emotional involvement come not only from mammillaries, and are consequently lost, but also directly from fornix, so emotional involvement is thus (at least partially) spared.

Hippocampal access to structures that activate the CNS may partly explain its "exceedingly low threshold for seizure activity" (Carpenter, 1991:375). Finally, the suggestion of Damasio (1989) and some others that hippocampus stores sensory experiences then later sends these back to sensory neocortex for permanent storage is biologically bizarre, despite being "consistent with the evidence".

The Amygdaloid Nuclear Complex

> "One might surmise ... that the fundamental task of the amygdala is to interpret sensory information in the context of species-specific objectives. A concomitant function might then be the evocation or potentiation of visceral and behavioral responses appropriate to this interpretation" (Amaral et al.,1992:54).

"The amygdala has all of the right connections with the cognitive neocortex and visceral brainstem to provide the link between them that is central to emotion" (Halgren, 1992).

Since it is generally considered, and strongly supported in this book, that the amygdaloid nuclear complex is the principal administrative centre for the elicitation of emotions it is given most attention in this appendix. (See Figs. C(6) and C(7))

Cortical connections. It must be borne in mind that much of this information has been obtained from non-human animals. Human details are largely unknown but presumed to be broadly similar. The basolateral nuclei are most developed in the human, no doubt to handle the enormous range and volume of emotional traffic required to cope with the complexities of the artefactual niche. The highly developed faculties of thinking, imagining, and understanding, which make humans appear qualitatively different from other species, in their operation so readily engage emotions that we must expect the substrate of emotionalism to be particularly elaborate in humans.

Connections with cortical regions in the human are probably much denser than indicated in the accompanying diagrams, which are based on findings in less encephalized mammals. Also, "the widespread (retrograde) projections of the amygdala ... to cerebral cortex suggest that this complex plays important roles in higher cognitive and motivational functions" (Carpenter, 1991:379).

The question arises as to what functions(s) return fibres serve, against the general flow of neural activity. An obvious suggestion is that it is in part for the modulation of upline activity to (1) increase the activity of the region from which impulses are coming, being the area of highest priority of the moment, and (2) to suppress the activity of other regions. Thus if a particular combination of 'instruments' of the emotional 'orchestra' is activated to produce a specific behavioral response to a particular life situation, other emotional responses of lower priority must be suppressed, and retrograde projections may in part do this. These retrograde projections are to much wider areas of cortex than supply the particular amygdaloid input, even as far back as V1 and V2 which have few projections to amygdala. This seems to be a general principle in CNS design (e.g., Zeki, 1993:330).

Tertiary sensory cortices have heavier projections to amygdala than primary cortices. For example, there is heavy projection from temporal visual cortex and little from occipital cortex. This is in keeping with the idea that with advanced encephalization more elaborate perceptual representations are possible (and *ipso facto* more elaborate imagery from memory) and therefore more and richer emotionalism is selectively advantageous; the size and complexity of amygdala increase in proportion to the advance in perceptual and cognitive capabilities. Herzog and van Hoesen (1976) report that "our findings reveal a far greater proportion of temporal neocortex than previously described contributes afferents to the amygdala, further strengthening the view that the amygdala occupies a key anatomical position linking the neocortex with the diencephalic structures".

Corticoamygdaloid projections are to the lateral nucleus, while return pathways to cortex are from basal and accessory basal nuclei; internal amygdaloid processing must take place for appropriate return signals.

Most of the projections from neocortex to amygdala originate in layer 3, less in layer 5 (Amaral et al, 1992:42). This suggests a different pathway from perceptual representations and imagery for emotional functions than for other cognitive functions.

No direct projections from primary and 'association' auditory cortices have been demonstrated (op.cit.:43) but there is evidence that such projections may occur via more rostral areas of superior temporal gyrus which project to the lateral nucleus. Since sound consciousness elicits some emotional feelings there must be connections from the auditory modality to amygdala or some other gateway to the emotional system.

Striatal connections. Projections to corpus striatum arise mainly from basolateral nuclei and "may integrate motor activities appropriate to emotional and motivational states" (Carpenter, 1991:379). But, alternatively, they may be concerned with the contraction of somatic musculatures via the extrapyramidal motor system to generate sensory impulses contributing to emotional feelings, and, in addition, to the laying down of learned responses to particular emotions. The concomitant evolutionary elaboration of neocortex, neostriatum, and neocerebellum suggests that together they provide the substrate for such learning capacity. Emotional *feelings* probably cannot be learned, but *responses* may be.

The amygdalothalamocortical loop. Projections to the mediodorsal MD nuclei of thalamus arise from most nuclei of amygdala but least from the phylogenetically older central and medial nuclei, possibly because the more highly evolved basolateral nuclei (most developed in humans) are required for the advanced emotional system of primates. In turn MD propagates to prefrontal cortical areas (reciprocally), but not to amygdala. This is further evidence that amygdala does not itself generate affect (emotional or feeling consciousness.) Frontal cortices have reciprocal connections with several amygdaloid nuclei, indicating 3-organ cooperative functioning, very likely in the control of facile emotionalism thereby allowing higher cognitive processing (especially thinking-to-understand) to proceed undistracted.

Access to primitive 'instruments' of the emotional 'orchestra'.
"... some of the best-studied outputs of amygdala are the projections from the central n. to the lateral hypothalamus and brainstem, and from the medial and accessory basal nuclei and amygdalohippocampal area to the medial hypothalamus ... these subcortically directed projections can affect both the hypothalamopituitary system and all levels of the parasympathetic and sympathetic systems, as well as other brainstem reflexes" (Amaral et al, 1992:56).

In attempting to determine the fundamental roles of the limbic system crucial pathways must be identified among the tangle of interconnections and traced to destinations that are essential participants in vital functions. This is not to imply that cybernetic mechanisms, which account for the bulk of neuronal interconnections, are somehow dispensable, but being support actors they may be ignored in the interest of conceptual clarity.

There are two main pathways from amygdala to effector outlets: the stria terminalis and the ventral pathway. Both relay in hypothalamic and brainstem centres which in turn control, directly and indirectly, visceral, cardiovascular, and (probably), via gamma lower motor neurons, somatic musculatures.

It has not been demonstrated that amygdala projects directly on feeling-generating neurons of the limbic system for the elicitation of emotions. (Its projection on the thalamic MD nucleus may be purely inhibitory.) Quadriplegic subjects are emotionally impoverished to the extent that there is no sensory input from structures cut off by the lesion, yet still express many emotions. They still retain somatic sensory input from head and neck and visceral input via vagus and upper sympathetic nerves. Some of the more ethereal human emotions, such as pity, nostalgia, compassion, appreciation of beauty, amusement, etc. may

Fig. C(6)   Amygdala's afferent connections — vertical, transverse section (see also frontispiece) (Amaral et al, 1992)

Note: Boxed sources provide input for elicitation of emotional and other effector responses. Unboxed sources provide modulatory input for complex control functions. Amygdala's internal processing interconnections are extremely complex (McDonald, 1992), as further indicated by the numerous transmitter substances and cell types identified (e.g., Fallon and Ciofi, 1992; Roberts, 1992).

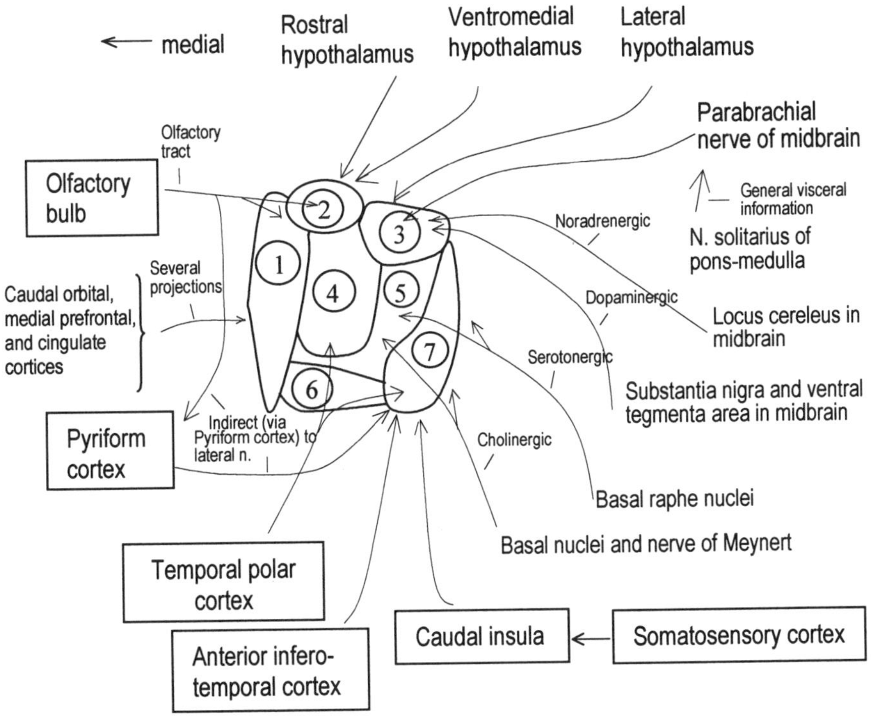

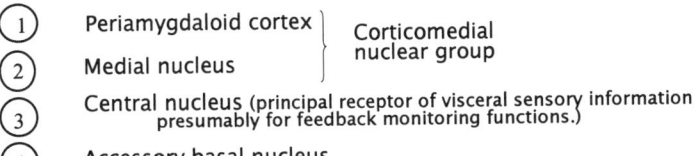

① Periamygdaloid cortex ⎫ Corticomedial
② Medial nucleus   ⎭ nuclear group
③ Central nucleus (principal receptor of visceral sensory information, presumably for feedback monitoring functions.)
④ Accessory basal nucleus
⑤ ⑥ Basal nuclei   ⎫ Well-developed in higher primates, especially humans
⑦ Lateral nucleus   ⎬ — presumably for recognizing the large number of
                     ⎭ situations of emotional significance and for the large number of computations required for selecting the downline components to be engaged for constructing the appropriate emotion.

Fig. C(7) Amygdala's efferent projections

"Targets of descending projections of amygdala are directly involved in the regulation of cardiovascular, respiratory, and gastric functions, all of which participate in the expression of fear and stress-related behavior" (Carpenter, 1991:379)

  Note 1: Boxed targets are way stations (`orchestral instruments') for the contraction of appropriate visceral, cardiovascular, and somatic musculatures to produce return sensory input to the consciousness-generating (feeling) elements of the limbic system, the particular blend of sensations constituting the particular emotion. The unboxed targets are for various control functions.
  Note 2: A sensory experience or even a brief image from memory may result in profound emotional feeling, e.g. of embarrassment (the effect of which is to trigger a cringing or hiding behavior, evolved as a result of its selective value; the various physiological side-effects (flushing of skin, tightening of neck and scalp musculatures, etc.) are inseparable from the generating process, being the only way nature could find for achieving this adaptive behavior.)

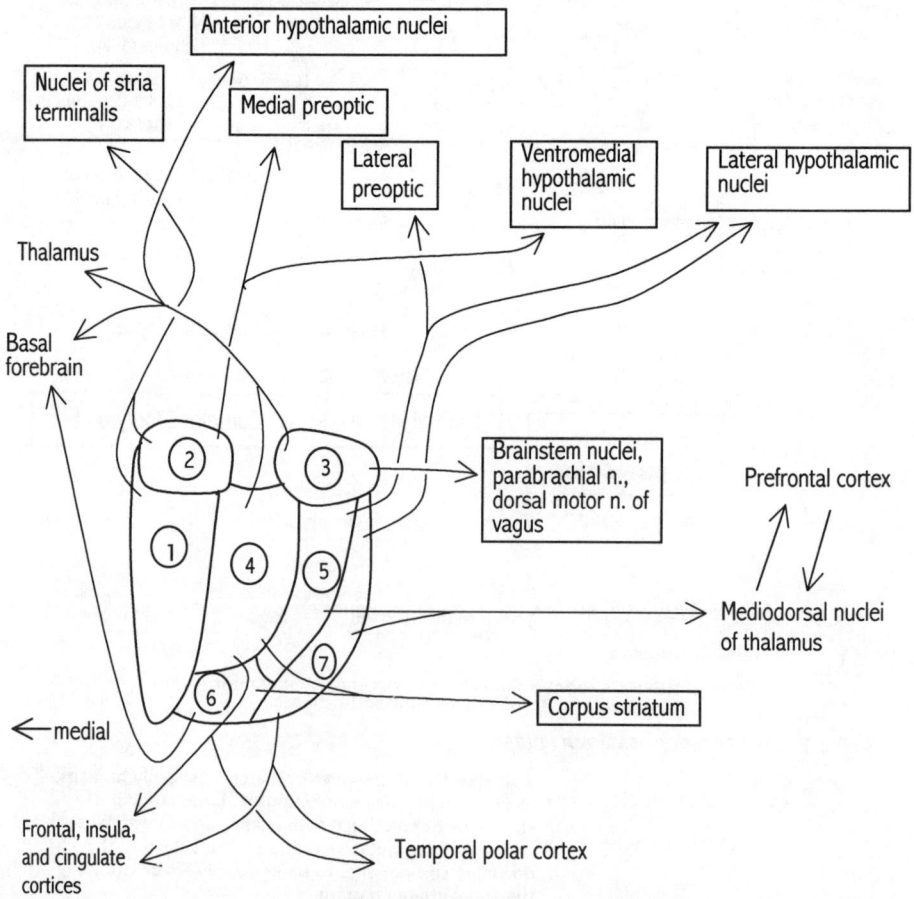

largely be elicited centrally with little contribution from peripheral sensory input, but no one has traced fibre connections responsible for any of these.

The Hypothalamus

The hypothalamus has extensive and complex connections as would be expected from its numerous functions. It should not be regarded as a single organ but a conglomeration of different organs occupying the same general region by reason of their evolutionary histories. Its different organs serve (1) basic homeostatic and regulatory functions via hormonal, reticular and autonomic systems, (2) elemental behavioral functions in response to primal life situations and vegetative needs affecting individual and group survival and reproduction, and (3) as elements coopted or utilized by the evolutionary process in development of an emotional system serving advanced behavioral functions. Each hemisphere has its own hypothalamus, separated from the other by the third ventricle (see frontispieces) but with common access to the pituitary gland.

Within and between each of the main sub-organs there is much cooperative functioning requiring control interconnections, in addition to the numerous external connections. When a higher function is activated a more primitive response may be unavoidably – and nonadaptively – involved, as the price paid for the higher good.

Most of the connections of hypothalamic nuclei are reciprocated; e.g., those to and from the brainstem reticular elements (all of which serve visceral functions). There are few and uncertain pathways from cerebral cortex, indicating that conscious experiences do not directly activate hypothalamic functions; or from thalamus, indicating that emotional feelings (i.e., feeling consciousness), if generated in part by thalamic structures (as suggested in this study), also do not activate hypothalamic elements but are effector on behavioral programs stored elsewhere, mainly in striatal and pallidal circuitries.

It is suggested that in emotionalism hypothalamic nuclei act as a set of relay instruments employed, mainly by amygdala, in the construction, via visceral, etc. musculatures, of emotional feelings, the feelings then acting to trigger or catalyse motor programs. Many of the vegetative manifestations that accompany especially the more primitive emotions are unavoidable side-effects of the activation of visceral, cardiovascular,

Fig.C(8)   Hypothalamic connections

(References: Barr and Kiernan, 1988; Carpenter, 1991.)

(A) Afferents

(Inputs from boxed structures are for activation of hypothalamic relays to brainstem nuclei for visceral functions and for contraction of visceral, cardiovascular, and somatic musculatures. Other inputs serve control functions.)

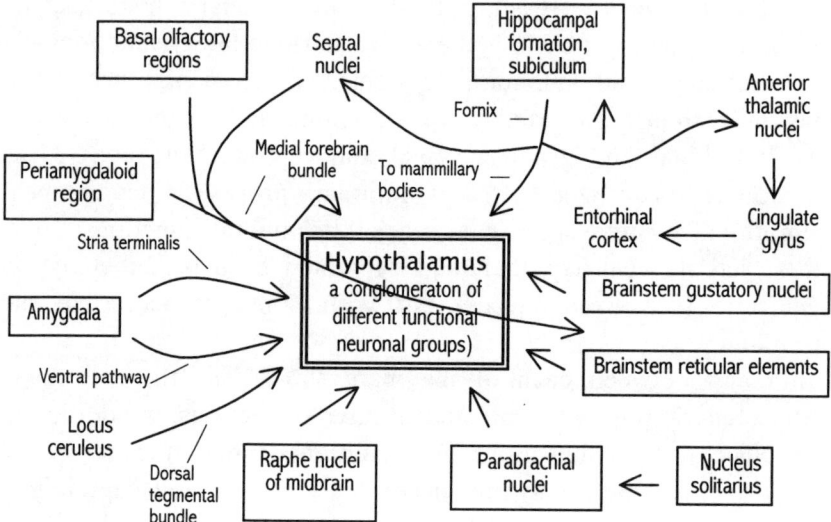

(B) Efferents

(Boxed targets control visceral functions and contraction of specific visceral, cardiovascular, and somatic musculatures. Unboxed targets are for control functions.)

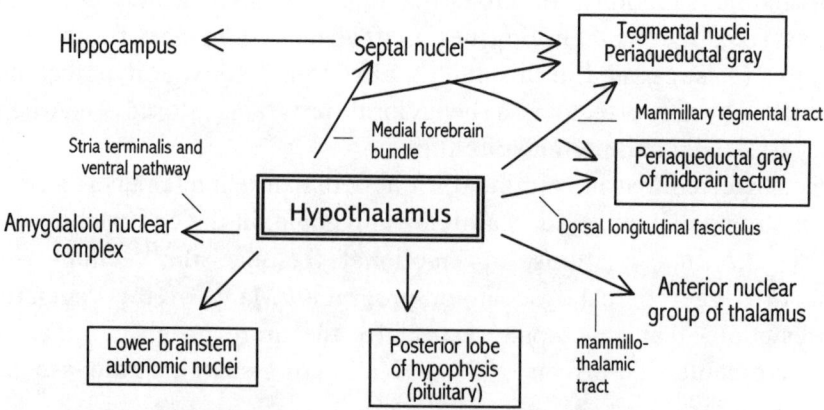

and somatic musculatures to provide the mix of sensory impulses required for the central generation of emotional feelings by brainstem and thalamic reticular elements and associated nuclei. Gastroduodenal ulceration, hypertension, coronary artery disease, and cardiac muscle fatigue are pathological examples of such side-effects.

Identified cellular groups constituting the anatomical hypothalamus include the mammillary, posterior, lateral, dorsal, dorsomedial, ventromedial, infundibular, anterior, and preoptic. They have been implicated (by electrical stimulation and ablation studies) in functions ranging from the purely homeostatic (such as maintaining optimal chemical and temperature levels), through those that employ complex behaviors for vegetative ends (such as seeking and consuming food), to those that are responsive to cognitive influences via, especially, amygdala and hippocampus.

But even the most narrow homeostatic functions have associated feelings and behaviors that are in some manner contributory to the goal; e.g., the animal will feel hot and seek shelter from the sun, or feel thirsty and seek and imbibe water.

The question arises as to what extent, if at all, the hypothalamic nuclei direct these ancillary behaviors and generate these feelings. Do hypothalamic nuclei generate feelings? Do they possess the motor program circuitries for musculo-skeletal actions such as suckling, seeking water, and copulation? Electrical stimulation or ablation of specific hypothalamic regions precipitates or eliminates many of these functions, but so does similar treatment to other brain structures.

Hypothalamic structures do not function in isolation. The advanced brain is descended from a unicellular organism: the single cell housed the functions of protection, nutrition, procreation, and the maintenance of the internal environment, in addition to the mechanisms that coordinated and prioritized these disparate functions. Every structure/function in advanced organisms is related by continuous descent to what was present at the unicellular stage. (With two possible exceptions: (1) Although bio-logic would seem to force us to conclude that some functional change in a preexisting structure resulted in the generation of consciousness which behaves as a form of energy of adaptive value to the organism, in view of the mystery of consciousness some doubt remains, and (2) symbionts, inclusion bodies, virions, and the like may become structurally part of a lineage and impart new functions).

The Anterior Thalamic Nuclei.

What are the functions of the anterior thalamic nuclei? The main nucleus receives the bulk of its input equally from the hippocampal formation and the mammillary bodies, the latter also receiving from the hippocampal formation. The anterior nuclei send the bulk of their output to areas of the cingulate gyrus, from which projections go to entorhinal cortex (which in turn projects to many structures, including the hippocampal formation.) The mammillary bodies project also to dorsal and ventral tegmental nuclei for downline visceral functions, and in turn receive visceral information from these nuclei.

By receiving from hippocampus and projecting to cingulate cortex the anterior nuclei may be concerned with emotional elicitations related to memory formation; possibly the anterior nuclei generate the emotions of interest and curiosity, which may act on the focusing mechanisms via connections with intralaminar thalamic nuclei. At the same time the hippocampal formation projects (also via fornix) on septal nuclei which project to widespread areas of neocortex using the activating neurotransmitter acetylcholine, which may play a part in memory formation.

So hippocampal participation in neocortical memory consolidation may be indirect by eliciting interest and curiosity 'in' the anterior thalamic nuclei and general cortical stimulation via septal nuclei.

Also, the mammillary nuclei by projecting on brainstem may indirectly activate locus ceruleus via tegmental nuclei to provide noradrenergic activity on wide areas of neocortex as well as hippocampus, further contributing to memory consolidation.

Fig. C(9) **Afferent and efferent connections of anterior thalamic nuclei**

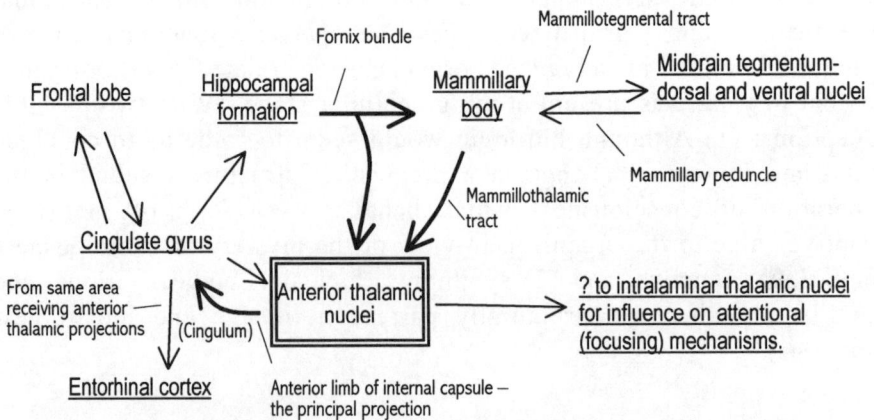

APPENDIX D

THE CORPUS STRIATUM AND ASSOCIATED STRUCTURES

"The striatum coordinates motor activities and postural muscle tone in all vertebrates, but the mechanism of action is poorly understood" (Sarnat and Netsky, 1981).

Anatomists, evolutionists, and clinicians have tended to use different terminologies:
Corpus striatum = caudate nucleus, putamen, and globus pallidus (and, with some authors, the nucleus accumbens)
Striatum = caudate n. and putamen = neostriatum
Pallidum = globus pallidus (lateral and medial segments) = paleostriatum
Lentiform nucleus = putamen and globus pallidus
Basal ganglia = corpus striatum, substantia nigra, subthalamic nucleus (and, with some authors, parts of amygdala, claustrum, and red nucleus)

The corpus striatum of each half of the brain lies deep in the substance of the hemisphere. It has three main parts – caudate, putamen, and globus pallidus – which are collections of nerve cells of different phylogenetic ages. Its older parts have hardwired motor program circuitries for innate behavioral responses to relatively unstructured sensory inputs.

As the evolutionary process added new circuitries providing more sophisticated responses to external situations, new levels were reached at which feelings, thought to be generated in reticular elements of the brain, participated by augmenting or catalysing responses. In addition, the neostriatum (coevolving with the cerebral neocortex and the neocerebellum) evolved the capacity to acquire behavioral programs appropriate to increasingly complex situations of emotional significance.

Associated with the corpus striatum in its motor functions are (1) the substantia nigra, which extends the length of the midbrain and is most developed in the human, (2) the raphe nuclei of the brainstem reticular formation, and (3) the subthalamic nucleus, also most developed in the human, lying between the thalamus and the globus pallidus. The nucleus accumbens, which lies adjacent to the ventromedial portion of the striatum, is ontogenetically more closely related to putamen and caudate than to septal nuclei as formerly thought, and also has projections to globus pallidus and substantia nigra. Gray (1995) gives it special status in interactions between the limbic system and basal ganglia.

The following observations highlight the significance of the basal ganglia in relation to the general thesis of this book:

(1) There are projections from almost all parts of neocortex to virtually all parts of striatum, and no part of striatum is under the sole influence of one neocortical area; this suggests that different levels of perceptual representation of the external world have access to innate response programs stored in corpus striatum – specific configurations of cortical cellular elements must have evolved to activate specific configurations of striatal cells, with extensive overlapping of such configurations: highly specialized synaptic and connectional properties allow cells to be shared by circuitries controlling quite different responses.

(2) Widely separated cortical areas overlap in their projections and overlap other striatal afferents; this is to be expected as different behaviors elicited from the corpus striatum have many common components, as do eliciting percepts in sensory cortices and eliciting emotions generated in the limbic system.

(3) A large variety of motor dysfunctions are associated with pathologies of different parts of the basal ganglia.

(4) It is likely, on the evidence of afferent projections, that striatal motor programs are of two general categories: One, non-emotional, responding to input from neocortex, consists of innate (some consciously and some non-consciously elicited) and learned program circuitries; the other, via intralaminar thalamic nuclei, responding to physical and emotional feelings which elicit or catalyse innate behaviors.

(5) Evidence suggests that the small non-limbic part of the striatum occupies the anterodorsolateral region, and the ventromedial caudate and the ventrocaudal putamen comprise the limbic striatum (Carpenter, 1991). The older striatum may be mainly concerned with innate emotional behaviors and the neostriatum with emotional-type responses to situations that have acquired emotional significance. (See note 10, below).

(6) The intralaminar thalamic nuclei, especially the rostral, receive heavy projections from the midbrain reticular formation (RF), and may be mainly concerned with emotive responses and modulation of emotionalism during cognitive functions, beside their proposed principal function (in higher primates) of controlling the selective generation of consciousness through their projections on the superficial layers of sensory cortices. The caudal nuclei, on the other hand, may be mainly concerned with vegetative and primitive innate responses.

(7) The projections of both substantia nigra and raphe nuclei on corpus striatum are inhibitory, as are collaterals from raphe to s. nigra, while projections from cortex and intralaminar thalamic nuclei are excitatory. Presumably the excitatory inputs engage specific responses while the inhibitory projections suppress unwanted responses and help coordinate the movement sequences. The precise operation of these influences is far from being understood. Numerous computations are possible; for example, an inhibitory projection on inhibitory interneurons may result in net effector activation.

(8) The general flow of neural activity is input to striatum (caudate and putamen), and from these to pallidum (globus pallidus), and from this to (a) thalamic relay nuclei, thence to motor cortex and motor neuraxis for physical responses, and (b) to neuraxis via projections on brainstem RF for distribution along the reticulospinal tract.

(9) Both globus pallidus and deep cerebellar nuclei project to ventral tier thalamic nuclei, thence to motor cortex, but these relays and their cortical targets are non-overlapping. The relays from cerebellum go to primary motor cortex (area 4) and the relays from pallidum to premotor and supplementary motor cortices.

Cerebellum and corpus striatum undoubtedly house the bulk of automatically performable motor programs, innate and acquired, controlling habits, skills, and emotionally driven behaviors, in addition to non-consciously elicited reflexive functions. But there is a puzzle here as neither of these motor systems has significant direct control over lower motor neurons in higher animals, although they may have had such control on the primitive reticular motor system before the evolution of special sense organs, thalamus, neocortex, and the pyramidal motor outlet (see (12), below).

Cooperative functioning between cerebellar and pallidal outputs may take place through interneurons in the ventral tier thalamic structures, as well as in red nucleus (Sarnat and Netsky, 1981:354).

(10) "Projections from basolateral amygdala to ventromedial caudate and ventrocaudal putamen suggest striatum may be divided into 'limbic' and 'nonlimbic' portions" (Carpenter, 1991:334). It is unclear what functions these projections serve. Since amygdala is not thought to generate feelings it may act as a relay to motor programs in striatum for feelings generated elsewhere in the limbic system, or it may suppress unwanted responses as an ancillary to its principal role of orchestrating the construction of appropriate emotions as postulated in Section 1.29.

(11) When a motor activity is performed action potentials appear in the basal ganglia before they appear in the cortical motor areas (Guyton,

1987:202). "There is much belief that the basal ganglia play an essential role in the initiation of most if not all motor activities..." (op.cit.:202). Furthermore, with the cerebral cortex removed basal ganglia "can still provide many aspects of motor control ... [though] much grosser and less determinitive" (op.cit.:202).

These observations strongly support the proposal that corpus striatum is excitatory on the motor system; that is, that it houses motor programs which are triggered (released) by percepts and emotions, as well as, probably, low-level, non-conscious triggers – it is not merely a modulatory system. Also, "...the establishment and execution of motor programs [are dealt with] in the basal ganglia" (Gray, 1995:1165). The projection from "ventral pallidum" to pedunculoportine nuclei (PPN) leads to motor activity (op.cit.:1167). Stimulation of the region of the PPN leads to walking activity. The PPN and associated reticular nuclei are the primitive residua of the pre-cerebral motor systems (Carpenter, 1991:212).

(12) Gamma-aminobutyric acid (GABA) is the principal neurotransmitter utilized by outward projections of corpus striatum, and is believed to be invariably inhibitory. How, then, can corpus striatum act as an effector structure, as we know it does from the facts that decorticated mammals and anencephalic infants perform primitive yet complex coordinated movements, and stimulating its different parts results in similar movements (Guyton, 1987:204).

Due to divergent evolution of the forebrain in the different vertebrate classes the lessons from comparative anatomy are of uncertain help. The hypopallium (primordial neostriatum) of reptiles and especially birds is the most massive part of their forebrains. It is presumably the command and executive centre for the major part of the motor behaviors of these classes, therefore must have full access to the motor neuraxis (Sarnat and Netsky, 1981:346). There is, however, evidence that only the ventral portion of this structure is homologous with mammalian corpus striatum.

Actually, the dorsal ventricular ridge of reptiles and birds (op.cit.:347,fig.12-7) receives the bulk of thalamic projections from sensory receptors, so may be the functional equivalent of sensory neocortex of mammals; and, in addition, it projections are similar, except that there are none on the motor neuraxis corresponding to the corticospinal tract of mammals (op.cit.:350-1). Projections from the dorsal ventricular ridge to the ventrolateral wall are consistent with the concept that the latter is the true homolog of mammalian corpus striatum and these projections correspond to the corticostriate projections of mammals.

Fig. D(1) Left hemisphere – lateral view

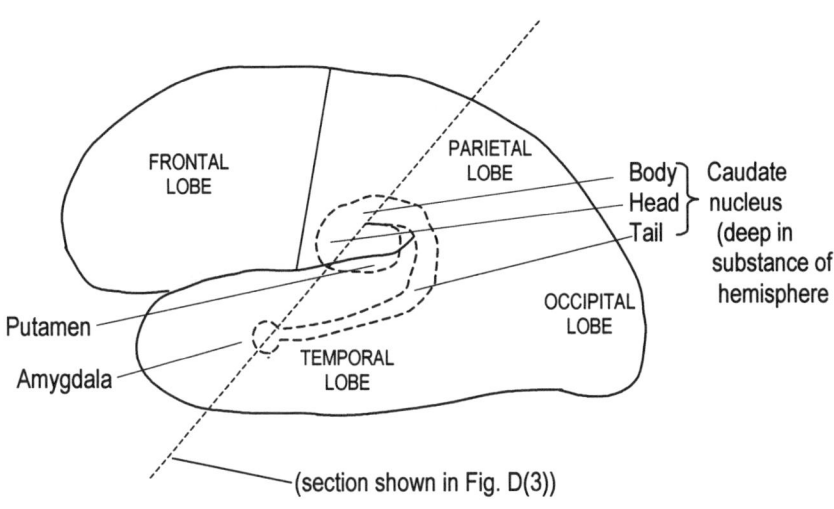

Fig. D(2) Lateral view of left corpus striatum

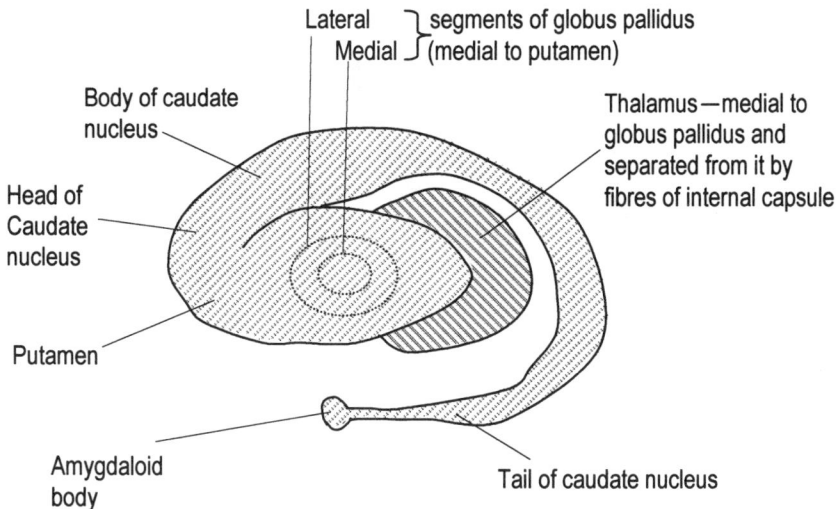

Fig.D(3) Transverse, semihorizontal section showing corpus striatum and related structure

(Note: Structures of the brain are too convoluted to be accurately represented in 2-dimensional diagrams. Some liberty is taken with the positioning of the structures in this sketch)

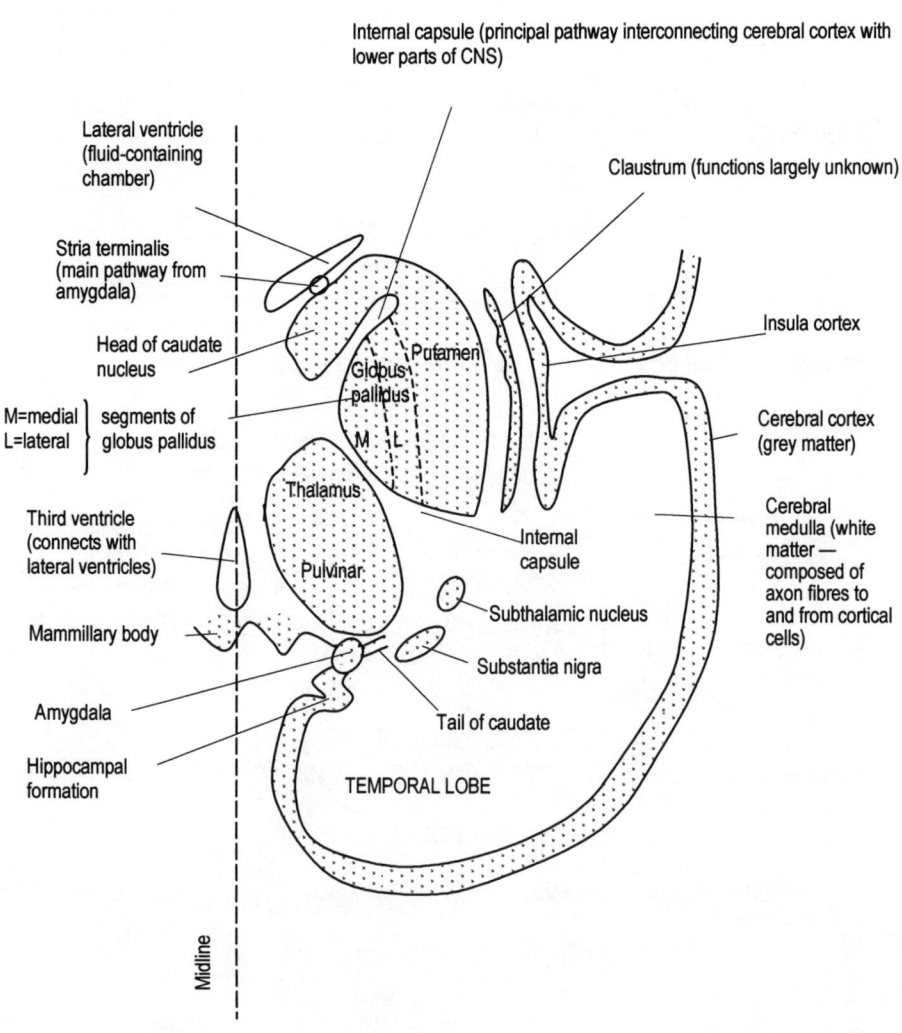

Fig. D(4)   **Input to corpus striatum. (The general flow of neural activity is to caudate, to putamen, to globus pallidus then out.)**

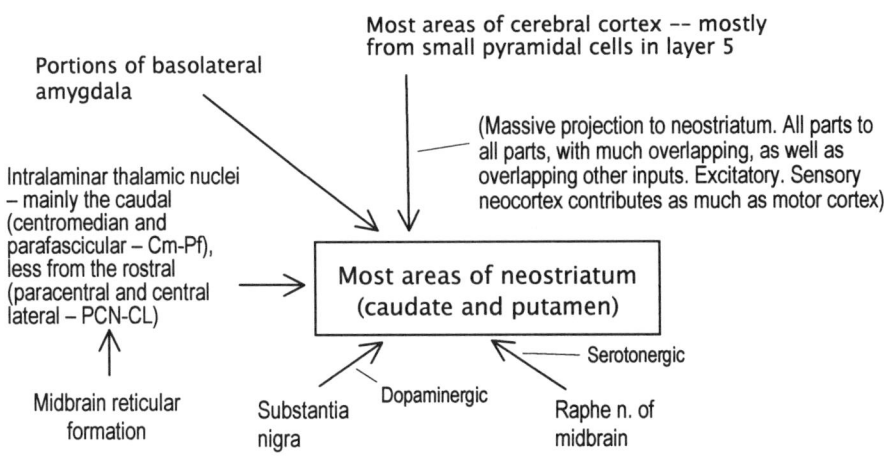

Fig. D(5)   **Corticostriatal projections**

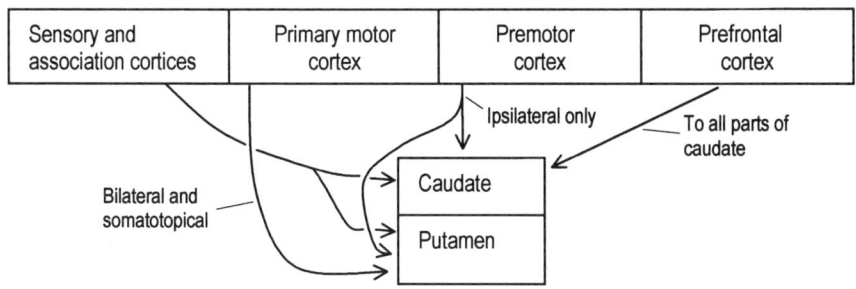

Note: Corticostriatal projections are excitatory. Also, basal ganglia are set in motion directly from sensory and sensory 'association' cerebral cortices (Guyton, 1987:202)

Fig. D(6) **Thalamostriatal projections**

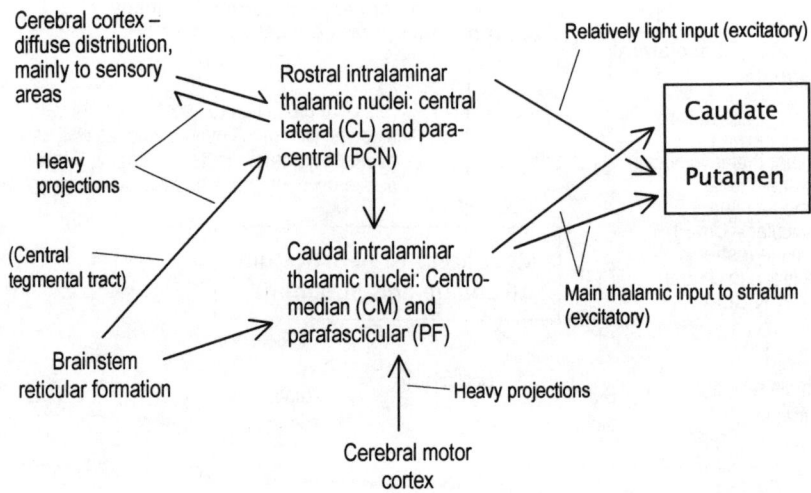

Fig. D(7) **Regulatory projections**

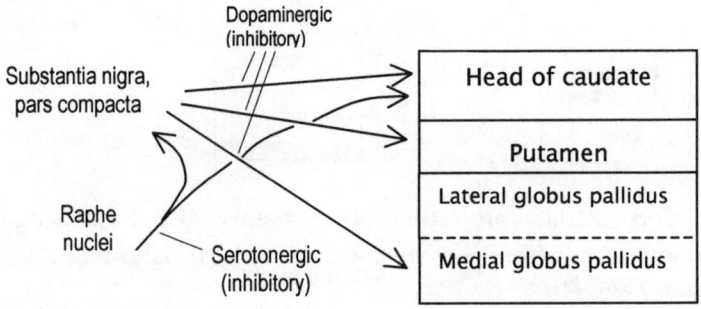

Fig. D(8) Output from corpus striatum

Note: GABA (gamma – aminobutyric acid) is a neurotransmitter released by axonal butons of various neurons throughout the nervous system and is always inhibitory on target neurons, so far as is known. Inhibitory action by corpus striatum and substantia nigra and thalamic relays to motor cortex is incompatible with the belief, supported by considerable evidence, that basal ganglia effect complex motor activities. Furthermore, according to Barr and Kiernan (1988:213-4) pallidothalamic projections cease functioning just before and during motor performance, yet substantia nigra to thalamus (non-overlapping with pallidothalamic) continues! Clearly, much needs to be learned about the functioning of these motor systems.

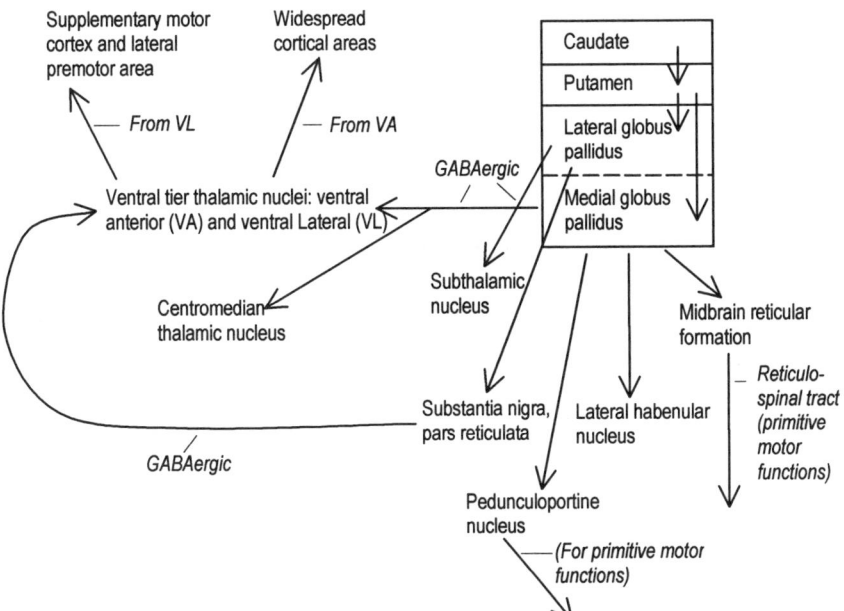

APPENDIX E

EVOLUTION OF THE BRAIN

Flow-chart Illustration

We may start at the evolutionary level roughly exemplified by Amphioxus (lancelet), a primitive chordate with a poorly differentiated neural tube, the cells (neurons) in its wall forming a network of connections commonly referred to as 'reticular'. It is provisionally accepted that the advanced mammalian nervous system arose through specialization of different parts of such a system.

Fig. E(1) **Early caudate stage**

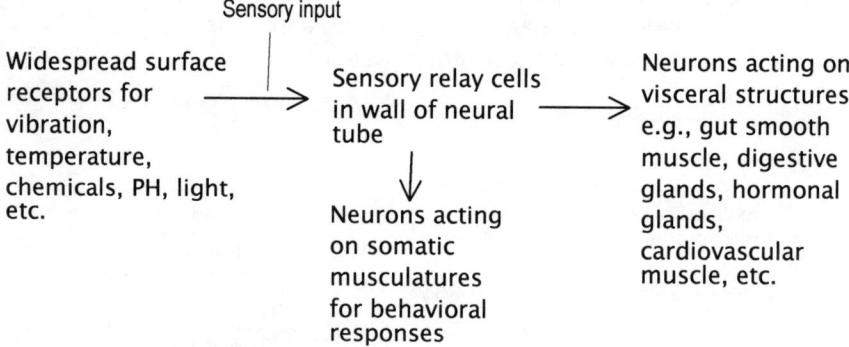

Fig. E(2) **As above, but also (at some stage)**

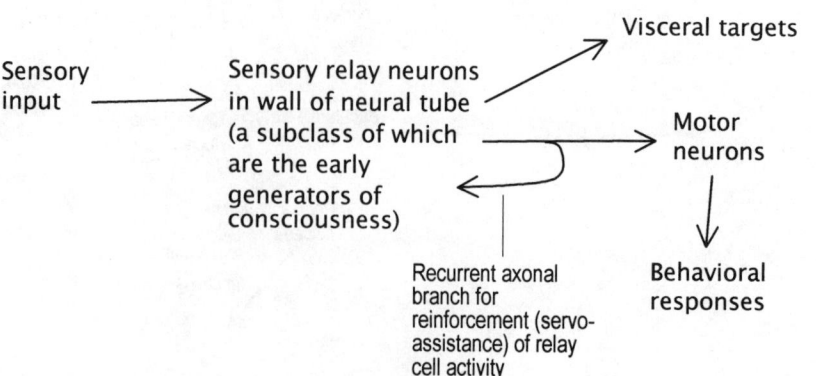

Fig. E(3) **Appearance of specialized receptors in 'head'**

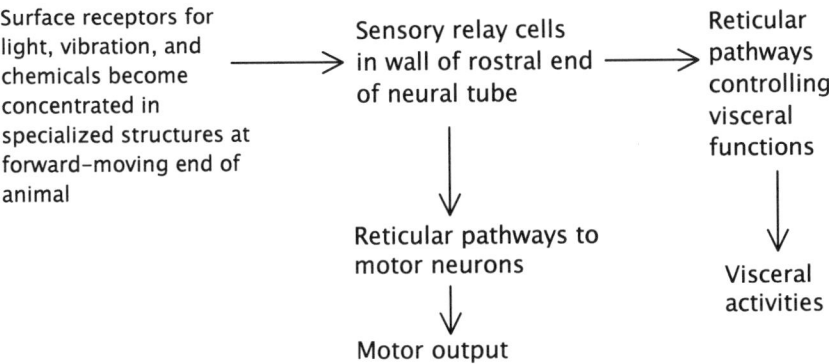

Fig. E(4) **Formation of thalamus and hypothalamus**

Both thalamus and hypothalamus are conglomerations of several different functional systems, each of which is the result of specialization of some primitive reticular function.

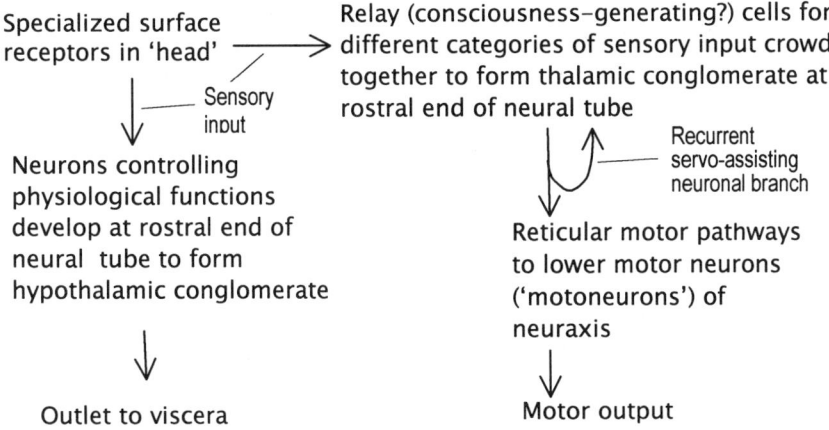

Fig.E(5) Evolution of the thalamo-cortical system

(a) Thalamus (T) ⎯⎯→ Effector outlets (Efo — limbic, diencephalic, reticulomotor)

(Thalamus may have been the earliest stage of CNS elaboration at which consciousness was utilized in representing external reality, albeit feebly. This implies that units of conscious energy generated at any moment coalesce to form a syncytial structure which may act in a unitary manner).

(b) T ⎯⎯→ Primary sensory cortex(PSC) ⎯⎯→ Efo
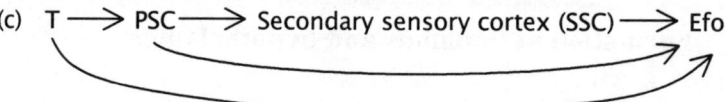

(As cortex evolved 'from' thalamus to provide more elaborate conscious representation of external reality it necessarily was provided stronger downline projections to the Efo's, which also underwent evolutionary elaboration.)

(c) T ⎯→ PSC ⎯→ Secondary sensory cortex (SSC) ⎯→ Efo

(d) T ⎯→ PSC ⎯→ SSC ⎯→Tertiary SC ⎯→ Efo

(The conscious representations become progressively more elaborate, as do effector systems, and connections more numerous. Primitive responses may still be mediated directly by the relatively sparse connections of the earlier stages, but in advanced brains these may tend to become vestigial)

(This theory of cortical evolution differs from that of Pandya and Barnes (1987) which is derived from the ideas of Sanides (1971,1972, which they cite) and which proposes that neocortical evolution started from two primordial areas, the hippocampal formation (archicortex) and the olfactory region (paleocortex), giving rise to the modern primate neocortex by separate developments)

Evolution of the Brain in Sketches

Note: In these sketches neither strict laterality nor relative positions is observed

The alimentary system of the primordial ancestor of vertebrates is presumed to have been a hollow tube open at both ends, with one-way passage of food and excreta. Movement of the organism was in the direction of the input end; i.e., 'forward' by definition. This end of the organism was most favourable for the positioning of specialized sense organs.

The neural tube developed from ectoderm and at the analogous evolutionary level of Amphioxus (lancelet) was almost undifferentiated. The central nervous system (CNS) at that stage consisted of a network of neurons in the wall of the neural tube allowing multisynaptic transmission of signals up and down for response to stimuli (vibration, temperature, chemical agents, reactivity, light, etc.) impinging on the general body surface. (Such multisensitivity is very ancient and is present even in unicellular organisms.)

In the following sketches the body is represented by an external outline and the neural tube by an internal outline. Neurons shown within the neural tube **are in the wall of the tube**; neurons external to the tube are peripheral nerves traversing the body tissues (from sensory nerve endings in skin and organs to the CNS, or from CNS to muscle and secretory organs).

Fig. E(6) **Neurons are depicted in the following manner:**

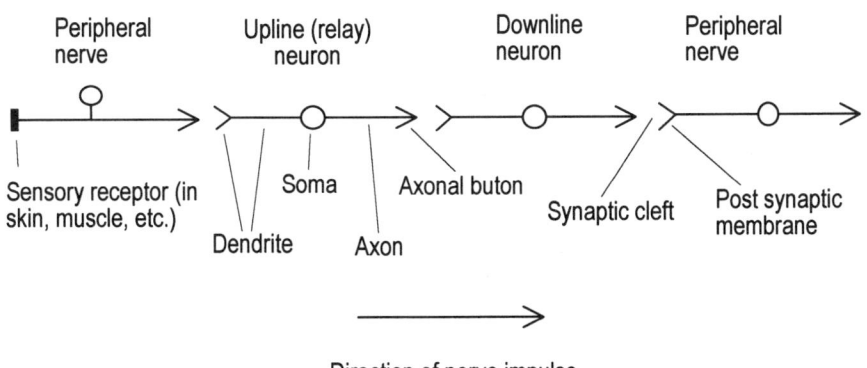

Fig. E(7) **Undifferentiated stage**

By convention the primitive CNS neural network is referred to as the 'reticular' system or 'formation' (RF). As different parts of the RF become specialized and take on new names the remaining parts continue to be known as the RF, but even these have become more-or-less specialized in advanced organisms.

Fig. E(8) **The specialization of rostral ectodermal cells for olfactory function heralds the differentiation of neural tube into 'brain' and 'cord'**

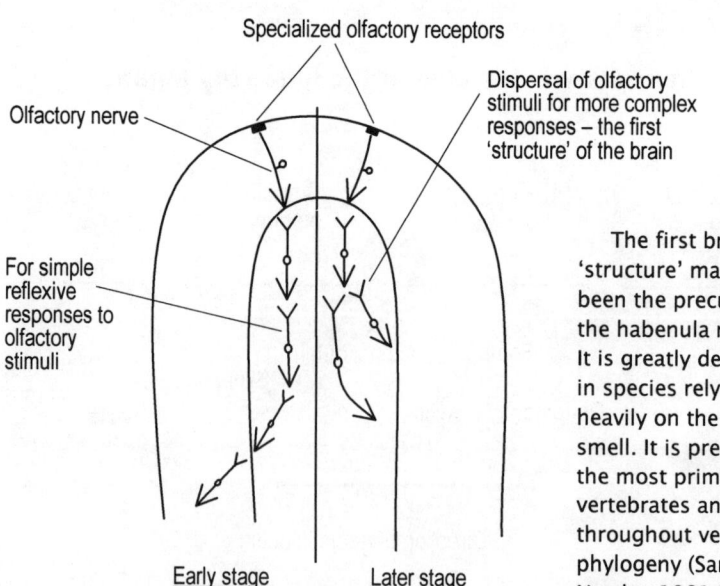

The first brain 'structure' may have been the precursor of the habenula nucleus. It is greatly developed in species relying heavily on the sense of smell. It is present in the most primitive vertebrates and throughout vertebrate phylogeny (Sarnat and Netsky, 1981:296-303)

Fig. E(9) Appearance of other sense organs in 'head'. Origin of thalamus.

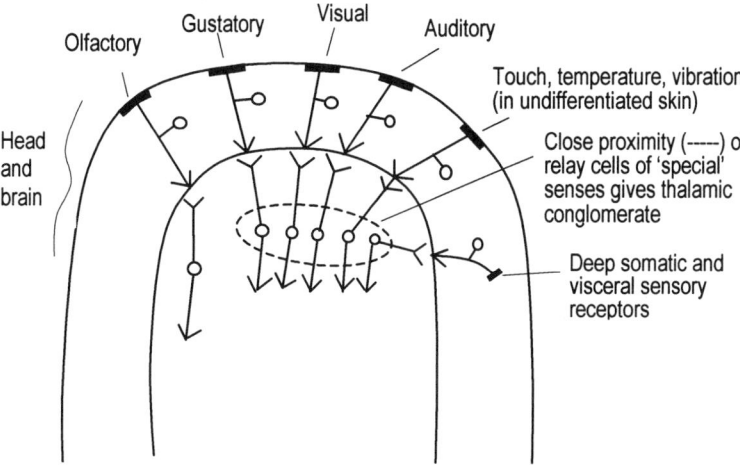

The olfactory relays are not part of the thalamic conglomerate. Note also that for special sense organs to develop from unspecialized epithelial cells the latter must have the potential to respond to different stimuli; this potential may have been present in the unicellular ancestor and lay dormant in the multicellular stage until niche factors and/or genetic changes brought them out.

Fig. E(10) Origin of pallidum and hypothalamus

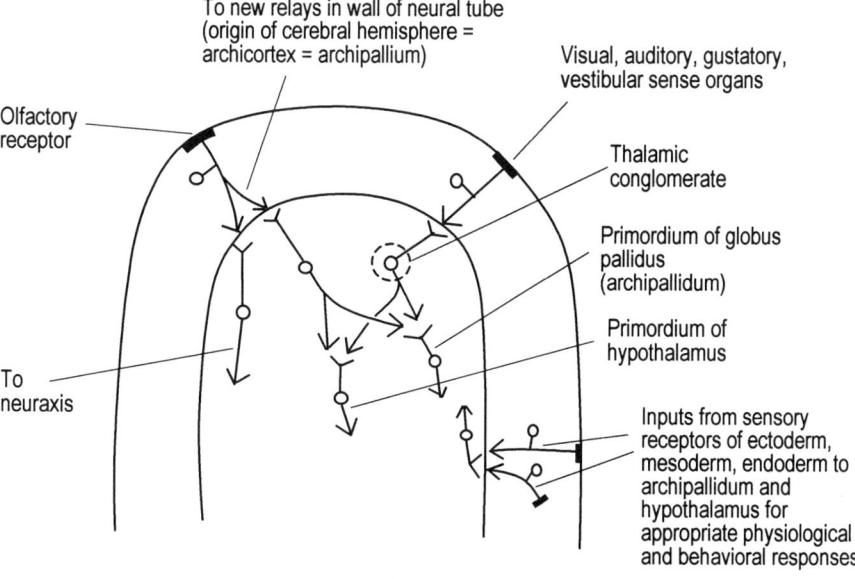

Evolved circuitries in the primordial pallidum (globus pallidus) respond to input from sensory sources to instigate behaviors more complex than simple reflexes. Similarly, the primordial hypothalamus contains circuitries controlling visceral and endocrine functions in response to particular sensory inputs.

Fig. E(11) (a) **Origin of olfactory bulb (and olfactory consciousness?)**
(b) **Origin of sensory consciousness of the 'special' senses?**

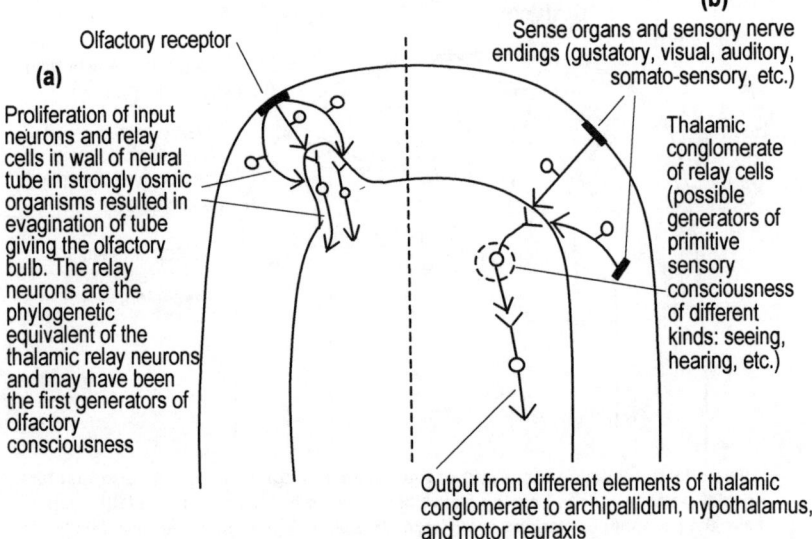

Fig. E(12) **Origin of archipallium (cerebral cortex) and memory function**

It is hypothesized that recognition memory derived from a servo-assisting mechanism as depicted in this sketch (and see text). Neuron M services a small fraction of the spectrum of a particular sensory modality. If it has been repeatedly activated its powers of transmission have been increased, and its activation threshold lowered. It may now be activated by minimal sensory input and thereby, via its recurrent branch, reinforce the activity of its upline thalamic relay, this constituting (or contributing to) 'recognition' of the stimulus. If the thalamic relay cell generates consciousness its reinforced activity will constitute conscious recognition, i.e., recognition memory.

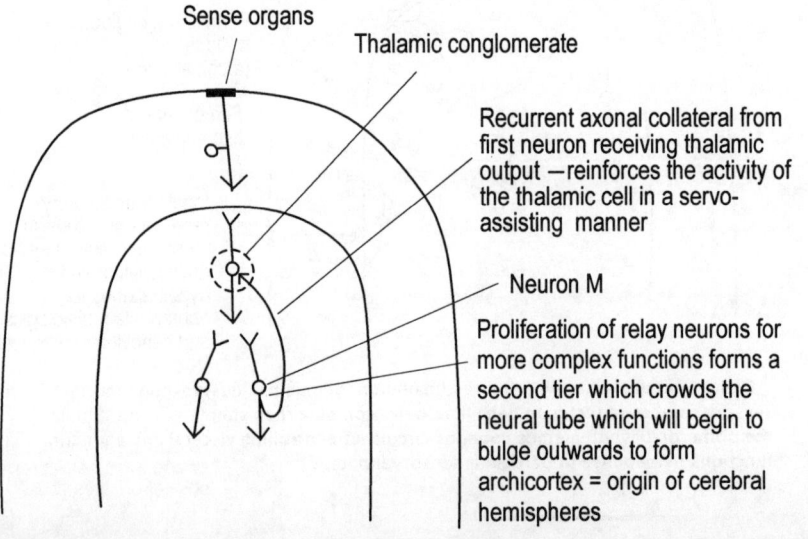

Fig. E(13) Origin and sites of generation of physical feelings

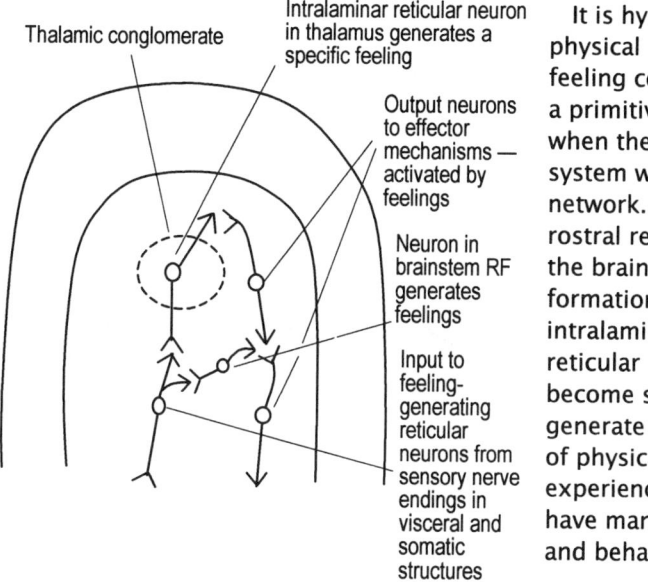

Thalamic conglomerate

Intralaminar reticular neuron in thalamus generates a specific feeling

Output neurons to effector mechanisms — activated by feelings

Neuron in brainstem RF generates feelings

Input to feeling-generating reticular neurons from sensory nerve endings in visceral and somatic structures

It is hypothesized that physical feelings (i.e., feeling consciousness) had a primitive origin, very likely when the central nervous system was a reticular network. We surmise that rostral reticular elements in the brainstem reticular formation (RF) and the intralaminar thalamic reticular system have become specialized to generate the many varieties of physical feelings experienced, which in turn have many physiological and behavioral effects

Fig. E(14) Origin of amygdala and emotions

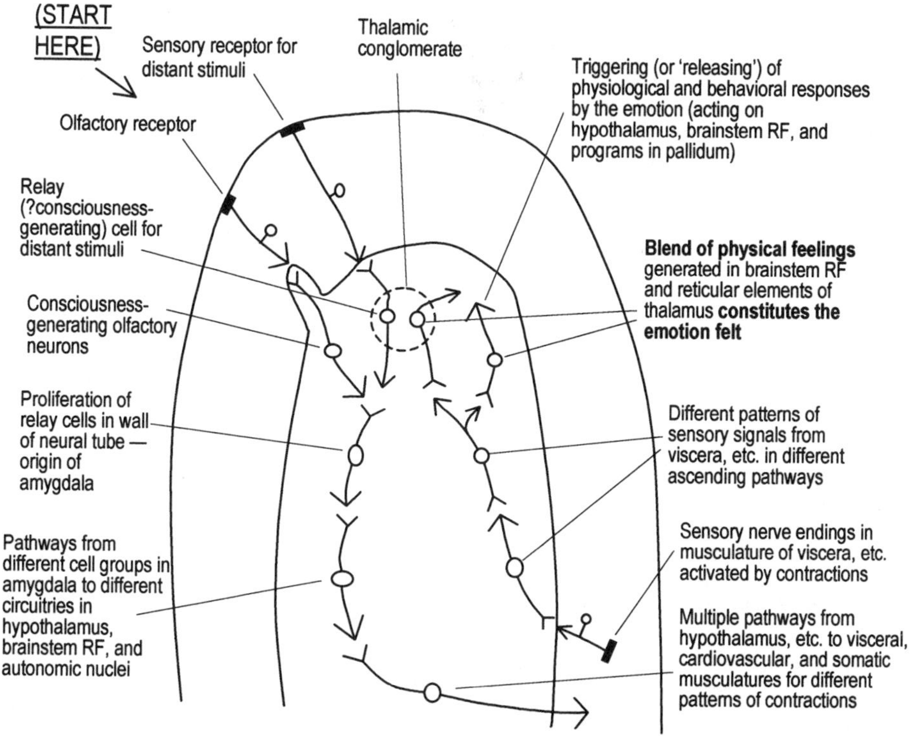

(START HERE) Sensory receptor for distant stimuli

Thalamic conglomerate

Olfactory receptor

Relay (?consciousness-generating) cell for distant stimuli

Consciousness-generating olfactory neurons

Proliferation of relay cells in wall of neural tube — origin of amygdala

Pathways from different cell groups in amygdala to different circuitries in hypothalamus, brainstem RF, and autonomic nuclei

Triggering (or 'releasing') of physiological and behavioral responses by the emotion (acting on hypothalamus, brainstem RF, and programs in pallidum)

Blend of physical feelings generated in brainstem RF and reticular elements of thalamus **constitutes the emotion felt**

Different patterns of sensory signals from viscera, etc. in different ascending pathways

Sensory nerve endings in musculature of viscera, etc. activated by contractions

Multiple pathways from hypothalamus, etc. to visceral, cardiovascular, and somatic musculatures for different patterns of contractions

Fig. E(15) Origin of neocortex and modern memory function

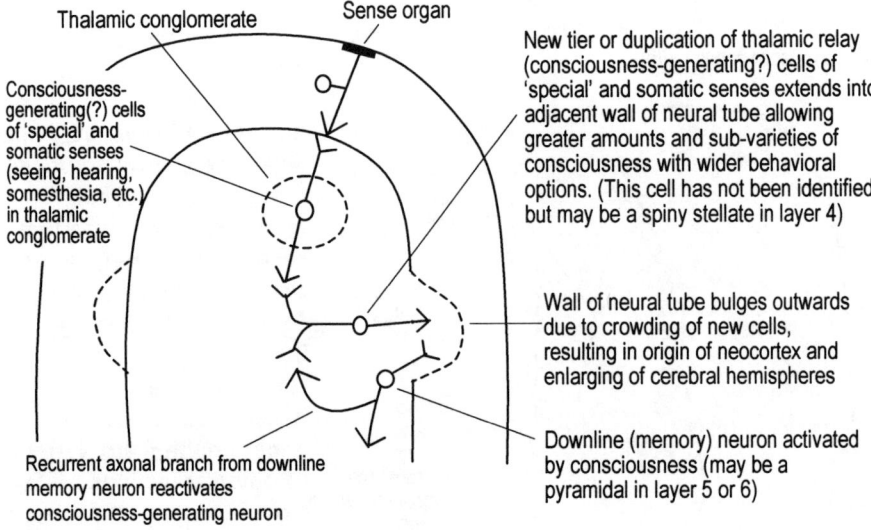

Fig. E(16) Further development of neocortex

The new tier of (consciousness-generating?) thalamic cells will carry with it the same onward projections of the original thalamic 'relay' cells: to paleo- and archicortex, and via these to hypothalamus, reticular elements in thalamic conglomerate (including the precursors of the anterior nuclear group and the mediodorsal nuclei), brainstem RF and autonomic nuclei, as well as the more direct outlet to the multisynaptic motor neuraxis. There will now be two sets of projections from thalamus: the original direct ones retaining primitive functions and undergoing relatively little further development, and the new indirect ones via neocortex undergoing massive further evolutionary development.

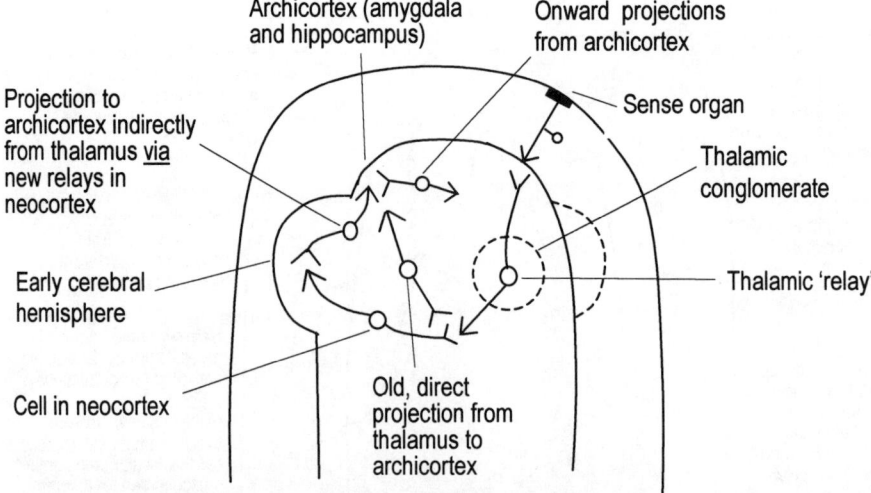

Fig.E(17) **Origin of motor projections from neocortex**

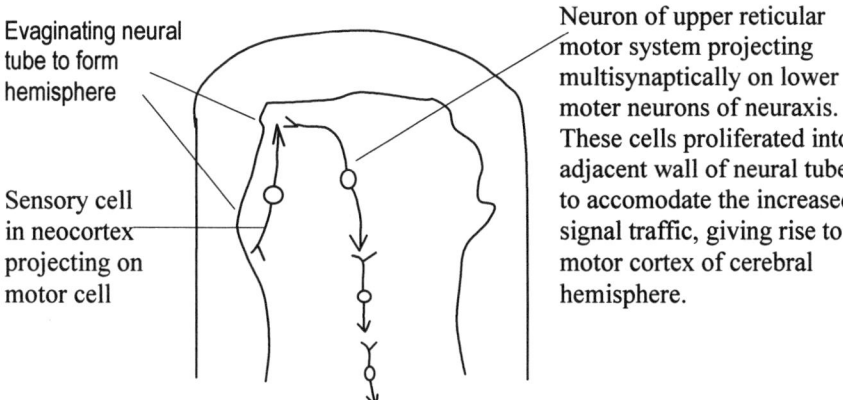

Evaginating neural tube to form hemisphere

Sensory cell in neocortex projecting on motor cell

Neuron of upper reticular motor system projecting multisynaptically on lower moter neurons of neuraxis. These cells proliferated into adjacent wall of neural tube to accomodate the increased signal traffic, giving rise to motor cortex of cerebral hemisphere.

Fig.E(18) **Conversion of multisynaptic cerebrospinal motor pathways to direct pyramidal motor system**

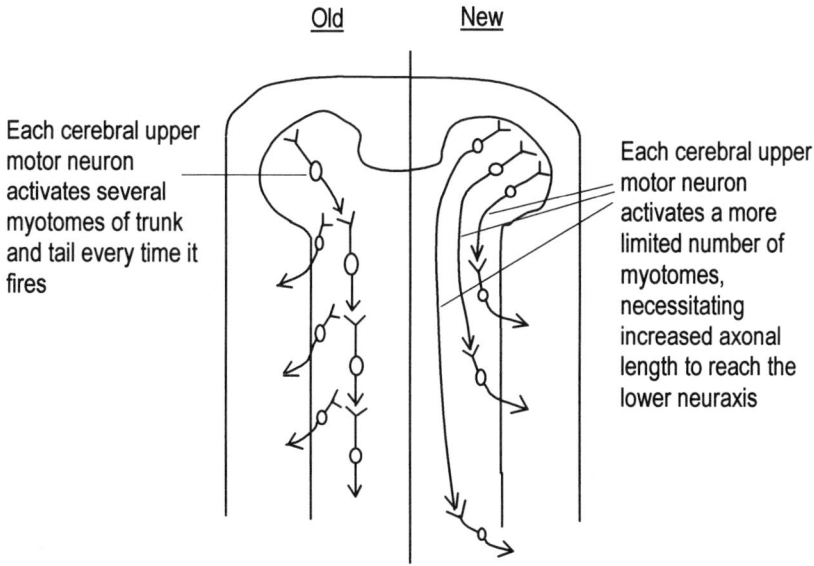

Old   New

Each cerebral upper motor neuron activates several myotomes of trunk and tail every time it fires

Each cerebral upper motor neuron activates a more limited number of myotomes, necessitating increased axonal length to reach the lower neuraxis

Fig. E(19) Origin of corpus striatum and cerebellum

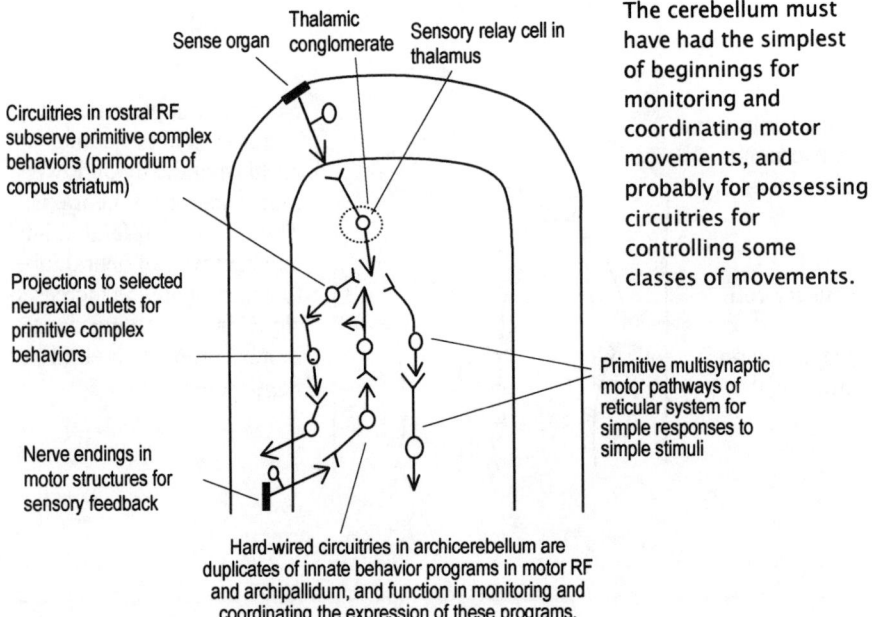

Sense organ — Thalamic conglomerate — Sensory relay cell in thalamus

Circuitries in rostral RF subserve primitive complex behaviors (primordium of corpus striatum)

Projections to selected neuraxial outlets for primitive complex behaviors

Nerve endings in motor structures for sensory feedback

Hard-wired circuitries in archicerebellum are duplicates of innate behavior programs in motor RF and archipallidum, and function in monitoring and coordinating the expression of these programs.

The cerebellum must have had the simplest of beginnings for monitoring and coordinating motor movements, and probably for possessing circuitries for controlling some classes of movements.

Primitive multisynaptic motor pathways of reticular system for simple responses to simple stimuli

Fig. E (20) The establishment of new motor programs in neocerebellum and neostriatum

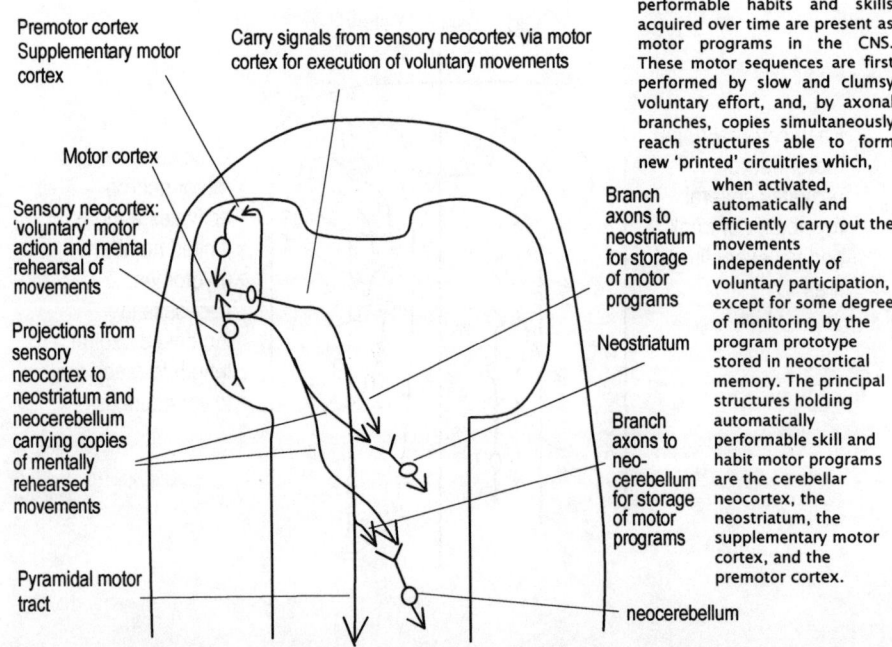

Premotor cortex
Supplementary motor cortex

Carry signals from sensory neocortex via motor cortex for execution of voluntary movements

Motor cortex

Sensory neocortex: 'voluntary' motor action and mental rehearsal of movements

Projections from sensory neocortex to neostriatum and neocerebellum carrying copies of mentally rehearsed movements

Pyramidal motor tract

Branch axons to neostriatum for storage of motor programs

Neostriatum

Branch axons to neo-cerebellum for storage of motor programs

neocerebellum

Vast numbers of automatically performable habits and skills acquired over time are present as motor programs in the CNS. These motor sequences are first performed by slow and clumsy voluntary effort, and, by axonal branches, copies simultaneously reach structures able to form new 'printed' circuitries which, when activated, automatically and efficiently carry out the movements independently of voluntary participation, except for some degree of monitoring by the program prototype stored in neocortical memory. The principal structures holding automatically performable skill and habit motor programs are the cerebellar neocortex, the neostriatum, the supplementary motor cortex, and the premotor cortex.

Fig. E(21) The olfactory system

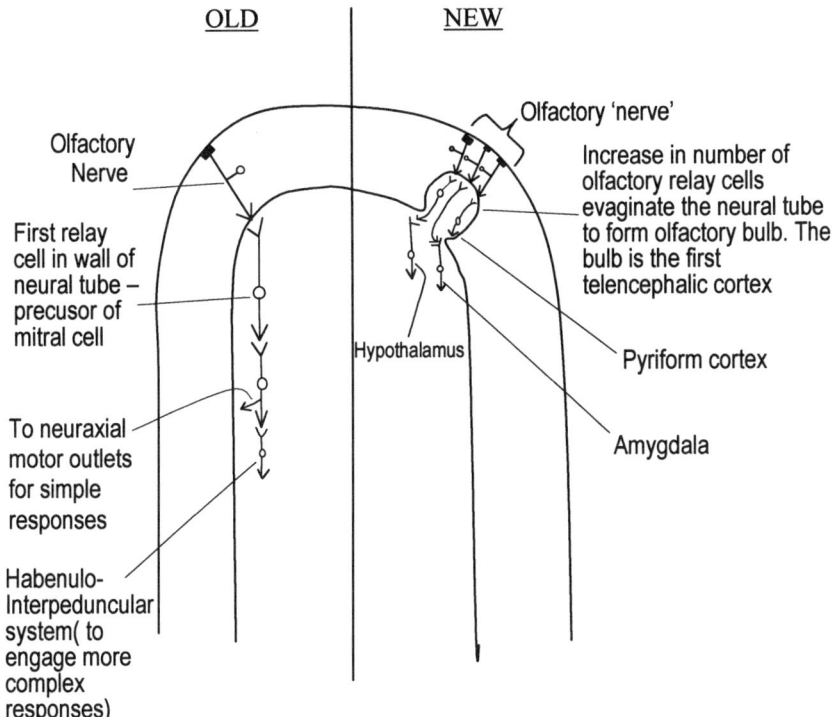

Note: There is much uncertainty over the origin and functioning of the olfactory system. In many primitive vertebrates the wall of the olfactory bulb is apparently typical multilayered archicortex and the mitral cell is equivalent to the thalamic sensory cell (and not, as has been suggested, to the retinal ganglion cell); this is supported by the existence of re-entrant ('centrifugal') fibres from other parts of the brain. Early olfactory consciousness may therefore be generated in the bulb, by mitral or granule cells. Pyriform cortex would therefore be the equivalent of primary sensory neocortex of the other modalities and would generate more complex olfactory consciousness. Its onward connections would allow functional integration with other systems of the brain for the global unification of consciousness and participation in mental and emotional processing, whilst other connections to physiological control systems in hypothalamus and brainstem retain primitive vegetative functions. (Sarnat and Netsky, 1981:330-6). "Complete removal of the lateral olfactory area [supplied by the lateral stria] hardly affects the primitive responses to olfaction" (Guyton, 1987:327.)

BIBLIOGRAPHY

Adler, Alfred: Mathematics and Creativity. New Yorker Magazine, 1972.

Adrian, Jasper, and Bremer, Eds.: Brain Mechanisms and Consciousness. Springfield, Ill., Charles C. Thomas, publisher, 1954.

Aggleton, J.P., Burton, M.J., and Passingham, R.E.: Cortical and subcortical afferents to the amygdala of the rhesus monkey (Macaca Mulatta). Brain Research, 190: 347-368. 1980.

Amaral, D.G. et al: Anatomical Organization of the Primate Amygdaloid Complex. In: The Amygdala, J.P. Aggleton, Ed. Wiley-Liss, N.Y. 1992.

Barbur, J.L., Watson, J.P., Frackowiak, R.S., and Zeki, S.: Conscious visual perception without V1. Brain 116, 1293-1302(1993).

Barr, M.L., and Kiernan, J.A.: The Human Nervous System. Fifth edition. J.B. Lippincott. Philadelphia, 1988.

Barrow, J.D.: What is mathematics? In: World Treasury of Physics, Astronomy, and Mathematics. Little-Brown, New York, 1991:546.

Beck, C.H., and Chambers, W.W.: Speed, accuracy, and strength of forelimb movements after unilateral paramidotomy in rhesus monkeys. Jour. of Comparative and Physiological Psychology. 70:1-22, 1970.

Beckers, G. and Zeki, S.: The consequences of inactivating areas V1 and V5 on visual motion perception. Brain (1995), 118, 49-60.

Bentivoglio, M.,et al: The intrinsic and extrinsic organization of the thalamic intralaminar nuclei. In: Cellular Thalamic Mechanisms, Bentivoglio et al, eds. Excerpta Medica, Amsterdam. Pp.221-237, 1988.

Beracochea, D.J. and Jaffard, R.: Effects of iboteric lesions of mammillary bodies on spontaneous and rewarded spatial alternation in mice. Jour. of Cognitive Neuroscience, Spring 1990:133.

Berlucchi, G, and Sprague, J.M.: The cerebral cortex in visual learning and memory, and interhemispheric transfer in the cat. In: The

Organization of the Cerebral Cortex. Eds. Schmitt, F.O. et al. MIT Press, 1981.

Bremer, F: The neurophysiological problem of sleep. In the cat during sleep with low voltage fast EEG activity. Jour. Neurophysiology, 25: 812-16, 1962.

Carpenter, M.B.: Core Text of Neuroanatomy. Baltimore: Williams and Wilkins, 1991.

Chalupa, L.M.: The nature and nurture of retinal ganglion cell development. In: The Cognitive Neurosciences.Ed. Gazzaniga. MIT Press, 1995.

Changeau, J.P.: Neuronal Man: The Biology of Mind. Pantheon Books, New York, 1985.

Chorobosky, J. and Penfield, W.: Cerebral vasodilator nerves and their pathways from medulla oblongata. Arch. Neurol. Psychiatry, 28: 1257, 1932.

Colonnier, M.: The electron-microscopic analysis of the neuronal organization of the cerebral cortex. In: The Organization of the Cerebral Cortex. Eds. Schmitt et al, MIT Press, 1981.

Cooper, L.N.: Distributed memory in the central nervous system: possible test of assumptions in visual cortex. In: The Organization of the Cerebral Cortex. Eds. Schmitt, F.U. et al. MIT Press, 1981.

Cosmides, L. and Tooby, J.: From function to structure: the role of evolutionary biology in cognitive neuroscience. In: The Cognitive Neurosciences. MIT Press, 1995: 1199.

Cowan, W.H.: Keynote. In: The Organization of the Cerebral Cortex. MIT Press, 1981: xi.

Cowey, A: Why are there so many visual areas? In: The Organization of the Cerebral Cortex. Eds. Schmitt et al, MIT Press, 1981.

Coren, S., Porac, C., and Ward, M.: Sensation and Perception, 2nd ed. Academic Press (Harcourt Brace Joranovich Publishers) 1984.

Damasio, A.R.: Time-locked multiregional retroactivation: A systems level proposal for the neural substrate of recall and recognition. Cognition, 33: 25-62, 1989.

Darwin, C.: On the Origin of Species by means of Natural Selection (1959). London: John Murray 4th ed, 1866.

Davenport, R.K., Rogers, C.M., and Russell, I.S.: Cross-modal perception in apes. Neuropsychologia, 11: 21-28, 1973.

Davis, M.: The role of amygdala in conditioned fear. In: The Amygdala. Ed. J.P. Aggleton. Wiley-Liss, New York, 1992: 253-306.

Davis, P.J., and Hersch, R.: The Mathematical Experience. Boston: Houghton and Miffin, 1982.

deGroot, J.: Correlative Neuroanatomy: Appleton and Lange, 1991.

Dennett, D.: Consciousness Explained. Boston: Little, Brown, 1991.

Desmedt, J.E.: Scalp recorded cerebral event-related potentials in man. In: The Organization of the Cerebral Cortex. MIT Press, Cambridge Mass. 1981.

Dewan, E.M.: Consciousness as an emergent causal agent in the context of control system theory. In: Consciousness and the Brain. Eds. Globus, G.G. et al. New York, Plenum Press, 1976.

Eccles, J. and Robinson, D.N.: The Wonder of Being Human. Boston: New Science Library, 1985.

Edelman, G.M.: Neural Darwinism. New York, Basic Books, 1987.

Edelman, G.M.: The Remembered Present – A Biological Theory of Consciousness. Basic Books, N.Y. 1989.

Emson, P.C., and Hunt, S.P.: Anatomical chemistry of the cerebral cortex. In: The Organization of the Cerebral Cortex. Eds. Schmitt, F.O. et al. MIT Press, 1981.

Evarts, E.V.: Activity of neurons in visual cortex of the cat during sleep with low voltage fast EEG activity. J. Neurophysiology, 25: 812-16, 1962.

Evarts, E.V.: Functional studies of the motor cortex. In: The Organization of the Cerebral Cortex. Eds. Schmitt, F.O. et al. MIT Press, 1981.

Fallon, J.H., and Ciofi, P.: Distribution of monamines within the amygdala. In: The Amygdala. Ed. J.P. Aggleton. Wiley-Liss, New York, 1992: 253-306.

Farah, M.J. et al: Brain activity underlying mental activity: event related potentials during mental image generation. Jour. Cogn. Neuroscience. Fall, 1989.

Feynman, P.P.: QED: The Strange Theory of Light And Matter. Princeton University Press, Princeton, N.J., 1985.

Forbes, H.S. and Wolff, H.G.: Cerebral Circulation. The vasomotor control of cerebral vessels. Arch. Neurol. Psychiatry, 19:1057, 1928.

Friedman, H.R., Janas, J.D., and Goldman-Rakic, P. : Enhancement of metabolic activity in the diencephalon of monkeys performing working memory tasks. Jour. of Cogn. Neurosc. Winter, 1990.

Gazzaniga, M.S., LeDoux, J.E., and Wilson, D.H.: Language, praxis, and the right hemisphere: clues to some mechanisms of consciousness. Neurology, 27:1144-7, 1977.

Gilbert, C.D. and Wiesel, T.N.: Laminar specialization and intracortical connections in cat primary visual cortex. In: The Organization of the Cerebral Cortex. Eds, Schmitt, F.O. et al. MIT Press, 1981.

Gilbert, C.D.: Dynamic properties of adult visual cortex. In: The Cognitive Neurosciences. Ed. Gazzaniga, MIT Press, 1995.

Glenn, L.L. and Steriade, M.: Discharge rate and excitability of cortically projecting intralaminar thalamic neurons during waking and sleep states. Jour. of Neurophysiology, Oct. 1982.

Glickstein, M. and Yeo, C.: The cerebellum and motor learning. Jour. Of Cogn. Neurosc., Spring, 1990.

Goldman, P.S. and Nauta, W.J.H.: An intricately patterned prefrontocaudate projection in the rhesus monkey. Jour. Comparative Neurology. 171:369-386,1977.

Goldman-Rakic, P.S.: Development and plasticity of primate frontal association cortex. In: The Organization of the Cerebral Cortex. Eds. Schmitt, F.O. et al. Cambridge, Mass.: MIT Press, 1981.

Goldman-Rakic, P.S.: Working memory and the mind. Scientific American. September, 1992.

Gray, J.A.: A model of the limbic system and basal ganglia. In: The Cognitive Neurosciences, Ed. M.S. Gazzaniga. MIT Press, 1995:1167.

Graybiel, A.M. and Berson, D.M.: On the relation between transthalamic and transcortical pathways in the visual system. In: The Organization of the Cerebral Cortex. Schmitt et al, eds. MIT Press, 1981.

Graziano, M.S. and Gross, C.G.: The representation of extrapersonal space: A possible role for bimodal, visual-tactile neurons. In: The Cognitive Neurosciences, Ed. M.S. Gazzaniga. MIT Press, 1995.

Griffin, D.R.: Animal Thinking. Cambridge, Mass. Harvard University Press, 1984.

Guyton, A.C.: Basic Neuroscience: Anatomy and Physiology. W.B. Saunders Company, 1987.

Hale, M.I.: The Mind: Its Origin, Evolution, Structure, and Functioning. Pittsburgh: Hale-van Ruth, 1989.

Halgren, E.: Emotional neurophysiology of the amygdala within the cortex of human cognition. In: The Amygdala. Ed. J.P.Aggleton. Wiley-Liss, New York, 1992:191-228.

Held, R., Leibowitz, H.W., and Teuber, H.L.: Perception. In: Handbook of Sensory Physiology, Vol.VIII. New York: Springer-Verlag, 1978.

Herzog, A.G. and van Hoesen, G.W.: Temporal neocortical efferent connections to the amygdala in the rhesus monkey. Brain Research, 115:57-70, 1976.

Hillyard, S.A., Mangun, G.A., Worldoff, M.G., and Luck, S.J.: Neural systems mediating selective attention. In: The Congnitive Neurosciences. MIT Press, 1995:665.

Houk, J.C.: Principles of system theory as applied to physiology. Medical Physiology, ed. V.B. Mountcastle, C.V. Mosby Co.,1980.

Hubel, D.H. and Wiesel, T.N.: Functional architecture of macaque monkey visual cortex. Proc.Roy.Soc.B198:1-59,1977.

Hume, D.: A Treatise of Human Nature. Oxford: Clarendon Press (1888).

Huxley, A.E.: Evolution from Molecules to Men: Prologue. Ed. Bendall, D.S., Cambridge University Press, 1983.

Ilinsky, L.A., Jouandet, M.L., and Goldman-Rakic, P.S.: Organization of the nigrothalamocortical system in the rhesus monkey. Jour. Of Comp. Neurol. 1985.

Ivry, R.B., and Keele, S.W.: Timing functions of the cerebellum. Jour. of Cogn. Neurosc. Spring, 1989.

Iwai, E., and Yukie, M.: Amygdalofugal and amygdalopetal connections with modality-specific visual cortical areas in macaques (Macaca fuscata, M. mulatta, and M. fascicularis). Jour. of Comparative Neurology, 362-387, 1987.

Jarvis, M.J., and Ettlinger, G.: Cross-modal recognition in chimpanzees and monkeys. Neuro-psychologia, 15:499-506,1977.

Jasper, H.H.: Problems of relating cellular of modular specificity to cognitive functions. In: The Organization of the Cerebral Cortex. Schmitt, F.O. et al, eds. MIT Press, 1981.

Johnson, M.H.: Cortical maturation and development of visual attention in early infancy. Jour. of Cogn. Neurosc., Spring, 1990.

Jones, E.G.: Some aspects of the organization of the thalamic reticular complex. Jour. of Comparative Neurol. 162:285-308, 1975.

Jones, E.G.: Anatomy of cerebral cortex: columnar input-output organization. In: The Organization of the Cerebral Cortex. Schmitt, F.O. et al, eds. MIT Press, 1981.

Kandel, E.R. and Hawkins, R.D.: The biological basis of learning and individuality. Scientific American, Sept. 1992.

Karten, H.J. and Shimizu, T.: The Origins of neocortex: connections and laminations as distinct events in evolution. Jour. of Cognitive Neuroscience, Fall, 1989.

Kass, J.H., Nelson, R.J., Sur, M., and Merzenich, M.M.: Organization of somatosensory cortex in primates. In: The Organization of the Cerebral Cortex. Schmitt, F.O. et al, eds. MIT Press, 1981.

Kass, J.H., The organization and evolution of neocortex. In: Higher Brain Functions. Wise, S.P. ed. New York, John Wiley, 1987.

Kent, E.W.: The Brains of Men and Machines. New York: McGraw-Hill, 1981.

Killacky, H.P.: General theory of cortical organization and expansion and specialization. In: The Cognitive Neurosciences, Ed. M.S. Gazzaniga. MIT Press, 1995:1249.

Kimura, D.: Neural mechanisms in manual signing. In: Sign Language Studies, 33:291-312, 1981.

Kinsbourne, M.: Models of consciousness: Serial or parallel in brain? In: The Cognitive Neurosciences, Ed. M.S. Gazzaniga. MIT Press, 1995:1321.

Kline, M: Mathematics and the Search for Knowledge. Oxford University Press, New York, 1985.

Kolb, B. and Whishaw, I.Q.: Fundamentals of Human Neuropsychology, 3rd ed. New York: W.H. Freeman and Co.,1990.

Kosslyn, S.M. et al.: Visual mental imagery activates topographically organized visual cortex: PET Investigation. Jour. of Cognitive Neurosc., Summer, 1993.

La Berge, D.: Computational and anatomical models of selective attention in object identification. In: The Cognitive Neurosciences, Ed. M.S. Gazzaniga. MIT Press, 1995:649.

Lassen, N.A. et al.: Brain function and blood flow. Scientific American, 239:62-71, 1978.

Lawrence, D.G., and Kuypers, H.G.: The functional organization of the motor system in the monkey. Brain, 91:1-36, 1968.

LeDoux, J.E.: Emotion, memory, and the brain. Scientific American, June, 1994; 1997 (Special Issue).

Legg, C.R.: Issues in Psychobiology. London and New York: Routledge, 1989.

Leggett, A.J.: The Problems of Physics. Oxford Uni. Press, 1987.

Levitan, I.B. and Kaczmarek, L.K.: The Neuron. New York and Oxford. Oxford University Press, 1991.

Lloyd, D.: Simple Minds. Cambridge, Mass. MIT Press, 1989.

Lund, J.S.: Intrinsic organization of the primate visual cortex, area 17. Schmitt, F.O. et al, eds. MIT Press, 1981.

Macchi, G. and Bentivoglio, M.: The thalamic intralaminar nuclei and the cerebral cortex. In: Cerebral Cortex. Jones and Peters, eds. Plenum Press, New York, 5:355-401, 1986.

Maunsell, J.H.R. and Newsome, W.T.: Visual processing in monkey extrastriate cortex. Annual Review of Neuroscience, 10:363-401, 1987.

Mayr,E.: Toward a New Philosophy of Biology. Cambridge, Mass. Harvard University Press, 1988.

McDonald, A.J.: Cell types and intrinsic connections of the amygdala. In: The Amygdala, J.P. Aggleton, Ed. Wiley-Liss, N.Y. 1992:67-96.

McElroy, W.D. and Seliger, H.H.: Firefly bioluminescence. In: Bioluminescence in Progress. Eds. Johnson, F. and Haneda, Y.

McNaughton, N.: Biology and emotion. Cambridge University Press, 1989.

Melzack, R. : Phantom limbs. In: Mysteries of the Mind. Scientific American, Special Issue, 1997.

Mills, R.: Space, Time, and Quanta. W.H. Freeman, N.Y., 1994.

Milner, B., Corkin, S., and Teuber, H.L.: Further analyses of the hippocampal amnesic syndrome: a 14-year follow-up study of H.M. Neuropsychologia:6:215-234, 1968.

Milnor, W.R.: Regional circulations. In: Medical Physiology, 14th Ed.. Mountcastle, V.B. ed. St.Louis: C.V.Mosby Co.,1980.

Mishkin, M., Malamut, B. and Bachevalier.: Memories and habits: Two neural systems. In: Neurobiology of Learning and Memory. Lynch, G. et al., eds, New York, Guilford Press, 1984.

Mountcastle, V.B. and Sastre, A.: Synaptic transmission. In: Medical Physiology, 14th Ed.. Mountcastle, V.B. ed. St.Louis: C.V.Mosby Co.,1980.

Muncaster, R.: A-Level Physics, 2nd ed. Stanley Thornes, Cheltenham, 1985.

Newcombe, F.: Neuropsychology of consciousness: a review of human clinical evidence. In: Brain and Mind. Oakley, D.A. ed. London and New York: Methuen and Co.,1985.

Oakley, D.A.: Animal awareness, consciousness, and self-image. In: Brain and Mind. Oakley, D.A. ed. London and New York: Methuen and Co.,1985.

Oakley, D.A. and Eames, L.C.: The plurality of consciousness. In: Brain and Mind. Oakley, D.A. ed. London and New York: Methuen and Co.,1985.

Oatley, K.: Representations of the physical and social world. In: Brain and Mind. Oakley, D.A. ed. London and New York: Methuen and Co.,1985.

Pandya, D.N., and Seltzer, B.: Association areas of the cerebral cortex. Trends in Neuroscience,5:386-390, 1982.

Pandya, D.N., and Barnes, C.L.: Architecture and connections of the frontal lobe. In: The Frontal Lobes Revisited. E.Perelman, ed. New York, IRBN, 1987:52.

Papez, J.W.: A proposed mechanism of emotion. Arch. Neurol. Psychiat. 38:725-743, 1937.

Pardo, J.V. et al.: Localization of a human system for sustained attention by positron emission tomography. Nature, 349:61-4, 1991.

Passingham, R.E., Perry, V.H., and Wilkinson, F.: The long-term effectsof removal of sensorimotor cortex in infant and adult rhesus monkeys. Brain 106:675-705, 1983.

Penfield, W: The Mystery of the Mind. New Jersey: Princeton University Press, 1975.

Poggio, G.F.: Central neural mechanisms in vision. In: Medical Physiology. 14th Ed.. Mountcastle, V.B. ed. St.Louis: C.V.Mosby Co.,1980.

Posner, M.I. et al.: Isolating attentional systems: a cognitive-anatomical analysis. Psychobiology, Vol.15(2) 107-121, 1987.

Preus, T.M.: The argument from animals to humans in cognitive neuroscience. In: The Cognitive Neurosciences, Ed. M.S. Gazzaniga. MIT Press, 1995:1227.

Pribram, K.H.: Problems concerning the structure of consciousness. In: Consciousness and the Brain. Eds. Globus, G.G. et al. New York, Plenum Press, 1976.

Reivich, M.: The use of cerebral blood flow and metabolic studies in cerebral localization. In: New Perspectives in Cerebral Localization. Thompson, R.A., and Green, J.R., eds. New York: Raven Press, 1982.

Robbins, T.W. and Everitt, B.J.: Arousal systems and attention. In: The Cognitive Neurosciences, Ed. M.S. Gazzaniga. MIT Press, 1995:703-720.

Roberts, G.W.: Neuropeptides: cellular morphology, major pathways, and functional considerations. In: The Amygdala. Ed. J.P.Aggleton. Wiley-Liss, New York, 1992:115-142.

Roland, P.E.: Cortical regulation of selective attention in man: A regional cerebral blood-flow study. Jour. of Neurophysiology, 48:1059-1078, 1982.

Roland, P.E. and Friberg, L.: Localization of cortical areas activated by thinking. Jour. of Neurophysiology, 53:1219-1243, 1985.

Roland, P.E. et al.: Positron emission tomography in cognitive neuroscience. In: The Cognitive Neurosciences, Ed. M.S. Gazzaniga. MIT Press, 1995:781.

Sarnat, H.B. and Netsky, M.G.: Evolution of the Nervous System. New York, Oxford: Oxford University Press, 1981.

Sawyer, W.W.: Mathematician's Delight. Pelican-Penguin Books, 1943.

Schmidt, C.F.: The Cerebral Circulation in Health and Disease. Springfield, IL: Charles, C. Thomas, 1950.

Searle, J.: Minds, Brains and Science. Cambridge, Mass.: Harvard University Press, 1984.

Shapiro, W., Wasserman, A.J., and Patterson, J.L.: Mechanism and pattern of human cerebrovascular regulation after rapid changes in blood CO2 tension. Jour. of Clinical Investigation, 45:915, 1966.

Shaywitz, S. and Shaywitz, B.: The Proceeds of the National Acadamey of Sciences, March 3, 1998.

Shepherd, G.M. (ed.): The Synaptic Organization of the Brain, 3rd edition. Oxford University Press, 1990.

Sherrington, C.J.: The Integrative Action of the Nervous System, 2nd ed. New Haven: Yale University Press, 1947.

Shimamura, A.P.: Memory and frontal lobe function. In: The Cognitive Neurosciences, Ed. M.S. Gazzaniga. MIT Press, 1995:803-824.

Smith, M.E.: Neurophysiological manifestations of recollective experience during recognition memory judgements. Jour. of Cogn. Neurosc. Winter, 1993.

Sokoloff, L. and Kety, S.S.: Regulation of cerebral circulation, Physiol. Review 40(Suppl.4)38:1960.

Sperry, R.W.: Mental phenomena as causal determinants in brain function. Eds. Globus, G.G. et al. New York, Plenum Press, 1976.

Sperry, R.W.: Forebrain commissurotomy and conscious awareness. Jour. of Medicine and Philosophy, 1977, Vol 2, No.2.

Squire, L.R.: Memory and Brain. New York: Oxford University Press, 1987.

Squire, L.R.: Memory and the hippocampus: a synthesis from findings with rats, monkeys, and humans. Psychological Review, 1992.

Steriade, M. and Glenn, L.L.: Neocortical and caudate projections of intralaminar thalamic neurons and their synaptic activation from midbrain reticular core. Jour. of Neurophysiology, 48:352-371, 1982.

Tooby, J. and Cosmides, L.: Mapping the evolved functional organization of mind and brain. In: The Cognitive Neurosciences, Ed. M.S. Gazzaniga. MIT Press, 1995.

Tranel, D. and Damasio, A.R.: Covert learning of affective valence does not require structures in hippocampal system or amygdala. Jour. of Cognitive Neurosc., Winter, 1993.

Weinberg, S.: Dreams of a Final Theory. Vintage Books, Random House, New York, 1993.

Welker, E. and Van der Loos, H.: Is areal extent of sensory cerebral cortex determined by peripheral innervation density? Experimental Brain Research, 63:650-654, 1986.

White, E.L.: Thalamocortical synaptic relations. Schmitt, F.O. et al., eds. MIT Press, 1981.

Wu, K. and Black, I.B.: Regulation of synaptic molecular structure. Jour. of Cognitive Neurosc., Spring, 1989.

Yingling, C.D. and Skinner, J.E.: Gating of thalamic input to cerebral cortex by nucleus reticularis thalami. In: Progress in Clinical Neurophysiology. Vol.1, J.E. Desmedt, ed. Basel: Karger, 1977:70-96.

Young, M.P.: Open questions about the neural mechanisms of visual pattern recognition. In: The Cognitive Neurosciences, Ed. M.S. Gazzaniga. MIT Press, 1995:467.

Young, J.Z.: An Introduction to the Study of Man. Oxford: Oxford University Press, 1971.

Young, J.Z.: Philosophy and the Brain. Oxford: Oxford University Press, 1971.

Zeki, S.: Colour coding in the cerebral cortex: the reaction of cells in monkey visual cortex to wavelength and colours. Neuroscience, 9:741-66, and 9:767-82, 1983(a).

Zeki, S.: The visual image in mind and brain. Scientific American, September 1992.

Zeki, S.: A Vision of the Brain. Oxford: Blackwell Scientific Publications, 1993.

☐

INDEX

accumbens nucleus 291, 253
acetyl choline 102, 352
Adler, A. 157
adrenergic activity 130
affect 180, 346
Aggleton, J.P. 209
agnosia 56
Amaral, D.G. 135, 343, 345-7
Amphioxus 106, 139, 362
amygdala Frontispiece 4, 59, 134, 192, 194, 209, 343-9
amygdalofugal pathways 209
anaesthesia 26, 232, 248, 323
anencephaly 356
angular gyrus 69, 70, 71
anterior thalamic nuclei 352(Fig.)
anthropomorphism 183, 309
anticipatory function 255
aphasia 162, 167
artefactual niche 7, 131, 135, 143, 144, 169, 171, 190, 211, 250, 310
artificial intelligence (AI) 222
attending (see focusing) 38, 131
auditory pathways 110, 111(Fig.)

Barbur, J.L. 49, 52
Barr, M.C. 56, 107, 109, 110, 140, 165, 205, 208, 210, 212, 241, 330, 331, 333, 340
basal forebrain nuclei 130
basal ganglia App.D
Barrow, J.D. 157
Beck, C.H. 292
Beckers, G. 50, 52, 72, 207
behavioral attending 85

behaviorism 28, 169
Bentivoglio, M 103
Beracochea, D.J. 343
Berlucchi, G. 51
Berson, D.M. 72, 219
Betz cells 159
binding problem 42, 65
Black, I.B. 254
blind-sight 50, 71
brain, evolution of App.E
Bremer, F. 138
Broca's area Frontispiece 1, 158
 aphasia 162, 165, 166

Carpenter, M.B. 51, 102, 104, 105, 107, 108, 166, 167, 194, 209, 291, 292, 299, 331, 335, 336, 343, 344, 345, 348, 355
cerebellum Frontispieces, 161, 290ff, 372
Chalupa, L.M. 229
Changeau, J.P. 11
Chomski, N. 163
cholinergic activity 102, 108, 130
Chorobski, J. 114
cingulate gyrus 336
Ciofi, P. 347
colliculo-pulvinar pathway 72, 89
colliculus, superior 200
Colonnier, M. 116, 221, 246
commissurotomy 50, 70
connectionists 223
conscious recognition 46
consciousness 27, App.A
 active 37

characterization of 30, 317
clinical assessment of 35
criteria for theory of 23, 25
division of 70, 222, 318
ego and 89, 318
elaboration of 58, 68, 80, 322
energetic nature of 16, 23, 79, App.A(318)
energy syncytium 264, 318
evidence for theory of 25
focusing of 85, 128, 130
generation of 41, 130
heuristic model of App.A
localization of 34, 36, 43, 60
loss of 36, 37, 321
modular unit 67
natural selection and 33
new blends of 62, 79
objective reality, and 73
olfactory 331
origin of 230
passive 37, 39, 82
recognition 46, 148, 149
representative 63, 91, 207
servomechanism, as 78, 207, 230, 327
sight 44, 49
sleep and 138
specific cells and 76
spectrum of 31, 318
status of 37
theories of 9-26
unification of 31, 59, 63, 67, 70, 189, 207, 222, 316
units of (see menton) 24, 31, 40, 86, 327
Cooper, L.N. 47
corpus callosum Frontispiece2, 50

corpus striatum 91, App.D, 353ff
cortex 60, 69, 76, 134, 212
association 64, 69, 108, 211
cytoarchitecture 212, Figs.1.32(1-3)
Cosmides, L. 76, 163
Cowan, W.H. 6
Cowey, A. 63
cross-modal matching 71
curiosity behavior 271ff

Damasio, A.R. 43, 56, 64, 265
Davenport, R.K. 71
Dennett, D 33
Desmedt, J.E. 33, 102
Dewan, E.M. 16
Dirac, P.A.M. 156
dopamine 102, Fig.1.12(4)
dopaminergic activity App.D
dreaming 177
  imaginative function and 177
dualism 22
dylexia 70

Eames, L.C. 21
Eccles, J. 314
Edelman, G. 21, 224, 254, 316
ego 89, 128, 177
emotional system 179, 193(Fig.), 344
  arguments for theory 192, 194
  basic functioning 92
  echo hypothesis 180
  evolution of 180, 188, 194
  feeling 179, 188
  'intellectual' emotions 122
  levels of elicitation 184,

185-7(Figs.), 197, 199, Apps.C,E
neuroanatomy of
recognition circuitries in 188, 191, 210
role of 92, 183, 195, 196
sites of generation 189
structure and pathways of 190, 191, 193(Fig.)
theoretical model 190, 199
Emson, P.C. 109, 116
enkephalins 140
entorhinal cortex 338, 339
epiphenominalism 26, 58, 142, 243, 325
Evarts, E.V. 25, 213
event related potentials (ERPs) 113
Everitt, B.J. 108
evolution, principles of 106, 120, 122, 150, 169, 179, 197, 201, 211, 224, 227ff, 312
of the human brain App.E, 133
of the human mind 310
stages of 225
experiential cells 27, 109
extrageniculate visual system 72, 89

Fallow, J.H. 347
Farah, M.J. 25
feeling 33, 200
    emotional 179
    evolution and 179, 190
    of interest and curiosity 122, 129
    physical 189, 190

sites of generation 189, 205
Feynman, R.P. 9
focusing of consciousness 37, 85, 101
competition for 99, 117, 118, 121, 123
evolution of 88, 91, 106
mechanisms 87, 94-100, 107, 119, 124
prefrontal cortex in 128
priority processing in 91, 118, 123
recognition of priority information 98, 116
sensory transmissions, control over 109
somatic orienting 114, 132
switch-focusing 128
vascular control 114
Forbes, H.F. 115
fornix 210
Friberg, L. 115, 130
Friedman, H.R. 77

GABA (gamma-aminobutyric acid) App.D, 109, 356
generalized thalamocortical (RA) system 102, 103
geniculocortical (visual) system 200
geniculostriate route 71
gigantocellular n. of RF 102, Fig.1.12(4)
Gilbert, C.D. 220, 247, 317, 323
Glenn, L.L. 26, 103, 108
Glickstein, M 122
Goldman-Rakic, P.S. 134, 135,

263, 279
Grabiel, A. 72, 219
Gray, J.A. 291, 354, 356
Graziano, M.S. 64
Griffin, D.R. 12
Gross, C.G. 64
Guyton, A.C. 9, 36, 56, 69, 101, 102, 136, 142, 167, 190, 205, 278, 291, 292, 333, 355, 356

habenula nucleus 366, Fig.E(8), 373
Hale, M.I. 311
hallucination 243
Halgren, E. 338, 344
Hawkins, R.D. 254, 256, 265
Held, R. 78
Herzog, A.G. 209, 345
Hilbert, D. 157
Hillyard, S.A. 113
hippocampal formation App.C, 210, 340, 341, 342
hippocampus Frontispieces, 59, 134, 208, 265-9
  memory and 265-9
Hubel, D.H. 26
Hume, D. 86
Hunt, S.P. 109, 116
Huxley, A.F. 12
hypothalamus 190, 208, 349-51, App.C(Fig.(8)

Ilinsky, L.A. 279
imaginative function 168, 171
  dreaming and 177
  evolution of 168
  mechanisms of 172
  thinking and 170, 171
  voluntary control of 171, 176
integration (see also conscious--ness: unification) 67,70, 75
intention, faculty of 282ff
intermodality connections 69
'interpretative' centres 75
intralaminar thalamic nuclei 77, 130
Ivry, R.B. 160
Iwai, E. 209

Jarvis, M.J. 71
Jasper, H.H. 26, 232, 248
Johnson, M.H. 232
Jones, E.G. 26, 103, 104, 222
Jouandet, M.L. 279

Kaczmarek, L.K. 68, 82, 231, 259
Kandel, E.R. 254, 256, 265
Kass, E.R. 77, 213
Keele, S.W. 166
Kent, E.W. 13
Kety, S.S. 114
Kiernan, J.A. 56, 107, 109, 110, 140, 165, 205, 208, 210, 212, 241, 330, 331, 333, 340
Killacky, H.P. 75
Kimura, D. 160
Kinsbourne, M. 29
Kline, M. 314
Kluver-Bucy syndrome 212
Kolb, B. 27, 41, 48, 49, 51, 56, 69, 72, 77, 162, 261,277, 289, 292, 321, 336
Kosslyn, S.M. 25
Kuypers, H.G. 292

LaBerge, D. 77, 89
lancelet (Amphioxus) 106, 139
language 157
  areas 158, 159
  central mechanisms 160, 164, 167
  imagery and 170
  structure of 161
  thinking and 157
Lassen, N.A. 165
lateral geniculate nucleus (LGN) 44, 52, 72, 219
Lawrence, D.G. 292
'leap-frog' principle 169, 228, 312
LeDoux, J.E. 188, 304
Legg, C.R. 25, 138
Leggett, A.J. 9
Levitan, I.B. 68, 82, 231, 259
limbic lobe 335
limbic system App.C, 134, 192
linear processing 88, 90, 131
linguistics 162
linkage systems of memory 237, 238, 259ff
  context 263
  external 237, 261
  internal 237, 260
  origin of 238
  time-sequential 263
localization of functions 61, 74, 247
  consciousness and 34
  problems of 74
  specific cortical cells in 76, 247
locus ceruleus 102, Fig.1.12(4), 130

Lund, J.S. 76, 213, 219, 247

Macchi, G. 103
magnetic resonance imaging (MRI) 70
mammillary bodies Frontispiece 4
mathematics 156
Maunsell, J.H. 63
Maxwell, J.C. 143, 156
Mayr, E. 229
McDonald, A.J. 347
McNaughton, N. 122, 250, 325
mediodorsal (MD) n. of thalamus 108, 135, 210, Fig.1.12(8)
Melzack, R. 288
Memory 58, 257
  basic plan 61
  consolidation of 266
  'declarative' 154, 255, 258
  expansion of capacity 257
  linkage systems of 220, 237, 259ff
  localization of 61
  odours, and App.B, 242
  origin of 230
  'procedural' 154, 258, 274
  recognition and 151, 241ff
  retrieval mechanism of 241ff
  servomechanism function of 230, 233, 241, 243, 245
mental processing 69, 248, 269, 308
  neuronal properties and 249
mentation vis-à-vis affect 180
menton 86, 287, 315, 318, 325, 329
Milner, B. 265

Milnor, W.R. 115
Mishkin, M. 77
modular units 67
monitoring 166, 167, 300-ff
  cerebellar 166, 167
  cerebral 167, 300ff
motor systems 275, 289
  emotionalism and App.D, 199
  program storage 289ff
  speech and 164-5
Mountcastle, V.B. 10, 104, 105, 135, 138, 139
Muncaster, R. 265
myxinoids (hagfish) 293

neostriatum 161
Netsky, M. 92, 105, 106, 120, 139, 197, 200, 201, 212, 213, 263, 290, 292, 293, 330, 332, 336, 340, 353, 355
neural network models 223
neural tube 204
Newcombe, F. 20
Newsome, W.T. 63
noradrenaline 102
noradrenergic activity Fig.1.12(4)
noticing function 49
  learning and 93

Oakley, D.A. 19, 21
Oatley, K. 20
odour consciousness 332
odour hallucinations 243
odour memory 242, 331
olfactory bulb 204, 330
olfactory system App.B

pain consciousness 206

  localization of 205, 206
Pandya, D.N. 76
parabrachial n. 210
paragenesis 229, 257, 259
parahippocampal gyrus 338, 339
Pardo, J.V. 114
parsimony 228
Passington, R.E. 292
pedunculoportine n.(PPN) 356, 361
Penfield, W 34, 114, 314
percept, generation of 43
perception 27, 41
  evolutionary biology of 41
piriform (pyriform) cortex 204
Posner, M.I. 131, 132
Poggio, G.F. 49
positron emission tomography(PET) 114, 115
prefrontal cortex 128, 133, 134
  limbic system and 134
  thalamus and 135
  thinking and 128, 133
premotor cortex Frontispieces, 290, 292
  motor programs and 290, 291
Preus, T.M. 163
Pribram, K.H. 17
problem solving 153
'processing', neural function of 69, 90, 308
prosopagnosia 56
pulvinar 44, 72, 89
purposeful behavior 271
putamen 64
pyramidal system 290ff, 371(Fig.E(18)

quadriplegia 197, 346

raphe nuclei   Fig.1.12(4), 102, 353
recognition consciousness 46, 148, 149
reflexivity, levels of   44, 91, 120, 147, 197, 231, 240, 256
Reivich, M. 114
reticular activating system (RAS) 77, 101, 102, 103
reticular formation (RF) 130, 138, 200, 297
reticular nucleus (RN) 104, 130
retinal projections 53, 72
Robbins, T.W. 108
Roland, P.E. 115, 130

saltationism 30
Sarnat, H.B. 92, 105, 106, 120, 139, 197, 200, 201, 212, 213, 263, 290, 292, 293, 330, 332, 336, 340, 353, 355
Sawyer, W.W. 314
Schmidt, C.F. 114
Searle, J.R. 18, 22
selective generation of con-
  -sciousness (see focusing) 85
self-consciousness   51, 86, 287-8, 318, 322
self, continuity of 325
self and world 73, 286
Seltzer, B. 76
sensation 27, 37, 39, 206
sensing 37
  active 37

passive 37, 39
septal area   Frontispiece 2, 96, 108, 334, 343, 352
serendipity in evolution   93, 150, 229
serotonergic activity
    App.D (Fig.4), Fig.1.12(4)
serotonin 102
Shapiro, W. 115
Shaywitz, S. 70
Shepherd, G.M.   68, 82, 238, 259
Sherrington, C.J. 230
Shimamura, A.P. 129, 263
Skinner, J.E. 110, 136
sleep 26, 138, 263
Smith, M.E. 244
Sokoloff, L. 114
somatic orienting 114, 132
speciation 229
Sperry, R.W. 14, 231
Sprague, J.M. 51
Squire, L.R. 210, 263, 265
stellate cells 109, 217
  non-spiny 217
  spiny 109, 217, 221
Steriade, M. 26, 103, 108
stria terminalis 209
substantia innominata 108
substantia nigra   Fig.1.12(4), 102, 343
subthalamic nucleus 353, 358
superior colliculus 200
supplementary motor cortex 161, 299
switch-focusing 128, 130
symbolism 155

teleonomy 7, 122, 250
terminological pitfalls 75
terminology 7, 75
thalamic intralamina nuclei 103
thalamus   Apps C&E, 59, 103,
          106, 135, 202, 291,
          331, 340
thinking 81, 128, 143, 222, 308
  basic process 81
  emotional system and   100,
          129
  imagery in 146, 171
  imagination and 171
  language and 157
  mechanism of 146
  switch-focusing in 128, 130
  understanding and   128, 129,
          143, 308
  symbolism in 155
Tooby, J. 76, 163
Tranel, D. 56, 189

uncinate fits 243
understanding function 81, 143,
          145, 152, 308
  evolution of 144, 308
  features of 145
  imagery and 152
  thinking and 143, 308
unification (see consciousness)
upward spiral principle   127,
          169, 188, 228, 311

vasoactive intestinal polypeptide
          (VIP) 109, 116, 247
van Hoesen, G.W. 209, 345
visual mechanisms 49, 55
  modular unit 67

extrageniculate 115
volition 137, 141, 274, 284

Welker, E. 54
Weinberg, S. 329
Wernicke's area
      Frontispiece 1, 59, 69, 70,
          71, 76, 159, 162, 163,
Whishaw, I.Q.   27, 41, 48, 49,
          51, 56, 69, 72, 77,
          162, 261, 277, 289,
          292, 321, 336
White, E.L. 217, 246, 247
Wiesel, T.N. 26, 220, 247, 323
Wolff, H.G. 115
Wu, K. 254

Yeo, C. 122
Yingling, C.D. 110, 136
Young, J.Z. 11
Young, M.P. 209
Yukie, M. 209

Zeki, S.   9, 21, 25, 27, 29,
          37, 41, 44, 49, 50, 52,
          63, 66, 109, 143, 189,
          207, 248, 316
zona incerta 105